Bilingualism 1

BILINGUAL EDUCATION & BILINGUALISM
Series Editors: Nancy H. Hornberger (University of Pennsylvania, USA) and Wayne E. Wright (Purdue University, USA)

Bilingual Education and Bilingualism is an international, multidisciplinary series publishing research on the philosophy, politics, policy, provision and practice of language planning, Indigenous and minority language education, multilingualism, multiculturalism, biliteracy, bilingualism and bilingual education. The series aims to mirror current debates and discussions. New proposals for single-authored, multiple-authored, or edited books in the series are warmly welcomed, in any of the following categories or others authors may propose: overview or introductory texts; course readers or general reference texts; focus books on particular multilingual education program types; school-based case studies; national case studies; collected cases with a clear programmatic or conceptual theme; and professional education manuals.

All books in this series are externally peer-reviewed.

Full details of all the books in this series and of all our other publications can be found on http://www.multilingual-matters.com, or by writing to Multilingual Matters, St Nicholas House, 31–34 High Street, Bristol BS1 2AW, UK.

BILINGUAL EDUCATION & BILINGUALISM: 125

Bilingualism for All?

Raciolinguistic Perspectives on Dual Language Education in the United States

Edited by
Nelson Flores, Amelia Tseng and Nicholas Subtirelu

MULTILINGUAL MATTERS
Bristol • Blue Ridge Summit

DOI https://doi.org/10.21832/FLORES0046
Library of Congress Cataloging in Publication Data
A catalog record for this book is available from the Library of Congress.
Names: Flores, Nelson, 1981- editor. | Tseng, Amelia, 1979- editor. | Subtirelu, Nicholas, 1986- editor.
Title: Bilingualism for All?: Raciolinguistic Perspectives on Dual Language Education in the United States/Edited by Nelson Flores, Amelia Tseng and Nicholas Subtirelu.
Description: Bristol, UK; Blue Ridge Summit, PA: Multilingual Matters, 2021. | Series: Bilingual Education & Bilingualism: 125 | Includes bibliographical references and index. | Summary: "This book adopts a raciolinguistic perspective to examine the ways in which dual language education programs in the US often reinforce the racial inequities that they purport to challenge. The chapters adopt a range of methodologies, disciplines and language foci to challenge mainstream and scholarly discourses on dual language education"— Provided by publisher.
Identifiers: LCCN 2020028245 (print) | LCCN 2020028246 (ebook) | ISBN 9781800410039 (paperback) | ISBN 9781800410046 (hardback) | ISBN 9781800410053 (pdf) | ISBN 9781800410060 (epub) | ISBN 9781800410077 (kindle edition)
Subjects: LCSH: Education, Bilingual—United States. | Educational equalization—United States. | Minorities—Education—United States. | Bilingualism—United States.
Classification: LCC LC3731 .B574 2021 (print) | LCC LC3731 (ebook) | DDC 370.117/50973—dc23 LC record available at https://lccn.loc.gov/2020028245
LC ebook record available at https://lccn.loc.gov/2020028246

British Library Cataloguing in Publication Data
A catalogue entry for this book is available from the British Library.

ISBN-13: 978-1-80041-004-6 (hbk)
ISBN-13: 978-1-80041-003-9 (pbk)

Multilingual Matters
UK: St Nicholas House, 31–34 High Street, Bristol BS1 2AW, UK.
USA: NBN, Blue Ridge Summit, PA, USA.

Website: www.multilingual-matters.com
Twitter: Multi_Ling_Mat
Facebook: https://www.facebook.com/multilingualmatters
Blog: www.channelviewpublications.wordpress.com

Copyright © 2021 Nelson Flores, Amelia Tseng and Nicholas Subtirelu and the authors of individual chapters.

All rights reserved. No part of this work may be reproduced in any form or by any means without permission in writing from the publisher.

The policy of Multilingual Matters/Channel View Publications is to use papers that are natural, renewable and recyclable products, made from wood grown in sustainable forests. In the manufacturing process of our books, and to further support our policy, preference is given to printers that have FSC and PEFC Chain of Custody certification. The FSC and/or PEFC logos will appear on those books where full certification has been granted to the printer concerned.

Typeset by Nova Techset Private Limited, Bengaluru and Chennai, India.
Printed and bound in the UK by Short Run Press Ltd.

Contents

Contributors　vii

Bilingualism for All or Just for the Rich and White? Introducing a Raciolinguistic Perspective to Dual Language Education　1
Nelson Flores, Amelia Tseng and Nicholas Subtirelu

1　The Intersectionality of Neoliberal Classing with Raciolinguistic Marginalization in State Dual Language Policy: A Call for Locally Crafted Programs　19
M. Garrett Delavan, Juan A. Freire and Verónica E. Valdez

2　Common Threads: Language Policy, Nation, Whiteness, and Privilege in Iowa's First Dual Language Program　40
Crissa Stephens

3　Dual Language and the Erasure of Emergent Bilinguals Labeled As Disabled (EBLADs)　63
María Cioè-Peña

4　Dueling Discourses in Dual Language Schools: Multilingual 'Success for All' versus the Academic 'Decline' of Black Students　88
Lisa M. Dorner, Jeong-Mi Moon, Edwin Nii Bonney and Alexandria Otis

5　Centering Raciolinguistic Ideologies in Two-Way Dual Language Education: The Politicized Role of Parents in Mediating their Children's Bilingualism　111
Sera J. Hernandez

6　Helping or Being Helped? The Influence of Raciolinguistic Ideologies on Parental Involvement in Dual Immersion　132
Jazmín A. Muro

7　Hebrew Dual Language Bilingual Education: The Intersection of Race, Language and Religion　156
Sharon Avni and Kate Menken

8　Raciolinguistic Positioning of Language Models in a Korean–English Dual Language Immersion Classroom　177
Jin Sook Lee, Wona Lee and Hala Sun

9 The Black and Brown Search for Agency: African American
   and Latinx Children's Plight to Bilingualism in a Two-Way
   Dual Language Program   199
   *Claudia G. Cervantes-Soon, Enrique David Degollado
      and Idalia Nuñez*

10 Who Gets to Count as Emerging Bilinguals? Adapting
   a Holistic Writing Rubric for All   220
   Margarita Gómez and Kristina Collins

11 One White Student's Journey Through Six Years of
   Elementary Schooling: Uncovering Whiteness and Privilege
   in Two-Way Bilingual Education   244
   *Suzanne García-Mateus, Kimberly A. Strong,
      Deborah K. Palmer and Dan Heiman*

   Conclusion: Bilingualism for All? Revisiting the Question   266
   Nelson Flores, Nicholas Subtirelu and Amelia Tseng

   Afterword: What is the Magic Sauce?   271
   Guadalupe Valdés

   Index   279

Contributors

Sharon Avni is Professor of Academic Literacy and Linguistics at Borough of Manhattan Community College of the City University of New York (CUNY). She is a Research Affiliate at the Jack, Joseph and Morton Mandel Center for Studies in Jewish Education at Brandeis University, and at the Research Institute for the Study of Language in Urban Society at the CUNY Graduate Center. Her scholarship examines the ideological, interactional and policy perspectives of Hebrew–English bilingualism and Hebrew acquisition in informal and formal educational contexts in the United States. Further information can be found on her website: www.sharonavni.com

Edwin Nii Bonney is a doctoral candidate in Educational Leadership and Policy Analysis at the University of Missouri-Columbia. His research includes recognizing and highlighting the languages, cultures and experiences of minoritized groups as a way to disrupt hegemonic English language practices and policies especially in Ghanaian education. He is also currently a researcher as part of the US Department of Education National Professional Development grant in Missouri called *Strengthening Equity and Effectiveness for Teachers of English Learners* (www.see-tel.org)

Claudia G. Cervantes-Soon is Associate Professor of Bilingual Education at Arizona State University. Her research interests center on critical ethnographic approaches to study the cultural production, pedagogical practices and enactments among historically marginalized communities in bi/multilingual, bi/multicultural and Mexico–US borderlands contexts. She draws on critical pedagogy, border/transborder epistemologies and anti-colonial Chicana feminist traditions to explore ways in which educators, youth and communities enact agency and forge empowered identities and new futurities.

María Cioè-Peña earned her PhD in Urban Education from The Graduate Center – City University of New York. She is a bilingual/biliterate researcher and educator who examines the intersections of disability, language, school–parent partnerships and public policy. Taking a sociolinguistic approach and stance, she pushes and reimagines the boundaries of *inclusive* spaces for minoritized children. Stemming from her experiences as a former bilingual special education teacher, María's research focuses on bilingual children with dis/abilities, their families and their ability to access multilingual and *inclusive* learning spaces within public schools.

Kristina Collins is a seasoned educator with 16 years of experience teaching children and adults in the Baltimore-Washington Area. At Loyola Universityof Maryland she is focused on preparing educators to become culturally and linguistically responsive teachers and reading specialists. She obtained her Bachelor's of Arts degree with honors in English with from the University of Maryland Eastern Shore. She received her Master of Science degree in Professional Writing with concentration in Teaching College Writing from Towson University. Kristina was the 2014 Loyola University Maryland Literacy Teacher of the Year.

Enrique David Degollado is a Post-Doctoral Scholar in Language Education at The University of Iowa. A Texas native, David taught 3rd- and 5th-grade bilingual education along the border in Laredo, where he was born and raised. David recently graduated from The University of Texas at Austin with a PhD in Curriculum and Instruction and a specialization in Bilingual/Bicultural Education. His research examines the ways in which the lived experiences of in-service bilingual education teachers inform their language and literacy ideologies and pedagogical practices.

Lisa M. Dorner is an Associate Professor of Education at the University of Missouri-Columbia: a teacher, researcher and life-long learner; a lover of language, intercultural connection and the idea of educación. Her work falls into three main areas: the politics/planning of bilingual education, educational policy implementation and immigrant family integration in 'new' spaces (like rural Missouri). She is especially interested in the development of language immersion education and how immigrant families and children navigate educational options. Lisa's work can be found in *American Educational Research Journal, Educational Policy* and *TESOL Quarterly* (forthcoming special issue 2020). Her website is lisamdorner.com.

M. Garrett Delavan is an Assistant Professor in transition from the School of Education at California State University San Marcos to the Department of Middle and Secondary Education at Georgia State University. He worked for 17 years as a public school teacher in language education. His first research focus is language education planning that creates equitable access to program types and class curriculum by opposing evolving forms of racism and classism embedded within marketization trends in education. His second research focus is ecojustice curriculum connections that will allow language learners to access the empowering awareness it will take to transform society for the better.

Juan A. Freire is an Assistant Professor in the Department of Teacher Education at Brigham Young University. He worked for several years as an elementary school teacher, both in Spain and in a Spanish–English dual language program in Utah. His research focuses on equity issues in dual language education, particularly concerns for English learners and other racialized students. In the field of dual language education, his research includes development of policy and planning as well as multicultural/bilingual classroom practices. He is a founding and governing board member of Esperanza Elementary, a Title 1 school in Utah with a whole-school Spanish–English two-way immersion program.

Suzanne García-Mateus is an Assistant Professor and the Director of the Monterey Institute for English Learners at California State University – Monterey Bay. A former two-way dual language bilingual teacher, she examines the intersection of race, language, identity and class through a critical lens in bilingual school contexts. Her interests include teacher preparation for urban and rural bilingual schools, bilingual education policy and Latinx family language practices and ideologies. As an advocate and activist with and for marginalized communities, she continues to promote bilingualism as a right and critical additive bilingual education programs across the US.

Margarita Gómez is an associate professor of literacy education at Loyola University Maryland where she teaches courses in processes and acquisition of literacy, assessment and instruction of literacy, and second language theory and assessment. Her research aims to better understand how classroom contexts play a critical role for culturally and linguistically diverse learners' writing development. Margarita earned her doctoral degree in Language, Learning and Literacy from Boston College. She previously taught at the elementary level in a bilingual school in California, and at an inclusion classroom in New York.

Dan Heiman is Assistant Professor of Bilingual Education in the Department of Teacher Education and Administration at the University of North Texas (Denton). A former bilingual/EFL educator in El Paso, TX and at the University of Veracruz (México), his research is grounded in critical ethnographic methods and examines how stakeholders make sense of and oftentimes resist neoliberal processes and policies in Two-Way Bilingual Education (TWBE). His interests include critical pedagogies in TWBE classrooms and bilingual teacher preparation, *acompañamiento* as language policy activism, and critical translanguaging pedagogies in K-16 contexts.

Sera J. Hernandez is Assistant Professor of Dual Language and English Learner Education at San Diego State University where she teaches graduate courses on language policy, multilingual education and biliteracy. She earned her PhD in Education from the University of California, Berkeley and has worked in public K-12 schools and universities for over 20 years. With an interdisciplinary academic background, Dr Hernandez's research bridges the fields of educational linguistics and the anthropology of education to examine the sociocultural, linguistic and political contexts surrounding educational language policies, bilingual teacher preparation, and bilingualism and biliteracy practices in the US and abroad.

Jin Sook Lee is Professor of Education at the University of California, Santa Barbara. Her research examines sociocultural factors that influence the learning and teaching processes of multilingual students and the maintenance and development of heritage languages among children of immigrant families. She co-edited *The Education of Language Minority Immigrants in the US* (Multilingual Matters, 2009) and *Feeling it: Language, Race and Affect in Latinx Youth Learning* (Routledge, 2018). She is a former Fulbright Scholar and her work has been supported by organizations such as the Foundation for Child Development, National Institute of Health and National Science Foundation.

Wona Lee is a lecturer of Korean in the East Asian Languages and Cultural Studies at the University of California, Santa Barbara. Her current research focuses on pedagogy of Korean/English bilingual teaching and curricula for adult Korean language learners. Her work has been published in the *Bilingual Research Journal*.

Kate Menken is a Professor of Linguistics and Director of Linguistics and TESOL Programs at Queens College of the City University of New York (CUNY). She is also a Research Fellow at the Research Institute for the Study of Language in Urban Society at the CUNY Graduate Center. Her research interests include language education policy, bilingual education, and the education of emergent bilinguals in US public schools. Further information can be found on her website: http://katemenken.org

Jeong-Mi Moon is a doctoral candidate in the department of Educational Leadership and Policy Analysis at the University of Missouri-Columbia. Her main research interest is educational policy for immigrant/language minority students in the United States as well as South Korea. Especially, she focuses on how school practices/policies regarding immigrant/language minority students shape their academic course-taking trajectories in high school.

Jazmín A. Muro is an Assistant Professor in the Department of Anthropology, Sociology & Criminal Justice at Regis University. Dr Muro received her PhD in Sociology at the University of Southern California and is in expert in qualitative research methods. Her work examines how race functions for Latinxs and their interactions with other racial/ethnic groups in multiple realms – including schools, romantic relationships and, most recently, gentrification. Her forthcoming book, *Consuming Difference: Latinxs, Language and Race Relations in California*, analyzes the race relations between Latinx and white families in Spanish/English dual immersion and is under contract with NYU Press.

Idalia Nuñez is an Assistant Professor of Language and Literacy at the University of Illinois Urbana-Champaign. She is a bilingual who grew up on the Texas-Mexico borderlands with experiences that have shaped and informed her understanding and interest in bilingualism, biliteracy and translanguaging. Her research focuses on recognizing the everyday cultural and linguistic resources of students of color, specifically from Latinx communities in order to leverage academic learning.

Alexandria Otis is a doctoral candidate in Educational Leadership and Policy Analysis at the University of Missouri. Her research includes examining gendered discourses in curriculum, supplementary text resources, and teacher–student interactions. She is currently an adjunct instructor in the education department at a small university in the Midwest.

Deborah K. Palmer is Professor of Equity, Bilingualism and Biliteracy in the School of Education at the University of Colorado Boulder. A former two-way dual language bilingual teacher, she conducts qualitative research using ethnography and discourse analysis in culturally/linguistically diverse settings. Her interests include bilingual education policy and politics; critical additive dual language bilingual education; teacher preparation for linguistically/culturally diverse teaching contexts; teacher advocacy and activism; and issues of language, power and identity in schools. She recently co-authored a book, published by Multilingual Matters: *Dual Language Bilingual Education: Teacher Cases and Perspectives on Large-Scale Implementation*.

Crissa Stephens is Assistant Teaching Professor at Georgetown University. Her community-based research focuses on identity, language policy, and social justice. She seeks to understand, map, and impact how policies and practices at play in education shape identity and access for multilingual people. In her critical ethnographic work, she partners with multilingual communities to center their experiences and transform language education towards equity.

Kimberly A. Strong is a doctoral candidate in the program Equity, Bilingualism and Biliteracy at the University of Colorado Boulder. Her research employs mixed methods and critical frameworks to understand and improve the school experiences of bilingual students and families, goals that are informed by her previous work serving bilingual communities in the education, government and nonprofit sectors. She is an educational consultant for the Congress of Hispanic Educators and teaches graduate courses for practicing teachers who work with culturally and linguistically diverse students. Her current research investigates how school accountability policies impact racially, economically, and linguistically marked learners.

Hala Sun is a doctoral candidate in Education at the University of California, Santa Barbara (UCSB), with specializations in Applied Linguistics and Writing Studies. Her research focuses on language classroom interactions in bilingual settings (Korean–English and Spanish–English English Learners), specifically examining the strategies and processes of hybrid semiotic practices. She teaches college-level writing and has recently been working on the evaluation of college STEM and Student Success programs, funded by the US Department of Education.

Verónica E. Valdez is an Associate Professor in the Department of Education, Culture, and Society at the University of Utah in Salt Lake City. She has over twenty years of experience working with culturally and linguistically diverse programs, teachers, students, families and communities in several states across the US. Her interdisciplinary research is focused on four interrelated and often overlapping strands: language learning efforts that foster multilingualism/biliteracy in school and out-of-school contexts; educational language policy and planning and its equity impacts for emergent bilinguals; Latinx learners and education; and teacher education and practices that promote the values of multilingualism, multiculturalism and social justice across educational settings.

Bilingualism for All or Just for the Rich and White? Introducing a Raciolinguistic Perspective to Dual Language Education

Nelson Flores, Amelia Tseng and Nicholas Subtirelu

In 2018, *Harper's Bazaar* published an article about the bilingualism of Princess Charlotte, the daughter of Prince William and Kate Middleton. The headline read 'Princess Charlotte may have just started nursery but can already speak two languages' (Fowler, 2018). The article, which was a glowing endorsement of her bilingualism, noted that she picked up Spanish from her nanny. That same year a woman was attacked on a London subway for speaking Spanish, with her assailants insisting that she should be speaking English in England (Dury, 2018). One would imagine that if the assailants had heard Princess Charlotte speaking Spanish they would have had a very different reaction.

Across the ocean in the United States we can see similar double standards and their effects. In 2017, Ivanka Trump posted a viral video of her daughter Arabella singing in Chinese (Klein, 2017). Comments about how cute she was coupled with enthusiastic emojis showed how impressed people were with her bilingualism. Two years later, an email sent by a Duke University professor to Chinese international students would also go viral. In her email she warned the students that some people were complaining about their use of Chinese in public areas and that they should only use English in order to avoid negative repercussions for their future careers (Kaur, 2019). Interestingly enough, nobody suggested that Arabella using Chinese would have negative repercussions for her. On the contrary, the overwhelming consensus was that her use of Chinese could only be good for her future.

While these examples may be extreme, the double standard that exists between white bilingualism and racialized bilingualism permeates the dominant discourses in mainstream educational debates in much more insidious ways as well. For example, Princess Charlotte entering preschool bilingual was universally celebrated. In contrast, in discussions of racialized bilingualism in schools it is much more common to hear about the 'problems' of increasing numbers of 'English Learners' (Gutiérrez & Orellana, 2006). In addition, while increased attention has been brought to purported cognitive benefits of bilingualism (Adescope *et al.*, 2010), it is still common for racialized bilingual students to be described as not fully proficient in either of their languages leading to cognitive deficiencies (Brooks, 2017; MacSwan *et al.*, 2002). Even bilingual education advocates often rely on these framings by arguing that bilingual education will provide racialized bilinguals a strong foundation in their L1 that they can then transfer to their L2 (Cummins, 2000). Yet unaddressed in this discourse is who determines what constitutes a strong foundation in an L1, what criteria are being used to make this determination and how it connects to a broader discursive history that has questioned the legitimacy of the language and literacy practices of racialized communities. That is, even as discourses surrounding bilingualism in general become more positive, the discourses surrounding the bilingualism of racialized students remain overwhelmingly negative with the assumption being that they may not even have a strong foundation in a language or languages that they may have heard since birth.

Dual language education programs that have the explicit goal of developing bilingualism and biliteracy of all participating students have often been proposed as a solution to these negative views of racialized bilingualism. While the first dual language program can be traced back to the 1960s, these programs have grown exponentially over the past 20 years (Boyle *et al.*, 2015). It is common for dual language education to be framed as inherently socially transformative and for their proliferation in recent years to be described as a natural means of developing more equitable spaces in public schools (Lindholm-Leary, 2000). In contrast to these more uncritical framings, in this book we adopt a *raciolinguistic perspective* that points to the contradictory role that dual language education plays in US society. Specifically, we situate the proliferation of dual language programs within the double standard described above that frames white bilingualism as inherently valuable and racialized bilingualism as inherently deficient.

This raciolinguistic perspective builds on Valdés' cautionary note that identified tensions within the movement to expand dual language education that began in the 1990s. Situating the emergence of dual language education within the broader racial stratification of US society Valdés (1997) noted that 'in implementing dual-language immersion programs, there must be sensitivity to the realities of intergroup relations in the communities surrounding schools to the fact that teachers are products of the society with all of its shortcomings, and to the fact that mainstream and minority children live in very different worlds' (1997: 419). She argued that 'educators need to carefully examine who the main beneficiaries of these language "resources" will be' (1997: 419). Specifically, in the context of Spanish–English dual language programs, she cautioned that power imbalances within these programs might lead to the needs of affluent white students and parents being favored over the needs of low-income Latinx students and parents. For example, in teaching and curricula, language instruction might be tailored to the needs of white second language speakers with little consideration of the consequences for Latinx Spanish speakers. More broadly, she cautioned that dual language education programs might increasingly be marketed as a form of elite bilingualism which would enrich affluent white children's educational experience and maximize their economic potential while doing little to improve the lives of Latinxs students.

Over 20 years later, her analysis appears prophetic as many of the dynamics she cautioned about have increasingly come to pass. Oyster-Adams Bilingual School in Washington, DC is a good example. The school has long been touted as an example of effective Spanish–English dual language education (Freeman, 1996). Fern (1995) writes that 'since it was inaugurated in 1971, Oyster has maintained a consistent record of high academic standards and student achievement' (1995: 497). Decades later, Oyster-Adams continues to be a widely respected dual language school, but the community it serves has undergone drastic changes. These changes were already underway in the early 1990s. Fern describes Oyster as serving two neighborhoods: one is composed of 'upper class diplomats, politicians, and other powerful professionals' and the other is 'Washington's barrio latino,' but she points that the 'barrio has undergone a tremendous gentrification, resulting in the displacement of the Latino population to the North and East, where housing costs are more accessible' (p. 501). Nonetheless, Fern notes that, during the 1992–93 academic year, 80% of the students at Oyster-Adams were identified as Hispanic and 40% participated in the free lunch program. Housing prices in the area around Oyster-Adams have continued to rise since the 1990s, and the result has been a decrease in the number of Latinx students and students from low-income families. During the 2017–2018 school year, 60% of the students were identified as Hispanic or Latino, and only 22% were categorized as economically disadvantaged (Tseng, 2017). Thus, due to the profound changes in the residential areas surrounding it, Oyster-Adams Bilingual School has become less accessible for students of color and students from less affluent families with a clear and direct impact on its dual language programming: difficulties recruiting students who speak Spanish at home (Williams, 2017) have pointed to how this shift toward the needs of affluent white communities has led to the gentrification of bilingual education with racialized bilingual students often systematically excluded from dual language programs (Valdez *et al.*, 2016). Yet, it is not just racialized bilingual students who are being excluded from these programs. African American students have also been systematically excluded because of deficit ideologies that suggest that they are not able to handle dual language education (Palmer, 2010) or have been marginalized within dual language classrooms because of their use of African American Language (AAL) (Zisselsberger & Collins, 2016). In addition, the creation of dual language programs in predominantly African American neighborhoods has been feared and resisted because of the ways that these programs contribute to the gentrification of schools and communities and the displacement of African American students (Stein, 2018). This book seeks to bring attention to these tensions in the hope of developing a vision for dual language education that most effectively promotes racial equity.

Developing a Raciolinguistic Perspective on Dual Language Education

The raciolinguistic perspective on dual language education developed in this volume builds on the five components of a raciolinguistic perspective laid out by Rosa and Flores (2017). Below we review each of these components and examine the ways that these principles are reflected in the various chapters of the volume. We discuss not just how the chapters reflect these components but also point to the ways that they extend them in new and productive ways by deepening our understanding of raciolinguistic dynamics that remain underexplored.

Historical and contemporary co-naturalization of race and language

The first component of a raciolinguistic perspective argues that 'contemporary raciolinguistic ideologies must be situated within colonial histories that have shaped the co-naturalization of language and race as part of the project of modernity' (Rosa & Flores, 2017: 3). In discussions of dual language education the most common way of documenting this history is through a focus on the hegemonic imposition of English. Scholars have often connected this imposition of English to the Americanization movement that emerged within the context of World War I (Wiley, 1998). Yet, efforts to eradicate African and Indigenous languages precede that by centuries (Spring, 2016) indicating the highly racialized nature of English hegemony throughout US history that has continued into contemporary society through xenophobic and nativist movements that seek to make English the official language and ban any form of bilingual education for racialized bilinguals (Macedo, 2000). While dual language programs have always stood in opposition to English-Only instruction, resistance to the hegemony of English can be challenging. Previous research has pointed to the ways that the broader societal context of English hegemony has often led English to have a higher status even within dual language programs that sought to equalize the status of the two languages (Babino & Stewart, 2017; Lopez, 2011; Palmer, 2007). A raciolinguistic perspective pushes this analysis even further by pointing to the broader racialization processes that further facilitate the hegemony of English within these programs. This is best illustrated by Cervantes-Soon, Degollado and Nuñez (Chapter 9) who point to the ways that the broader school structures of a low-income segregated school including a culture of surveillance and high student mobility that led students to be added to the dual language program throughout the school year negatively impacted the status of Spanish in the program and increased the use of English. They add to existing literature on English hegemony in dual language programs by suggesting that the colonial legacy that produces the highly racialized surveillance apparatus of low-income segregated schools and the instability that characterizes the lives of many students in these schools can further increase the hegemony of English regardless of any goals that a program may have.

Yet, the historical co-construction of language and race extends beyond English hegemony into dominant conceptualizations of bilingualism that permeate debates surrounding bilingual education generally and dual language education specifically. As a product of the War on Poverty, at the core of the Bilingual Education Act (BEA) passed in 1968 was the culture of poverty thesis that posited that the primary challenge confronting Latinxs and other racialized bilinguals was linguistic – namely that they had linguistic deficiencies – and that bilingual education would help to fix these linguistic deficiencies and allow them to assimilate into mainstream society (Sung, 2017). While dual language programs typically strive to reject such deficit-oriented perspectives, they have inherited from the BEA the assumption that the main challenge confronting racialized bilinguals is linguistic marginalization rather than white supremacy and global capitalism. The result is often an uncritical celebration of diversity that does little to challenge the status quo. This can be seen clearly in Stephens' chapter (Chapter 2) where she points to the ways that media representations of a dual language program indicated that white families were applauded for their participation while Latinx families were pressured into putting their children into English-Only programs. This chapter also illustrates the ways that Latinx children are often framed as resources for the learning of white children – learning that these children and their families can then, in turn, use to further marginalize Latinx children and their families in the school community and the broader society.

While chapters in this book utilize a raciolinguistic perspective to examine the historical and contemporary marginalization of Latinxs in dual language education, they also point to the historical factors that lead to the marginalization of other racialized communities within the contemporary context of dual language education. A particularly strong focus across the chapters is documenting the marginalization of African American students and connecting this marginalization to the history of anti-Blackness that has shaped contemporary US society. As Dorner, Moon, Bonney and Otis (Chapter 4) illustrate, even in a context where there is an explicit focus on expanding dual language education to meet the needs of African American students, raciolinguistic ideologies can serve to undermine these efforts by suggesting that African American students need to fully master English before being able to learn an additional language.

In short, the chapters in this volume illustrate the ways that dual language programs, as products of broader racialized histories, often serve to reinforce the relations of power that they purport to challenge. Specifically, each of the chapters shows in their own ways how framing social transformation solely within the linguistic realm obscures the fact that language is always already racialized. Delavan, Freire and Valdez (Chapter 1) succinctly describe this as *propertied white aurality* which connects the ways that language is heard to the apparatus of white supremacy and capitalism. From this perspective, language uptake cannot be divorced from the broader political economy that positions speakers as legitimate or illegitimate users of language before they even utter a word.

Perceptions of racial and linguistic difference

The second component of a raciolinguistic perspective draws attention to the constructed socio-historical nature of raciolinguistic perception, and the fact that ideologies of difference single out racialized groups as distinctive in comparison to the unmarked white norm. In particular, it draws attention to the white perceiving subject and the ways that this subject position, shaped by centuries of colonialism, over-determines the language practices of racialized communities to be deficient and in need of remediation. Importantly, this white perceiving subject position is not simply inhabited 'by white individuals but rather by whiteness as an historical and contemporary subject position that can be situationally inhabited both by individuals recognized as white and nonwhite' (Rosa & Flores, 2017: 8). In addition, it is not just inhabited by people but can also be inhabited by 'nonhuman entities such as institutions, policies, and technologies associated with linguistic profiling' (Rosa & Flores, 2017: 8). That is, the white perceiving subject is an ideological position that has been produced by a long history of colonialism that has sought to police the language practices of racialized communities while celebrating these same language practices when utilized by white people. Put differently, a basic component of hegemonic whiteness is the ability for one's language practices to always be perceived as the norm while a basic component of racialization is for one's language practices to always be perceived as deviating from the norm.

A raciolinguistic perspective has brought specific attention to two instantiations of this white perceiving subject. The first instantiation are discourses of languagelessness that suggest that racialized bilinguals are not fully proficient in either of their two languages (Rosa, 2016). These discourses of languagelessness shaped the foundation of early debates related to bilingual education as can be seen with the emergence of the term *semilingual* in the 1970s to describe racialized bilingual students in bilingual programs who were deemed to be not fully proficient in either English or their home language based on their performance on standardized assessments (Heath, 1984). While the discourse has since shifted away from semilingualism toward a discussion of their perceived lack of mastery of *academic language*, the underlying framework has remained the same – that the language practices of racialized bilingual students are inadequate for school success and require modification. Previous research has illustrated the ways that these discourses of languagelessness have served to marginalized racialized students, even raising questions as to their fit for dual language education (Chaparro, 2019; Palmer, 2010). Chapters in this book build on this previous work in ways that further theorize the connection between language and race in producing these discourses of languagelessness even within contexts that purport to value bilingualism.

Dorner, Moon, Bonney and Otis (Chapter 4) document this circulating ideology in the case of African Americans and the ways that this was used to suggest that African American students were not capable of thriving within a dual language context. Gómez and Collins (Chapter 10) point to the ways that this gets enacted in daily practice at a school serving large numbers of African American students where teachers actively resist recognizing AAL as a legitimate form of communication even within a context that purportedly celebrates linguistic diversity. Lee, Lee and Sun (Chapter 8) go even further by examining the ways that raciolinguistic ideologies can impact the perceptions of the language practices of racialized bilingual teachers. Specifically, they describe how Korean parents perceived the Korean–American teachers to be inadequate in English because they were not white and inadequate in Korean because they did not grow up in Korea. This raises questions related to how to prepare racialized bilingual teachers within a context where their bilingualism is policed and perceived to be deficient in comparison to their white counterparts.

A second instantiation of the white perceiving subject is related to the ways that whiteness affords language users the ability to have their bi/multilingualism framed as inherently good. Previous research has documented the ways that white privilege has often led to white students and their families dominating the classroom and school community (Burns, 2017; Heiman & Murakami, 2019; Muro, 2016; Palmer, 2011; Valdés,

1997). This can also be seen in the case study of a white child in a dual language program offered by García-Mateus, Strong, Palmer and Heiman (Chapter 11). In particular, her Spanish language skills were celebrated to the point where she was deemed a Spanish language model even though she was not observed using Spanish on a regular basis. In contrast, her Latinx classmates who came from bilingual homes and likely were exposed to Spanish more regularly were often not positioned as Spanish language models. This, in turn, gave her enough confidence to question the expertise of her Latinx peers and even question the Spanish expertise of her teacher. Meanwhile her Latinx peers never really had the opportunity to be truly recognized as language models of any language.

Together, the chapters in this volume point to the ways that hegemonic perceptions of language ability are inextricably connected to the racial position of the speaker. Racialized speakers are perceived as deficient in relation to the white peers even when engaged in ostensibly similar linguistic practices. This raises important questions about how best to prepare bilingual teachers to work in a context fraught with power dynamics that may serve to marginalize the students that dual language programs were originally designed to support. Recent calls for adding an explicit focus on the development of critical consciousness offer an important first step in beginning to develop structures and practices that challenge these power dynamics (Cervantes-Soon *et al.*, 2017). Yet, questions of who has the authority to facilitate this work around critical consciousness is important to consider. If racialized bilingual teachers are often scrutinized in ways that their white counterparts are not, it may be difficult for them to push these conversations forward because of their perceived lack of linguistic proficiency. In addition, low-income segregated schools with punitive disciplinary cultures may lack the appropriate infrastructure for developing such critical conversations leaving these conversations to emerge in more privileged settings. In this way, the chapters in this volume allude to the ways that challenging the white perceiving subject will inevitably require broader structural change that complement changes in pedagogical approaches to facilitate more critical conversations in dual language classrooms.

Regimentation of racial and linguistic categories

The third component of a raciolinguistic perspective argues that the co-naturalized ideological relationship between language and race is socially constructed, deriving from historical and ongoing processes of 'raciolinguistic enregisterment, whereby linguistic and racial forms are jointly constructed as sets and rendered mutually recognizable as named languages/varieties and racial categories' (Rosa & Flores, 2017: 10). Assumed differences between racialized groups and the unmarked white norm are regimented through social expectations and interaction.

The repeated naming of categories regiments them while erasing processes and practices that do not fit into the raciolinguistic norms. Importantly, social associations take on a life of their own: as stereotypes or racial emblems, they 'need not correspond to empirically verifiable linguistic practices' (Rosa & Flores, 2017: 12).

One example of raciolinguistic enregisterment that is prominent in dual language education is the enregisterment of entire languages as belonging to particular types of people. Most common is for Spanish to become associated with low-income Latinx students and English to become associated with affluent white students in ways that erase the heterogeneity of Spanish and English speakers. As Hernandez (Chapter 5) describes, this raciolinguistic enregisterment of English and Spanish is often connected to broader discursive constructions that typically connect whiteness and English speaking within dual language programs to 'bravery' and 'confidence' with the implication being that Latinidad and Spanish speaking makes dual language education a less brave and confident choice. There is no acknowledgement of the bravery and confidence that it must have taken for the low-income Latinx caregivers being served by the program to immigrate to a new country or to choose to have their children participate in a dual language program in a xenophobic society. Interestingly, the same discourse of bravery and confidence is not often attributed to AAL speakers who participate in dual language programs with Gómez and Collins (Chapter 10) illustrating the ways that these students are often framed as problems whose language practices need to be fixed. Indeed, as they suggest, the more explicit focus on language that characterizes dual language programs may actually increase the raciolinguistic policing that African American students experience.

These chapters also point to ways that the one-the-ground raciolinguistic reality doesn't neatly conform to the raciolinguistic enregisterment that connects whiteness with affluence and English and racialization with poverty and languages other than English. For example, Muro (Chapter 6) challenges the binary of low-income Latinx and affluent white by examining the experiences of middle-class Latinxs. In many ways, the school context she describes seems to fit in with dominant notions of raciolinguistic enregisterment that connect Latinxs with poverty and Spanish and white people with affluence and English. Yet, middle-class Latinxs participating in the program did not fit neatly into this dichotomy and often experienced racialization as Latinxs even as they had class privilege and proficiency in English. Their class privilege and proficiency in English often led them to ally themselves more with affluent white parents than they did with low-income Latinx immigrant parents. In addition, Avni and Menken (Chapter 7) complicate notions of white people in dual language programs through their exploration of a Hebrew–English dual language program. The program served a primarily working-class Jewish student population, which challenges dominant notions of raciolinguistic enregisterment in multiple ways. For one, the students were working class and not affluent. Secondly, the partner language was a language that they had familial connections to rather than one that ostensibly belonged to another group. Both of these coalesced for Jewish families into a discourse that suggested that the Jewishness of the program could provide a safe space for students to explore their heritage within a society with a long history of anti-Semitism. Together these chapters point to the complexity of the on-the-ground raciolinguistic reality of dual language programs and the ways that simplistic raciolinguistic categories erase the dynamic reality of these programs and classrooms. At the same time, they also point to the ways that dual language education in and of itself does not and cannot erase raciolinguistic hegemony, but instead often reproduces it, furthering the regimentation of racialized identities at the expense of educational equity.

Racial and linguistic intersections and assemblages

The fourth component of a raciolinguistic perspective addresses racial and linguistic intersections and assemblages with other forms of social differentiation. This component builds on the work of Black feminists who sought to bring attention to the intersection of racial and gender oppression (Combahee River Collective, 1986; Crenshaw, 1989) alongside recent developments in critical social theory that emphasizes that intersectionality is an 'assemblages of signs that bundle together to position individuals in various ways depending on the context, but also reflect longstanding processes of raciolinguistic subject formation that profoundly shape and often overdetermine individual presentations of self and perceptions of Others' (Rosa & Flores, 2017: 16). A major intersectional assemblage that has already received some attention in the dual language education literature is between race, language and social class. This intersection can be seen in the ways that dual language programs are being marketed to affluent white communities as illustrated by Delavan, Freire and Valdez (Chapter 1) as well as by Stephens (Chapter 2). This same intersection is also at play in documenting the experiences of Latinx middle class families who because of their class privilege often find that their political interests align more with affluent white families as illustrated by Hernandez (Chapter 5) and Muro (Chapter 6).

Chapters in this volume also bring attention to other intersectional assemblages beyond race, language and social class. One major intersection that has not received much attention in the literature to date is the intersection between language, race and disability. Cioè-Peña (Chapter 3) provides compelling evidence of the ableist assumptions that goes into dual language policies and programming and the ways that these assumptions systematically exclude racialized bilinguals with disabilities from participation in these programs. She challenges those of us interested in promoting racial equity within dual language education to adopt *critical disabilities raciolinguistic perspectives* that combine insights from critical disability studies with a raciolinguistic perspective to ensure that dual language education programs are inclusive of *all* racialized students, including those classified as having disabilities.

Another major intersection that has not received much attention in the literature to date is the intersection between language, race, and religion. This can be found in Avni and Menken's chapter (Chapter 7) where they document the experiences of working-class Jewish students in a Hebrew–English dual language program. In their chapter they unpack the relationship between Jewishness and whiteness and reveal that white Jewish and non-Jewish Black caregivers had different understandings of whiteness. Non-Jewish Black parents noted the white privilege afforded to Jewish families in the form of social and educational access. Meanwhile, white Jewish caregivers described their affinity to the program based on religious and ethnocultural connections rather than through overtly racial discourses. This speaks to the complex relationship between Jewishness and whiteness while also speaking to the unique experiences of working-class white families in dual language education. This perspective on whiteness opens a new direction for future investigation.

In short, the chapters in this volume move beyond a focus on the intersection of language and race to bring attention to the other forms of social differentiation that impact the experiences of racialized bilinguals in dual language education. One way that they do this is by moving the conversation beyond the white/Latinx binary and its accompanying assumptions of social class and language dominance that has dominated the research to date. To be clear there are many dual language contexts that include primarily low-income Spanish dominant Latinxs and primarily affluent English-dominant white students and many of the chapters in this volume reflect that reality. That said, many dual language contexts do not fit neatly into this dichotomy. Adopting an intersectional assemblage perspective offers tools for accounting for this complexity in ways that offer insights on how best to promote racial equity within contexts of multiple overlapping systems of privilege and oppression.

Contestations of racial and linguistic power formations

The final component of a raciolinguistic perspective 'refocuses our theory of social change away from the modification of the linguistic behaviors of racialized populations toward a dismantling of the white supremacy that permeates mainstream institutions as a product of colonialism' (Rosa & Flores, 2017: 17). Building on Valdés' cautionary note, this component challenges the assumption that dual language programs are inherently socially transformative. While she situated her critique within the long history of deficit perspectives that have shaped the educational experiences of Mexican American students, this principle makes a more general claim about the working of white supremacy in US society. Specifically, it adopts a materialist view of white supremacy that argues that the rise of global capitalism would not have been possible without the exploitation and genocide of racialized communities, including through the trans-Atlantic slave trade, the white settler colonial genocide of indigenous people and economic imperialism. White people were able to pass on the wealth that they had been able to accumulate through the exploitation and genocide of racialized communities to their children who passed it on to their children and so on and so forth leading to the racial inequalities that persist today (Harris, 1992).

Despite the materialist basis of existing racial inequalities, typical efforts to challenge racial inequalities in contemporary societies focus primarily on changing the attitudes of individuals (Melamed, 2011: 37). In this way, modern society can be characterized as a society of 'racism without racists' with individual white people not feeling individually racist but still benefiting from the multiple generations of wealth accumulation that has provided them with access to material resources denied racialized communities worldwide (Bonilla-Silva, 2014). This is certainly the case in mainstream views of dual language education that typically suggest that having students learn a different language and culture will increase their sociocultural competence and appreciation of diversity (Howard *et al.*, 2018). The implication is typically that this increased competence and appreciation will lead students and families participating in dual language programs to become agents of social change. Yet, García-Mateus, Strong, Palmer and Heiman (Chapter 11) suggest that simply participating in a dual language program may not lead white students to become agents of social change in a straightforward way and may, inadvertently, even further cement their white privilege. Cervantes-Soon, Degollado and Nuñez (Chapter 9) further observed the many challenges of focusing on sociocultural competence and appreciation of diversity within a broader dysfunctional schooling context produced as a consequence of segregation and concentrated poverty. In this way, any effort to promote sociocultural competence must be situated within broader efforts to challenge segregation and poverty. Cioè-Peña (Chapter 3) pushes even further by pointing to the impact of the systematic exclusion of students labeled with disabilities on the development (or lack thereof) of sociocultural competence of dual language students. If dual language students are less likely to be in inclusive contexts can we really say that they are developing the sociocultural competence needed for a diverse world?

In line with this insight, the chapters in this volume also illustrate the limits of the focus on individuals in dismantling racial hierarchies. Specifically, a materialist view of white supremacy points to the limits of recent efforts to commodify bilingual education within the contemporary context of neoliberal educational reform (Flores & García, 2017). In a context of intense racial stratification, commodifying programs is going to benefit those who are already privileged. This sobering reality is powerfully demonstrated by Delavan, Freire and Valdez (Chapter 1) in their chapter that offers us a glimpse into the gentrification of dual language education in Utah. They document the ways that efforts to sell dual language programs to affluent white communities systematically excludes racialized bilingual students who would most benefit from access to these programs. Looking at the case of a dual language school in Los Angeles, Muro (Chapter 6) documents the power dynamics that exist between white parents and Latinx parents and the ways that the white parents (alongside some middle-class Latinx parents) dominated the agenda of the school. These chapters clearly demonstrate that there is nothing inherently transformative about efforts to promote dual language education and that, on the contrary, these programs can serve to reproduce and even exacerbate existing racial and social class hierarchies.

These findings do not suggest to us that we should abandon effort to promote dual language education. Instead, we see this volume as a 'loving critique forward' (Paris & Alim, 2014) for efforts to expand dual language education. Our concern is not with the goal of expanding dual language education per se. It is with expanding dual language education in ways that are not connected with broader efforts to dismantle racial hierarchies. These efforts need to be multiscale, transforming education in individual interactions, classroom practices, community connections, school culture and curriculum, and broader policies affecting students and education. Armed with a more representative critical understanding, we will be better positioned to effect materially anti-racist social change and less likely to inadvertently reproduce racial injustice.

Outline of the Book

The book consists of 11 chapters written by scholars who were asked to apply a raciolinguistic perspective to research that they have undertaken related to dual language education. The first four chapters deal with the systematic exclusion of racialized populations from dual language programs. The first chapter by Delavan, Freire and Valdez offers a birds-eye view of Utah's state-wide effort to expand dual language education. They point to the ways that this top-down expansion has privileged the needs of affluent white communities in ways that systematically marginalize and exclude the many racialized bilingual students in the state who would benefit from such programs. In Chapter 2, Stephens shifts the focus away from state-level policies toward media representation describing Iowa's first dual language program. She argues that while this media representation offered a counterpoint to the increasing xenophobia of the Trump presidency, it promoted an uncritical celebration of bilingualism while ignoring the stark social status differences between white and Latinx students and families who participated in the program. Both chapters conclude with calls for resisting the trend of situating the expansion of dual language education within neoliberal discourses of preparation for the global economy and resituating issues of equity and heritage in ways that support schools and communities in developing grassroots dual language initiatives that re-center the needs of racialized communities.

Chapters 3 and 4 offer accounts of systematic exclusion that expand beyond a focus on racialized bilingualism. In Chapter 3, Cioè-Peña introduces the intersection of racialized bilingualism with disability. Using New York City as a case study, she analyzes the ways that policies that promote dual language education systematically exclude racialized bilingual students who are labeled as disabled. She suggests that New York City dual language policy simultaneously utilizes a discourse of integration while justifying the continued segregating of racialized bilingual students labeled as disabled in ways that deny them access to these programs. In Chapter 4, Dorner, Moon, Bonney and Otis expand the conversation beyond racialized bilinguals by focusing attention on African American students. They document the journey of a charter school network that began with the expressed mission of promoting dual language education in the African American community. The chapter traces how as the school began to confront high stakes testing that the discourse of the school gradually shifted from one that emphasized issues of equity to one that emphasized supposed linguistic deficiencies of African American students eventually undermining the goals of the program. Both chapters point to the impact of standardized assessments and the labels that officially and unofficially emerge from them on the access – or lack thereof – of racialized students to dual language education.

The next four chapters pay particular attention to the role of parents and families in dual language education programs. Chapters 5 and 6 examine the intersection of raciolinguistic discourses with parent participation across and within schools with Spanish/English dual language programs. In Chapter 5, Hernandez examines the role of race and social class in facilitating or hindering parent engagement in two public DLI schools in California, one in a district which deliberately integrates students of different racial, linguistic and economic backgrounds, and one in a district which segregates students along these axes. She shows that teachers, administrators and parents themselves reproduced white-privileging discourses of worth and agency, and importantly points out that a mentality of 'classed whiteness' was shared by middle-class Latinx parents. In Chapter 6, Muro investigates disparities in white and Latinx parent participation in a single Spanish/English DLI program in California. She also found that race and social class affected their participation and the perception of their involvement and agency, with Latinx parents perceived as in need of help and white parents perceived as valued helpers. Her findings also unpacked diversity and tension amongst Latinos by pointing to the delicate balance experienced by middle class Latinxs who often found themselves more politically aligned with their affluent white peers than their low-income Latinx peers. In Chapter 7, Avni and Menken examine the intersection of race, language and religion in a dual language Hebrew–English program serving white Jewish and non-Jewish Black children in NYC, taking on an unusual case of religious language ideologies in public DLI schools. They found that the program promoted diversity but, being limited to essentialist ethnolinguistic ideologies, also reproduced racism and marginalization. These studies show us that raciolinguistic ideologies are not a one-to-one mapping onto racialized bodies but intersectional, and viewed differently depending on subject positionality. As such, they draw attention to important diversity which remains underexplored in raciolinguistic perspectives on dual-language education.

Chapters 8, 9 and 10 bring more attention to the role of teachers in dual language education. In Chapter 8, Lee, Lee and Sun examine the raciolinguistic ideologies that shape both parent and teacher perception of what constitutes a good language model in a Korean–English dual language program. The Korean parents utilized what the authors called a 'native gaze' that suggested that the Korean American teachers were not adequate models of either Korean or English. In contrast, the teachers used their own life experience as a point of entry for positioning Korean American students whose language practices more closely mirrored theirs as better models than students who arrived to the school from Korea. In Chapter 9, Cervantes-Soon, Degollado and Nuñez offer a case study of one teacher's classroom in a school that primarily serves a low-income Latinx and African American student population. They examine the ways that the efforts of the teacher to create a culturally and linguistically sustaining classroom are undermined by the broader school culture of punitive surveillance alongside the fact that several students were placed into his class after the school year began. The result was increased use of English and increasingly unengaging Spanish lessons that did not promote language learning or appreciation. While Chapter 9 describes the journey of a teacher who was initially open to embracing language diversity, in Chapter 10 Gómez and Collins point to the difficulties that come with trying to change teachers' deep-seeded raciolinguistic ideologies. They describe their efforts to raise the status of AAL in a dual language school that serves a primarily African American student population and the massive resistance they confronted from teachers who refused to recognize AAL as ever appropriate for a school setting. Both chapters point to the ways that the work of dual language teachers is shaped by the broader sociopolitical context that both shapes how they view language diversity and what is possible for them to do in their classrooms to value language diversity.

In Chapter 11, García-Mateus, Strong, Palmer and Heiman bring attention to the role of students in dual language education. In particular, they trace the journey of one white student in a dual language program over the course of her six-year elementary school experience. They point to the ways that her white privilege has shaped her experiences in the program and illustrate how a program that does not systematically work toward the development of critical consciousness may lead white students who participate in dual language programs to use their newly acquired bilingualism in ways that further cements their privileged place in the broader society as opposed to in the struggle for social change. This conclusion mirrors Guadalupe Valdés' 1997 cautionary note, which she revisits in the concluding chapter.

Together this volume seeks to connect theory and practice in ways that illustrate the implications of a raciolinguistic perspective for more robustly understanding the recent expansion of dual language education in the United States. Yet, it is important to recognize that while colonialism was a global project that continues to affect the present, it has played out differently in different contexts. This volume seeks to better understand how this legacy has shaped bilingual education in one country. That said, it is our hope that this volume provides insights for scholars who are interested in thinking through the implications of a raciolinguistic perspective on bilingual education in other contexts as well. In short, we hope that this volume opens up a broader conversation of if and how a raciolinguistic perspective might offer insights for analyzing bilingual education around the world.

References

Adescope, O., Lavin, T., Thompson, T. and Ungerleider, C. (2010) A systematic review and meta-analysis of the cognitive correlates of bilingualism. *Review of Educational Research* 80, 207–245.

Babino, A. and Stewart, M. (2017) 'I like English better': Latino dual language students investment in Spanish, English and bilingualism. *Journal of Latinos and Education* 16, 18–29.

Bonilla-Silva, E. (2014) *Racism Without Racists: Colorblind Racism and the Persistence of Racial Inequality in America*. Lanham: Rowman & Littlefield.

Boyle, A., August, D., Tabaku, L., Cole, S. and Simpson-Baird, A. (2015) *Dual Language Education Programs: Current State Policies and Practices*. Washington, DC: U.S. Department of Education.

Brooks, M. (2017) 'She doesn't have the basic understanding of a language': Using spelling research to challenge deficit conceptualizations of adolescent bilinguals. *Journal of Literacy Research* 49, 342–370.

Burns, M. (2017) 'Compromises that we make': Whiteness in the dual language context. *Bilingual Research Journal* 40, 339–352.

Cervantes-Soon, C., Dorner, L., Palmer, D., Heiman, D., Schwerdtfeger, R. and Choi, J. (2017) Combating inequalities in two-way immersion programs: Toward critical consciousness in bilingual education spaces. *Review of Research in Education* 41, 403–427.

Chaparro, S. (2019) But mom! I'm not a Spanish Boy: Raciolinguistic socialization in a Two-Way Immersion bilingual program. *Linguistics and Education* 50, 1–12.

Combahee River Collective (1986) *The Combahee River Collective Statement: Black Feminist Organizing in the Seventies and Eighties*. Albany, NY: Kitchen Table Women of Color Press.

Crenshaw, K. (1989) Demarginalizing the intersection of race and sex: A Black feminist critique of antidiscrimination doctrine, feminist theory and antiracist politics. *The University of Chicago Legal Forum* 1989, 139–167.

Cummins, J. (2000) *Language, Power and Pedagogy: Bilingual Children in the Crossfire*. Clevedon: Multilingual Matters.

Dury, C. (April 2018) Woman attacked on London Underground for speaking Spanish. *Independent*. See https://www.independent.co.uk/news/uk/home-news/london-underground-attack-woman-speaking-spanish-tube-hair-pull-racist-a8303771.html

Fern, V. (1995) Oyster school stands the test of time. *Bilingual Research Journal* 19, 497–1512.

Flores, N. and García, O. (2017) A critical review of bilingual education in the United States: From basements and pride to boutiques and profits. *Annual Review of Applied Linguistics* 37, 14–29.

Fowler, D. (January, 2018) Princess Charlotte may have just started nursery but can already speak two languages. See https://www.harpersbazaar.com/uk/culture/culture-news/a15153245/princess-charlotte-bilingual-spanish-nursery-nanny/

Freeman, R. (1996) Dual-language planning at Oyster bilingual school: 'Its much more than language.' *TESOL Quarterly* 30, 557–582.

Gutiérrez, K. and Orellana, M. (2006) The 'problem' of English learners: Constructing genres of difference. *Research in the Teaching of English* 40, 502–507.

Haney Lopez, I. (1996) *White by Law*. New York: New York University.

Harris, C. (1993) Whiteness as property. *Harvard Law Review* 106, 1710–1791.

Heath, S. (1984) Linguistics and education. *Annual Review of Anthropology* 13, 251–74.

Heiman, D. and Murakami, E. (2019) 'It was like a magnet to bring people in': School administrators' responses to the gentrification of a two-way bilingual education (TWBE) program in central Texas. *Journal of School Leadership* 29, 454–472.

Howard, E., Lindholm-Leary, K., Rogers, D., Olague, N., Medina, J., Kennedy, D., Sugarman, J. and Christian, D. (2018) *Guiding Principles for Dual Language Education* (3rd edn). Washington, DC: Center for Applied Linguistics.

Kaur, H. (January, 2019) A Duke professor warned Chinese students to speak English. See https://www.cnn.com/2019/01/28/health/duke-professor-warns-chinese-students-speak-english-trnd/index.html

Klein, B. (February, 2017) First granddaughter sings Chinese new year song in Mandarin. See https://www.cnn.com/2017/02/02/politics/ivanka-trump-daughter-mandarin/index.html

Lindholm-Leary, K. (2000) *Biliteracy for a Global Society: An Idea Book on Dual Language Education*. Washington, DC: George Washington University.

Lopez, M. (2011) Children's language ideologies in a first-grade dual-language class. *Journal of Early Childhood Education* 12, 176–201.

Macedo, D. (2000) The colonialism of the English only movement. *Educational Researcher* 29, 15–24.

MacSwan, J., Rolstad, K. and Glass, G.V. (2002) Do some school age children have no language? Some problems of construct validity in the pre-LAS español. *Bilingual Research Journal* 26, 395–420.

Melamed, J. (2011) *Represent and Destroy: Rationalizing Violence in the New Racial Capitalism*. Minneapolis: University of Minnesota Press.

Muro, J. (2016) 'Oil and water?' Latino-white relations and symbolic integration in a changing California. *Sociology and Ethnicity* 2, 516–530.

Palmer, D. (2011) Middle-class English speakers in a two-way immersion bilingual classroom: 'Everybody should be listening to Johnny right now…'. *TESOL Quarterly* 43, 177–202.

Palmer, D. (2010) Race, power, and equity in a multiethnic urban elementary school with a dual-language 'strand' program. *Anthropology & Education* 41, 94–114.

Palmer, D. (2007) A dual immersion strand programme in California: Carrying out the promise of dual language education in an English-dominant context. *International Journal of Bilingual Education and Bilingualism* 10, 752–768.

Paris, D. and Alim, H. (2014) What are we seeking to sustain through culturally sustaining pedagogy? A loving critique forward. *Harvard Educational Review* 84, 85–100.

Pearl, A (1997) Cultural and accumulated environmental deficit models. In R. Valencia (ed.) *The Evolution of Deficit Thinking: Educational Thought and Practice* (pp. 132–159). Washington DC: The Falmer Press.

Rosa, J. (2016) Standardization, racialization, languagelessness: Raciolinguistic ideologies across communicative contexts. *Journal of Linguistic Anthropology* 26, 162–183.

Rosa, J. and Flores, N. (2017) Unsettling race and language: Toward a raciolinguistic perspective. *Language in Society* 46, 621–647.

Spring, J. (2016) *Deculturalization and the Struggle for Equality: A Brief History of the Education of Dominated Cultures in the United States*. New York: Routledge.

Stein, P. (July, 2018) Are dual-language programs in urban schools a sign of gentrification? *The Washington Post*. See https://www.washingtonpost.com/local/education/are-dual-language-programs-in-urban-schools-a-sign-of-gentrification/2018/07/03/926c4a42-68c2-11e8-9e38-24e693b38637_story.html?utm_term=.5049bdd806f5

Sung. K. (2017) 'Accentuate the positive; eliminate the negative': Hegemonic interest convergence, racialization of Latino poverty, and the 1968 bilingual education act. *Peabody Journal of Education* 92, 302–321.

Tseng, A. (2017) Heritage languages in a global city: Language maintenance, urban displacement, and educational equity. Fourth National Symposium on Spanish as a Heritage Language. University of California, Irvine, Irvine, California. February 16–18.

Valdés, G. (1997) Dual-language immersion programs: A cautionary note concerning the education of language-minority students. *Harvard Educational Review* 67, 391–429.

Valdez, V., Freire, J., and Delavan, M. (2016) The gentrification of dual language education. *The Urban Review* 48, 601–627.

Wiley, T. (1998) The imposition of World War I era English-Only policies and the fate of German in North America. In T. Ricento and B. Burnaby (eds) *Language and Politics in the United States and Canada: Myths and Realities* (pp. 211–241). New York: Routledge.

Williams, C. (2017, 28 Dec) The intrusion of White families into bilingual schools: Will the growing demand for multilingual early-childhood programs push out the students these programs were designed to serve? *The Atlantic*.

Zisselsberger, M. and Collins, K. (2016) Whose language is legit? Intersections of race, ethnicity and language. *Journal of Cases in Educational Leadership* 19, 51–61.

1 The Intersectionality of Neoliberal Classing with Raciolinguistic Marginalization in State Dual Language Policy: A Call for Locally Crafted Programs

M. Garrett Delavan, Juan A. Freire and
Verónica E. Valdez

In 2008, the US state of Utah kicked-off a new policy initiative that was promoted as providing Utah students access to a one-size-fits-all model of dual language (DL) education backed with financial support. In this chapter, we draw on a raciolinguistic lens to analyze how this state-level language education policy commodified DL, how it promoted its proliferation and for whose benefit. In the process, we seek to join the theoretical conversation around raciolinguistics, which Alim (2016: 5) defines as 'the interdisciplinary field of "language and race"'. We argue that an intersectional raciolinguistic perspective on the Utah DL policy can be an illustrative case study of the operation of the colonizing cultural phenomenon of *propertied white aurality* – our concept for how language use is heard and structured within capitalism and white supremacy. When Utah's DL policy and the pattern of placement of its programs are looked at through this raciolinguistic lens, what comes to the fore is that racialization must be connected to socioeconomic classing in order to fully explain the inequitable access to DL for historically marginalized families, an intersectional analysis that reflects Leonardo's concept of raceclass (2012) and Harris' (1993) idea of whiteness as property in US legal history. The significance of the findings is broader than just Utah because a number of states in the US have noticed and even emulated its DL model. Utah's model follows the policy logic of the foreign language lineage of second language education that draws on the Canadian foreign language immersion model, whose traditional focus has been on building multilingualism within majority language speakers of the national context (Lambert & Tucker, 1972), whereas we follow the bilingual education lineage, which centers the cultural and linguistic interests and needs of raciolinguistically marginalized students (Valdez *et al.*, 2016a).

Despite its reputation as a heavily white state, Latinx individuals constitute 14% of the state's population, roughly matching their presence in the US as a whole (US Census, 2019a, 2019b). With 30% of Utah's population under 18 years of age versus 22.4% nationally (US Census, 2019a, 2019b), it is important to note that Utah's public schools are 26% students of color (with Latinx, Pacific Islanders representing the largest groups) and 7.5% of students are designated as 'English language learners,' with Spanish being the largest minoritized language represented in schools (Utah State Board of Education [USBE], 2019). Nationally, about half of the public-school population are students of color, and 9.6% are designated as 'English language learners' (National Center for Education Statistics, 2019). Overall, Utah had the second fastest growth rate of residents who spoke a language besides English at home – 20% between 2010 and 2016 – spurred by children of immigrants (Camarota & Zeigler, 2017). Spanish is followed by Pacific Islander languages (Tongan and Samoan) in prominence, with 15% of school-age children speaking a language other than English in the home, including Native American languages, such as Navajo (US Census, 2019b). This significant and geographically dispersed presence in Utah of multilingual racialized communities is often overlooked, evidence of which lies in the fact that, historically, Utah's public school system has faced US Office of Civil Rights investigations over racial discrimination, including lack of attention to language-minoritized students, that continued to 2017 (Sayers, 1996; Stevens, 2018).

Our chapter is divided into four sections: First, we offer a theoretical framework that elaborates how socioeconomic classing is just as tied to linguistic positioning and racialization as those latter two are to each other. Next, we describe the data set on which we base this chapter. Third, we use an intersectional raciolinguistic framework to reanalyze our previous findings on Utah DL in ways that make this US state's cautionary tale even more relevant to other contexts, whether in the US or internationally. Three themes emerged for how Utah's policy has demonstrated raciolinguistic classing, and we deliberately chose economic metaphors to name them in order to emphasize the pattern of economic discourse camouflaging the racial calculation: *Mass production* of DL programs by innovating a top-down, state-level one-size-fits-all model rather than a co-constructed process at the district and school community level that is responsive to local demographics and community needs; *mass marketing* of the economic benefits of elite multilingualism and multiculturalism for all to promote the DL policy to privileged audiences; creating *mass displacement* of equity and heritage discourses and of historically marginalized students from DL. Finally, we offer a way forward for those who want DL in their locale to avoid perpetuating the status quo. We argue that, allowing equitable space to remain open for locally crafted DL programs that respond to their communities' racialized and classed positionalities allows all students to benefit from the proliferation of DL to more learners, not just the privileged.

Joining the Raciolinguistics Conversation with an Emphasis on Classing

We understand culture, policy, and pedagogy through a lens of discourses – ways of construing the world and human practices that either perpetuate or contest social power arrangements. Consequently, for this chapter, we read raciolinguistic understandings (and many of the prior ideas its users have drawn on) as a complementary lens to critical discourse analysis as a theoretical orientation or, stated broadly, 'analysis of the codes of power' (Flores & Rosa, 2015: 165). We follow Rogers and colleagues (2016: 1216) in defining critical discourse analysis in education (descriptively rather than prescriptively) as a theoretical orientation used to connect more local processes to societal processes 'through description, interpretation, and explanation' of discursive phenomena. Our particular point of entry into the conversation theorizing raciolinguistic discourse is Flores and Rosa's (2015: 168–169) call for 'shifting language education from inadvertently perpetuating the racial status quo to participating in struggles against the ideological processes associated with the white speaking and white listening subject,' two concepts that build on the model of the white gaze, that is, the white point of view. To speak of the cultural centrality of the white speaking and white listening subject more succinctly (and parallel to the white gaze) we use the concept of *aurality* – that is, the act or sense of hearing. *White aurality* (Thompson, 2017) is thus the seemingly natural or common-sense privileging of (a) how one talks/sounds in order to perform whiteness and (b) how whiteness acts as an unmarked norm against which language varieties are legitimated or othered. White aurality allows us to succinctly summarize how white supremacy in the US and around the world also operates through how ways of speaking are (de)valued.

Rosa and Flores (2017: 636) deepen this analysis by proposing that such a raciolinguistic perspective can perceive ways in which language varieties and racial categories were discursively co-imagined historically and are continually reproduced together in contemporary spaces such as bilingual education. They see possibilities for intersectional analysis with this lens where 'assemblages of signs and identities configured in particular contexts' are studied for how they produce consequences and for whom; building on Zeus Leonardo's (2012) raceclass perspective, Rosa and Flores highlight the interconnected, evolving histories of classism plus racism (capitalism plus white supremacy) that have often played out through the medium of language. We take up this call by reading Utah's DL model and associated policies as just such an assemblage of identity-bearing discourses. Because socioeconomic class was so clearly linked to race and linguistic positionality in our prior findings, reexamining and resynthesizing Utah's assemblage of DL policy and its promotion immediately suggested that we spend time theorizing the concept of a *propertied* (economically privileged) version of the gaze/aurality concept. Just as other scholars have used 'propertied gaze' as a means to efficiently talk about the point of view of classes above the poor, whether middle class or elites (Bergland, 2000), *propertied aurality* summarizes the ways in which capitalism and classing valorize, other, and standardize people's language varieties and repertoires.

There are three points we would like to add to the conversation around the intersection of white aurality with capitalism and classing. First, the raciolinguistic framework has analysis of propertied aurality built into it, which should not be overlooked by those who take it up. If we are to 'account for the workings of white supremacy within global capitalism' or simply 'racial capitalism' (Rosa & Flores, 2017: 640–641) then the Utah case demonstrates what a mistake it would be not to take seriously the moments when classing or marketing discourse becomes a key theme in one's data. Yet we do not mean to imply that all raciolinguistic inquiry must forefront classing in order to be valid. Rosa and Flores (2017) allude to Bonfiglio's (2002) powerful discursive history of the shift of the dominant US accent from the Northeast accent to the (Mid)West accent during the first half of the 20th century. The US standard moved away from centers of wealth rather than toward them, as had happened in other industrialized nations. The only explanation that sufficed was the ideological portrayal of the (Mid)West as the nation's least racially 'contaminated' space, a new 'heartland' of whiteness and non-immigrant-ness. Considering this context of standardization in the US around white aurality much more than propertied aurality, we are not making a claim that economics or class are always central, only that one should test for whether they are one of the central forces intersecting.

Second, a raciolinguistic perspective is grounded in a critique of the endurance of colonialism in the present moment. We understand colonialism as an inherently economic or classed process that subsequently produced the discourses of racialization and standardized language that endure to this day as propertied white aurality. Moore (2015) advocates for a theory of capitalism as a new knowledge paradigm that began to alter landscapes and consume resources at an accelerated rate after 1450.

A new cash crop system of agriculture was the original laboratory of the *mass production* economic model – one of our key analytical metaphors – and it co-emerged with racialization, slavery and colonization. Built into the fabric of the new economic logic was another of our key analytical metaphors: the *mass displacement* of 'in the way' or 'disposable' populations who were forced into labor, deprived of territory and exposed to European diseases. Yet the mass displacement was also discursive and cultural: ways of living, languaging and thinking were directly or indirectly pushed to the margins of social space through the propertied white aurality of the colonizing population.

Racialization and white supremacy became the legitimizing discourse for the globalization of this once localized system of economic and cultural value. Omi and Winant (2015: 115) argue that a racial system that was merely brutal sociocultural sorting in the first few centuries of colonization became 'newly difficult to justify' amidst the Enlightenment's discourses of rights and freedoms that the ascendant economic elites were asserting; hence race was biologized and naturalized through new scientific discourses. Simultaneously, the solidification of the nation-state form in the 1700–1800s further fossilized language in ways that produced a more fully hegemonic, monolingual (and racialized) ideology of languages. Hutton (2000) argues that European linguists began at that time to theorize the affinity among Indo-European languages and the concept of an Aryan (supreme, white) race. These 'tribal beliefs of academic linguists' infused white supremacy discourse with an even deeper connection to language via 'fictive identities that fused language and race as political myths' of the nation-state era (Hutton, 2000: 70–71). In some sense, white supremacy and language standardization operated as a marketing campaign to 'sell' the legitimacy of the colonial order, the capitalist class system, and the new 'democratic' nation states run by the business class rather than the aristocracy. Literal, undifferentiated mass marketing of products had its heyday between the 1880s and 1950s in the US (Tedlow & Jones, 2014), but all commodities of the capitalist era were marketed in some way in the media forms of the era. Mass marketing attempts to sell products with a homogenous appeal to an entire market without considering the diversity of tastes or needs within it, which necessarily includes some form of privileging (or constructing) a sense of what the majority wants; it is the opposite of niche or segmented marketing, which targets – or, arguably, *creates* – particular sectors of the market with more differentiated messages (Tedlow & Jones, 2014). Marketing is clearly a form of discourse by which people are invited or persuaded into subjectivities of need for or affinity with particular commodities. The effect of the choice of mass rather than niche marketing is to participate in reinforcing a dominant, majoritarian subjectivity as superior or normal. Mass marketing in the US thus used and reinforced propertied white aurality.

Third, a key theme that emerged from our work on Utah DL policy was that economic discourses were clearly overshadowing discourses of educational equity around race and linguistic positionality. In order to make sense of that pattern, we needed to research and communicate with our readers about how a recent revalorization of multilingualism in the US that frames Utah's 2008 DL policy rode the wave of discourse of the neoliberal (free-market) era of capitalism. The irony of our findings in Utah was that its neoliberal discourse strategy was 'impure' because neoliberalism coincides better with niche marketing and the commodification of diversity and (school) choice. What explains this contradiction is the intersectionality with white supremacy and aurality. As we will detail, a homogenized DL model as product, marketed to the white majority and their interests, made the space of DL a 'safe neighborhood' ready for the influx of privileged students that we have termed *gentrification* (Valdez *et al.*, 2016b). Yet neoliberal discourse was already entwined with white supremacy prior to being taken up within language education circles. Hohle (2015) traces the historical trajectory by which working class whites began to give up on the welfare state, that is, on community investment and wealth redistribution through Keynesian taxation and government expenditure. He found that business leaders' neoliberal discourses did not initially appeal to working class whites. However, in the wake of *Brown v Board*, 'the language of neoliberalism' gained racially charged traction as a 'result of the white response to the black struggle for civic inclusion' where discourse became 'organized around the white-private/black-public binary' (Hohle, 2015: 4). These findings corroborate Omi and Winant's (2015) reading of the rise of neoliberalism to include economic elites fomenting the electoral politics of white resentment over the gains of the US Civil Rights Movement, which was pioneered by then President Nixon and others in coded, colorblind terms like crime, drugs, and public assistance. Flores (2017) summarizes evidence like this as demonstrating that neoliberalism's relationship to racialization is not unidirectional, but that it was (is) both shaped by and produced (produces) forms of racism.

Perhaps the most overarching finding of our work on Utah DL policy was that it articulated what we called a *globalized human capital* (GHC) framework at the expense of discourses about creating educational equity by drawing on students' language and heritage. A GHC framework refers to a dominant, neoliberal, language-education discourse that values the production of 'multilingual workers to compete in the global marketplace' (Valdez *et al.*, 2016b: 606). The GHC framework operates beyond the US; for example, Flores (2013) argues that plurilingualism in the European Union emerged from a neoliberal perspective seeking 'for flexible workers and lifelong learners to perform service-oriented and technological jobs as part of a post-Fordist political economy' (2013: 501). Equity/heritage discourses had largely dominated the development of DL programs in Utah and the US prior to the new policy. Similar equity/heritage discourses have shaped the intercultural or indigenous bilingual education movement in Latin American countries supported by leftist governments that distanced themselves from neoliberalism; this intercultural bilingual education movement has opposed previous assimilationist and colonial educational models (López, 2014).

We chose human capital as a cornerstone concept of the neoliberal era because it conceptualizes people first and foremost as instruments or actors of economic planning – homo economicus – and education as enhancing this economic value (Pierce, 2013). Neoliberal discourse often claims the power of marketization as a socially equalizing and inclusive force, but the promise of economic equality through neoliberalism's 'solutioneering' is seldom fulfilled (Atasay & Delavan, 2012), and it tends to superficialize and commodify any inclusion of multiculturalism or pluralism (Flores, 2017) such that non-whiteness is valued through a selective process governed by how much such inclusiveness also benefits white identities; this reflects critical race theory's concept of interest convergence, that is, the societal pattern where policy changes beneficial to those racialized as communities of color often occur largely because they coincide with the interests of those racialized as white (Bell, 1980; Sung, 2017). Cervantes-Soon (2014) and Valdés (2018) both remind us that two-way immersion has the interest-convergence danger of commodifying Latinx linguistic and cultural knowledge for easy appropriation by the beneficiaries of propertied, white aurality. The conflict between the equity/heritage and GHC discourse frameworks embodies the intersection of classing with race and linguistic positionality because economic concerns in the Utah DL assemblage functioned to distract the policy's audience from questions of equity for raciolinguistically marginalized communities. Ultimately, we argue that DL policies (via grassroots pushback) may be able to better balance the frameworks, rather than allowing GHC to trump and distract from all else. The imperative step would be allowing for locally crafted DL programs to flourish in spaces outside the homogenizing pressures of mass production, marketing and displacement.

The Data Set

This chapter re-examines our Utah DL policy findings through a raciolinguistic lens based on our previous research conducted from 2010 to 2015 published across four articles (Delavan *et al.*, 2017; Freire *et al.*, 2017; Valdez *et al.*, 2016a, 2016b). Our overall analysis of Utah's state-centralized DL policy incorporated critical discourse analysis, content analysis, visual analysis and two-sample independent *t* tests to examine policy documents, promotional materials, print media and state reported demographic data about the schools housing DL programs across the state. In this chapter, we list the key documents we reviewed across our four publications (see publications for citation information on data sources). Our

DL policy review focused on five key policy documents: Utah Senate Bill 80; Utah Senate Bill 41; Utah Administrative Code R277-488 [Administrative Rule]; the Utah Dual Language Immersion text [DL Overview]; and the 2013 Critical Languages: Dual Language Immersion Education Appropriations Report [the Legislative Report]. The state promotional materials were accessed through the Utah State Board of Education (USBE) website and included promotional brochures for DL programs across the five partner languages, the USBE's DL websites, two articles written by USBE officials, and two interviews done with USBE officials and published online. Our analysis of media sources centered on articles from five major newspapers with the largest circulation in the state published from 2005 to 2011: *Standard-Examiner*, *Salt Lake Tribune*, *Deseret News*, *Daily Herald* and *The Spectrum*. The final element of our data set was state-reported data from Utah's 2014–2015 school year state aggregated student enrollment spreadsheet of all Utah public schools and the 2014–15 school year list of Utah DL programs supplemented with follow-up contact on DL program characteristics made with the listed schools housing DL programs. One comprehensive DL demographics database was created that contained school and district name, partner language, total student enrollment, year the program began, type of DL program, student enrollment by race, student enrollment by English learner designation and student enrollment by free and reduced lunch status which was used for our statistical analysis.

Findings

The proliferation of DL programs around the US and other countries can be a positive goal to advance multilingualism, but a raciolinguistic lens allows us to see that certain policy initiatives may be sacrificing other important goals in service of the speedy production and broad marketing and proliferation of DL. Using the metaphors of mass production, mass marketing and mass displacement in the next three sections we illustrate how a raciolinguistic lens highlights the intersectionality of race, language, and class in the Utah DL policy and its implications for who benefits from it.

DL mass production

The Utah DL case suggests the metaphor of an attempt to mass produce a commodity. Utah's mass production of DL education was characterized by a top-down, state-level, one-size-fits-all logic articulated by legislation that also offered financial support. Utah's planning for DL proliferation fit the metaphor of mass production in three principal ways. First, Utah was the first state to centralize DL planning in this way. Prior DL planning in the US had operated largely at a district, school and community level with some state support. The innovation of this state-level DL planning brought Utah national attention with at least 30 states communicating with USBE state officials or visiting DL programs in Utah schools. Second, there was an explicit 2010 USBE goal of establishing 100 DL programs by 2015 with 30,000 students enrolled, a quick scale up unprecedented in the US that was met in the 2014–2015 school year (Freire *et al.*, 2017). Senate Bill 80 in 2008 served as the starting gun that opened state-centralized DL programs across Utah, leading to the establishment of 119 programs as of the 2018–2019 school year. This is in a state with only approximately 1% of the nation's population.

Third, the policy created a standardized model as a majoritarian product for a mass market seen without internal diversity. The state established Utah DL as a product, prescribed by policy as a one-size-fits-all model whose characteristics and supporting structures prioritized the needs and concerns of the white, propertied, English-speaking beneficiary. Based on conversations with state officials, we learned that the original discussions that set the final Utah DL policy in motion contemplated an exclusive focus on one-way world language immersion programs also known as foreign language immersion, which reinforces the idea of DL as a majoritarian product. Utah's final DL policy decision made this majoritarian product slightly more neoliberally multicultural and inclusive by specifying two sub-models: one-way world language immersion programs that served mainly English-monolinguals and two-way immersion programs that was inclusive of students whose dominant language was the partner language in balanced ways. In the words of the 2012 legislation, one-way 'consists of English language speakers with limited to no proficiency in the foreign immersion language' and two-way 'consists of a **majority** of English language speakers and a **minority** of language speakers other than English' (Valdez *et al.*, 2016b: 615, emphasis ours). This was an important exception to an overall discourse of one-size-fits-all, but it was immediately presented in ways that reinforced the overall majoritarian pattern. Another key majoritarian aspect of the model was the choice of the 50:50, two-teacher approach. Utah policy stipulated that only 50:50 programs would receive state support until grassroots pressure forced the inclusion of 90:10 and similar models in 2018 (Freire *et al.*, in press). The explicit rationale of the original policy was that a 50:50, two-teacher approach was ideal to allow for only half of all teachers involved to need proficiency in the partner language. This would thus (a) facilitate the desired quick scale up and (b) function as a strategy for preempting pushback from current monolingual anglophone teachers expecting to be displaced. In both these cases, satisfying those with a majoritarian aurality was the main concern. A subtext of the choice of the 50:50 approach, however, was its widely acknowledged appeal to English-monolingual families considering DL for their children. Calderón and Minaya-Rowe (2003: 29) write of 90:10 programs, 'Schools with this model sometimes experience "second-grade parent panic," where English-speaking parents panic because their children are not receiving [enough] formal reading instruction in English'. Freire and Delavan (under review) analyze how the 50:50 approach functions symbolically to meet English hegemony's discursive demand for no less than half of instructional time. Thus, the equality (rather than equity) discourse signaled by a one-size-fits-all, 50:50 model constitutes the illusion and false promise of fairness in a fashion very similar to colorblindness: In a context of English hegemony, equal time to languages hardly translates into educational fairness for language groups. In this case again, it was the fears of propertied, white aurality that were preempted or assuaged rather than any concerns of historically marginalized constituencies. English hegemony is also a significant factor in bilingual education programs outside the US. In Europe, English hegemony in CLIL and foreign-language programs is alive and well 'despite the Council of Europe's recommendations to protect linguistic and cultural diversity' (Hélot & Cavalli, 2017: 485).

The teacher qualifications specified by the policy for Utah's two-teacher DL model were skewed toward requiring higher levels of skill for teachers teaching the partner language than for those teaching English, further evidence that the standardized model was majoritarian in focus. Although all DL teachers were required to have an 'elementary Utah teaching license,' this was the only requirement for English DL teachers as they were not required, only 'strongly recommended' to have an English as a Second Language (ESL) endorsement. On the other hand, partner language DL teachers in all program models were required to also have a 'world language endorsement in the immersion language and a dual language immersion endorsement' offered by Utah higher education institutions from a world languages perspective. These elements of teacher qualifications deprioritized the interests of those othered by propertied, white aurality by elevating a majoritarian, world language education approach to teacher preparation over a bilingual education or ESL approach.

The last piece of evidence was the choice of languages specified by the legislation. Though this at first may appear to be driven by variety, this selection seemed more driven by an effort to make the policy resemble choices traditionally available in world language education along with languages seen as those of so-called rising economies like Brazil's. A key USBE official stated in an interview, 'We selected Mandarin Chinese, French, and Spanish because they are three really important international business languages' (Valdez et al., 2016a: 862). This approach indicated that language choices were driven by a homogenizing propertied white aurality attuned to an undifferentiated majority audience, which preempted a focus on locally spoken languages associated with lack of property or a threat to the white demographic majority. Mehisto's (2015: xx–xxi) piece on Utah DL policy states:

Utah's programme is driven by political vision and the belief that skill in more than one language is central to increasing the state's economic advantage in a global economy. . . . The use of several languages in the Utah programmes may also help counterbalance fears in some circles that Spanish may at some point become the dominant language of the state.

Utah's process towards the now arguably national mass production of DL was supported by a highly strategic state-level mass marketing effort that we describe next.

DL mass marketing

The strategy for proliferation of the Utah DL model included mass marketing of the program to change attitudes about it and appeal to a broad audience. This occurred through a comprehensive state-level mass-marketing apparatus in which the state board of education (with the support of state legislators, the governor's office and the state office of economic development) produced promotional materials and gained media coverage that broadcast state discourses. However, by its very emphasis on broad appeal it ignored racial, linguistic and class differences among segments of the market and homogenized its message toward one audience; thus, by default and invisibly to much of the general public, it became a niche marketing effort for the interests and concerns of privileged white, propertied, English-monolingual constituents, a population previously part of white flight out of urban public schools and largely disinterested in the bilingual education happening there.

The state marketing apparatus began its efforts by adopting a GHC economic argument to promote DL. This served several purposes but was particularly used to elevate the value of elite (formally learned) multilingualism over folk multilingualism learned informally outside of schooling (De Mejía, 2002). In a conservative, majority white racial context, in which the state enacted English-only legislation in 2000 in the wake of nationwide negative perceptions of bilingual education that swept the US in the late 1990s, Utah's turn toward multilingualism through DL would require a significant change in public perception. The mass-marketing efforts thus were focused on changing public attitudes away from English hegemony toward multilingualism, a trait associated negatively with the local folk multilingualism of immigrant communities of color. This negative association was evident in statements such as when *The Daily Herald* wrote, 'Not to be confused with controversial bilingual education designed to mainstream non-English-speaking children, subjects taught in a foreign language are designed to make a child fluent in speaking and writing two languages' (Dobnik, 2007: A3). To facilitate a shift in public attitudes, neoliberal GHC discourses were used to promote the *market( ) ability* DL offered its participants in the global marketplace and served to disguise the white supremacy and continued reproduction of social inequalities embedded within the neoliberal policies endorsed by the GHC discourse (Valdez *et al.*, 2016a).

Supposedly egalitarian market( )ability was really about putting white, propertied, English-speaking constituents ahead in the job market by preparing them to gain access to middle-class bilingual jobs not everyone can get. If raciolinguistically othered students did advance economically via the policy, the market( )ability discourse worked to ensure that it happened in ways that were not ultimately a threat to the dominance of propertied white aurality. Evidence of this was that despite the existence of two-way programs under the policy, Spanish-speaking families were not targeted by the promotional materials in any way. For example, this less privileged constituency and the existence of two-way programs were silenced (that is, omitted) in Spanish brochures with discourse such as, 'You'll be delighted how quickly your child becomes a comfortable and competent Spanish speaker' (Freire *et al.*, 2017: 285).

This GHC market( )ability discourse was reflected across Utah print media's DL messaging. For example, our analysis of 164 articles from five Utah newspapers from 2005 to 2011 showed an increasing number of neoliberal GHC value statements in the context of Utah's DL programs as enriching options for privileged students, while value statements around equity and heritage discourses decreased. Two examples of statements meant to spur this columbusing rediscovery of multilingualism (Flores, 2015) were themes such as 'the world is too small not to be at least bilingual and to not offer your child that opportunity to develop bilingualism, you are really depriving them,' and 'to engage in commerce, we have to be able to speak the language of our customers' (Valdez *et al.*, 2016a: 870–871). A raciolinguistic analysis of how Spanish and its current and future speakers were constructed by Utah policy discourses thus points to the fact that local, folk, working-class Spanishes were by and large not heard to exist as part of a larger societal pattern of propertied white aurality in which (a) multilingual homelives are part of what constructs non-whiteness, (b) varieties of Spanish associated with whiteness and property (in Spanish-dominant countries) are what schools tend to endorse and (c) policy that prioritizes those subjects/persons co-constructed in these ways as white and Standard-English-dominant gets read as normal and commonsensical rather than politically entrenched.

The elevation of the value of elite multiculturalism was another messaging strategy to make DL more appealing to white, propertied, English-monolingual constituents. It was evident in images on state promotional brochures we accessed between 2012–2019 used for the mass marketing of the five different language programs available in the state-centralized DL initiative. The French and German brochures had images of all visually white students in classroom settings wearing regular clothes and holding books. Figure 1.1a offers the human image used in the German brochure. On the other hand, the brochure photographs promoting the Portuguese, Spanish and Chinese DL programs included images of children who were

(a)   (b)

(German DL Brochure)   (Spanish DL Brochure)

Figure 1.1 Excerpts from Spanish and German Utah state DL brochures used to mass-market DL

Note. Panel A is an image from the state German DL brochure accessed through the state DL website that illustrates unexoticized, unmarked language according to white aurality. Panel B's image from the state's Spanish DL brochure accessed through the state DL website exhibits exoticized, marked language according to white aurality.

visually Latina/o or African American, sometimes at the exclusion of any visually white students. However, children who were visually Latino/a or African American were exoticized and/or depicted in non-academic ways performing cultural activities and/or wearing cultural costumes stereotypically associated with the language promoted echoing the colonial narratives of the exotic other and neoliberal multiculturalism's narratives of an 'authentic' other (Flores, 2017). In fact, the Spanish DL brochure image as seen in Figure 1.1b, similar to the Portuguese and Chinese brochure images, sent a message of promoting exoticization for the consumption of white children. This commodification and exploitation of historically marginalized students' languages and cultures in the DL promotional materials was a strategy utilized to make the Other more attractive and integration with the Other safe by positioning them in ways that converged with the interests and concerns of those privileged by propertied, white aurality and gaze.

This elite multilingualism and elite multiculturalism messaging were complemented with the state promotion of the Utah model of DL nationally and statewide as the 'mainstreaming' of DL that would include all. The use of this inclusiveness discourse was evident in the following excerpt written by Utah state DL officials in a national DL publication reporting that Utah was, 'mainstreaming dual language immersion programs for students of diverse abilities across all socioeconomic, ethnic, rural, urban, large and small school communities throughout the state.' In addition, these same state officials presented at national bilingual education conferences including a presentation titled, *It takes a village to raise multilingual-multicultural children: One state's story to mainstream dual language instruction,* explicitly calling for the mainstreaming of DL education by treating the planning and implementation of DL programs similarly to the

Starbucks initiative. This presentation emphasized the need for the field of DL to emulate the success of Starbucks by taking a similar mass production, marketing, and distribution approach to DL, like they had done. These efforts served to raise the national profile of Utah's DL initiative and its position in the global economy, and thus elevated the value DL held as an exclusive commodity to be accessed in the state. Overall, the mass marketing strategies used by the state failed to deliver inclusiveness and instead deflected and diverted attention away from the equity heritage concerns associated with students and communities historically marginalized in public schools based on their racialization, language repertoire and/or their non-propertied status as discussed in more detail in the next section.

Mass displacement of equity heritage concerns and constituencies

In our earlier discussion on the mass production of DL, we showed that it was designed to be a majoritarian product. We argued that Utah's DL education initiative positioned DL as a commodity and as a tool to gentrify the metaphorical bilingual education neighborhood. This gentrification process, a contemporary version of colonization, displaced racial, linguistic and class-based equity heritage discourses as well as the access of historically marginalized populations to DL programs. The only instances in which historically marginalized students were included were when their interests happened to converge with the interests of the white, propertied English-monolingual constituent. Thus, the propertied white aurality used in the construction of Utah's DL policy documents, state promotional materials and media discourses had mass-displacement effects for equity/heritage discourses and historically marginalized constituents. Next, we focus on the mechanisms of the DL gentrification process normalized into the state education apparatus that displaced the people and discourses marked as Other by a propertied, white aurality.

Even when the DL policy seemed to be counterhegemonic and included general equity discourses that pointed toward the policy's inclusiveness, they were problematic due to the absence of references to local heritage languages or local historically marginalized communities. There were three examples discussed earlier in our mass-production section that illustrate how the DL policy itself contributed to this displacement. First, the only types of DL programs acknowledged in the policy texts were one-way world language immersion programs and two-way immersion programs. Developmental bilingual education programs (also known as a type of one-way DL) serving students designated by schools as English learners who speak the partner language, were not legitimized as a DL option. Second, Utah's DL policy imposed the 50:50 approach as the only language allocation target allowed in the state despite research showing that the 90:10 approach provides benefits when compared to 50:50, including reclassification rates for students designated as English learners and both academic performance and partner language proficiency for all students (Collier & Thomas, 2017; Lindholm-Leary & Genesee, 2010). Lastly, the DL teacher credentialing requirements specified in Utah's DL policy were distinctly different for DL teachers of English versus teachers of the partner languages, such that DL teachers were required to be much more equipped to address the second language learning needs of English-monolinguals than those of students designated as English learners. These students were raciolinguistically constructed as non-white, English learners and non-propertied; hence, they were also constructed in the policy as a less deserving focus of teacher training.

This displacement was also evident in the languages chosen as the DL partner languages. For example, the original 2008 DL legislation specified four languages: Mandarin Chinese, Spanish, French and Navajo. However, the state education office quietly replaced Navajo, a local language and the language of the Dine' people of the Four Corners region, with Portuguese in 2012 on the list of languages from the original legislation and erased it from its narration of Utah's DL history, discursively silencing Navajo from the DL conversation while retaining those languages identified through white aurality to bring economic benefit to the global marketplace. This illustrates how the needs and interests of historically marginalized students were displaced in the DL mass-production process.

The displacement process also extended to an attempt to have pre-existing bilingual education instruction in the state conform to the new model. The state DL model was enforced rather than simply recommended, meaning other forms of DL 'production' such as existing bilingual education programs in the state and custom or locally crafted DL programs, were marginalized or incentivized and persuaded to conform in an effort to quickly spread Utah's DL model and disrupt critiques about the lack of diversity in its DL programs. Except for two Title I public charter schools with high numbers of historically marginalized students, state officials succeeded in moving all existing bilingual education programs to the state model. Under a white aurality climate with new financial incentives on offer, most schools transitioned without objections with few exceptions. This points to the economic power backing Utah's DL movement and its usefulness to displace the existing network of local bilingual education programs in the state serving the largest number of historically marginalized constituents and their equity heritage interests while appropriating them to serve the white aurality of the state's interests.

The state's DL mass-marketing efforts discussed earlier promoted GHC discourses that positioned elite multilingualism and elite multiculturalism as outcomes of DL that would have privileged constituents well positioned for the global marketplace. These efforts also perpetuated displacement of historically marginalized constituents, particularly Spanish and its speakers, by exoticizing them, while also deflecting, silencing, and erasing equity heritage discourses and constituencies from the marketing efforts. This was evident in the Utah version of a documentary called *Speaking in Tongues* that the state used to promote DL. The USBE took excerpts from the full documentary and combined them with a speech by a former Utah Governor, who was a strong supporter of DL and discussed the benefits of bilingualism. The original documentary gave equal time to a total of four protagonists. The two protagonists included were an African American boy and a white boy adding Chinese as a second language, and those not included by the USBE version were a Mexican American boy who entered his Spanish DL program as a proficient Spanish speaker and a Chinese American girl recovering her family's Chinese language (Delavan *et al.*, 2017). Thus, the USBE's edits to the original documentary clearly performed silencing: Spanish and maintenance or heritage reasons for learning languages were not highlighted while the foreign language reasons for learning languages were left in and centered. Thus, as discussed in the previous section, we view the DL promotional materials' depiction of linguistically and racially marginalized youth as only soccer players and performers of traditional cultural dances and practices as problematic, positioning these youth as the exotic, non-threatening and commodified Other that are there in service to the state's interests. These racialized discourses serve as examples of the racing of languages while also languaging Asians and Latinas/os through white aurality.

The placement of DL programs in the most privileged schools in Utah provided additional evidence of this mass-displacement trend. First, our statistically significant findings showed clear differences between the student composition in the eight schools housing DL programs – including one-way developmental bilingual education programs – before implementation of the state DL model (1978–2004) and the 87 schools selected after its full implementation in 2009. State model programs were more often located in schools with students who were whiter '(MD = −0.3298, 95% CI [−0.5378, −0.1217], $t(7.53) = -3.70$, $p < 0.01$, two-tailed based on unequal variances),' more propertied '(MD = 0.2930, 95% CI [0.1334, 0.4526], $t(93) = 3.65$, $p < 0.01$, two-tailed)' and more English-monolingual '(MD = 0.1789, 95% CI [0.0448, 0.3130], $t(7.41) = 3.12$, $p < 0.05$, two-tailed based on unequal variance)' (Valdez *et al.*, 2016b: 619–620). Second, the high proportion of programs implemented under the policy that were one-way world-language immersion programs rather than two-way (serving linguistically marginalized students) was another indicator of the demographic displacement. In 2014, three fourths of Utah's 106 DL programs were one-way world language immersion with only one-fourth being two-way. Due to the state's delegitimization of the one-way developmental bilingual education DL option, this automatically restricted the number of enrollment slots made available to students designated as English learners. Propertied white aurality was what made these decisions seem logical and ethical to many, despite mass displacement of those designated as English learners from a form of education that had historically served their needs first and foremost. Utah DL policy's emphasis on 'mainstreaming' DL education from a world language immersion perspective and in serving privileged students while excluding students marginalized through propertied white aurality thus constituted both demographic and discursive displacement that resembled colonial histories.

Concluding Discussion

Our findings from Utah, where economic discourses are being used to distract from issues of equitable access to DL for racially and linguistically marginalized students, show the importance of why economics and classing are included in raciolinguistic perspectives in the field of DL. It is true that the intertwined racial and linguistic discrimination against some families kept them from appearing politically important to policymakers in comparison to the ideal policy target of families who are at the top of the raciolinguistic spectrum – white, English-monolingual speakers. Yet it is also true that this process was enclosed on both ends by class-stratified economic processes: on the one hand, past colonialism driven by early capitalism, on the other, a columbusing rediscovery of multilingualism driven by current capitalism (Flores, 2015). Past colonialism led to logics of linguistic racialization and language standardization that are still in operation as propertied white aurality. Current capitalism (neoliberalism) leads to a discourse of enrichment education as an entitlement of those who are propertied (middle-class or above) or at least those who did the 'right shopping' for a public school that could set their students apart from the crowd or put them ahead of their supposed competitors. It is therefore not accidental that Utah policy resembled the mass production, mass marketing and mass displacement of capitalist and colonial processes.

Despite containing only about 1% of the US population, the case of Utah matters. This state resembles many parts of the US and the globe in its significant but underutilized potential for equity/heritage-driven language planning. The case of Utah also matters because of how influential the Utah DL model has become. Recent research on DL policy has found that several US states are following Utah in adopting centralized policy at the state level (Boyle *et al.*, 2015). Freire and Delavan (under review) have found that Delaware, Georgia, Indiana and Wyoming have initiated centralized DL models in the same fashion as Utah that continue to marginalize 90:10 and other models of equitable language allocation even as Utah has reversed course on that restriction in response to grassroots pressure. Like Flores and Rosa (2015) and Rosa and Flores (2017) we believe optimistically that educators can critique propertied white aurality without abandoning efforts to increase access to effective language education for all students. We hope that our work is not discouraging to educators because we see the potential for raciolinguistic perspectives on policy to empower advocates of an equity/heritage framework for DL to continue their work with more conviction. The main implication we want to impress upon readers is that communities, schools and districts who want locally crafted, custom-made programs outside a state policy paradigm of mass production, marketing and displacement should have the right to be supported by the state in doing so. If DL programs have been treated in Utah (and emulating states) as if they were commodities or cash crops (Cervantes-Soon, 2014; Heller, 2003), an alternative vision for DL policy would support DL programs that resemble sustenance farming, grassroots gardens that help local multilingual communities sustain themselves. In her critique of the ban on bilingual education in Massachusetts, Ross (2007: 1510) argued that it constituted a *tyranny of the majority*:

> mandating a uniform method of instruction for all children in all communities ... [lacks] flexibility to recognize and accommodate the many legitimate interests at stake, including individual children and their families, minority groups, local communities, and the democratic interest of the general public.

In an alternative vision to *mass* DL policy that is more democratically protective of minoritized identities and interests, *locally crafted* programs would not just be tolerated on the margins but equally centered alongside majoritarian interests. Several recommendations would support this goal of local DL crafting.

First, states should structure DL policy so that professionals trained in the bilingual education lineage have an equal seat at the table with professionals trained in the foreign language lineage (Valdez *et al.*, 2016a) such as by specifying within policy documents that both types of professionals should be involved in decision making. Professionals from the bilingual education lineage generally train educators to have much deeper understanding of equity, advocacy, community engagement and raciolinguistic understandings. These professionals can then guide states in following our other recommendations because they will have been trained to address power differentials among the constituencies served by the policy. Moreover, such professionals will not only help prevent restrictive DL policies from fossilizing, but they will also tend to promote sociopolitical consciousness as the fourth goal of DL education (Freire, 2020) in ways that remind DL educators and students to self-advocate. Second, states should do active outreach to communities that might benefit from DL and support them in locally crafting one if there is interest. This is an alternative vision from passively awaiting applications from interested and empowered districts and communities. Professionals trained in the bilingual education lineage can help guide states to especially prioritize outreach to those communities that are already multilingual or might want to revitalize an endangered language. Third, local communities should be empowered to lead the program design, meaning that professionals employed through the state policy should act as advisors and financial supporters. This can create DL programs that are more responsive, more enduring, and more attractive to historically marginalized parents and students.

Economic goals in DL policy should only be one of several considerations and should not be prioritized at the expense of (or to distract from) the equity and justice considerations that should always remain centered. The top-down DL education policy propelling DL mass production in the US is prone to replicate and perpetuate social injustices for historically marginalized students unless deliberate efforts are made to address the specific ways raciolinguistic ideologies shape language policy implementation. Scholars, educators and community members need to be cautious of any attempts similar to Utah state officials' efforts to 'mainstream' DL education unless new policies guarantee equitable opportunities for locally crafted programs that empower their communities.

References

Alim, H.S. (2016) Introducing raciolinguistics: Racing language and languaging race in hyperracial times. In H.S. Alim, J.R. Rickford and A.F. Ball (eds) *Raciolinguistics: How Language Shapes our Ideas About Race* (pp. 1–30). New York, NY: Oxford University Press.

Atasay, E. and Delavan, G. (2012) Monumentalizing disaster and wreak-construction: A case study of Haiti to rethink the privatization of public education. *Journal of Education Policy* 27 (4), 529–553.

Bell, D. (1980). Brown and the interest-convergence dilemma. In D. Bell (ed.) *Shades of Brown: New Perspectives on School Desegregation* (pp. 90–106). New York, NY: Teachers College Press.

Bergland, R.L. (2000) The puritan eyeball, or, sexing the transcendent. In T. Fessenden, N.F. Radel, M.J. Zaborowska (eds) *The Puritan Origins of American Sex* (pp. 105–120). New York, NY: Routledge.

Bonfiglio, T.P. (2002) *Race and the Rise of Standard American*. New York, NY: Walter de Gruyter.

Boyle, A., August, D., Tabaku, L., Cole, S. and Simpson-Baird, A. (2015) *Dual Language Education Programs: Current State Policies and Practices*. Washington, DC: US Department of Education.

Calderón, M.E. and Minaya-Rowe, L. (2003) *Designing and Implementing Two-way Bilingual Programs: A Step-by-Step Guide for Administrators, Teachers, and Parents*. Thousand Oaks, CA: Corwin Press, Inc.

Camarota, S.A. and Zeigler, K. (2017, October 24) *65.5 Million US Residents Spoke a Foreign Language at Home in 2016 [Report]*. Center for Immigration Studies. https://cis.org/report

Cervantes-Soon, C.G. (2014) A critical look at dual language immersion in the new Latin@ diaspora. *Bilingual Research Journal* 37 (1), 64–82.

Collier, V.P. and Thomas, W.P. (2017) Validating the power of bilingual schooling: Thirty-two years of large-scale, longitudinal research. *Annual Review of Applied Linguistics* 37, 203–217.

De Mejía, A. (2002) *Power, Prestige, and Bilingualism: International Perspectives on Elite Bilingual Education*. Clevedon: Multilingual Matters.

Delavan, M.G., Valdez, V.E. and Freire, J.A. (2017) Language as whose resource?: When global economics usurp the local equity potentials of dual language education. *International Multilingual Research Journal* 11 (2), 86–100. doi: 10.1080/19313152.2016.1204890

Dobnik, V. (2007, September 3) More US schools teaching in two or more languages. *The Daily Herald*, p. A3.

Flores, N. (2015) *Has bilingual education been columbused?*, blog. See https://education-allinguist.wordpress.com/2015/01/25/columbising-bilingual-education/ (accessed 26 May 2019).

Flores, N. (2017) From language-as-resource to language-as-struggle: Resisting the coke-ification of bilingual education. In M.-C. Flubacher and A. Del Percio (eds) *Language, Education and Neoliberalism: Critical Studies in Sociolinguistics* (pp. 62–81). Bristol: Multilingual Matters.

Flores, N. (2013) The unexamined relationship between neoliberalism and plurilingualism: A cautionary tale. *TESOL Quarterly* 47 (3), 500–520.

Flores, N. and Rosa, J. (2015) Undoing appropriateness: Raciolinguistic ideologies and language diversity in education. *Harvard Educational Review* 85 (2), 149–171.

Freire, J.A. (2020) Promoting sociopolitical consciousness and bicultural goals of dual language education: The transformational dual language educational framework. *Journal of Language, Identity, and Education* 19 (1), 56–71.

Freire, J.A. and Delavan, M.G. (under review) 50:50 takeover as a companion strategy for gentrifying dual language bilingual education programs: Will one-size-fits-all language allocation use equality to trample equity? *Language Policy*.

Freire, J.A., Delavan, M.G. and Valdez, V.E. (in press) Grassroots resistance and activism to one-size-fits-all and separate-but-equal policies by 90:10 dual language schools en comunidades Latinas. *International Journal of Bilingual Education and Bilingualism*.

Freire, J.A., Valdez, V.E. and Delavan, M.G. (2017) The (dis)inclusion of Latina/o interests from Utah's dual language education boom. *Journal of Latinos and Education* 16 (4), 276–289. doi: 10.1080/15348431.2016.1229617.

Harris, C.I. (1993) Whiteness as property. *Harvard Law Review* 106 (8), 1707–1791.

Heller, M. (2003) Globalization, the new economy, and the commodification of language and identity. *Journal of Sociolinguistics* 7 (4), 473–492.

Hélot, C. and Cavalli, M. (2017) Bilingual education in Europe: Dominant languages. In O. García, A. Lin and S. May (eds) *Bilingual and Multilingual Education, Encyclopedia of Language and Education* (3rd edn) (pp. 471–488). Cham, Switzerland: Springer International Publishing. doi: 10.1007/978-3-319-02258-1_26.

Hutton, C. (2000) Race and language: Ties of 'blood and speech', fictive identity and empire in the writings of Henry Maine and Edward Freeman. *Interventions: International Journal of Postcolonial Studies* 2 (1), 53–72.

Hohle, R. (2015) *Race and the Origins of American Neoliberalism*. New York, NY: Routledge.

Lambert, W.E. and Tucker, G.R. (1972) *Bilingual Education of Children: The St. Lambert Experiment*. Rowley, MA: Newbury House.

Leonardo, Z. (2012) The race for class: Reflections on a critical raceclass theory of education. *Educational Studies* 48 (5), 427–449.

Lindholm-Leary, K. and Genesee, F. (2010) Alternative educational programs for English learners. In California Department of Education (eds) *Improving Education for English Learners: Research-Based Approaches* (pp. 323–367). Sacramento, CA: California Department of Education Press.

López, L.E. (2014) Indigenous intercultural bilingual education in Latin America: Widening gaps between policy and practice. In R. Cortina (ed.) *The Education of Indigenous Citizens in Latin America* (pp. 19–49). Bristol: Multilingual Matters.

Mehisto, P. (2015) Introduction: Forces, mechanisms, and counterweights. In P. Mehisto and F. Genesee (eds) *Building Bilingual Education Systems* (pp. xv–xxvii). Cambridge: Cambridge University Press.

Moore, J.W. (2015) *Capitalism in the Web of Life: Ecology and the Accumulation of Capital.* New York, NY: Verso Books.

National Center for Education Statistics (2019) English language learners in public schools. Retrieved from https://nces.ed.gov/programs/coe/indicator_cgf.asp

Omi, M. and Winant, H. (2015) *Racial Formation in the United States.* New York, NY: Routledge.

Pierce, C. (2013) *Education in the Age of Biocapitalism: Optimizing Educational Life for a Flat World.* New York, NY: Palgrave Macmillan.

Rogers, R., Schaenen, I., Schott, C., O'Brien, K., Trigos-Carrillo, L., Starkey, K. and Chasteen, C.C. (2016) Critical discourse analysis in education: A review of the literature, 2004 to 2012. *Review of Educational Research* 86 (4), 1192–1226.

Rosa, J. and Flores, N. (2017) Unsettling race and language: Toward a raciolinguistic perspective. *Language in Society* 46 (5), 621–647.

Ross, L.B. (2007) Learning the language: An examination of the use of voter initiatives to make language education policy. *New York University Law Review* 82 (5), 1510–1546.

Sayers, J. (1996) Accidental language policy: Creating an ESL/Bilingual teacher endorsement program in Utah. *TESOL Quarterly* 30 (3), 611–615. https://www.jstor.org/stable/i285101

Stevens, T. (2018, February 27) Feds are investigating 23 potential civil rights violations at Utah elementary and high schools, according to new searchable list. *Salt Lake Tribune.* See https://www.sltrib.com/news/education/2018/02/24/feds-are-investigating-23-potential-civil-rights-violations-at-utah-elementary-and-high-schools-according-to-new-searchable-list/ (accessed 6 May 2019).

Sung, K.K. (2017) 'Accentuate the positive; eliminate the negative': Hegemonic interest convergence, racialization of Latino poverty, and the 1968 Bilingual Education Act. *Peabody Journal of Education* 92 (3), 302–321.

Tedlow, R.S. and Jones, G.G. (2014) *The Rise and Fall of Mass Marketing.* New York, NY: Routledge.

Thompson, M. (2017) Whiteness and the ontological turn in sound studies. *Parallax* 23 (3), 266–282.

US Census Bureau (2019a) *QuickFacts: United States.* See https://www.census.gov/quickfacts/fact/table/US

US Census Bureau (2019b) *QuickFacts: United States; Utah.* See https://www.census.gov/quickfacts/UT

Utah State Board of Education [USBE] (2019) Fall enrollment by demographics, October 1, 2018–2019 [Enrollment/Membership Report]. See https://www.schools.utah.gov/data/reports?mid=1424&tid=4

Valdés, G. (2018) Analyzing the curricularization of language in two-way immersion education: Restating two cautionary notes. *Bilingual Research Journal* 41 (4), 388–412.

Valdez, V.E., Delavan, G. and Freire, J.A. (2016) The marketing of dual language education policy in Utah print media. *Educational Policy* 30 (6), 849–883. doi: 10.1177/0895904814556750

Valdez, V.E., Freire, J.A. and Delavan, M.G. (2016) The gentrification of dual language education. *The Urban Review* 48 (4), 601–627. doi: 10.1007/s11256-016-0370-0.

2 Common Threads: Language Policy, Nation, Whiteness, and Privilege in Iowa's First Dual Language Program

Crissa Stephens

Introduction

This chapter applies a raciolinguistic perspective (Flores & Rosa, 2015; Rosa & Flores, 2017) to media representations of the first bilingual education program in the state of Iowa, a context where populations of language minoritized students are newly expanding. Utilizing an intertextual and interdiscursive analysis (Fairclough, 1992; Johnson, 2015), I trace and discuss the ways in which language, race and national origin have been framed historically in public discourse and policy in Iowa against an ever-evolving backdrop of whiteness. I then situate the media representations of bilingual education within historical and current political context at national, state and local levels to reveal discursive links between monoglot ideology, nativism and white supremacy that persist even as bilingual education is celebrated in Iowa. In revealing these ideological threads and their material effects, the chapter also identifies potential points for transformation in local context towards more equitable language education.

Language Policy in Demographic Shift

Presently, much of the knowledge base about the social processes surrounding dual language (DL) education draws from research based in urban centers with sizeable, long-established populations of multilingual residents. However, nonmetropolitan sites across the country that have not traditionally been home to large populations of students classified as English Language Learners (ELLs) are seeing demographic and linguistic shift with rapid growth in language minoritized student groups (Alim,

2016; Baker & Hotek, 2003; Wortham *et al.*, 2015). With this shift comes the charge of educating language minoritized students classified as English Learners in public schools through equitable policy and practice (US Department of Justice and US Department of Education, 2015).

In Iowa, one such site and the focus of this study, the population of students classified as English Learners students in the public school system has increased by 292% in the past 20 years, while the number of predominantly English-speaking students has decreased (Johnson *et al.*, 2018). The demographic shift in Iowa has been heavily driven by changes in the state's labor force in the agricultural and meat packing industries (Grey & Woodrick, 2005). These changes have significantly reconfigured the linguistic, racial and cultural makeup of small and large towns across the state. While the necessity for equitable educational language policy implementation surges in these contexts and others like it across the country, there is less empirical knowledge of the social processes, ideological and structural settings, and cultural politics (Dumas *et al.*, 2016) that influence DL policy and implementation in these contexts. Additionally, the rapid demographic and linguistic shift highlights the challenge of underdeveloped policy infrastructures in the education system to equitably serve new populations of students classified as English Learners. At the same time, this shift opens up possibilities for transformation in creating these infrastructures equitably where they previously did not exist (Hamann *et al.*, 2001).

As an entry point into understanding the national, regional and community-level public discourses surrounding DL education programming in Iowa, I undertook an initial study of media representations of the state's first DL educational program, implemented in the small town of West Liberty, IA (population 3700 approx.). Because of the social role of media in mediating society back to itself (Matheson, 2005) through the pretense of objectivity (Fairclough, 2014), I turned to media representations of DL education circulating at the community level in Iowa to see what discourses were relevant in regional context. My findings were that news reporting on West Liberty's program overwhelmingly touted it as *award-winning* and *community-building*. These claims were substantiated in news reporting by references to educational research on language development (e.g. interdiscursive connections to Cummins, 1979 and Collier & Thomas, 2004) and reports of positive impacts on test scores.

The positive reporting on DL education in this rural context ran counter to previous findings of studies of media coverage on bilingual programs, which showed that bilingual education and issues of sociolinguistic diversity have often been portrayed in a contentious, negative light in news media around the world (Johnson, 2005; Rickford, 1999; Waller, 2012). In contrast to the findings of previous studies, news reporting on West Liberty's DL program utilized educational research findings about language acquisition and discourses of the benefits of bilingual education (see Flores, 2016 for discussion) were also disseminated. Like many DL programs around the country, the program's wait list for predominantly English-speaking students is long and keeps the program in demand. Both white[1] and Latinx residents and educators express contentment with the character and climate of the community through intertextual connections to their speech featured in news reports.

This original study of media representations of DL education was undertaken before the primary season for the presidential election of 2016, which mobilized controversial discourses about immigration as well as accompanying policy on a national level. Given the prevalence in public discourse of an ideological bundle linking language, brownness and national status for Latinxs (Rosa, 2015) and the political action taken by the Trump administration targeting various constituents of this bundle through both rhetorical and material action, I was interested to see how the DL program and its representation in the media were impacted at a local level. The sociopolitical context of Iowa, a rural state Trump won in the general elections with 51.1% of the vote, makes it an interesting backdrop for examining discourses around bilingual education in polemical times. After the election of Donald Trump and the first eight months of his administration, I updated the analysis of news article representations of the DL program and conducted two follow-up interviews with an administrator and educator in West Liberty to learn their perspectives on how the program had weathered policy changes and national discourses that targeted the multilingual students in their program in intangible and material ways.

DL Education Policy: Language, Race, and Social Transformation

The literature on bilingual education argues that it can be implemented as an 'identities project' (Freeman, 1998). In other words, the discourses and practices implemented around language and education can instantiate and support multilingual identity positions that run counter to dominant, monoglot ideologies and discourses of social positions along lines of race and language (Flores, 2016). However, DL can also serve as a site of (re)production for these same dominant discourses when it fails to transform the white supremacist status quo (Flores & García, 2017; Palmer, 2015; Valdés, 1997). In the present study, I show how the DL program in West Liberty is associated with effects to both of these ends across different layers of social activity. I operate under the premise that truly equitable approaches to DL education require transformation in the underlying system of white supremacy alongside the premise that meaningful social transformation can also take place through bottom-up social action in schools.

The challenges and possibilities related to implementing equitable DL education and the development of language policies in contexts of demographic shift do not exist in a historical or structural vacuum. The workings of white supremacy, power and privilege in the education system have been theorized in various ways, including as an underlying system of social privilege and oppression (Lensmire *et al.*, 2013; Liu, 2017). Within such a system, whiteness is an ever-evolving category shaped by historical and political context (Omi & Winant, 2014) and those who receive its benefits do so by their relative proximity to this shifting, contextually sensitive standard (Liu, 2017).

The creation and implementation of educational policies are influencing factors stemming from and contributing to this social context (Dumas *et al.*, 2016). In addition to delineating what is considered equitable and inequitable and brokering access to linguistic, cultural, and material resources for both white students and students of color, educational language policies can contribute actively to how racial ideologies and the social systems they implicate are constructed and sustained (Dumas *et al.*, 2016) or transformed. Therefore, there is need for an examination of the ways educational policy is connected to and produced by larger social structures (Milner, 2008). In line with this thinking, the present study takes a critical eye to the work of language policy implementation in benefitting or marginalizing those whose educational experiences it is designed to regulate (Tollefson, 1991, 2015).

A raciolinguistic perspective (Rosa & Flores, 2017) is particularly useful for more explicit theorization of the ways in which language and race are co-constructed within the power dynamics of larger sociopolitical structures and institutions such as policies and schools. As Flores (2016) has articulated, today's iterations of hegemonic whiteness are not necessarily monolingual, and this is the case when the social benefits of bilingualism proportioned through the education system accrue asymmetrically to predominantly English-speaking white students participating in DL programming (Valdés, 1997). By locating 'the co-naturalization of race and language in relation to longstanding histories of colonialism and nation-state formation' (Rosa & Flores, 2017: 15) a raciolinguistic lens provides theoretical explanation for the historical processes and shifting categories of whiteness that have shaped public discourse and language policy in the context of Iowa. These historical foundations and their contributions to the social foundations of DL education today cannot be accounted for when race and language are perceived as mutually exclusive, straightforwardly separable categories.

Methods: Connecting Past to Present, National to Local

In this chapter, I draw upon the original and updated studies of news coverage of the DL program, situating them within analysis of historical public discourse and educational policy regarding multilingualism in the state of Iowa. In order to trace the connections between historical discourse, language policy and local perspectives on educational programming, I utilize intertextual analysis (Fairclough, 1992; Johnson, 2015), which examines the way texts are shaped by and incorporated into other texts throughout and across space and time, allowing definition of both present and historical social forces visible in language. The analytical technique of tracing intertextual connections (where the language of one text is incorporated directly into another) and interdiscursive connections (where texts draw upon the same habitual way of representing knowledge about something (Foucault in Hall, 2001) makes visible which discourses are pertinent to the construction of bilingual education policy activity. Following Johnson (2015), I utilized intertextual and interdiscursive analysis methods to map the ways that discourses of DL education travel across historical and current layers of social action and identify which discourses circulate and are relevant in a particular context. Specifically, I focused on how discourses of bilingual education in Iowa were represented in local, regional, state and national news. I then situated this analysis within a historical analysis of policy and public discourse in the state and present analysis of one administrator and one educator's perceptions from within the program.

Data included 40 news articles about West Liberty's DL education program through 2014 with the later addition of the two local news articles written between 2014 and 2016 and qualitative interviews with one administrator and one educator in the program undertaken in the spring of 2016 and 2017. I updated the data from local news reporting to include articles published between 2014 and into mid-2016 to learn whether and how the discourses in these reports changed in accordance with national discourse on immigration, race, power and privilege. All the data from news sources were analyzed again in light of historical data from public discourse and current language policy in Iowa. This cross-section of data across time and social context (Hult, 2010) provided a multilayered glimpse across time and space of how discourses about bilingual education circulate within and around policy, the newspaper, the district office and the classroom.

A Historical Look at Nativism, Monoglot Ideology and Whiteness in Iowa's Political Discourse and Language Policy

Like the US as a whole, the Midwest state of Iowa where this research took place has a long history of multilingualism (Johnson *et al.*, 2018), though it is typically perceived today as a predominantly English-speaking context. Iowa's indigenous languages are often overlooked in education programs and policy, in keeping with the groundwork laid by processes of white settler colonialism (Veracini, 2017). This groundwork is upheld by the semiotic process of erasure (Bucholtz & Hall, 2005; Irvine & Gal, 2000) which upholds dominant language ideology in linguistically diverse settings. Historically, the land of Iowa was home to autochthonous Sioux languages such as Chiwere and later the Algonguin language of Mesquakie-Sauk. The name *Iowa* itself comes from the Chiwere language. Much of the available historical information about bilingual education in Iowa bypasses this indigenous linguistic history in accordance with the white settler colonial narrative that white Europeans were the first to establish settlements, followed by a second wave of 'immigrants' (Goebel, 2017). In keeping with this narrative, historical accounts of multilingual education in Iowa focus heavily on German–English bilingual programs, which were common practice in parts of the state until the use of foreign languages was made illegal towards the end of World War I.

In a critical analysis, Johnson *et al*. (2018) demonstrate how nativism and a monoglot standard (Silverstein, 1998) are intertwined throughout Iowa history in both public discourse and policy; a finding that corroborates the claims of various studies of language ideology and power at the national level (Flores, 2014; Subtirelu, 2013; Wiley & Wright, 2004). The implicit link between nativism, monoglot ideology and the shifting standard of whiteness is not to be overlooked, as raciolinguistic ideologies are instrumental in upholding a monoglot standard. Flores and Rosa (2015) point out that the monoglot standard, which positions 'idealized monolingualism in a standardized national language as the norm to which all national subjects should aspire' (2015: 151) works to perpetuate raciolinguistic ideologies that position the language of racialized groups as inferior and subject to social norms set by whiteness, regardless of whether associated claims are borne out by empirical linguistic data.

Language discrimination accompanied by physical violence against German Americans was prevalent in various places across the country around the time of WWI (Flores, 2014; Thompson, 2017). Iowa is the only state to have legally codified this discrimination through passage of a law outlawing the use of languages other than English. The Babel Proclamation, Iowa's law outlawing the use of non-English languages in institutions and the public square, became law on May 23, 1918. The Babel Proclamation criminalized noncompliance with a nativist, monoglot norm. In announcing this policy, Iowa governor Warren L. Harding proclaimed the following:

> Every person should appreciate and observe his duty to refrain from **all acts or conversation which may excite suspicion or produce strife** among the people…every word and act will **manifest his loyalty** to his country and his solemn purpose to aid in achieving victory for our army and navy and the permanent peace of the world. (Harding, 1918)

Conversation in a language other than English, regardless of the topic, equals a powerful, anti-national social act in Harding's discourse.

Inherent in this act, according to Harding, is the ability to excite suspicion and produce strife. Harding's speech draws overtly on a discourse of fear and his words link this fear to military victory (or, by implication, defeat). This logic plays on a longstanding link between ideologies of national identity, nativist policy, and English (Hill, 2009; Subtirelu, 2013) to construct an ideological framework where even the sounds of non-English, regardless of the content of the speaker's message, can be made to index subterfuge of American military efforts. This Proclamation had additional material effects through its regulation of educational language policy, where the teaching of non-English languages was also prohibited (Schissel, 2019).

In 1918, president Teddy Roosevelt spoke from the steps of Iowa's capitol, expressing his support of the Harding's Babel Proclamation and representing a voice for this discourse at the national level:

> This is a nation – not a polyglot boarding house…There can be but one loyalty – the stars and the stripes; one nationality – the American – and therefore only one language. (Quoted in O'Toole, 2006)

In his speech about language, Roosevelt also makes an interdiscursive connection to nativist ideology through his positioning of multilingual identities in the United States as unestablished, unmoored, maybe even passing through: residents of a boarding house. Like many before and after him, his speech equates language with loyalty and nation. The language of both Roosevelt and Harding connects these ideologies to policy practices that bear material effects: the criminalization of multilingualism and the prohibition of bilingual education.

Language policy in Iowa was not spared from the social effects of these ideologies. A few years after the passage of the Babel Proclamation, these discourses made their way into an Iowa Supreme Court Decision regarding education policy:

> The **harmful effects of non-American ideas**, inculcated through the teaching of **foreign languages**, might…be avoided by limiting teaching below the eighth grade to the medium of English. (Supreme Court of Iowa, 1921 in Mertz, 1982)

Again, the ideological links between nativist, monoglot ideology, language education, and educational policy is made evident in the language of this ruling about educational language programming. Here, a Whorfian folk theory (Flores, 2014; Mertz, 1982), in this case the idea that non-American ideas are inherently associated with any language other than English, is on display in policy as *harmful effects of non-American ideas* are meant to be limited by denying Iowa children the right to learn through their full linguistic repertoires. Again, a purported link between linguistic repertoire and content of ideas is constructed in the service of a restrictive educational policy decision.

These rulings were effectively working at the intersection of language, race, national identity and ethnicity to target German Americans. A raciolinguistic perspective is helpful in understanding how a ruling about language constituted a ruling about race and ethnicity which worked to uphold a system of white (Anglo) supremacy and privilege at the time. The Iowa Supreme Court ruling on language education specifically targeted Iowans excluded at the time from the historically contextualized, evolving social category of whiteness (Omi & Winant, 2014) in the midwestern US by virtue of their simultaneous bilingualism and German ethnicity while concomitantly allowing access to bilingualism for predominantly English-speaking Iowans. This is made evident in the allowance for the teaching of foreign languages starting at the eighth grade, the age when foreign language instruction typically began for predominantly English-speaking students in Iowa schools.

Public Discourse in Iowa's Present

In later periods of US history – particularly around and following the Civil Rights era (Bonilla-Silva, 2001) – these overtly nativist and white supremacist ideologies went, as Hill (2009) terms it 'underground,' and became taboo in normative public discourse. However, they remained alive as ever (Bonilla-Silva, 2001), reappearing overtly in the speech of prominent public figures, including the President of the United States during the present study (Santa Ana *et al.*, 2019). The election cycle of 2016 served as a site of mobilization for nativist discourses at a national level that connect interdiscursively to those that have historically circulated in the state of Iowa. Because of Iowa's strategic role in national politics, many of these discourses received visible public support at rallies held and broadcasted in the state, which Trump won in the general election.

The rhetoric and social identity positions of Donald Trump himself illuminate the historical and current discursive threads that bind monoglot ideology, nativism, public policy and white supremacy at the national level. During a nationally broadcasted Republican presidential primary debate, Trump tapped into the power of this rhetoric as he argued:

> We have a country where, to assimilate, you have to speak English…To have a country, we have to have assimilation. We've had people over the years for many, many years saying the same thing. This is a country where we speak English, not Spanish. (Speech transcribed by Teague Beckwith, 2015).

Essentially, Trump's language here does the ideological work of constructing a monoglot ideology, connecting the identity of *a country* with *English* and constructing a national identity where multiple languages are mutually exclusive (even as the federal government of the United States does not have an official language policy).

Because Trump's imagined country is one in which *we* do not speak Spanish, the roughly 41 million Spanish speakers in the US today, including the families whose children are educated in West Liberty's DL program, are positioned as outsiders, not constituents of the country. Though Trump's speech overtly references identity categories of language and national identity, it does so in concert with an underlying discourse of white supremacy wherein Spanish-speaking Latinx Americans, particularly those of Mexican origin, are specifically targeted. Rather than referencing any language that is not English and implicitly targeting a specific racial or ethnic group as past policies and public discourse analyzed herein had done, Trump – whose own grandfather predominantly spoke German when he arrived to the US as an immigrant (Blair, 2001) – names Spanish specifically as the language *we* do not speak.

Trump's voice draws upon discourses traveling through the voices of others in US history such as Theodore Roosevelt (Johnson *et al.*, 2018) and Noah Webster (Flores, 2014) to reinforce this monoglot, nativist, white supremacist discourse. A link between language, country, and race in Trump's discourse is further realized through his position as one of the early advisory members of US English, an organization with overt white supremacist origins made public in a leaked memo by one of its co-founders, Steve Tanton (Johnson *et al.*, 2018). Rosa (2014) describes the semiotic process visible throughout the examples discussed thus far as the construction of ideological bundles at the intersections of language, race, immigration and national identity; one bundle links the identity positions of American, whiteness and English, while the other links identity positions of immigrant, brownness and languages other than English. Historically, these discourses have appeared more subtly in educational policies, practices, and enforcement in Iowa. Interestingly, Trump makes overt reference to and use of the historical tradition of these discourses – *we've had people over the years for many, many years saying the same thing*. Through this language, Trump makes an overt interdiscursive connection to historical figures spearheading past, and present movements in favor of English-only and to his own political involvement with white supremacist language activism (Johnson *et al.*, 2018).

Iowa Language Policy Today

The language of Iowa's official English policy bears similar traces of monoglot ideology and nativism, ideologically linking linguistic identity with race, immigration and nationality even as it adopts less overtly nativist discourses. Iowa's English Reaffirmation Act of 2002 (SF 165), motivated by advocacy from US English, made English the official language:

> Iowa is comprised of individuals from different ethnic, cultural, and linguistic backgrounds. Iowa encourages the assimilation of Iowans into

Iowa's rich culture. **Throughout the history of Iowa and of the United States, the common thread binding individuals of differing backgrounds together has been the English language**...In order to encourage every citizen of this state to become more proficient in the English language, thereby facilitating participation in the economic, political, and cultural activities of this state and of the United States.

Like Trump's speech quoted above, a lynchpin of the argument set up by this language, is a discourse of assimilation. This language of official state policy positions English as a common thread – an instrument of unity for Iowans – thereby obscuring the disunity, strife and violence stemming from enforcement of the English norm in Iowa history. 'Who counts as an *Iowan?*', is a question this language leaves unanswered even as it positions the English language as a characteristic of Iowans. The policy names as a subject *every citizen of this state* whether *Iowan* or not. The goals stated are English proficiency, and participation in economic, political and cultural activities of the state and nation. Notably, interdiscursive connections to these same goals appear in other Iowa language education policy documents through the guidance for the Seal of Biliteracy in Iowa, as a part of its world language program (Iowa Department of Education, 2019) and in the West Liberty Dual Language program's publicly articulated goals (West Liberty Community School District, 2019).

While it did not extinguish bilingual education, the official English policy represented a legislative win for US English (Johnson *et al.*, 2018) and another codification of monoglot ideology in Iowa history. More insidious is its codification of an imagined link between Iowa's culture, whiteness and English. In SF 185, English is positioned as a tool for unity through assimilation and participation, just as it is in Trump's speech from the second debate. The burden of assimilation is on an imagined non-English-speaking Other and the charge is to assimilate into *Iowa's rich culture*. The white settler colonial narrative (Goebel, 2017) is propagated through the link constructed between English and Iowa's culture *throughout the history of Iowa and of the United States*. This phrase subtly rewrites history through a settler colonial narrative (Goebel, 2017) and erases Iowa's original languages and indigenous speakers of color, implying that both Iowa and US history started with the English of white European settlers. Finally, in the language of this policy, a discourse of unity, *the common thread binding individuals of differing backgrounds* works to silence multilingual voices and erase the use of diverse linguistic repertoires in concert with a history of attempts by the state to suppress these things.

In terms of educational language policy, State Code 280.4, the current law governing the education of Iowa's ELLs, is less restrictive, but nonetheless bears traces of the discourse of the dominance of English:

The **medium of instruction** in all secular subjects taught in both public and nonpublic schools shall be the **English language**, *except* when the use of a foreign language is deemed appropriate in the teaching of any subject or when the student is Limited English Proficient. When the student is Limited English Proficient, both public and nonpublic schools shall provide special instruction, which shall include but need not be limited to either instruction in English as a second language or transitional bilingual instruction until the student is fully English proficient or demonstrates an ability to speak, read, write, and understand the English language. [Iowa Code 280.4, p. 3]

In state law the goals of bilingualism and biliteracy are not found nor is there mention of bilingual education in the form of DL programming. The language education programming options that appear are ESL (where English is the medium of instruction) or Transitional Bilingual Education (where students receive bilingual instruction for a period before transitioning to English). Iowa Code 280.4 does not name bilingualism as an asset, and English mastery is positioned as the standard through the suggestion that the use of other languages in instruction should continue until English proficiency is achieved. In spite of the dominant positioning of English in policy and politics in Iowa, the language of this policy opens up a wide space for interpretations and implementations of various types of language programming through its use of the qualifiers *except when* and *need not be limited to*. It is this space which allowed West Liberty educators to advocate for a DL model in their schools where none had previously existed.

Carving Out Discursive Space for Iowa's First DL Program

While previous implementations of state language education policy had encompassed only English-based educational models, in 1997, West Liberty educators found a means of serving their longstanding population of multilingual, Latinx residents through the creation of the state's first Spanish-English DL program. The population of the town is majority Latinx but nearly mirrors the 50/50 ratio of Spanish and English speakers often held up as ideal for DL programs. Educators advocated for and initiated the program in order to best serve their student population after attending an education conference in the state's capital where they learned about the benefits of DL education. These educators pitched the DL model to administration, sought federal grant funding, and recruited bilingual teaching staff through an exchange program with Spanish and Mexican universities. Since then, the program has enjoyed support and accolades within the state for its approach to language education.

One means of spreading positive characterizations of the program has been national, state, and local media coverage in news articles. My earlier study on media representations of the DL program in West Liberty found that the language of the news painted a favorable picture of DL education by touting its positive social impact. The themes of community building, academic success as measured by test scores and biliteracy outcomes, and interdiscursive connections to educational research about advantages of bilingualism and biliteracy appeared in the news reports. For example, the following excerpt from a news article is representative of the community-building theme in news reporting on the program:

> In many ways, West Liberty is unique with its **cohesiveness within the community**. The addition of the state's first Dual-Language Program to the school district will only **help bring the English and Spanish speakers closer together**. (Hamilton, 2000: C14)

This news reporting primarily utilizes the discourse of social success through English found in Iowa language policy (discussed below) and reframes it as a product of bilingualism and biculturalism through DL language programming. In this sense, news reporting about bilingual education in Iowa challenges the history of overtly monoglot legislation and educational policy. At the time of the initial study, these discourses also ran counter to findings of the existing body of national and international studies of language policy and the media (Johnson, 2005; Rickford, 1999; Tarasawa, 2009; Waller, 2012), which pointed out techniques employed by the media to portray DL education and the valuing of sociolinguistic diversity in language policy implementation in an unfavorable light. At the same time, this characterization fits within what Flores (2016) identifies as a liberal multicultural discourse within which diversity and unity are celebrated, but the underlying system of white supremacy can remain intact.

In response to the success of this program, two other bilingual programs were established in Iowa school districts with recent and significant demographic shift in their multilingual populations. Presently, one more public district and several private schools are in the process of adding DL programming for a total of eight DL programs in the process of being implemented in Iowa. These new programs have drawn upon and utilized the success of West Liberty's model as a support for the expansion of DL programming, demonstrating the positive effect springing from the actions taken to propagate DL in West Liberty. The successful implementation of DL programming in a context which previously had none makes discourses of successful bilingual and bicultural education programming available and viable in the local context of policy interpretation – something that had not existed in the state prior to the advent of this program. The implementation of DL programs gained momentum in the state alongside these news communications about the program's success.

DL as a Shelter from Political Tension

The positive characterizations of West Liberty's program continued in the two news articles written after the 2016 presidential election. In these articles, West Liberty's DL program is positioned as both as a bastion of diversity and a shelter from political tension over immigration:

> Undisputed **tension on immigration** issues exists across party lines throughout the nation, including Iowa. However, in the last ten years, one rural Eastern Iowa city continues to prove **diversity can thrive.**
>
> 'I think **you can find political tension almost anywhere**,' said High School Principal Brenda Arthur-Miller.
>
> However, Arthur-Miller said this is **not the case** in her district.
> As the city with Iowa's first dual language program, **learning two languages is as cherished as learning how to walk**. (Vidal, 2017)

Here, the DL program is positioned as a counterpoint to tense national immigration discourse, aligning with previous media reports of the DL program's community-building benefits. The discourse of the article employs an interesting simile between language learning and learning to walk, positioning bilingualism through DL programming as a natural, innate process. This represents an interdiscursive connection to an orientation towards *language as right* (Ruiz, 1984), because, by extension of the simile, denying someone the right to DL would be synonymous with prohibiting an infant from learning to walk. The discourses about linguistic diversity here diverge from those found in historical public discourse, SF 165, and even Code 280.4. In the language of this news article, knowing two languages is synonymous with thriving and the success of DL education is associated with unity that defies the political majority in the state in the midst of political tension. Put differently, DL is positioned here as a common thread of unity in juxtaposition with which SF 165 (the official English law) which ascribes English with the role of social unifier.

One national news article written after Trump's election features manifest intertextual connections to the words of a West Liberty student about language and the community. *Yes!*, a source self-described as reporting on 'alternative ways of thinking that can produce a more equitable and Earth-friendly world' (Yes! media, 2019) quoted Luz, a high school student as saying:

> 'I feel safe here, because I know almost everybody in town.'
>
> She said she's felt different in other parts of Iowa.
>
> '**I just don't feel the same environment** – I feel intimidated. I always fear being discriminated in other towns, because of being Hispanic, because I don't know how they are. **I don't know if they're a racist town**' (Elkhatib, 2017).

Then, the article features Luz's words about the linguistic discrimination she fears her mother will face outside of the small community of West Liberty:

> 'When I go outside of town, I'm protective in a certain way, especially of my parents, of my mom,' she says. 'I fear that someone might say

something mean to her, and that **she won't be able to say anything back to defend herself**, so I'm kind of protective in that way' (Elkhatib, 2019)

The co-mapping of race and language in her experience of the local context of West Liberty and of the regional context of Iowa is visible in Luz's language. She doesn't know if other towns are *racist towns* and her main fear in these towns is that someone *might say something mean* to her mother, *who won't be able to say anything back*. In this account, language is a coherent part of how racism operates and maintains power. Like the quotes from administrators featured in news articles, Luz's language also describes the community as a place where she does not fear discrimination or feel intimidated. While Luz doesn't name the DL program as the reason for this safety, both of the news articles position the program as one of the material ways in which West Liberty has created shelter and sanctuary for its Latinx population.

Voices on the Ground: Discourses from Within the Program

This portrait of the DL program's impact was echoed by qualitative interviews with local actors to ascertain what educators in the program had to say. In updating the initial 2014 study, I sought to expand analysis to include discourses found in the characterizations of educators who work in DL program. To situate analysis of the media reporting in historical and present perspective, I interviewed an administrator, the DL program coordinator, as well as a classroom social studies teacher to learn their views on the ways the program had weathered the discourses mobilized throughout the election cycle as well as the immigration policy changes associated with the presidential election of 2016.

In my interview with Bryan, a social studies teacher, he explained:

> I will say it's been **a lot more positive than I expected...** think there have been a lot of legitimate concerns related to immigration and that, but I think overall **we haven't experienced the same level** of the Trump Effect [Interview, 3.21.18].

Here, Bryan's characterization echoes that of Vidal's article (2017), coinciding with claims made by Vidal's reporting and through manifest intertextual connections (Fairclough, 1992) to the quoted speech of the high school principal. *The Trump Effect* Bryan refers to is the documentation of heightened instances of racialized acts targeting language minoritized, LGBTQ, and students of color in schools across the country in association with Trump's election (Costello, 2016).

Though Bryan's language linking this social effect to the DL program associates it with a positive social impact in one facet of white supremacist society, he also points out ways in which communications about the benefits of the program have been asymmetrical for its white students and Latinx students:

> It was originally sold to the state as a program to address a need for English Language Learners, like **this was our plan for ELLs,** and but it was sold to the community as 'this is an **enrichment opportunity for our Anglo families**'

First, when describing the process of arguing for the implementation of DL education where it previously had not been an option, he employs the term *sold,* an interdiscursive connection to the positioning of language as a commodity (Heller, 2010; Subtirelu, 2017). Within this discourse, bilingualism was described as a resource to be utilized for the state's Department of Education looking to show success as increased standardized test scores and to the white families in the community, looking to increase their social capital through multilingualism. The powerful decision-makers in this account are the state and the white families, not the Latinx families without whose linguistic resources a bilingual program would be untenable in the context of West Liberty.

Additionally, the discourses running through Bryan's account exemplify critical race theory's construct of interest convergence (Bell, 1980) wherein whites are willing to promote non-discriminatory educational policies when they stand to benefit and their social position goes unchallenged (Milner, 2008). Though the underlying power imbalance related to language and race visible in Bryan's account of community decision-making around language policy is not unique to West Liberty's DL program (Cervantes-Soon *et al.*, 2017), it is even more apparent in light of the demographic makeup of West Liberty, where Latinxs outnumber whites.

To further contextualize the discourses pointing to DL's potential role in social transformation, cohesion and thriving diversity repeated in the recent language of news coverage of the program, I asked Bryan about his perceptions of the program's role:

> **Crissa**: Would you say the program has had a transformational effect in the community in some ways?
>
> **Bryan**: Again, I'd say it's had a **bigger effect on the Anglo families**. I have had some families express to me that they're happy that the program is there for their kids, but *we also have a number of parents- when their child starts struggling in English- will pull their kids out, so that their kids can do more in English. I think the families are more focused on the English acquisition.*

An interdiscursive tension is visible here. Bryan's conceptualization of what is happening on the ground in the DL program's enrollment patterns diverges from the predominant discourses found in the news media reports, which tout the program's successfulness for all students in developing biliteracy and biculturalism. While the media reporting espouses the values of liberal multicultural education through DL programming, it does not highlight the asymmetries within these claims Bryan highlights.

The phenomenon Bryan describes, while deserving of further research, does align with the foundation visible throughout the historical discourse, official English policy and educational policy in the state of Iowa. First, the underlying foundation of white supremacy in the state's discourse about language education remains unchallenged – *it's had a bigger effect on the Anglo families*. Secondly, while Latinx families express contentment about the bilingual option for their kids, Bryan perceives that English is a more pressing concern which ultimately impacts participation in the DL program for Latinx families. The discourse of asymmetry seen in this speech between the value of English for Latinx families versus the value of bilingualism for white families aligns with raciolinguistic patterns demonstrated in research around the country showing how bilingualism is undervalued when it comes from the mouths of people of color but accrues as a social benefit to white people (Cervantes-Soon *et al.*, 2017; Flores & Rosa, 2015; Rosa, 2015; Subtirelu, 2017). Bryan credits the program with positive social impact (shelter from The Trump Effect). At the same time, his language here points to a pattern visible in past Iowa language policies where white families benefit disproportionately from bilingual education.

Discussion: Untangling the Past for Transformation in the Present

In the case of Iowa and of its first DL program, intertextual analysis of a long history of public discourse alongside historical and present language policies demonstrates that the discourses of monoglot ideology, nativism and evolving structures of white supremacy still align with educational phenomena today. A raciolinguistic lens reveals the shifting norms of whiteness throughout Iowa history that enable these ideological threads not only to shape discourse and institutional practices around national origin and language, but also to uphold a historically contextualized societal category of whiteness (Hill, 2009; Omi & Winant, 2015) which today includes Iowans of German heritage but excludes Spanish speakers. It is within this socio-historical foundation that the various discursive representations of West Liberty's bilingual program can best be contextualized and demographic inequalities within the program can be understood. In the case of Iowa and of its first DL program, analysis of a long history of public discourse alongside historical and present language policies demonstrates that the discourses of monoglot ideology, nativism and evolving structures of white supremacy may still align with educational phenomena today.

Historical and current regulation of Iowa's languages has produced various generations of speakers of color and borne material effects such as the historical loss of bilingual education, criminalization and the potential for disproportionate benefit to white families in DL programs. Today, Iowans of German heritage enjoy the privileges of whiteness in Iowa and some currently benefit from bilingual education in West Liberty. Many others currently express views that new Latinx immigrants should not speak Spanish and point to their ancestors as a model of English learning for immigrants. Thompson (2018) argues that these viewpoints are often argued based on fictionalized accounts of history that ignore how German Americans and their language were racialized through policy and practice during this historical period. Where violent processes of white settler colonialism erased both indigenous languages and populations earlier in Iowa's history, a more subtle process of erasure (Irvine & Gal, 2000) obscures both the racialization of and violence inflicted upon German Americans on the basis of language and ethnic origin and undergirds the preservation of hegemonic whiteness (Matías *et al.*, 2014) through language policy.

Another way in which hegemonic whiteness may be maintained today is visible through examination of English dominance and multilingualism in the discourses of policy, public speech, and media. Current messages about the value of bilingual education for Latinx residents at the state level in Iowa and the local level in West Liberty's program are contradictory. Discourses in past and present public discourse, official language policy, and educational language policy in Iowa draw upon a discourse of social success and economic participation through English. Ultimately, policy language and some positive media representations construct their arguments for or against bilingualism from the same discursive basis even if these discourses are sometimes used to argue for bilingualism and biliteracy as opposed to English-only policy and education. Prominent English-only discourses and discourses of bilingualism in Iowa tend to draw from what Valdez *et al.* (2016) identify as a discursive framework constructed through the values of global human capitalism as opposed to an equity/heritage discourse which values equity for language minoritized students and the right to maintain non-English heritage languages.

When educators exerted agency to create the state's first bilingual program against this monoglot backdrop, new discourses of thriving diversity and social success through bilingualism were introduced. Media reports associate the program with antiracist social benefits, such as community-building and providing a shelter from the Trump Effect. Some of these reports feature manifest intertextual connections to the language of Latinx students in the DL program whose language affirms these benefits (e.g. Elkhatib, 2017). However, Bryan's characterization of demographic patterns within the program suggest that the underlying foundation of white supremacy which enables white students to receive disproportionate social benefit from bilingualism may remain intact and there is need of continued work towards transformation.

By situating today's media representations of the benefits of the DL program within their historical foundations alongside a comprehensive, raciolinguistic analysis of the relevant power governors (Liu, 2017) – institutions such as state legislatures, schools and powerful individual actors that come together to produce marginalization and uphold a social system that disproportionately benefits white people – the ways that discourses of nativism, monoglot ideology and white privilege can intertwine with DL programs become visible. Once this underlying foundation is visible, it can be addressed, and steps toward dismantling it must include continued antiracist social action (Flores, 2017; Flores & Chaparro, 2017; Lensmire *et al.*, 2013). Research can and should continue to reveal these powerful historical foundations and highlight a path forward towards transformation in these power dynamics.

Positive media reporting on the program as well as the policy implementation actions of educators who seek social benefit for Latinx families in their community stand in contrast to monoglot language in policy and past public speech about language. While these discourses are a counterpoint to the monoglot discourses of past and present policy and political speech to positive social effect, it could also be argued that these public communications fit within what Flores (2016) has identified as a discourse of liberal multiculturalism where diversity is celebrated but hegemonic whiteness remains unchallenged. According to Flores (2016), addressing the harmful effects of this discourse entail taking a critical look at whiteness and how it works through the educational system to undermine equal benefit for Latinx students. Building on critical whiteness scholarship (Matías *et al.*, 2014), this process involves institutions examining and upending norms of whiteness as well as white stakeholders who are willing not only to interrogate how their own positions and imaginations about Latinx students may function to sustain inequalities in bilingual education. It also requires white stakeholders to recognize the power dynamics that empower raciolinguistic ideologies and to identify their own location within them in order to devise effective antiracist activism (Lensmire *et al.*, 2013; Matías & Liou, 2015) in their local context.

For educators who are committed to bilingual education's potential for social transformation like Bryan and many others in West Liberty, one action point is revealed in Bryan's account of powerful stakeholders to whom DL program was *sold*. He mentions the buy-in DL proponents sought from the state as well as from white families, two entities that stand to benefit from existing systems rooted in hegemonic whiteness and a discourse of global human capital. This is consistent with Valdez *et al.* (2017) argument that there has been a shift in recent years in the audience of print media representations of bilingual education towards white stakeholders. Missing is a characterization of the Latinx families, who ultimately provide the linguistic resources that make the bilingual program possible (Ricento, 2005), as powerful stakeholders for whom effort should be exerted in *selling* the program. This pattern of positioning white families and legislators as the most powerful decision-makers when creating community buy-in for DL has been demonstrated elsewhere (Cervantes-Soon *et al.*, 2017; Valdez *et al.*, 2017). In West Liberty, Bryan recognizes this and is continuing the transformational work towards fighting this dynamic.

Transformation, then, might take the form of community members coming together to positioning Latinx families as powerful stakeholders and decision-makers (Olivos, 2004) in DL, fomenting what Solorzano and Delgado Bernal (2001) term *transformational resistance*. This is a form of social action rooted in a critical consciousness of systematic patterns and inequalities, such as those identified in the present analysis, that is 'political, collective, conscious, and rooted in a sense that social change is possible' (Solorzano & Delgado Bernal, 2001: 321). As a white scholar, it is my intention to speak to the role of white stakeholders in this process without centering perspectives and power dynamics rooted in whiteness. White stakeholders must first recognize their own social locations within a system of disproportionate social benefit, then seek to upend it. They might carry out the business of transformational resistance in their dealings with the media by uncovering and centering the perspectives of Latinx families in the program, inciting action through media communications towards the goal of supporting and upholding Latinx families' goals for their children's education.

These media relations should move away from the values discourse of global human capitalism that currently underpins policy and media communications about language in Iowa to re-center an equality/heritage discourse recognizing language as a right (Ruiz, 1982) for Latinx students. In addition, communication with the media should be geared toward exposing and countering the social forces that threaten this right. Researchers might join in the process of transformational resistance by revealing the assumptions and underpinnings of hegemonic whiteness and uncovering discourses, policies, practices, and structures in education that position Latinx students as 'struggling in English' (alluded to in Bryan's account) rather than as people with a right to bilingualism and by identifying steps to transform them.

Note

(1) In keeping with a raciolinguistic perspective and a primary argument of this chapter, where whiteness is co-naturalized with English in the US context, I use the term *white* to refer to predominantly white, English-speaking students in the DL program. Educators in West Liberty use the term *Anglo*, which connotes both phenotype and English language usage.

References

Alim, H.S. (2016) Introduction raciolinguistics: Racing language and langauging race in hypperacial times. In H.S. Alim, J.R. Rickford and A.F. Ball (eds) *Raciolinguistics: How Language Shapes Our Ideas About Race* (pp. 1–32). Oxford University Press.

Baker, P.L. and Hotek, D.R. (2003) Perhaps a blessing: Skills and contributions of recent Mexican immigrants in the rural Midwest. *Hispanic Journal of Behavioral Sciences* 25 (4), 448–468.

Bell, D. (1980) Brown v. Board of Education and the interest convergence principal. *Harvard Law Review* 93, 518–533.

Blair, G. (2001) *The Trumps: Three Generations that Built an Empire*. New York: Simon and Schuster.

Bonilla-Silva, E. (2001) *White Supremacy and Racism in the Post-Civil Rights Era*. Boulder, CO: Lynne Reiner Publishers.

Bucholtz, M. and Hall, K. (2005) Language and Identity. In A. Duranti (ed.) *A Companion to Linguistic Anthropology* (pp. 369–394). Oxford: Blackwell.

Cervantes-Soon, C.G., Dorner, L., Palmer, D., Heiman, D., Schwerdtfeger, R. and Choi, J. (2017) Combating inequalities in two-way language immersion programs: Toward critical consciousness in bilingual education spaces. *Review of Research in Education* 41 (1), 403–427.

Collier, V. and Thomas, W. (2004) The astounding effectiveness of dual language education for all. *NABE Journal of Research and Practice* 2 (1), 1–20.

Costello, M.B. (2016) The Trump effect: The impact of the presidential campaign on our nation's schools. *Southern Poverty Law Center*, See https://www.splcenter.org/20161128/trump-effect-impact-2016-presidential-election-our-nations-schools#pdf

Cummins, J. (1979) Cognitive/academic language proficiency, linguistic interdependence, the optimum age question and some other matters. *Working Papers on Bilingualism*, No. 19, 121–129.

Dumas, M.J., Dixson, A.D. and Mayorga, E. (2016) Educational policy and the cultural politics of race: Introduction to the special issue. *Educational Policy* 30 (1), 3–12.

Elkhatib, B. (2017) Tiny town in the heartland creates homegrown sanctuary: Residents of Iowa's first Hispanic-majority town don't need sanctuary city policies to support their immigrant neighbors. *Yes! Magazine*. See https://www.yesmagazine.org/people-power/tiny-town-in-the-heartland-creates-homegrown-sanctuary-20170501

Fairclough, N. (1992) Intertextuality in critical discourse analysis. *Linguistics and Education* 4 (3), 269–293.

Fairclough, N. (2014) *Language and Power*. Abingdon: Routledge.

Flores, N. (2014) Creating republican machines: Language governmentality in the United States. *Linguistics and Education* 25 (1), 1–11.

Flores, N. (2016) A tale of two visions: Hegemonic whiteness and bilingual education. *Educational Policy* 30 (1), 13–38.

Flores, N. (2017) Developing a materialist anti-racist approach to language activism. *Multilingua* 36 (5), 565–570.

Flores, N. and Chaparro, S. (2017) What counts as language education policy? Developing a materialist anti-racist approach to language activism. *Language Policy* 17, 365–384.

Flores, N. and García, O. (2017) A critical review of bilingual education in the united states: From basements and pride to boutiques and profit. *Annual Review of Applied Linguistics* 37, 14–29.

Flores, N. and Rosa, J. (2015) Undoing appropriateness: Raciolinguistic ideologies and language diversity in education. *Harvard Educational Review* 85 (2), 149–172.

Freeman, R. (1998) *Bilingual Education and Social Change*. Clevedon: Multilingual Matters.

Goebel, M. (2017) Settler colonialism in postcolonial Latin America. In E. Cavanagh and L. Veracini (eds) *The Routledge Handbook of the History of Settler Colonialism* (pp. 139–152). Abingdon: Routledge.

Grey, M.A. and Woodrick, A.C. (2005) Latinos have revitalized our community: Mexican migration and Anglo Responses in Marshalltown, Iowa. In V. Zúñiga and R. Hernández-León (eds) *New Destinations: Mexican Immigration in the United States* (pp. 133–154). New York: Russell Sage Foundation.

Hall, S. (2001) Foucault: Power, knowledge and discourse. In S.J. Wetherell, M. Taylor and S. Yates (eds) *Discourse Theory and Practice: A Reader*. London: Sage.

Hamann, E., Wortham, S. and Murillo, E.G.J. (2001) *Education and policy in the new Latino diaspora. Education in the New Latino Diaspora*. New York: Ablex Publishing.

Hamilton, R. (2000, Feb. 25) West Liberty revels in town's ethnic diversity. *Press-Citizen*.

Harding, W.L. (1918) '*Original Copy of the Babel Proclamation.' German Iowa and the Global Midwest*. State Historical Society of Iowa, Des Moines, IA. See http://germansiniowa.lib.uiowa.edu/items/show/313

Heller, M. (2010) The commodification of language. *Annual Review of Anthropology* 39 (2010), 101–114.

Hill, J.H. (2009) English-Language Spanish in the United States as a site of symbolic violence. In J.A. Cobas, J. Duany and J.R. Feagin (eds) *How the United States Racializes Latinos: White Hegemony and Its Consequences* (pp. 116–133). Boulder, CO: Paradigm Publishers.

Hult, F.M. (2010) Analysis of language policy discourses across the scales of space and time. *International Journal of the Sociology of Language* 2010 (202), 7–24.

Iowa Code 280.4

Iowa Department of Education (2019) *Biliteracy Seal*. See https://educateiowa.gov/pk-12/instruction/biliteracy-seal

Irvine, J.T. and Gal, S. (2000) Language ideology and linguistic differentiation. In P.V. Kroskrity (ed.) *Regimes of Language: Ideologies, Polities and Identities* (pp. 35–83). Santa Fe, NM: School of American Research Press.

Johnson, D.C. (2015) Intertextuality and language policy. In F.M. Hult and D.C. Johnson (eds) *Research Methods in Language Policy and Planning: A Practical Guide* (pp. 166–180). Chichester: Wiley.

Johnson, D.C., Stephens, C. and Lynch, S. (2018) The past is prologue: Language policy and nativism in new immigrant contexts. *Journal of Language and Politics* 17 (3), 366-385.

Johnson, E. (2005) WAR in the media: Metaphors, ideology, and the formation of language policy. *Bilingual Research Journal* 29 (3), 621–640.

Lensmire, T.J., McManimon, S.K., Dockter Tierney, J., Lee-Nichols, M.E., Casey, Z.A., Lensmire, A. and Davis, B.M. (2013) McIntosh as synechdoch: How teacher education's focus on white privilege undermines antiracism. *Harvard Educational Review* 83 (3), 410–432.

Liu, W.M. (2017) White male power and privilege: The relationship between white supremacy and social class. *Journal of Counseling Psychology* 64 (4), 349–358.

Matheson, D. (2005) *Media Siscourses: Analyzing media texts*. Milton Keynes: Open University Press.

Matías, C.E. and Liou, D.D. (2015) Tending to the heart of communities of color: Towards critical race teacher activism. *Urban Education* 50 (5), 601–625.

Matías, C.E., Viesca, K.M., Garrison-Wade, D.F., Tandon, M. and Galindo, R. (2014) 'What is critical whiteness doing in OUR nice field like critical race theory?' Applying CRT and CWS to understand the white imaginations of white teacher candidates. *Equity & Excellence in Education* 47 (3), 289–304.

Mertz, E. (1982) Language and Mind: A Whorfian Folk Theory in United States Language Law. *Sociolinguistics Working Paper* 93. See http://ccat.sas.upenn.edu/~haroldfs/540/theory/mertz1.html

Milner, H.R. (2008) Critical race theory and interest convergence as analytic tools in education policies and practices. *Journal of Teacher Education* 59 (4), 332–346.

Olivos, E.M. (2004) Tensions, contradictions, and resistance: An activist's reflection of the struggles of Latino parents in the school system. *The High School Journal* 87 (4), 25–35.

Omi, M. and Winant, H. (2014) *Racial Formation in the United States*. Abingdon: Routledge.

O'Toole, P. (2006) *When Trumpets Call: Theodore Roosevelt After the White House*. Simon and Schuster.

Palmer, D.K. (2015) Middle-class English Speakers in a two-way immersion bilingual classroom: 'Everybody should be listening to Jonathan right now.' *TESOL Quarterly* 43 (2), 177–202.

Ricento, T. (2005) Problems with the 'language-as-resource' discourse in the promotion of heritage languages in the USA. *Journal of Sociolinguistics* 9 (3), 348–368.

Rickford, J. (1999) The Ebonics controversy in my backyard: A sociolinguist's experiences and reflections. *Journal of Sociolinguistics* 3, 267–266.

Rosa, J. (2015) Nuevo Chicago? Language, diaspora, and Latina/o panethnic formations. In L. Martin-Rojo and R. Marquez-Reiter (eds) *A Sociolinguistics of Diaspora: Latino Practices, Identities and Ideologies* (pp. 34–47). Abingdon: Routledge.

Rosa, J. and Flores, N. (2017) Unsettling race and language: Toward a raciolinguistic perspective. *Language in Society* (im), 1–27.

Ruiz, R. (1984) Orientations in language planning. *NABE Journal* 8 (2), 15–34.

Santa Ana, O., Antonio Juárez, M., Resêndez, M., Hernández, J., Gaytan, O., Cerón, K., Gómez, C. and Hirose, Y. (2019) Documenting the president's verbal animus against immigrants to defend DACA grantees: Final report of the UCLA DACA defense group. UCLA César E. Chávez Department of Chicana and Chicano Studies. See https://www.thepresidentsintent.com/our-findings

Schissel, J. (2019) *Social Consequences of Testing for Language Minoritized Bilinguals in the United States*. Multilingual Matters.

Silverstein, M. (1998) Monoglot 'standard' in America: Standardization and metaphors of linguistic hegemony. In D. Brenneis and R. Macaulay (eds) *The Matrix of Language: Contemporary linguistic anthropology* (pp. 284–306). Boulder, CO: Westview Press.

Solorzano, D.G. and Delgado Bernal, D. (2001) Examining transformational resistance through a Critical Race and LatCrit theory framework: Chicana and Chicano students in urban context. *Urban Education* 36 (3), 308–342.

Subtirelu, N.C. (2013) 'English… it's part of our blood': Ideologies of language and nation in United States Congressional discourse. *Journal of Sociolinguistics* 17 (1), 37–65.

Subtirelu, N.C. (2017) Raciolinguistic ideology and Spanish-English bilingualism on the US labor market: An analysis of online job advertisements. *Language in Society* 46 (4), 477–505.

Tarasawa, B. (2009) Mixed messages in media coverage of bilingual education: The case of Atlanta, Georgia. *Bilingual Research Journal* 31 (1–2), 23–46.

Teague Beckwith, R. (2015) Full text of the second presidential debate. *Time*. See http://time.com/4037239/second-republican-debate-transcript-cnn/

Thompson, M.R. (2017) *Narratives of Immigration and Language Loss: Lessons Learned from the Great American Midwest*. Lexington Books.

Tollefson, J.W. (1991) *Planning Language, Planning Inequality: Language Policy in the Community*. Longman.

Tollefson, J.W. (2015) Historical-structural analysis. In F.M. Hult and D.C. Johnson (eds) *Research Methods in Language Policy and Planning: A Practical Guide* (pp. 140–151). Malden: Wiley Blackwell.

US Department of Justice (DoJ) & Department of Education (ED) (January 7, 2015) *Dear Colleague Letter: English Learner Students and Limited English Proficient Parents*. See www.ed.gov/OCR

Valdés, G. (1997) Dual-language immersion programs: A cautionary note concerning the education of language-minority students. *Harvard Educational Review* 67 (3), 391–429.

Valdez, V.E., Delavan, G. and Freire, J. (2016) The marketing of dual language education policy in Utah print media. *Educational Policy* 30 (6), 849–883.

Veracini, L. (2017) Introduction: Settler colonialism as a distinct mode of domination. In E. Cavanagh and L. Veracini (eds) *The Routledge Handbook of the History of Settler Colonialism* (pp. 1–8). Abingdon: Routledge.

Vidal, G. (November 9, 2017) Programs in education form cross-cultural blend in Iowa's first 'minority majority' town. CBS 2 Iowa. See https://cbs2iowa.com/news/local/programs-in-education-form-cross-cultural-blend-in-iowas-first-minority-majority-town

Waller, L.J. (2012) Bilingual education and the language of news. *Australian Journal of Linguistics* 32 (4), 459–472.

West Liberty Community School District (2019) Dual Language Program. See https://www.wl.k12.ia.us/district/dual-language-program/

Wiley, T.G. and Wright, W.E. (2004) Against the undertow: Language-minority education policy and politics in the 'age of accountability.' *Educational Policy* 18 (1), 142–168.

Wortham, B.S., Clonan-Roy, K., Link, H. and Martínez, C. (2015) The new Latino diaspora: The surging Hispanic and Latino population across the country has brought new education challenges and opportunities to rural and small town America. *Phi Delta Kappa* (March 2013), 14–19.

Yes! Media (2019) About Yes! Journalism for people building a better world. See https://www.yesmagazine.org/about

3 Dual Language and the Erasure of Emergent Bilinguals Labeled As Disabled (EBLADs)

María Cioè-Peña

The discourse within mainstream America has traditionally positioned bilingualism as an impediment to full English proficiency and, subsequently, assimilation. At the same time, researchers across different fields have documented the varying ways in which bilingualism can be a boon for individuals with increases in cultural capital, economic opportunities and even brain function (Cioè-Peña, 2017). Although this research has existed for decades, this information was not known to most laypeople, creating a knowledge gap which likely contributed to the growth and expansion of racialized English-only movements across the country. However, during the last 10 years the mainstream media has contributed greatly to shifting the narrative around bilingualism, making these advantages much more visible, known and relatable to mainstream Americans. As such, what once was viewed as a limitation for some (i.e. immigrants and people of color) is now viewed as a potential gain for others (White monolingual English speakers). This new awareness has led to the reversal of English-only laws in some states and to a renewed interest in bilingual education, particularly Dual Language (DL) programs.

Traditional bilingual programs, which originated from grassroots efforts and were designed and geared for minoritized children, have often been rejected as an educational setting (Flores & García, 2017; Martínez-Álvarez, 2018). Two-way DL immersion programs, on the other hand, have been embraced by neoliberal efforts which aim to increase access to language learning for English-dominant children (Calderon & Carreon, 2000; García Mathewson, 2017; Kelly, 2016; Stein, July 3, 2018; Valdés, 1997). As such DL is promoted as a medium that brings together speakers of minoritized and majoritized languages and makes them bilingual and biliterate. This bringing together of children from diverse backgrounds is also thought of as an inclusive setting where students from differing linguistic, ethnic and socioeconomic backgrounds learn alongside each other. Not only do children gain another language, they also gain new world views and cultural understandings. However, the inclusiveness of DL is accessible only to a particular kind of student: one who can make measurable academic and linguistic gains.

In order to gain access to a DL program a student must meet several criteria. First and foremost, they must be neurotypical. This need to be neurotypical is reflected in 'the lack of special education supports' within DL programs as well as the systemic counseling out that parents of Emergent Bilinguals Labeled As Disabled (EBLADs) encounter (Martínez-Álvarez, 2018). This last point may be reflective of ableist ideologies that view students with disabilities (SWD) as deficient and DL spaces as rigorous thus inappropriate for SWD regardless of their linguistic experience (Drysdale *et al.*, 2015; Gutierrez-Clellen, 1999; Harry & Klingner, 2007; Martínez-Álvarez, 2018). As such, students with dis/abilities, who are disproportionately Black, Latinx and Indigenous, remain overwhelmingly excluded from DL. While some could argue that DL is unintentional in its exclusivity, the reality is that explicit efforts to be fully inclusive have not been adopted. This oversight may be rooted in the fields focus on attaining legitimacy, sustainability and longevity. Like other alternative learning settings, in order for DL programs to continue to not only exists but also thrive, they must deliver on the promises of academic and linguistic growth. As a result, most programs resort to recruiting the most coveted student: the White, middle class, typically developing child. This archetype of academic excellence is sought after in hopes that they will bring the skills and resources that many students are color are said to need (Franko, 2018; Rabe Thomas, 2018).

This chapter will look at how the promises of DL have EBLADs[1] as well as share how old tropes about language confusion continue to ostracize this subset of minoritized students from their multilingual peers even as the research indicates that they show the same gains. This chapter will also discuss the ways in which DL programs uphold ideas grounded in ableism[2] and White supremacy,[3] ultimately benefiting from the alienation of emergent bilinguals labeled as dis/abled. In order to do this, this chapter will focus on how DL within the context of New York City, the largest and most diverse school district in the country, is failing emergent bilinguals labeled as dis/abled. While NYC is viewed as this rich and diverse metropolis, it continues to host one of the most segregated education systems in the country. The high rate of racial, linguistic, socioeconomic and ableist segregation amongst NYC schools mirrors that of districts around the United States and the world. This segregation persists even as the city's educational czars: the mayor-appointed school chancellors, continue to make national headlines for their social justice initiatives. In particular, both Carmen Fariña and Richard Carranza, with the support of Mayor Bill DeBlasio, have made increasing access to bilingual programming a cornerstone of their administrations. And still, EBLAD students continue to experience linguistic isolation. As such the NYC context allows us to explore how a school district that is so supportive of multilingualism and of social justice can continue to relegate some students to margins? The answer lies in a cause that is not unique to NYC: disjointed educational policies and ideologies.

Educational programming in NYC is governed by both city, state and federal policies, as a result this setting offers a unique opportunity for gathering rich data. As such, this chapter uses publicly available data such as educational policies, academic scholarship, organizational reports, city demographic, newspaper articles and school websites. Additionally, in order to show how the macro impacts the micro, the chapter also presents school level data (interviews, reports, and correspondence) that was gathered by the City University of New York-New York State Initiative on Emergent Bilinguals (CUNY-NYSIEB), a project I was a part of. All of these data were analyzed using critical discourse analysis (Fairclough, 2013) and textual analysis (Allen, 2017). These methods were enacted in order to understand how ideas about race, language and disability are not only shared within them but how they influence public discourse and thought.

Theoretical Framework

This work is dependent on an intersectional lens, which lays bare the fact that the injustices faced by multiply minoritized people are unique and specific to their experiences rather than any of the singular identity markers they embody (Crenshaw, 1991; Hankivsky, 2014). That is to say that, the injustices faced by EBLAD students are distinct and potentially more profound than those experienced by neurotypical emergent bilinguals[4] or by White children with dis/abilities. This intersectional lens can be described as a critical disabilities raciolinguistic (CDR) perspective. As such, this perspective is informed by an integration of two existing theories: Raciolinguistics and dis/ability critical race studies (DisCrit), in order to develop a framework that is suitable for understanding the experiences of this multiply marginalized population.

The central theory enacted in this work is the theory of raciolinguistics which posits that understandings of language are tied to the racialization of the speaker and vice versa (Alim *et al.*, 2016). This explains the ways in which bilingualism is valued in majoritized groups but devalued for minoritized and othered people (Flores & Rosa, 2015; Rosa & Flores, 2017). This is clearly articulated by Flores and Rosa (2015):

> a raciolinguistic perspective seeks to understand how the white gaze is attached both to a speaking subject who engages in the idealized linguistic practices of whiteness and to a listening subject who hears and interprets the linguistic practices of language-minoritized populations as

deviant based on their racial positioning in society as opposed to any objective characteristics of their language use. (2015: 151)

While a raciolinguistic perspective pushes us to consider issues of devaluation on the grounds of race and perception it does so while unintentionally upholding ableist rhetoric. For example, by addressing language as that which is 'spoken' and 'heard,' raciolinguistic perspectives endorse oral communication over other means of communication, such as sign language, that are not based in sound/word production but whose users are no less racialized. To the contrary, non-verbal communicators are subjected to additional categorizations, devaluation and subjugation. Additionally, in grounding the conversation on the 'White gaze[5]' without accounting for normative ideologies raciolinguistics ignores the labels and pathologies enacted by the 'White gaze' that subsequently erase racialized acts and rewrites them as matters of disability. This oversight allows arguments that are framed within the realm of capacity and capability rather than race or language to remain unchallenged. As such, the linguistic practices of people of color with disabilities (POCwD) can continue to be qualified as 'deviant' on the basis of disability rather than race. By focusing on language and race without considering ability, raciolinguistics, as it is currently conceived, does not consider the ways in which its own strength-based and body-centered discourse can be used to further marginalize POCwD. Nonetheless, this gap can be mitigated with the adoption of a critical disabilities' framework such as DisCrit.

Like raciolinguistics, DisCrit calls attention to the social construction of value and appropriateness, with a particular focus on race and ability. According to Annamma and Morrison (2018):

> DisCrit exposes how ability is distributed and withheld based on race through policies and practices. Additionally, DisCrit recognizes interlocking marginalizing processes which target multiple dimensions of identity. In other words, we are all actively abled or disabled based on our multiple identities. The closer we are to the desired norm (e.g. white, male, cis-gender, heterosexual), the more likely we are to be imagined as capable, regardless of our behavioral and academic interactions (Broderick & Leonoardo, 2016). (2018: 72)

In this way, and similar to how raciolinguistics discusses ability within the context of language, DisCrit examines ability within the context of the body and its perceived (dis)functions. As such, Discrit is concerned with the ways in which pathologization acts as a surrogate for racialization. Another way to conceive this is by understanding the ways in which disability labels have been constructed to support White people by granting them access to services but to suppress people of color by enforcing segregated educations and denying them access to services (Annamma *et al.*, 2013). Still, DisCrit's considerations of race are based on phenotypical presentations and only tangentially address issues of language.

While DisCrit researchers have identified the ways in which students that were once segregated on the basis of race are now segregated on the basis of ability – with the catalyst being an altruistic one rather than a racist one – it fails to recognize the ways in which integration can also result in linguistic oppression because in order to be included the EBLADs must align themselves to a different measure of normativity: English monolingualism.

In melding raciolinguistics and DisCrit, a CDR perspective argues that not only is the speaker subject to the White gaze but more specifically to the White normative gaze. Unlike the White gaze which can only be attributed to racially majoritized speakers and listeners, the White normative gaze challenges even racially minoritized speakers/listeners to interrogate the ways in which they idealize the linguistic practices of 'normal (White) people' while interpreting the linguistic practices of POCwD as deviant. As such, the idolizing happens not just in relation to how much the speaker approximates whiteness but also by how much they approximate normalcy. A CDR perspective also pushes us to confront the ways in which disability labels have been used as surrogates for both racial and linguistic categorizations, replicating the same oppressive outcomes with searing accuracy. A CDR perspective requires that we apply the understandings that just as race and language are social constructs so too are disability categories. Just as race and language practices are representative of human diversity so too are physical and neurological variances (Annamma *et al.*, 2013).

Without acknowledging the normative stance, regardless of one's positionality, normative speakers/listeners are able to, without guilt or reservation, subject EBLADs to raciolinguistic subjectivities on the grounds of ability without examining the racial-normative practices they are enacting and promoting. Similarly, the White gaze can also enact policies that are linguistically oppressive under the guise of inclusion. In short, centering white supremacy without accounting for normative hegemony allows people to disassociate themselves from the oppression in question while ignoring the violence they are enacting on the grounds of mitigating a disability even though the disability is acting as a surrogate for race.

A CDR perspective is necessary in order to fully understand the educational experiences of EBLADs. While both raciolinguistics and DisCrit aim to address the systemic violence that children of color endure, individually, they fall short because they fail to account for a significant part of a child's identity and positionality. Thus, by integrating them into a CDR perspective we have the potential to fully appreciate and support EBLAD children, recognizing that current bilingual and special education practices are fragmented, often asking them to deny a part of themselves and ultimately, denying them the opportunity to navigate through the world as a whole person. As such, a CDR perspective is also meant to show the polymorphic nature of the oppressor's gaze – the ways in which it adapts in order to guarantee the othering and oppression of minoritized groups. Ultimately, a CDR perspective aims not to depict EBLADs as the sum of their parts but rather as whole beings whose racial, linguistic, physical and neurotypical diversities cannot be teased apart.

Language and Disability Supplant Race

In 1954, the supreme court of the United States struck down notions of separate but equal and ordered that schools be racially integrated. Nearly 65 years later and most schools remain as segregated now as they were then (E. A. K. Harris, Josh, May 2, 2018; The Civil Rights Project, May 15, 2014). While many politicians and educators continue to publicly denounce segregation on the basis of race, many continue to support 'need'-based segregation. As such, segregated learning spaces persist because racial segregation has been replaced with segregation on the basis of language and disability, yet still grounded around ideas of White intellectual superiority (Connor & Ferri, 2005; Ferri & Connor, 2005). In many ways, special education, traditional bilingual education and English as a second language (ESL) have become the 'for colored only' learning spaces while mainstream and gifted and talented programs remain overwhelmingly 'for whites only.' This is evident in the overrepresentation of African American, Latinx and Native American students within special education, as well as the disproportionate enrollment of emergent bilinguals in transitional and sheltered ESL programs in contrast to their disproportionately low representation in G&T programs (Division of English Language Learners and Student Support; Kramarczuk Voulgarides, Fergus, & King Thorius; Pirtle; Sullivan; Sullivan & Bal). However, rather than being viewed as discriminatory, this kind of segregation is viewed as both necessary and benevolent (Dev & Dev, 2015). Similarly, DL spaces then function as the gifted and talented learning spaces where 'model minorities[6]' can learn alongside much-coveted White students. In many ways, DL not only promotes these ongoing models of segregation, it thrives because of them.

All labels that are placed on students serve the purpose of distinguishing them from the norm (Lauchlan & Boyle, 2007; Scheff, 2017). A few labels are representative of being above the norm: gifted and talented, valedictorian, honor student, bilingual. However, most school-based labels are used to indicate those whose academic performances are considered to be subpar: English language learners, culturally and linguistically diverse, special needs. The primary purpose of these labels is categorization and treatment: when we can identify the problem, we can identify the treatment. However, this focus on intervention is based on a system of standards where White, heteronormative, neurotypical, middle-class values are seen as the norm. Thus, the treatments are always focused on approximating a very rigid definition of 'normal' and on moving students closer to 'a regular class.' As such, traditional bilingual education serves as a transitional space where emergent bilinguals can develop their English competency with the end goal of moving into a 'regular class' code for 'monolingual English class.' Similarly, students labeled as disabled receive services in different settings with the goal of moving to the least restrictive environment (LRE): the general education classroom, where they can 'learn alongside their [typically developing] peers' (Wishart *et al.*, 2007). In all of these instances, the educational model rationalizes segregated learning spaces as transitional and temporary and wholly focused on moving children to monolingual general education classrooms. However, the reality is that those who do not make the necessary improvements on prescriptive measures like standardized testing, or subjective measures like teacher evaluations, are destined for alienated learning spaces for their entire educational experience.

Using a CDR perspective we can understand that just as language is racialized, so too is behavior. Students from culturally and linguistically diverse backgrounds are educated in segregated spaces at alarming rates, this is a result of their racialization more so than their performance or behavior. Even while bilingual education programs continue to grow in places like New York City (NYC) – which has nearly quadrupled its bilingual programming in the last five years, emergent bilinguals, SWD and EBLADs continue to be overwhelmingly educated in English-only settings:

> the vast majority of the city's roughly 142,000 non-native English speakers take most of their classes in English. Only about 18 percent of those students are enrolled in bilingual programs, down from about 40 percent in 2002, according to [(Menken & Salorza, 2012)]. The majority of those programs are transitional bilingual, with just 154 of the city's 1,600 traditional public schools offering dual-language programs. (Wall, April 4, 2016)

As a result, in 2016–2017, only 4.9% of New York City's 160,624 emergent bilingual students were educated within DL programs (Division of English Language Learners and Student Support, 2017). In comparison, 10% of emergent bilinguals were placed in transitional bilingual education (TBE) while 83% were relegated to English as a New Language (ENL) classes (Division of English Language Learners and Student Support, 2017). The increase in DL programing has not led to increased access to emergent bilinguals: in 2013–2014, 4.5% were instructed in DL, 15.4% in TBE, and 79.2% in stand-alone ESL/ENL programs (Department of English Language & Student, 2015). So, while the New York City Department of Education (NYCDOE) has publicly promoted the increase in DL and bilingual programing, emergent bilingual access to it has sharply decreased. This means that the 4.9% of emergent bilinguals that are enrolled in DL programs are the only emergent bilinguals in NYC who have access to racially, and socioeconomically diverse classrooms that will result in bilingualism and biliteracy. Additionally, while the number of EBLADs has increased from 23.3% in 2013–2014 to 24.7% in 2016–2017, the overwhelming majority of these students are educated in segregated special education, English-only settings (Department of English Language & Student, 2015; EngageNY, 2017).

As previously, mentioned racial segregation continues to be a large issue within NYC schools, and this is no less true within special education. The overrepresentation of culturally and linguistically diverse students within special education is a long-standing issue recognized by both disability and bilingual education advocates (Cartledge *et al.*, 2016; Connor, 2017; Klingner & Artiles, 2003; O'Connor & Sonia DeLuca, 2006; Samson & Lesaux, 2009; Zhang *et al.*, 2014). However, these discourses are grounded in ideas of disability and bilingualism as mutually exclusive. As such, throughout most of the United States students are identified as either 'English language learners,' a label that completely erases their multilingual practices and reduces the child's identity to a linguistic need, or as 'a student with disability', a label that absolves a child of a complex identity and reduces them to a medicalized other (Baglieri *et al.*, 2011). Both of these labels focus on needs rather than capacities. These labels also serve as call whistles to educators (and other learners) that let them know the student is different and in need of intervention. Perhaps it is in avoidance of being viewed as doubly deficient that the bilingual education community has gone to great lengths to clarify that a language need is not a disability. However, ideology that focuses solely on racism while dismissing ableism further others children who are labeled as disabled while simultaneously diminishing their access to bilingual learning spaces. If bilingual education is for children who have language needs and language needs are not a disability than a child with a disability does not belong in a bilingual setting – that space will not be able to meet their disability needs. This ideology of division functions as a way to both negate and sustain the exclusion of EBLADs from DL. Upon closer look one would notice that while race is no longer the primary tool for exclusion, disability is functioning as its surrogate. This lack of true intersectionality and superficial understanding of inclusion is also reflected throughout bilingual education resources.

Disabilities within Dual Language Guides and Policies

One of the most explicit ways that SWD are excluded from DL programs is by being excluded from DL theories and policies. After engaging in textual analysis of bilingual education materials and policy documents, it is evident that disabilities are rarely discussed, and when they are it is not in a way that would result in the inclusion of children with disabilities within bilingual spaces.

Within the 'Guiding Principles for Dual Language Education' (Howard *et al.*, 2007), a DL anchor document spanning 124 pages, disabilities is only mentioned twice, both times within the same paragraph and following a paragraph addressing the participation of African American students in DL:

> Some educators have questioned whether low-income African American students should participate in dual language education programs because of the achievement gap that often exists between this group and European Americans. While there is little research on the literacy and achievement of African American children in immersion programs, there is some research to indicate that these children are not negatively affected and may, in fact, realize positive outcomes in their achievement and attitudes (Holobow *et al.*, 1991; Lindholm, 1994; Lindholm-Leary, 2001).
>
> As is true in immersion education (Genesee, 1987), students with special education needs or learning disabilities are typically accepted into dual language programs (Cloud *et al.*, 2000; Lindholm-Leary, 2001). The only caveat is the scenario in which students have a serious speech delay in their native language; in these cases, the decision for admittance is carefully conducted on an individual basis. Further, according to the panel of experts (personal communication, June 16, 2003), students are typically not moved out of the dual language program because of special education or learning disability needs that are diagnosed after the student enrolls. (Howard *et al.*, 2007: 33–34)

In discussing the needs of SWD alongside African American students an opportunity is created for racial bias to cross over into ableism. Although not explicit, there aforementioned passage facilitates a collusion between race and neurodiversity that while situated in different paragraphs have the same outcome: validating the exclusion of African American students and SWD from DL. The participation of AA in DL is framed within the context of academic potential which is juxtaposed with mentions of the 'achievement gap' – a racially coded term and ideology. This belief in the 'achievement gap' is also at the core of the overrepresentation of African American children in SpEd. This passage also introduces class as a factor, which again can be used as a substitute for race while producing the same segregationist outcomes for these students. On the other hand, the academic potential of SWD within DL is completely missing, instead there we are introduced to rationalizations of why and how some SWD should be counseled out of DL. While, Howard writes that SWDs are not often removed from DL on the basis of their disability, she fails to address the fact that their disability influences the way educators perceive their linguistic abilities of SWD thus allowing them to remove SWD from DL, not on the basis of disability but on the basis of linguistic performance.

The discourse around and about these two subgroups highlights the ways in which race and neurodiversity are seen as mutually exclusive and either tangentially addressed or purposefully ignored within DL. In many ways, mentioning these students in this way serves as an attempt to include them in the program without actually offering guidance on how to do that thus subversively denying them entry into DL programs. Howard's guide was crafted as a pedagogical and administrative tool that would help school administrators and educators establish DL programs in their schools. One could argue that it was not her responsibility to consider the inclusion of EBLADs given their specialized education needs and that at the time of publication, 2007, inclusive education nor bilingual education had the presence they do in the current educational landscape. However, the exclusion of SWD in the guide are echoed within more formal policy documents like New York state's Commissioner's Regulations Part 154 (CR Part 154).

CR Part 154 are the 'regulations [that] describe the services and supports to which English language learners (ELL), their parents and teachers are entitled [to]' (United Federation of Teachers, 2014). The commissioner's regulations have always existed but in 2014, in response to a growing Culturally and Linguistically Diverse (CLD) demographic, new testing regulations were introduced which brought along big changes. The most noticeable change was an increase in access to bilingual programs for emergent bilingual students. As per the mandate of the ASPIRA decision in 1972, CR Part 154 has always decreed that if a school has 20+ 'English language learners' with a shared home language across two grade levels then a bilingual program option must be made available to those students (Colón-Collins, 2016). However, in 2014, this requirement of 20+ students was amended to cover an entire district, as such school districts were

> required to annually estimate ELL enrollment before the end of each school year, and create a sufficient number of Bilingual Education programs in the district, if there are 20 or more ELLs *district wide* of the same grade level who speak the same home language. (New York State Education Department, 2014)

This resulted in increased access to bilingual programs for children across varying communities within singular school districts. Thus, while the NYCDOE has spoken about the increase of bilingual program options as a just educational practice, in many ways the expansion of bilingual education programs and the inclusion of emergent bilinguals in DL is much more a reflection of compliance than equity.

While on the surface CR Part 154 presents an opportunity to increase access to bilingual education for all emergent bilingual students, upon closer inspection one can see that EBLADs were not considered a part of that 'all'. Within CR Part 154, parts 1, 2 and 3, disability is discussed within three specific contexts: identification, decertification and evaluation. Within the regulations, disability is first presented within the confines of ensuring that linguistic variance is not confused with a disability.

This is primarily done in the interest of reducing the overrepresentation of emergent bilinguals within special education. It is also a pushback on educational standards that have positioned limited English proficiency with limited intellectual capability. The second context for disability with CR Part 154, focuses primarily on the role a student's disability plays in determining their participation in yearly English language proficiency testing. It is expected that all students who are identified as ELLs take an initial – New York State Identification Test for English Language Learners (NYSITELL) – and subsequent yearly assessment – New York State English as a Second Language Achievement Test (NYSESLAT)– to determine their continued qualification as an ELL. While this measure is meant to keep school districts accountable by measuring student progress, it also is used to determine whether a student is still classified as an ELL and as such still has access to ELL designated services such as bilingual education and ESL/ENL programs. Which leads to the third context of discourse for disability: decertification. The CR Part 154 also provides guidelines that schools can follow in order to decertify a student as an ELL if they have a disability. Unlike typically developing students whose classification is based on their measured performance on the aforementioned assessments, EBLADs can be declassified as an ELL by the Committee on Special Education (CSE) or by the individual district during its annual review of dually classified students (Colón-Collins, 2016). As such the CSE or the district can then say that an EBLAD's academic limitations are a consequence of their disability and not their ELL status. As a result, the EBLAD gets declassified as an ELL, becomes a standard student with a disability and is denied access to ELL programing. The final way that CR Part 154 denies EBLADs' access to bilingual programing is by failing to include bilingual special education (BSE) as a program option for bilingual students.

Still, while a student needs to be classified as an ELL in order to be guaranteed access to ELL service related programs such as ESL/ENL or TBE, a student does not have to be an ELL to be part of a DL program (Infante, nd). Because DL classes typically comprised at least 50% of students who are English proficient, ELL status cannot be a requirement for participation. However, because DL programs specifically aim to develop the bilingualism and biliteracy of all students, EBLADs can be denied entry both for not being an ELL and for not being English dominant. That means that when a pool of students is being gathered to form the 'home language' group, EBLADs who have been declassified are not included because they are not flagged as one of those '20 or more students' needing additional home language support in order to advance their academic or linguistic development (Colón-Collins, 2016). Similarly, when the cohort of English dominant students is being constructed, EBLADs do not meet the necessary criteria of being linguistically or academically strong enough to encourage or support the development of their neurotypical ELL peers nor would they supply the much needed racial or socioeconomic qualities needed to create an integrated program.

In the end, the absence of SWD from bilingual education guides and policies is just another way in which DL programs benefit from the continued racial- and disability-based segregation of EBLADs. In framing DL programs as places of success, achievement and growth, those who are socially framed as deficient are never considered much less given access to those same opportunities. In this way, disability takes on a lot of the same race-based arguments that devalue not only the learning capacity of marginalized students but also discounts any contribution that they could make to the learning of others. As such, it disguises racism as disability service while producing the same outcomes. Still, these polices which exclude children with disabilities are curious particularly at a time when DL is not only framed as a space for academic achievement but also as emblematic of the cross-cultural future.

Dual Language for Integration... into what?

Traditional bilingual education programs are often viewed as scaffolds or stepping stones to monolingual English learning spaces. This is evident in the propensity of bilingual education programs in the elementary grades in contrast to the dearth of BE in middle schools and high schools as well as the expansion of TBE programs (New York City Department of Education, 2018a). As such, most bilingual education classes are populated by emergent bilinguals who originate from non-English-speaking households. Due to this focus on English development, most traditional bilingual classes host students who may represent national diversity but share a racial/ethnic identity. For example, in many neighborhood elementary schools a bilingual (Spanish/English) class will consist of students with ties to El Salvador, Guatemala, Dominican Republic, Puerto Rico and Mexico. These students can represent varying degrees of racial phenotypes but on all official school documents they are classified as Latinx. So, while there is some cultural diversity, their place in the world is the same and the role of their home language is to serve as a transitional tool to English proficiency vis a vis linguistic assimilation. In the end, most bilingual learning spaces are not linguistically, ethnically, racially or even socio-economically diverse.

This lack of diversity can have a negative impact on the academic, social and linguistic development of minoritized students (Stuart Wells, 2014). For this reason, many view DL as the most promising and potentially socially just bilingual program model:

> Officials and some advocates view dual-language programs as a tool for integration by drawing middle-class families eager to have their children

speak two languages into neighborhood schools that they otherwise may not have considered. (Veiga, January 17, 2018)

For many, integration is the answer to social inequality. Bringing together students from diverse backgrounds – more importantly, by integrating students of color with White students – is viewed as the first step towards dismantling systems of oppression. Yet, most integrative opportunities reify power differentials and often lead to greater sources of inequity such as gentrification or minority erasure. The reason for this is because the way in which integration is achieved is often by giving White, middle-class families what they want above what linguistically minoritized students need (Valdés, 1997).

Take the example of Anna Silver, PS 20, in New York City. PS 20, a former CUNY-NYSIEB site school, is an elementary school located between the Lower East Side and the East Village neighborhoods of Manhattan. These are two neighborhoods that have historically been populated by immigrant communities, from the Jews at the turn of the century to Puerto Ricans in the 1970s and Asians in the early 2000s (Foner, 2014). However, as gentrification has expanded in NYC these communities have been pushed out of these neighborhoods, often to growing immigrant neighborhoods in Brooklyn (Hum, 2014). Throughout this time, bilingual education has been limited or non-existent at Anna Silver. However, this changed in 2010. In 2010, Anna Silver started its first DL program which on the surface could be viewed as a great gain for both the Latinx and Chinese communities that surround the school. However, this program did not focus on the languages of the community: Spanish, Fujianese, or Cantonese; this was a DL Mandarin program, a language that was quickly gaining political and economic power in the United States (All People's Initiative, December 2009; Semple, October 21, 2009; Urciuoli, 1991). The push for a DL program at PS 20, as in many other locations, came from a vocal minority of White middle-class parents in the area who saw bilingualism as a necessary social and economic advantage for their children (Cioè-Peña, 2014; Gramanzini, 2018; E. A. Harris, October 8, 2015; Liem, 2016). And so in 2010, with Latinx students making up 63% of its student body, the DL Mandarin program opened its doors (Office of Information and Reporting Services, February 5, 2011; PS 20 – Parent Teacher Association, 2019). It would take five years and a new chancellor before Anna Silver would open a DL Spanish program, by then the Latinx population in the school had dropped by 25% and the White population had increased by 65%.

Additionally, while Anna Silver housed several inclusive and self-contained special education classes none of the DL programs were designed for, nor accessible to, students with disabilities, all of which were African American or Latinx (Cioè-Peña, 2014). This lack of inclusivity is reflective of the segregation that is present in practice, policy and ideology. If we do not fathom the possibility that SWD can thrive in a DL setting than we do not consider them in the development of DL programs or classes. Similarly, if the driving force behind the development of a DL program are the White neurotypical parents of White neurotypical children than the programs will be reflective of their interests and designed to serve that population first and foremost. This is also true of a DL program that is implemented with the hopes of attracting this type of student and family. By 2014, the Latinx principal of Anna Silver possessed enough of the raciolinguistic perspective needed to recognize the need for a Spanish DL program in a Latinx community. Her position was one primarily concerned with restoring the status of the Latinx community within the school by maximizing, developing and supporting their linguistic repertoire while honoring both their local and global contributions, history and culture. Still, there remained a lack of normative awareness which allowed her to consider the development of a mainstream DL class without recognizing that the population most of in need of this type of inclusivity and support were the school's SWD. This lack of intersectionality (especially from within racialized communities) is how the alienation of EBLADs and students of color with disabilities continues, without notice and without critique.

Dual Language: A Tool for Exclusion

DL, as it is currently implemented, is imperfect with regards to its inclusion of SWD. Still, many DL advocates would argue that DL brings together children from diverse backgrounds, including some SWD, and as such *is* an inclusive space. Envisioned as a linguistically rich, socioeconomically, racially and ethnically diverse space, DL appeals to educators and districts not only for its capacity to support bilingualism and biliteracy but also as a means for racial integration (Freeman, 1996; Gándara & Aldana, 2014). DL programs do have the potential to facilitate and uphold racial integration initiatives. However, DL will never fulfill this promise if educators continue to overlook

> the overrepresentation of students of color in segregated special education settings. In 2015, 11 percent of white students and 10 percent of American Indian or Alaska Native students with disabilities were educated in regular classrooms for less than 40 percent of the day, compared to 21 percent of Asian students and 17 percent of black students. (Potter, 2018: 1)

Although this issue is often discussed within the realm of SpEd, this form of hyper-segregation is also replicated within bilingual settings, especially BSE. Even though BSE programs do exists, unlike traditional bilingual programs where parents can opt their children into them, access to BSE settings is entirely at the discretion of school professionals who are part of the Committee on Special Education (Advocates for Children of New York, 2017). Having a committee decide whether an emergent bilingual child with a disability 'needs' to be educated bilingually is in sharp contrast to the fact that neurotypical White, English-dominant children are accepted into DL programs solely on the basis of interest and desire as opposed to necessity. Within special education, an EBLAD's bilingualism is not conceived of as an indication of their talents but rather as an affirmation of their deficits.

On par with national trends, in NYC during the 2016–2017 year, 19,262 children of color were referred for initial special education evaluations (New York City Department of Education, 2017; Office of English Language Acquisition, 2017). Of this group, 5,140 students were identified as being emergent bilinguals but only a fifth had access to a language of instruction other than English (New York City Department of Education, 2017). Access to bilingual education was even lower for students who had already received special education services for at least three years. In addition, unlike their typically developing counterparts, SWD who do not come from linguistically diverse households are never considered for placement in a bilingual setting. The reason for this is because they are not identified as having a 'linguistic need' which would validate such a placement. In other words, unless a SWD also has an identifiable language need, as defined by their ELL status, there is no perceived benefit in placing them in a bilingual setting. Given this fixation on the labels and needs of the learners, BSE is not viewed as a space of opportunity and promise as are mainstream DL classes. On the contrary, BSE programs are viewed as educational spaces for those who are most impaired and neediest thus warranting segregation on two fronts: disability AND language. This multipronged devaluation of EBLADs also allows for them to be regularly subjected to multitiered systems of segregation, as is reflected in the range of BSE options that they can be placed in.

NYC public schools host two types of BSE programs: DL and TBE, these are further fragmented into integrated co-teaching (ICT) classes and self-contained classe.[7] That is to say that, aside from traditional ENL settings, there are four potential placement options for an EBLAD: TBE ICT, TBE Self-contained, DL ICT and DL self-contained. However, the truth is that an EBLAD student doesn't have equal access to these different program options. In reviewing the 2019 'Bilingual Education Programs List – Manhattan' one would learn that there are 126 bilingual classes (from Pre-k to High School) in the borough of Manhattan. On the surface this seems like a robust amount. However, upon closer analysis we can start to notice how ableism supplants racism as the bilingual education gatekeeper. Of the 126 bilingual classes only a third (47 classrooms) serve SWD. The overwhelming majority of those 47 BSE classes are TBE (30 classes), of which only 5 are ICT. On the other hand, 12 out of the 14 DL classes that serve SWD are ICT. This signals two things: first, most EBLADs are still being served within TBE programs designed for increasing English proficiency rather than bilingual development. As is evidenced by the fact that 75% of the general education bilingual programs are DL compared to only 29% of the BSE programs. Secondly, most EBLADs receive services in segregated classrooms. As is noted by the fact that 60% of the BSE classes are 12:1:1 or 6:1:1 self-contained, segregated classes compared to 29% of the monolingual English special education classes (New York City Department of Education, 2018b).

While the foremost way that EBLADs and students of color are restricted from accessing bilingual educations is through limited seat availability, the second way is through program categorization. As part of the Individuals with Disabilities Education Improvement Act, SWD should be educated in the LRE[8] as much as possible (National Council on Disability, 2018). Access to the LRE varies greatly by disability category (McLeskey *et al.*, 2010). As such, students who are classified as having a specific learning disability are more likely to be placed in an inclusive or mainstream class compared to students classified as having emotional or behavioral disorders and intellectual disabilities who are more likely to be placed in more restrictive settings (McLeskey *et al.*, 2010). Additionally, the data show that students of color are more often than not diagnosed with emotional disturbance and intellectual disabilities (Shifrer; US Department of Education, 2007). These disability labels, which are highly subjective and racialized, result in more restrictive settings for students of color with disabilities. On the other hand, emergent bilinguals are more likely to be diagnosed with a specific learning disability or speech and language impairment, labels that typically result in increased access to LREs, the added label of English Language Learner is used to legitimize more restrictive placements for EBLADs (Shifrer, 2018; US Department of Education, 2007).

For example, in 2015, there were more Latinx students identified as having a disability than not, and more SWD were classified as Limited English Proficient, yet most access to mainstream bilingual learning was reserved for typically developing peers (Stiefel *et al.*, 2017). In addition, because there are so few BSE classes, BSE is considered a specialized program and a more restrictive setting because it requires that most students attend a school beyond their local community/district. As such placing students in BSE then goes against the mandates for inclusion (Ed.gov; Kurth *et al.*, 2014; McLeskey *et al.*, 2012; New York City Department of Education, 2016; Ryndak *et al.*, 2014). As a result, parents are often discouraged from sending their children to another district and instead are offered alternatives which at their core offer monolingual English placements with supplementary services like an alternate placement paraprofessional (a temporary bilingual paraprofessional who serves as a linguistic scaffold for a child, usually for only one year), and/or ESL/ENL classes (Advocates for Children of New York, 2017; New York City Department of Education, 2014).

Ultimately, schools use disability and language as tools for segregation in lieu of race. As such, they are able to promote DL programs as integrative initiatives while discounting the participation of children with disabilities – a category that is overwhelmingly composed of racially and ethnically minoritized students. As a result, they are able to maintain the status quo while enacting a progressive and inclusive façade. In many ways DL programs benefit from these subversive means of segregation because it raises their prestige on the grounds of social altruism and academic achievement when in reality, they are just another tool for the systemic oppression of doubly disenfranchised learners.

Conclusion

The erasure of EBLADs is quiet but efficient. It does not happen all at once but rather in stages. First, the individual child is stripped of their home language by being labeled an ELL. Next, their identity as an ELL is coupled with a more profound and urgent need: disability. Once reduced to a multiplicity of need, the EBLAD is written out of DL education by having their linguistic needs excluded from policy. In removing them from discourse, an opportunity is created whereby their linguistic dexterity is absent from the data, from programming, from instruction. Finally, by placing them in monolingual settings or transitional bilingual settings they are denied the ability to hold onto, communicate and grow in their home language. This final step is what ultimately renders them silent in their home (language).

This fragmentation of EBLADs takes place because, neither they nor their educational needs are being viewed holistically. Instead, different experts align themselves to different categorizations of the child in order to advance their own agenda. In other words, bilingual education researchers focused solely on the promotion and advancement of bilingualism are insensitive to the ways in which their brand of 'advancement' and 'acceptance' constructs bilingualism as a privilege rather than a need or inherent right, resulting in the exclusion of POCwD from multilingual spaces. Similarly, researchers focused on the needs and rights of people with disabilities are so invested in inclusion that they often endorse cultural and linguistic erasure in an effort to create access to the mainstream. Both of these camps, with their own set of good intentions, pave the paths to exclusion.

By viewing disability and language as separate, educational researchers and professionals are able to parse and rank the needs of the child and while this may seem like the most practical way to support the child, it is incredibly harmful. Not only are there negative consequences based on which need is addressed first, it also has major consequences for both POCs and PWDs. By placing disability and CLD in a dichotomy, researchers and educators fail to create any true and lasting form of progress for any minoritized person because they continue to support the fragmentation of people and as such continue to uphold White supremacist ideals of normalcy. In other words, you can achieve some semblance of success and inclusion into the mainstream if you are CLD and otherwise 'normal' OR White and disabled, but you cannot be both CLD and disabled. If we truly want to create an inclusive and just society then we must refute the entire White normative gaze. We must enact intersectional ideologies regardless of the populations we work with and for. As such, DL advocates; teachers, researchers and chancellors, cannot focus solely on the gains that their movement offers CLD communities. Doing so continues to reify siloed educational policies and outcomes, as has been the case in NYC. In order to avoid superficial manifestations of inclusion, DL advocates must also be attuned to the ways in which DL promotes injustice by upholding and promoting the racialization and pathologization of others. They must then commit to mitigating these intersectional issues.

There are several ways in which educators and policy makers can respond to the unjust educational trajectories of EBLADs. First, we must demand that districts committed to developing and growing DL programs reserve a minimum percentage of seats for CLD students with disabilities. While, we can celebrate districts, like the NYCDOE, on their commitment to expanding DL programs, we must also question which students will benefit from that growth and take stock of the answer. As such, we must ensure that the opportunity to develop as a bilingual individual is available for all who want to, regardless of their classifications. Secondly, if we know that CLD students are overrepresented in special education, rather than focusing solely on resolving disproportionality, we should also focus on making the services mandated by special education accessible in multilingual and multicultural ways. This work must be done in tandem. That is to say that an EBLAD should be able to have their learning, linguistic and cultural needs met simultaneously. Special education is a service not a place, as such there should be no limitations on the kind of classroom where a student with a special education need can/should be placed. Research shows that children with disabilities are most successful in the LRE (Connor *et al.*, 2008; Danforth, 2014; Obiakor *et al.*, 2012). Research also shows that CLD children learn best in classrooms that are driven by culturally relevant and culturally sustaining pedagogies (Ladson-Billings, 1995; Paris, 2012; Paris & Alim, 2017). We also know that CLD students are most successful in settings that celebrate and uphold their complex linguistic repertoires (García *et al.*, 2016). As such, no EBLAD child should have any part of their identity denied in exchange for academic success. True success comes from honoring, nurturing and supporting the whole child. Finally, the field of bilingual education needs to move beyond disproportionality. What the discourse around disproportionality does is raise awareness about the number of children who are labeled without questioning or dismantling the labels themselves. Minoritized students will continue to be pathologized, categorized and underserved so long as we continue to view labels and the subsequent 'special' classes and programs as the primary way to respond to children who fall outside of the White normative gaze.

DL programs are promoted as a place of promise, as a space where children from varying linguistic, socioeconomic and racial backgrounds can learn alongside each other and, perhaps more importantly, from each other. However, as long as the definition of integration continues to focus on race and class while ignoring neurodiversity DL will remain an ableist and elitist educational space. Access to bilingualism and biliteracy should be available to all children not just those who possess sociocultural features that are positioned as most valuable (White, middle class, neurotypical), nor those who can least offend the White normative gaze. Until, DL can find ways to make space for all learners at the margin, it will continue to be nothing more than another way to deny emergent bilinguals, regardless of ability, all of the things it promises to their English-proficient counterparts. As such, it will not improve the education of emergent bilinguals as much as it will continue to amplify the voices of the power majority (at the detriment of EBLADs).

Notes

(1) The use of the term emergent bilinguals labeled as dis/abled (EBLAD) rather than English language learners with dis/abilities or English language learners with special education needs aims to dismantle the double deficit model that is produced by combining the term English language learner, which fails to acknowledge the linguistic resources that a student brings, with the terms 'with disabilities' or 'special education needs,' which negate the social and structural power dynamics that are at play, making dis/ability a result of individual failure rather than systemic inequality. By using the terms EBLAD an attempt is made at acknowledging a student's full linguistic potential as well as emphasizing the imposing nature of labeling and categorizing children. While the disproportionality and overrepresentation of culturally and linguistically diverse students is a real issue, this chapter is meant to tease out the ways in which these students, regardless of the appropriateness of their labels, are being underserved and ignored by dual language programs. Additionally, disability pride is an important component of disability discourse, however, these students do not own these labels for themselves. Instead, these labels are imposed upon them by external forces. The term EBLAD is meant to reflect the imposition, and subsequent miseducation as a result of, these labels rather than the appropriateness of them.
(2) According to the Center for Disability Rights, 'Ableism is a set of beliefs or practices that devalue and discriminate against people with physical, intellectual, or psychiatric disabilities and often rests on the assumption that disabled people need to be "fixed" in one form or the other' (n.d.). As such, 'an [ableist] perspective asserts that it is preferable for a child to read print rather than Braille, walk rather than use a wheelchair, spell independently rather than use a spell-checker, read written text rather than listen to a book on tape, and be friends with nondisabled kids rather than with other disabled kids' (Hehir, 2007).
(3) According to (Gillborn, 2006), 'white supremacy is conceived as a comprehensive condition whereby the interests and perceptions of white subjects are continually placed centerstage and assumed as "normal"' (2006: 318). This hegemonic understand of Whiteness as greatness infiltrates all parts of society, from the mundane (i.e. microaggressions) to the grand (i.e. world politics).

(4) The author's preferred term is emergent bilingual. However, English Language Learner or ELL will be used whenever it relates to policy and student classifications.
(5) While the word *gaze* is colloquially defined by its relationship to sight, the use of it within this framework is not considered ableist in nature given that it is being used to describe an apparatus of power on a systemic level rather than the individual and physical act of seeing. For more see Foucault's *The Birth of the Clinic* (1994) and *Discipline and Punish; The Birth of the Prison* (1995).
(6) The term 'model minority' here is meant to evoke an understanding of how culturally and linguistically diverse emergent bilinguals are stratified based on their usefulness to their white peers. Speaking a language other than English is not sufficient. In order to be a part of a DL program the CLD student also has to fit the part of the model minority. They must have *good* home language literacy/proficiency (often defined by their fidelity to linguistic rules and boundaries), be academically strong and behaviorally manageable. Any student who does not meet this model, would defeat the purpose of their inclusion by not only failing to serve as a good language mediator but also by drawing heavily from the resources meant to support White emergent bilinguals. Additionally, the use of the label model minority brings attention to how the inclusion of select CLD students in DL programs serves in upholding and maintaining the fallacy of meritocracy that is at the center of White supremacy and ableism (Yi & Museus, 2015).
(7) In an ICT class, SWD are integrated into classes predominantly occupied by typically developing students (in NYC there is an unofficial use of a 60/40 ratio of GenEd to SpEd students per class). The students who are traditionally placed in ICT classes tend to be those who approximate normalcy the most. Additionally, we know that statistically children of color, particularly Black and Latinx children are more likely than their White peers to be placed in self-contained/segregated settings (Ferri & Connor, 2005).
(8) The least restrictive environment is defined as the (monolingual) general education classroom, all other settings are considered more restrictive with hospital and home placements counting as the most restrictive. For more see (Osborne & Dimattia, 1994).

References

Advocates for Children of New York (2017) *English Language Learners and Special Education*. Retrieved from New York, NY. See https://www.advocatesforchildren.org/sites/default/files/library/bilingual_special_ed.pdf?pt=1

Alim, H.S., Rickford, J.R. and Ball, A. (eds) (2016) *Raciolinguistics: How Language Shapes Our Ideas About Race*. Oxford University Press.

All People's Initiative (December 2009) Fuzhounese in the New York Metro Area. In A. P. s. Initiative (ed.). New York, NY: ethNYcity.

Allen, M. (2017) Textual analysis. In M. Allen (ed.) *The SAGE Encyclopedia of Communication Research Methods*.

Annamma, S.A., Connor, D. and Ferri, B. (2013) Dis/ability critical race studies (DisCrit): Theorizing at the intersections of race and dis/ability. *Race Ethnicity and Education* 16 (1), 1–31. doi:10.1080/13613324.2012.730511

Annamma, S. and Morrison, D. (2018) DisCrit Classroom Ecology: Using praxis to dismantle dysfunctional education ecologies. *Teaching and Teacher Education* 73, 70–80. See https://doi.org/10.1016/j.tate.2018.03.008

Baglieri, S., Valle, J.W., Connor, D.J. and Gallagher, D.J. (2011) Disability studies in education: The need for a plurality of perspectives on disability. *Remedial and Special Education* 32 (4), 267–278. doi:10.1177/0741932510362200

Broderick, A.A. and Leonardo, Z. (2016) What a Good Boy. *DisCrit-Disability Studies and Critical Race Theory in Education*, 55–67.

Calderon, M. and Carreon, A. (2000) A two-way bilingual program: Promise, practice, and precautions. Report No. 47. Center for Research on the Education of Students Placed At Risk, Baltimore, MD. Retrieved from https://files.eric.ed.gov/fulltext/ED447706.pdf

Cartledge, G., Kea, C.D., Watson, M. and Oif, A. (2016) Special education disproportionality: A review of response to intervention and culturally relevant pedagogy. *Multiple Voices for Ethnically Diverse Exceptional Learners* 16 (1), 29–49. doi:10.5555/2158-396X.16.1.29

Cioè-Peña, M. (2014) *Anna Silver School Visit Reflections Fall 2014.*

Cioè-Peña, M. (2017) Disability, bilingualism and what it means to be normal. *Journal of Bilingual Education Research & Instruction*.

Cloud, N., Genesee, F. and Hamayan, E. (2000) *Dual Language Instruction: A Handbook for Enriched Education*. Boston, MA: Heinle & Heinle.

Colón-Collins, L. (2016) CR Part 154 Comprehensive plan for the education of English language learners/multilingual learners. In *The State Education Department/Office of Bilingual Education and World Languages*.

Connor, D.J. (2017) Who is responsible for the racialized practices evident within (special) education and what can be done to change them? *Theory Into Practice* 56 (3), 226–233. doi:10.1080/00405841.2017.1336034

Connor, D.J. and Ferri, B.A. (2005) Integration and inclusion: A troubling nexus: Race, disability, and special education. *The Journal of African American History* 90 (1/2), 107–127.

Connor, D.J., Gabel, S.L., Gallagher, D.J. and Morton, M. (2008) Disability studies and inclusive education – Implications for theory, research, and practice. *International Journal of Inclusive Education*, 12 (5–6), 441–457. See https://doi.org/10.1080/13603110802377482

Crenshaw, K. (1991) Mapping the margins: Intersectionality, identity politics, and violence against women of color. *Stanford Law Review* 43 (6), 1241–1299. See https://doi.org/10.2307/1229039

Danforth, S. (ed.) (2014) *Becoming a Great Inclusive Educator* (Vol. 1). Peter Lang.

Department of English Language, L. and Student, S. (2015) School Year 2013–2014 Demographic Report. See https://docplayer.net/6870844-Department-of-english-language-learners-and-student-support-school-year-2013-2014-demographic-report.html

Dev, P. and Dev, P.C. (2015) Teacher perspectives on suitable learning environments for students with disabilities: What have we learned from inclusive, resource, and self-contained classrooms? *The International Journal of Interdisciplinary Social Sciences: Annual Review* 9 (1), 53–64. doi:https://doi.org/10.18848/1833-1882/cgp/v09/53554

Division of English Language Learners and Student Support (2017) *English Language Learner Demographics Report for the 2016–17 School Year*. Retrieved from New York, NY. See https://infohub.nyced.org/docs/default-source/default-document-library/2016-17-demographic-report-v10_remediated.pdf

Drysdale, H., van der Meer, L. and Kagohara, D. (2015) Children with autism spectrum disorder from bilingual families: A systematic review | SpringerLink. *Review Journal of Autism and Developmental Disorders* 2 (1). doi:10.1007/s40489-014-0032-7

Ed.gov. IDEA – Building The Legacy of IDEA 2004. In: US Department of Education.

Engage, N.Y. (2017) *New York State Demographics*. Retrieved from Albany, NY. See https://www.engageny.org/file/151526/download/nyseslat-2018-ell-demographic-slides.pdf

Fairclough, N. (2013) *Critical Discourse Analysis : The Critical Study of Language* (2nd edn). Routledge.

Ferri, B. and Connor, D.J. (2005) Tools of exclusion: Race, disability, and (re)segregated education. *Teachers College Record – Teach Coll Rec,* 107 (3), 453–474. doi:10.1111/j.1467-9620.2005.00483.x

Flores, N. and García, O. (2017) A critical review of bilingual education in the United States: From basements and pride to boutiques and profit | annual review of applied linguistics | Cambridge Core. *Annual Review of Applied Linguistics* 37, 14–29. doi:10.1017/S0267190517000162

Flores, N. and Rosa, J. (2015) Undoing appropriateness: Raciolinguistic ideologies and language diversity in education. *Harvard Educational Review* 85 (2), 149–171. doi:10.17763/0017-8055.85.2.149

Foner, N.R., Jan, Duyvendak, W. and van Reekum, R. (2014) *New York and Amsterdam.* New York, NY: NYU Press.

Franko, K. (2018, 2018/04/27/T21:47:08Z) District move to keep white students cites 'racial balance'. *AP NEWS.* See https://apnews.com/6e9683d05e00491db18774 82693430c4, See https://www.apnews.com/6e9683d05e00491db1877482693430c4

Freeman, R.D. (1996) Dual-language planning at Oyster Bilingual School: 'Its Much More Than Language.' *TESOL Quarterly* 30 (3), 557–582. doi:10.2307/3587698

Gándara, P.C. and Aldana, U.S. (2014) Who's segregated now? Latinos, language, and the future of integrated schools. *Educational Administration Quarterly* 50 (5), 735–748. doi:10.1177_0013161X14549957

García, O., Johnson, S.I. and Seltzer, K. (2016) *The Translanguaging Classroom: Leveraging Student Bilingualism for Learning* (1st edn). Philadelphia: Caslon Publishing.

García Mathewson, T. (2017, 2017-07-31) Rising popularity of dual-language education could leave Latinos behind. *Hechinger Report.* See https://hechingerreport.org/rising-popularity-dual-language-education-leave-latinos-behind/

Genesee, F. (1987) *Learning Through Two Languages.* Cambridge: Newbury House.

Gillborn, D. (2006) Rethinking white supremacy: Who counts in 'WhiteWorld'. *Ethnicities* 6 (3), 318–340. doi:10.1177_1468796806068323

Gramanzini, G. (2018) Dual language programs are riding high in New York City. *i-Italy.*

Gutierrez-Clellen, V.F. (1999) Language choice in intervention with bilingual children. *American Journal of Speech-Language Pathology* 8 (4). doi:10580360000800040291

Hankivsky, O. (2014) Intersectionality 101. *Cal* 64 (1), 238.

Harris, E.A. (October 8, 2015) Dual-language programs are on the rise, even for native English speakers. *The New York Times.*

Harris, E.A.K., Josh. (May 2, 2018) Why are new york's schools segregated? It's not as simple as housing. *New York Times.*

Harry, B. and Klingner, J. (2007) Discarding the deficit model. *Educational Leadership* 64 (5), 16.

Hehir, T. (2007) Confronting ableism. *Educational Leadership* 64 (5), 8–14.

Holobow, N., Genesee, F. and Lambert, W.E. (1991) The effectiveness of a foreign language immersion program for children from different ethnic and social class backgrounds: Report 2. *Applied Psycholinguistics* 12, 179–198.

Howard, E.R.S.J., Christian, D., Lindholm-Leary, K. and Rogers, D. (2007) *Guiding Principles for Dual Language Education.* Washington, DC: Center for Applied Linguistics.

Hum, T. (2014) *Making a Global Immigrant Neighborhood: Brooklyn's Sunset Park.* Philadelphia, Pennsylvania: Temple University Press.

Infante, A. (nd) *Parents' Bill of Rights For New York State's English Language Learners.* Albany, NY: The [New York] State Education Department; The University of The State of New York. See http://www.nysed.gov/common/nysed/files/bilingual/ParentsBillofRights_EnglishLanguage_FINAL.pdf

Kelly, L.B. (2016) Interest convergence and hegemony in dual language: Bilingual education, but for whom and why? | SpringerLink. *Language Policy* 17 (1), 1–21. doi:10.1007/s10993-016-9418-y

Klingner, J.K. and Artiles, A.J. (2003) When should bilingual students be in special education? *Educational Leadership* 61 (2), 66.

Kramarczuk Voulgarides, C., Fergus, E. and King Thorius, K.A. (2017) Pursuing equity: Disproportionality in special education and the reframing of technical solutions to address systemic inequities. *Review of Research in Education* 41 (1), 61–87. doi:10.3102/0091732x16686947

Kurth, J.A., Morningstar, M.E. and Kozleski, E.B. (2014) The persistence of highly restrictive special education placements for students with low-incidence disabilities. *Research and Practice for Persons with Severe Disabilities* 39 (3), 227–239. doi:10.1177/1540796914555580

Ladson-Billings, G. (1995) Toward a theory of culturally relevant pedagogy. *American Educational Research Journal* 32 (3), 465–491. See https://doi.org/10.3102/00028312032003465

Lauchlan, F. and Boyle, C. (2007) Is the use of labels in special education helpful? *Support for Learning* 22 (1), 36–42. doi:10.1111/j.1467-9604.2007.00443.x

Liem, P.C. (2016) [Anna Silver School Leadership Team].

Lindholm, K.J. (1994) Promoting positive cross-cultural attitudes and perceived competence in culturally and linguistically diverse classrooms. In R.A. Devillar, C.J. Faltis, and J.P. Cummins (eds) *Cultural Diversity in Schools: From Rhetoric to Practice* (pp. 189–206). Albany: State University of New York Press.

Lindholm-Leary, K.J. (2001) *Dual Language Education*. Clevedon: Multilingual Matters.

Martínez-Álvarez, P. (2018) Dis/ability labels and emergent bilingual children: Current research and new possibilities to grow as bilingual and biliterate learners. *Race, Ethnicity and Education* 22 (2), 174–193. doi:10.1080/13613324.2018.1538120

McLeskey, J., Landers, E., Williamson, P. and Hoppey, D. (2010) Are we moving toward educating students with disabilities in less restrictive settings?. See http://dx.doi.org/10.1177/0022466910376670. doi:10.1177_0022466910376670.

McLeskey, J., Landers, E., Williamson, P. and Hoppey, D. (2012) Are we moving toward educating students with disabilities in less restrictive settings? *The Journal of Special Education* 46 (3), 131–140. doi:10.1177/0022466910376670

National Council on Disability (2018) *The Segregation of Students with Disabilities*. See https://ncd.gov/sites/default/files/NCD_Segregation-SWD_508.pdf

New York City Department of Education (2014) *Family Guide to Special Education Services for School-Age Children – A Shared Path to Success*. New York, NY: New York City Department of Education.

New York City Department of Education (2016) Least Restrictive Environment In.

New York City Department of Education (2017) *Local Law 27 of 2015 Annual Report on Special Education*. Retrieved from New York, NY. See https://www.sinergiany.org/sites/default/files/2018-CityCouncilReportSY17.pdf

New York City Department of Education (2018a) *2017–2018 Anticipated Bilingual Education Programs*. See https://data.cityofnewyork.us/Education/2017-2018-Anticipated-Bilingual-Education-Programs/ydbx-4ufw

New York City Department of Education (2018b) *Annual Special Education Data Report, School Year 2017-2018*. New York, NY. See https://infohub.nyced.org/docs/default-source/default-document-library/annual-special-education-data-report-sy-17-18.docx?Status=Temp&sfvrsn=538f6981_2

New York State Education Department (2014) *Ensuring Equal Educational Opportunities for English Language Learners*. Albany, NY: New York State Education Department. See http://www.k12.wa.us/migrantbilingual/k20/ensuringequaleducationalopportunitiesell.pdf

O'Connor, C. and Sonia DeLuca, F. (2006) Race, class, and disproportionality: Reevaluating the relationship between poverty and special education placement. *Educational Researcher* 35 (6), 6–11.

Obiakor, F.E., Harris, M., Mutua, K., Rotatori, A. and Algozzine, B. (2012) Making inclusion work in general education classrooms. *Education and Treatment of Children* 35 (3), 477–490. See https://doi.org/10.1353/etc.2012.0020

Office of English Language Acquisition (2017) *Students with Disabilities Who Are English Learners*. Retrieved from Washington, D.C. See https://ncela.ed.gov/files/fast_facts/05-19-2017/ELStudentsWithDisabilities_FastFacts_4p.pdf

Office of Information and Reporting Services, N.Y.S.E.D. (February 5, 2011) *PS 20 Anna SIlver School Report Card: Accountability and Overview Report 2009–10*. Retrieved from New York. See https://data.nysed.gov/files/reportcards/archive/2009-10/AOR-2010-310100010020.pdf

Osborne, J., Allan G. and Dimattia, P. (1994) The IDEA's least restrictive environment mandate: Legal implications. *Exceptional Children* 61 (1), 6–14. doi:10.1177_001440299406100102

Paris, D. (2012) Culturally sustaining pedagogy a needed change in stance, terminology, and practice. *Educational Researcher* 41 (3), 93–97. See https://doi.org/10.3102/0013189X12441244

Paris, D. and Alim, H.S. (2017) *Culturally Sustaining Pedagogies: Teaching and Learning for Justice in a Changing World*. New York: Teachers College Press.

Pirtle, W. (April 23, 2019, 2019-04-23) The other segregation. *The Atlantic*. See https://www.theatlantic.com/education/archive/2019/04/gifted-and-talented-programs-separate-students-race/587614/

Potter, H.Q., Kimberly. (2018) *Significant Disproportionaility Comments* (p. 3). Washington, D.C. The Century Foundation.

PS 20 – Parent Teacher Association (2019) PS 20 The Anna Silver School.

Rabe Thomas, J. (2018, 2018/10/15/T22:30:44 + 00:00) Do magnet schools need white students to be great? *The CT Mirror*. See https://ctmirror.org/2018/10/15/magnet-schools-need-white-students-great/

Rosa, J. and Flores, N. (2017) Unsettling race and language: Toward a raciolinguistic perspective. *Language in Society* 46 (5), 621–647. doi:10.1017/S0047404517000562

Ryndak, D.L., Taub, D., Jorgensen, C.M., Gonsier-Gerdin, J., Arndt, K., Sauer, J., … Allcock, H. (2014) Policy and the impact on placement, involvement, and progress in general education critical issues that require rectification. *Research and Practice for Persons with Severe Disabilities* 39 (1), 65–74. doi:10.1177/1540796914533942

Samson, J.F. and Lesaux, N.K. (2009) Language-minority learners in special education rates and predictors of identification for services. *Journal of Learning Disabilities* 42 (2), 148–162.

Scheff, T. (2017) Updating labelling theory: Normalizing but not enabling. *Nordic Journal of Social Research*, 1. doi:https://doi.org/10.7577/njsr.2044

Semple, K. (October 21, 2009) In Chinatown, sound of the future is Mandarin. *New York Times*. See https://www.nytimes.com/2009/10/22/nyregion/22chinese.html

Shifrer, D. (2018) Clarifying the social roots of the disproportionate classification of racial minorities and males with learning disabilities. See https://doi.org/10.1080/00380253.2018.1479198. doi:10.1080/00380253.2018.1479198

Stein, P. (July 3, 2018) Are dual-language programs in urban schools a sign of gentrification?: One D.C. elementary school is divided about the future of its campus. – ProQuest. *The Washington Post*. See https://search-proquest-com.ezproxy.montclair.edu/docview/2063574647/BCD7085994454373PQ/1?accountid=12536

Stiefel, L.S., Menbere, Schwartz, A.M. and Gottfried, M. (2017) Is special education improving? Evidence on segregation, outcomes, and spending from New York City. In *IESP Working Paper #02-17*. New York, NY: Institute for Education and Social Policy – NYU Steinhardt.

Stuart Wells, A. (2014) *Seeing Past the 'Colorblind' Myth of Education Policy: Why Policymakers Should Address Racial/Ethnic Inequality and Support Culturally Diverse Schools*. Retrieved from Boulder, CO.

Sullivan, A.L. (2011) Disproportionality in special education identification and placement of English language learners. See http://dx.doi.org/10.1177/001440291107700304, 77 (3), 317–334. doi:10.1177_001440291107700304

Sullivan, A.L. and Bal, A. (2013) Disproportionality in special education: Effects of individual and school variables on disability risk. *Exceptional Children* 79 (4), 475–494. doi:10.1177/001440291307900406

The Civil Rights Project (May 15, 2014) UCLA Report Finds Changing US Demographics Transform School Segregation Landscape 60 Years After Brown v Board of Education [Press release]. See https://www.civilrightsproject.ucla.edu/news/press-releases/2014-press-releases/ucla-report-finds-changing-u.s.-demographics-transform-school-segregation-landscape-60-years-after-brown-v-board-of-education

US Department of Education, O. o. S. E. P. (2007) *Number and percentage of children ages 3 to 5 and ages 6 to 21 served under the Individuals with Disabilities Education Act (IDEA), by race/ethnicity and type of disability: 2007*. See https://nces.ed.gov/pubs2010/2010015/tables/table_8_1b.asp

United Federation of Teachers (2014) *ELL Services [Changes to CR Part 154]*. New York, NY: United Federation of Teachers.

Urciuoli, B. (1991) The political topography of Spanish and English: The view from a New York Puerto Rican neighborhood – URCIUOLI – 1991 – American Ethnologist – Wiley Online Library. *Journal of American Ethnological Society* 18 (2), 295–310. doi:10.1525/ae.1991.18.2.02a00060

Valdés, G. (1997) Dual-language immersion programs: A cautionary note concerning the education of language-minority students. *Harvard Educational Review* 67 (3), 391–430. doi:10.17763/haer.67.3.n5q175qp86120948

Veiga, C. (January 17, 2018, 2018-01-17) New York City will add dual language options n pre-K to attract parents and encourage diversity. *Chalkbeat*. See https://www.chalkbeat.org/posts/ny/2018/01/17/new-york-city-will-add-dual-language-options-in-pre-k-to-attract-parents-and-encourage-diversity/

Wall, P. (April 4, 2016, 2016-04-04) City to add dozens of dual-language programs as they grow in popularity. *Chalkbeat*. See https://www.chalkbeat.org/posts/ny/2016/04/04/city-to-add-dozens-of-dual-language-programs-as-they-grow-in-popularity/

Wishart, J.G., Willis, D.S., Cebula, K.R. and Pitcairn, T.K. (2007) Collaborative learning: Comparison of outcomes for typically developing children and children with intellectual disabilities. *American Journal of Mental Retardation* 112 (5), 361–374. doi:10.1352/0895-8017(2007)112[0361:clcoof]2.0.co;2

Yi, V. and Museus, S.D. (2015) Model minority myth. In *The Wiley Blackwell Encyclopedia of Race, Ethnicity, and Nationalism* (pp. 1–2).

Zhang, D., Katsiyannis, A., Ju, S. and Roberts, E. (2014) Minority representation in special education: 5-year trends. *Journal of Child and Family Studies* 23 (1), 118–127.

4 Dueling Discourses in Dual Language Schools: Multilingual 'Success for All' versus the Academic 'Decline' of Black Students

Lisa M. Dorner, Jeong-Mi Moon, Edwin Nii Bonney and Alexandria Otis

A network of one-way dual language (DL) schools in the Midwest, the Language Immersion Charter Schools (LICS, a pseudonym), was designed with an audacious vision that went beyond the three typical goals of DL education. In addition to academic achievement, biliteracy and sociocultural competence (Howard *et al.*, 2018), LICS made social equity central to its vision. Specifically, the founders aimed to design racially integrated DL schools. Like other foreign language or 'one-way' immersion programs, LICS was designed primarily for students from the same language background (Tedick & Wesley, 2015), but they included a special focus on serving African-American youth.

In the early 2000s, LICS opened three elementary programs, each using a different language of instruction for about 90% of the school day (Mandarin, Spanish or French). The schools met their demographic goal, annually enrolling 50–60% Black students who spoke English as their home language. Moreover, in the initial years, the network was led by women of color, including an African-American bilingual French speaker, a native Spanish speaker from Mexico, a native Mandarin speaker from China and a second-generation immigrant from India. However, like many charter schools (Consoletti, 2011; Paino *et al.*, 2014), LICS struggled with finances, operations and meeting grade-level standards on state tests. In later years, the network's Board and Sponsor – the local university that reviewed and accredited charter schools in the area – increasingly expressed concerns that the language immersion model was not working and especially not for the majority of LICS's students; they explicitly named Black and low-income children from the city as their challenge.

In turn, we designed this study to examine the discourses surrounding LICS's founding and development. Using a raciolinguistic perspective, we sought to understand how relationships between language, race, and power became institutionalized in these DL schools; we were especially curious how LICS positioned and served Black students, who typically have less access to DL programs (Wall *et al.*, 2019). Applying critical discourse analysis (CDA) (Fairclough, 2010) to 21 artifacts designed by LICS's educational leaders, especially the network's Director and university Sponsor, we asked: What discourses defined LICS's goals over time? How were Black students positioned, as the schools competed to enroll children and remain open with declining test scores?

LICS's original goals to serve racialized minorities – to equalize educational opportunities for Black students via language immersion schools – was laudable. However, the vision that DL education was for 'all students' co-existed and was in tension with a variety of other racialized discourses. Specifically, data analyses show how accountability pressures toward English proficiency *standards* and the proclaimed low literacy, or *languagelessness*, of Black students were used to defend a major change for the organization. In Year 10, LICS moved from a 90/10 'full immersion' model to a 50/50 model, thereby reducing the time students spent studying languages other than English. In turn, as described in the following section, this project drew from the raciolinguistic perspective to examine 'how the racialized relationship between ideologies of standardization and languagelessness' enacted 'forms of societal exclusion' (Rosa, 2016: 164) for African-American children who were striving to become multilingual.

Conceptual Framework

In this chapter, we apply a raciolinguistic perspective (Rosa, 2016; Rosa & Flores, 2017) to study the structures and discourses that create language hierarchies, which could shape and ultimately exclude racialized students at DL schools. We focus specifically on the intersecting ideologies of *languagelessness* and *standardization* in DL education, and how these ideas may compete with *social equity*, which has been a central goal of bilingual education for decades (Cervantes-Soon *et al.*, 2017). Our review of research and theories suggest that the voices and positions of white, middle-class English speakers – to which minoritized and racialized children are often compared as *languageless* – and educational policy, especially goals of accountability that promote *standardization* (Menken & Solorza, 2014), contribute to the racialization of students and, in turn, hamper DL's vision of social equity.

Linguistic hegemony and languagelessness

The ideology of languagelessness asserts that certain individuals and particular groups have 'limited linguistic capacity' (Rosa, 2016: 163). For instance, despite being bilingual and having creative linguistic repertoires (Martínez, 2017), Latinx students in the US are often positioned as lacking proficiency in either English or Spanish (or both), especially by schools in terms of academic language (Flores & Rosa, 2015). Similarly, although 'Black talk' has been recognized as 'Spoken Soul' in the US – an 'expressive instrument in American literature, religion, entertainment and everyday life' (Rickford & Rickford, 2000: 4) – linguistic profiling haunts African Americans to this day (Baugh, 2003). Classifications of Black and Brown youth set up comparisons between them and the imagined white standard language learner, thereby positioning students of color as linguistically deficient and inferior (Rosa, 2016). In turn, racialized subjects are often portrayed as without any language at all (Flores & Rosa, 2015; Rosa, 2016).

Linguistic hegemony in DL

Simply put, DL education in the US context aims to develop multilingualism by teaching academic content via a language other than English for at least 50% of students' instructional time (Howard *et al.*, 2018). However, even in multilingual DL education, languages other than English are sometimes perceived as inappropriate for rigorous instruction. In one rural Midwest community that finally managed to implement a 50/50 model, white parents initially accepted Spanish for social interactions but resisted its use for instruction. In turn, teachers provided instruction in Spanish for only 30 minutes per day, rather than half the day, as they wished; they focused on English instruction because they feared white parents might not enroll their children otherwise (Paciotto & Delany-Barmann, 2011). Meanwhile, in a Colorado DL school, white parents, whose children had attended the school, connected the heritage language of immigrant students to the school's low academic performance, with one parent explicitly stating that the school's curriculum and standards 'went down' when the DL program and multilingual education started (Pearson *et al.*, 2015: 13). In another context, even parents and administrators whose primary concern was promoting social equity implied that white children in DL schools were sacrificing academic rigor; it was a 'compromise' for them to attend school with multilingual Latinx students (Burns, 2017: 348).

Languagelessness and positioning in DL

In DL, the English language spoken by racialized minorities is often positioned as nonstandard or 'wrong' (Valdés, 2002: 194). Moreover, Black students are rarely centered or enrolled in DL programs (Valdés,

2018). In Thomas and Collier's (2012) research on over 85,000 students in 11 schools in North Carolina, only 24% of the DL program students were Black, while 39% of the 'non-DL' population in the study's schools were Black. The reasons might include: no special consideration is given to Black students in DL as they are regarded as native English speakers (Nicoladis *et al.*, 1998); researchers presume that English-speaking students in DL are white, resulting in ignoring Blacks' presence or absence; and deficit orientations, ideologies and inequitable DL policy implementation likely hinder their enrollment (Henderson, 2019; Wall *et al.*, 2019). Some educators worry about the exposure of designated English Learners to Black English (Valdés, 2002), while others believe that the English spoken by Black students adds challenges to their education, with educators claiming Black students need to learn both 'standard English' *and* 'a third language' (Palmer, 2010: 109). Ironically, failure to acknowledge and value the linguistic practices of racialized minorities in DL run counter to its goals, reinforcing deficit orientations toward racialized minorities as their linguistic practices are perceived as 'wrong, incorrect, or sloppy uses of the standard language' (de Jong, 2016: 10).

Racializing students in terms of their linguistic proficiencies/deficiencies is related to how they are positioned in DL programs, where a variety of views on racialized minorities can exist simultaneously. On the one hand, heritage language speakers are positioned as partners who exist *for* white/English-dominant students to learn language and culture (Muro, 2016; Palmer, 2010), or even as economic assets to help secure federal subsidies (Burns, 2017). On the other hand, they may be perceived as academic and social problems, as suggested above, and ultimately positioned as the main indicators of failing schools (Pearson *et al.*, 2015). The problem of any of these interpretations is that racialized minorities are defined by others through limited, deficit and often exploitative lenses.

Standardization

Rosa (2016) stresses that the ideologies of languagelessness and standardization intertwine to disrupt schooling for racialized students. The idea of standardization in language education comes from the long-standing value placed on monolingualism as the natural state of being, flowing from the *one language, one nation, one people* ideology quite prevalent in the US. In turn, the linguistic repertoires of multilingual individuals are devalued, and in fact, positioned as problems to be solved (Gutiérrez & Orellana, 2006). Moreover, there is an imagined, desired *standard* (white) English, such that language spoken by Black people, in particular, is often stigmatized and given as the reason for their lack of societal inclusion, access and socioeconomic mobility (Alim *et al.*, 2016; Baugh, 2003). Such a perspective suggests that individual linguistic deficiency is the problem to be fixed, as opposed to the structural, systemic or political issues that may negatively impact DL sustainability (Rosa & Flores, 2017).

Standardization through accountability in DL

Accountability, which can disorient DL education and shift a focus from multilingualism to English (Dorner & Layton, 2013), is especially pronounced in programs that serve racialized minorities and are under pressure to meet certain standards on state tests. For instance, a Philadelphia public school serving 84% Latinx and 13% Black students, which had a new DL program K-2, faced possible takeover by a charter organization due to low test scores (Flores & Chaparro, 2018). During this time of instability, several teachers left, including bilingual ones, and the school had to reduce the DL program to K-1. In turn, test results and subsequent actions (designed to *standardize*) reduced students' access to rich language education. With fewer DL classes, some former DL students transferred to English-only education. Moreover, due to continued surveillance and takeover fears, the remaining DL teachers privileged English instruction (Flores & Chaparro, 2018).

In summary, the raciolinguistic perspective shifts our attention from individual, racialized speaking subjects to the institutions and policies that categorize linguistic practices. Analyses of those institutions and policies can reveal how raciolinguicism is reproduced, and in Meshulam and Apple's words, how even in the 'most antiracist of schools, issues of race and racism persist' (2014: 650).

Methods

We designed this study as a CDA, situated within an ethnography, to understand the relationships between language, race and power in DL schools, especially what kinds of ideologies gain prominence throughout a school's development and how they shape Black students' educational experiences. Drawing data from a research collaboration with the LICS, we asked: What discourses defined LICS's goals over time? How were Black students positioned, as the schools competed to enroll children and remain open with declining test scores?

Researcher positions

This study comes from a long-time community-research partnership developed between the founders of the LICS network and first author Lisa. Lisa became interested in language education equity as a previous teacher of English as a foreign and second language in Japan and Chicago, and as a white, US-born parent raising her own children bilingually. Her collaboration with LICS began as a longitudinal ethnography focused on its creation, especially parents' engagement in the schools' opening

(Dorner, 2015). Over nine years, the partnership evolved to support research and professional development, which included ethnographic studies in classrooms (Dorner & Layton, 2014), surveys on school climate (Aguayo & Dorner, 2017) and family engagement projects (Bonney et al., 2019).

Given such close connection to the schools, it was critical to have co-authors from other backgrounds and experiences for this analysis. Jeong-Mi comes from South Korea, has lived in the US for five years, and has two children in English-only district public schools. She has contributed alternate perspectives on race and language, having grown up in a linguistically minoritized, multilingual community within a country that is perceived to be mono-ethnic/linguistic. Meanwhile, Edwin is a multilingual speaker of three home/native languages – English, Twi, Ga – and Spanish, which he learned at school and abroad. He has shared his experience researching educational discourses of English standardization and hegemony in Ghana. Finally, Alexandria, a white woman, has worked for seven years as an elementary teacher in a private school that offers Mandarin, French and Spanish classes to mostly white and some international students; she has studied and is interested in how phonemic awareness and dialect impact how children learn to read and spell.

LICS Context and history

LICS opened in the 2000s, part of the growth of both DL education and charter schools across the US. As discussed earlier, LICS was conceived and built by an African-American educator (Reina, a pseudonym) who had reclaimed her French heritage language and who dreamed and dared to provide multilingual education for students like her: Head Start graduates who rarely had opportunities to develop bilingualism from an early age. After meeting with like-minded educators and parents, and collaborating with local power brokers, Reina learned that area school districts did not have the resources or wherewithal to develop innovative, equitable DL education as she desired. In turn, she partnered with former policymakers, community advocates, teachers, and parents to develop a non-profit, the LICS. Together, they opened four charter schools: three K-5 elementary programs, which offered Spanish, French and Mandarin approximately 90% of each school day, and one middle school, which offered instruction in these three languages so students could continue to develop their bilingualism.

Two of the LICS schools opened in a converted warehouse in the center of the city in what we call Year 1; each included kindergarten and first grade, and they planned to grow one grade per year. Per local charter school law, LICS could enroll children from the entire city school district, across neighborhood boundaries. To ensure enrollment of African-American and low-income city residents, LICS offered busing for city students. LICS also enrolled white children from the surrounding suburbs per the city's integration policies. Such policies and efforts helped LICS meet its goals to be racially diverse.

Over the schools' first nine years, the student demographics remained remarkably stable, though the size of the schools fluctuated over time. Each year LICS enrolled about 50–60% Black students, 30–35% white, 5–10% from Spanish-speaking backgrounds, 5–10% multiracial, and 55–65% who received free or reduced lunch. While the city's foreign-born population hovered around 6% at the time of this study, 15–20% of children at LICS had an immigrant parent. Notably, these simple census/racial identifiers belie the complex demography of the school population. LICS students came from a range of diverse backgrounds: There were Canadian-American (white) children whose parents had lived in Chile and had native-like fluency in Spanish; siblings whose mom was an Italian immigrant and whose US-born dad was the son of a German mother and Indian father; African-American youth whose relatives migrated to the city as part of the Great Migration; and Central American newcomers whose family members had mixed documentation/legal status. Socioeconomic status ranged from homeless to the highest income brackets.

Start-up charter schools are ever in flux, and LICS was no exception. Quick early growth from adding a grade each year and initial excitement over the unique opportunity contrasted with later shrinkage, shaped by challenging school conditions as well as new competition, like other charter schools opening nearby. Over the years, the schools experienced growing pressure from their sponsor and the state to improve finances, operations and comparatively low standardized test scores, especially of low-income and Black students. By Year 7 of the network's existence, the board announced the departure of their founding director, with news reports citing that the board voted unanimously to replace Reina. (No specific reasons were given.)

Leadership changed continually in Years 7–10, after having had the same director and school-level leaders from Year 1–6. After being led by white consultants and a Black interim director in Year 7, LICS had two different full-time white directors as well as new school-level leadership each Year 8 to 10. Then, the director in Year 9 proposed changing LICS's 'full immersion,' or 90/10 design, to a 50/50 model, thereby reducing the amount of time students spent learning in the partner languages from around 90% to 50%. In addition, per the new approach, students would have to demonstrate proficiency in their home language (for most students, English) before studying in another language. As further explicated in findings, for many Black students, this meant delaying their exposure to other languages until they received certain scores on English proficiency exams. By Year 10, none of the founding leadership – neither central office staff nor principals – remained, and only one leader spoke one of the schools' languages as his first/native language. None were individuals of color.

Data

Drawing from nine years of data, we chose to analyze the most consequential public documents that defined LICS and documented its progress over time: the LICS charter, charter renewal, year-end reports from LICS directors, and annual reviews by the university sponsor (see Table 4.1). Given changes at the sponsoring organization, we only had access to annual reviews from Years 5–9, when more formal and defined review processes were instituted. Our goal in choosing these documents from the broader ethnographic data set was to have similar data from each year that described and defended LICS to its community, the public and policymakers.

Data analysis

Given her prior ethnographic research at LICS, data analysis began with Lisa journaling and then sharing experiences with her co-authors, including her perceptions of accountability, students of color and

Table 4.1 LICS documents

Year	Documents		
0+	Charter application		
1	Recruitment presentation	Annual 'State of LICS'	Director's mid-year report
2	Recruitment presentation	Annual 'State of LICS'	
3		Annual 'State of LICS'	
4		Annual 'State of LICS'	
5	Charter renewal	Annual 'State of LICS'	Sponsor annual review
6		Annual 'State of LICS'	Sponsor annual review
7	New Director profile	Annual 'State of LICS'	Sponsor annual review
8		End-of-year letter from new Director (in lieu of 'State of LICS,' which no longer happened)	Sponsor annual review
9	Two documents explaining new programming from Director		Sponsor annual review

Note: + prior to opening

discourses at LICS over time (Dorner, 2015; Dorner & Layton, 2013). Next, Lisa, Edwin and Jeong-Mi separately analyzed the initial charter, openly coding for LICS's vision. When the group came together, they noted the following original goals related to the raciolinguistic perspective. LICS aimed to:

- Design an urban school with high expectations and high literacy for all children – *social equity*.
- End 'word poverty' of African-American students – *languagelessness*
- Recognize English varieties, but meet standardized proficiencies – *standards*.
- Regularly measure performance of students, teachers, etc. – *standards*.

With this backdrop, we employed tools from CDA. CDA broadly argues that discourses – which are evident through language and text – represent social practices, ideologies and identities striving for power and recognition (Fairclough, 2010). In turn, the next major step of analysis was to code each document for any discourses that represented these ideologies: social equity, languagelessness and standardization. We also had an 'other' category to place other items that might not fit directly in this schema; we began to note how many documents highlighted LICS's financial and organizational challenges.

For the second major step of analyses, we looked closer at the discourses employed in the documents. We drew from Fairclough's (2011) definition of the 'orders of discourse:' genres (ways of interacting), discourses (ways of representing) and style (ways of being). Specifically, we studied the 'discourse' or way of representing *standardization* in the documents, asking questions like: What kinds of standards or proficiencies were presented, desired and valued? What and who was being measured, with what kinds of data? We also examined 'style' or ways of being (identities) tied to students of color: How were students positioned in terms of the schools' goals? Who was LICS for? How were Black students and their languages/linguistic proficiencies described? In the analyses, we noted which discourses were used in arguments about developing and changing LICS's instructional program, and we noted what and who were absent in LICS's arguments.

As we worked through the analyses, we found the following discourses and ideologies at LICS: (1) Public education is a public good, which was presented in the form of: multilingual education should be accessible to all *(ideology of social equity)*. (2) Schools must be held accountable to standards, in this case, especially students' linguistic and academic proficiency *(ideology of standardization)*. (3) There is an achievement gap in this country; specifically, we have a 'language gap' (Avineri *et al*., 2015) that negatively impacts the education of Black and low-income children *(ideology of languagelessness)*. Comparing discourses that represented these ideologies over time demonstrates the racial and linguistic tensions in designing DL schools for social equity.

Findings

As with any institution, there existed various, competing ideas at LICS. The three core ideologies and their related discourses were remarkably stable over time, with LICS leadership (the schools' Directors and Sponsor) presenting each of these almost every year. To review, we found: (1) a concern to provide language immersion education to *all* youth (*social equity*); (2) a value on standard measurement or outcomes (*standardization*); and (3) the goal to address an achievement gap, most often named as low literacy and test scores of Black youth (*languagelessness*). These ideologies drove the arguments for (1) developing the school, i.e. we need to bring rich multilingual education to Black kids, who otherwise have low literacy rates; (2) creating the strongest schools, i.e. we need to measure everything, especially kids' individual proficiencies, to a high standard; and (3) implementing a new model in LICS's later years, i.e. we need to employ a 50/50 model, rather than the 90/10 model, primarily because our Black kids are failing. Table 4.2 lists which documents reflected each ideology.

As shown in the following sections, although each ideology existed across time, the space dedicated to the different discursive arguments

Table 4.2 The prevalence of each ideology at LICS

	Social equity	Languagelessness	Standardization
Years 0–6[+] Ten documents by founding director	Charter application (0)* Recruitment (1) Mid-year report (1) Recruitment (2) State of LICS (3) State of LICS (4) Charter renewal (5) State of LICS (6)	Charter application (0) Charter renewal (5)	Charter application (0) Mid-year report (1) State of LICS (1) Recruitment (2) State of LICS (2) State of LICS (4) Charter renewal (5) State of LICS (5) State of LICS (6)
Years 7–9 Five documents by subsequent directors	State of LICS (7) New director profile (7) End of year letter (8) New program email (9) New program FAQs (9)	New director profile (7) New program email (9) New program FAQs (9)	State of LICS (7) New program email (9) New program FAQs (9)
Years 5–9 Five documents by university Sponsor	Annual review (5) Annual review (6) Annual review (7) Annual review (8) Annual review (9)	Annual review (5) Annual review (6) Annual review (7) Annual review (8) Annual review (9)	Annual review (5) Annual review (6) Annual review (7) Annual review (8) Annual review (9)

[+] Year 0 = when LICS as a non-profit began, while Year 1 = the opening year of the schools
* The number in parentheses is the year of the document.

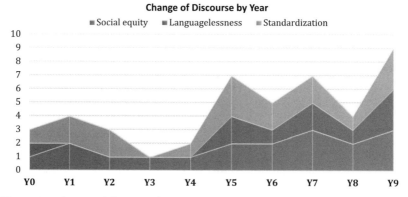

Figure 4.1 Change of discourse by year

changed as the leadership changed. Most significant, the *'languagelessness* of Black youth' was more prominent in the later years (5–9), while *social equity* was the most consistent (see Figure 4.1). In addition, the later Director's arguments about changing LICS's programming in Years 8–9 neglected to mention the material reality of the schools. Specifically, annual reviews spent significant space presenting the operational and financial challenges facing LICS, but such challenges were never publicly named by the new director as a reason to change the instructional program in Year 10. Instead, Black youth were framed as the deficiency, as what needed to be fixed for the schools to meet state standards. LICS leadership employed these discourses as they proposed to 'give' English (as opposed to other languages) to Black students, so more of them could perform proficiently on the annual state tests, in English. In turn, the intersection of *standardization* and positioning youth as *languageless* became the rationale to implement a new 50/50 model at LICS, which ultimately had the power to exclude Black students from participation in rich language education and dampen LICS's efforts toward social equity.

LICS at the beginning: Social equity for all (Black) youth

> *'Each LICS school will resemble a true multilingual society in which individuals interact in the language(s) which are most comfortable to them.'* (Charter application)

LICS founders – especially the founding Director – consistently pronounced the core value of social equity, proclaiming that multilingual education should be accessible to all, and all children can succeed in language immersion education. As demonstrated in the following paragraphs, LICS leaders defined who they meant by the phrase 'all children:' they primarily aimed to serve Black children and low-income youth from the city who had not had previous opportunities to learn another language in primary schooling. 'All children' was a discursive move to suggest the development of an inclusive and integrated space in a very segregated urban context. However, in making an argument for integrated and equitable multilingual education, they also began to define Black youth as *languageless*.

All children

Recruitment documents highlighted the goal of serving 'all children' equitably. LICS presentations for Years 1 and 2 used the following phrases (emphases ours):

> 'Mission: To position all children for success in local and global economies through holistic, intellectually inspiring language immersion programs.' (Years 1, 2)

> 'We practice excellence for all.' (Year 1)

> 'Transportation provided for all city residents.' (Years 1, 2)

> 'Before and after care are free for all families.' (Years 1, 2)

> 'We recruit a student body that reflects the diversity of the region.' (Year 2)

> We serve '53% Black, 27% White, 7% Hispanic, 7% Multi-ethnic' students. (Year 2)

> We have 'Four pillars for success: innovative curriculum, parent excellence, professional development, social equity' (Year 2)

This idea of 'all children' was also reflected in the original charter. For example, the description for school leader positions stated: Principals will hold 'an unswayable belief that all students can achieve at high levels.' Under the section on 'Student Achievement Standards,' the first major sub-section was titled: 'Success for All Students.'

In addition, these unswayable beliefs were presented in 'State of LICS' annual presentations to LICS parents. For example, in Year 5, slide 13/17 called 'language immersion instruction for all students' a 'non-negotiable' (Figure 4.2). In Year 6, this same slide was moved to an earlier point in the presentation (4/14), posted right after the title page and the organization's mission and vision. Such forward movement suggests a renewed focus on this non-negotiable, highlighting the importance of rich multilingual education for all students. Moreover, starting Year 4, the annual 'States of LICS' presented by the founding director used pictures of students from LICS (not stock photos) that highlighted predominantly Black youth learning, playing and working with teachers. In short, 'all children' in this context meant inclusive communities serving mostly Black students.

> **Living our non-negotiables daily**
>
> Language immersion instruction for all students
>
> IB instruction for all students
>
> Speaking to people with kindness and respect– remember students are people too.
>
> Hungry for feedback

Figure 4.2* Language immersion instruction for all is non-negotiable
* IB stands for International Baccalaureate, the curricular framework LICS used at the time

All children further defined as Black and languageless

While the phrase 'all children' was inclusive to Black students, as found in the charter (Year 1), it appeared alongside discourses that reflected the ideology of *languagelessness*. Specifically, to make the argument for language immersion to serve all students in this urban area, the founding director wrote (emphases ours):

> LICS 'is designed to enable each pupil to achieve the standards because of three key research-based program design components:
>
> - ending word poverty among low-income and African-American populations through language immersion instruction,
> - increasing social capital through informal learning, and
> - maintaining integrated racial and socio-economic school populations in heterogeneously grouped classes.'

The charter then spelled out three arguments. First, it referenced 'all students' once again, claiming that no matter one's level or variety of English, students can succeed in language immersion education: 'Immersion instruction will allow all of the students to have common learning experiences and progress towards a new goal regardless of their home language or parents' level of education' (charter, Year 1). While this is a nod to an anti-deficit perspective of multilingual youth, the second and third arguments turned to linguistic and cognitive deficiencies of minoritized students.

Referencing Hart and Risley's (2003) 'ground-breaking research' on 'word poverty,' the second argument in this section of charter argued that language immersion education would help fill literacy and linguistic gaps for low-income and African-American students. The third argument continued this deficit discourse, stating that Black students also lack 'social capital' and need 'integrated schools' to fight a 'decline in cognitive function' (charter, Year 1). The charter continued: 'The enrollment ideal is to have heterogeneous groups of children in each class, combating the typical cognitive and academic decline of low-income African-American children during elementary school' (charter, Year 1). The words used here suggest that Black children in majority-Black schools typically had weak cognitive and academic outcomes as a result of being surrounded by Black peers; joining 'heterogeneous' (white) classrooms could combat such typical decline. This kind of language positions Black students and *their* typical decline as the issue to be solved; such discourse centers students as the problem, rather than highlighting the societal, structural, legal and ethical issues – the entrenched institutional racism – that have led to such 'decline.' It is also telling that the charter application leaves out a discussion of the rich language varieties and histories of Black America. The term 'African-American' itself was used six times, but never to highlight Blacks' resiliency, academic strengths, or linguistic dexterity. Four instances positioned Black youth as lacking literacy or cognitive capacity, while the other two instances simply reported city and school demographics.

Although Hart and Risley's work has been discredited (McKenna, 2018), the belief that many low-income and Black students come to school 'without words' is robust. Even at LICS – a school system designed to equalize opportunity for Black youth by providing access to rich language education – the founding charter relied upon a discourse that ignored the linguistic repertoires and capacities of Black students. In summary, both *social equity* and *languagelessness* drove the arguments for creating LICS. Ideologies of *languagelessness* and *standardization*, then, grew stronger as the schools developed, with new (white) leadership.

The annual reviews begin: Students must reach standard proficiencies

To develop LICS over the years, LICS leadership and policymakers argued for holding their students, teachers and community members to high standards. As shown in the following paragraphs, accountability discourses were quite prevalent, as LICS measured or promised to collect a range of data on nearly everything, including: students' academic proficiencies, parents' satisfaction and teachers' abilities (see Dorner & Layton, 2013).

First, a glance at the kind of data included in the State of LICS annual presentations by the director highlights the schools' focus on data, and also suggests how accountability concerns shifted over the years from a focus on parent engagement/satisfaction to students' standardized test scores:

- Parent satisfaction survey; Students' English and Spanish proficiency (Year 1);
- Parent satisfaction survey (Year 2);
- Campus climate surveys (of parents, teachers and students) (Year 4);

- Students' standardized test score growth – '25% growth in English on state tests from 3rd–4th grade' – as well as student literacy goals, with a focus on bilingualism: 'Absolute Priority: 80% of students reading on grade level in L1 and L2' (Year 5);
- Enrollment statistics, a repeat of Year 5's statement regarding student growth, and a new goal for bilingualism: '80% of all 7th graders will be proficient/advanced in L1 and L2' (Year 6);
- Parent satisfaction survey; students' standardized test scores in English only (Year 7).

In these public presentations, both the founding and subsequent directors highlighted data. For instance, from Years 1–6, Director Reina presented results of parent and school climate surveys, suggesting a focus on holding LICS accountable to its families, teachers and students. Later, she made increasing mentions of student standardized test scores and goals to measure 'proficiency' in both 'L1 and L2,' holding LICS accountable to their focus on bilingualism. Then, in Year 7, the year after Reina left, the interim director gave the first public presentation of graphs that compared LICS's state standardized test scores to city and state results, while in Years 8-9, the newly hired director argued for using a wide range of data in decision-making. Specifically, while she no longer held annual community events to present the 'State of LICS,' she did write letters to the community. In one letter explaining their search for a new language immersion model, she explained: 'When I use the word "data" here, I am not just referring to student test scores on the state assessment given each spring. We have examined much more….' Then, she listed: parent and staff surveys, focus groups, classroom and technology resources, financial statements and data on student enrollment, attrition and conduct.

On the one hand, the discourses of the directors and sponsor suggest that data, writ large, were central to the schools. On the other hand, looking across all documents suggests that *student data and standardized scores on tests given in English* ultimately became the most significant concern. While directors' reports in the early years started by reporting family survey results, the later years primarily provided data on student achievement, merely stating that other kinds of data were valued. Likewise, in later Years 5–9, each annual review by LICS's sponsor always contained an analysis of student achievement, with data and graphs that compared LICS students to peers at nearby city schools. Notably, when the sponsor's annual reports presented academic achievement, they never reported students' growing proficiency in Spanish, French, or Mandarin; they always represented students' achievement using state standardized test scores in math and English language arts. Drawing out results like this is the very act of 'norming' or standardizing Black children (the majority of LICS's student population) against others, in this case the white, English-speaking subject.

Moreover, the presentation of data in the Sponsor's annual reviews – especially in the summaries that listed LICS's 'areas of strengths' and 'areas of improvements' – often specifically stated 'African-American,' 'low-income,' or 'disadvantaged' students were not performing at a proficient level. For example, the areas of improvement in nearly each executive summary named the challenge of educating African-American students as follows:

- LICS needs to 'improve academic performance of African-American population.' (Year 5, summary);
- 'Students who come to LICS behind in English remain behind. LICS needs to focus attention on meeting the literacy needs of these students.' (Year 6, summary);
- 'Black students performed significantly lower than white students on all state tests.' 'Students who are behind in L1 [English] should receive interventions to strengthen their proficiency in English.' (Year 6);
- In Math and English Language Arts state tests, 'All schools' African American and Super Sub group students scored significantly lower than LICS's total.' (Year 7);
- 'Student achievement outcomes for the schools' more disadvantaged students are weak.' (Year 8, summary).

In Year 9, the state experienced a delay in sharing students' standardized test scores, so the annual review analyzed norm-referenced tests instead. In this review, for the first time, the Sponsor did *not* have a statement that Black students were not meeting proficiency standards – either because the data did not disaggregate students by race or because there was no significant difference to mention. However, the review still proclaimed the need for a new language immersion model due to low test scores of Blacks and low-income students, as discussed in the next section.

LICS at a language(less) crossroad: Arguing for the 50/50 model

As the charter school Sponsor and state accountability systems strengthened over time, and LICS had more standardized test scores to analyze (because their students had aged and started taking state exams), the ideologies of standardization and languageless intertwined. LICS leaders and policymakers relied on related discourses to argue for changing from a 90/10 to a 50/50 model.

After hiring her, the sponsor encouraged the new director in Years 8–9 to explore new instructional approaches in DL education that included more time for English. The need for enhanced English education within their language immersion model was mentioned explicitly in the annual reviews starting Year 6, in the area analyzing LICS's Vision:

- 'Beginning in kindergarten, students who are behind in L1 [English] should receive interventions to strengthen their proficiency in English.

LICS should also consider introducing English instruction for all students in grade 1.' (Year 6);
- 'In light of state test outcomes – especially those of LICS's low-income students on English Language Arts – all stakeholders should revisit the vision of a full language immersion school to consider its viability for the students served by the schools.' (Year 7);
- 'The school needs to determine the best language immersion model for the students served by the school.' (Year 8).

In turn, the new director used various data to explore other language immersion models. Ultimately, she made the following statements regarding the reasons for the future implementation (Year 10) of a 50/50 model (emphases ours):

- 'In coming to understand the data, it made great sense to try to identify a language immersion instructional model that was grounded in research and educational best practices ... and, most importantly, one that demonstrated positive outcomes on student achievement in both languages for students from underserved communities. It also would be desirable to find a model that had wide adoption in public schools serving a diverse student body....' (Year 9).
- 'Question: Why does LICS want to implement a different language immersion model? Answer: Our students are not learning or growing in the basic subjects of English, math and science. While the full language immersion model was compelling, over time it became clear that for the majority of our students, the new language skills came at the expense of learning in math, English, and science. About 75% of LICS students enter LICS below grade level in literacy and math. Test scores show our low-income students of color are not getting up to grade level as quickly as other students. This is called an achievement gap. We need a model that will teach all children the target language and also teach them the basics. We know that students who have strong reading skills in their first language (English) will be able to transfer skills much more easily to the target language. Therefore, it makes sense to teach LICS students to read in English first.' (Year 9).

In these communications, the new director reflected the same kind of discourses that the founding director had, from a focus on *social equity* to *standardization* and *languageless*. In the first quote above, for example, she aimed to ensure that LICS served a 'diverse student body' well, a nod to the idea of access and equity in serving 'all (Black) children' discourse described by the founders.

The second quote, however – which was buttressed by subsequent communications and interactions with LICS stakeholders – more strongly reflected the discourses of *languagelessness* and *standardization*. As suggested by these communications, in the new 50/50 model, students would have to demonstrate proficiency in their home language first, thereby delaying their exposure to other languages. For the US-born Black students at LICS, this meant that they would not receive Spanish, French or Mandarin literacy instruction until they passed a certain proficiency level in English. Such a statement positioned them, again, as *without language* until they could prove a certain *standard*.

Moreover, this recommendation was not grounded in the field of US world-language immersion education, which recommends more, not less, attention on the non-English language; this is recommended to combat the unequal power/political status and hegemony of English in US society and because 'research demonstrates that more time in English does not result in better English language outcomes in immersion' (Tedick & Wesley, 2015: 27). LICS's leaders and policymakers in the later years also did not pay attention to linguistic studies of African-American Language (AAL) or the richness of 'Spoken Soul,' mentioned earlier, and how a language school might build upon such linguistic dexterity. Instead, the idea of 'transfer' applied here was drawn from the field of bilingual education, which argues that developing US *im/migrant* (not US-born, English-speaking) students' literacy in their home languages, first, supports their eventual academic achievement in English (e.g. Umansky *et al.*, 2016). No matter the research base, a very real tension here – and one facing more than just language immersion schools (Delpit, 2011; Paris, 2016) – was how to ensure all (Black) students had access to the language of power ('standard English'), and whether explicit instruction in standardized (white) English prior to another language would serve them well. There was no clear answer, though there were very real discourses that shaped LICS's thinking on these issues.

Over time, as LICS educators and policymakers wrestled with these tensions, the ideology of *languagelessness* remained. What is most striking is that the director's communications placed the failure of the schools on Black students and their presumed inabilities to meet state standards, rather than the structural, historical issues facing both Black youth in the city and this particular charter school. Specifically, the majority of the sponsor's annual reviews named myriad challenges in LICS's finances, operations, governance, special education provisions and teacher professional development. For example, in the executive summary of Year 7, 22 lines of text suggested 'areas of improvement' in 'culture, leadership, governance, and finances,' whereas only 11 lines went to 'student achievement.' The New Director Profile in Year 7 summarized these challenges:

> The primary challenges facing LICS are associated with the lack of a stable, effective administration during the last few years,' including 'lack of strong leadership,' 'breakdown of operating systems...drop-off

procedures, textbook ordering, supply acquisition, communication with parents about school policies and practices, and the development of an annual budget.... (New Director Profile, Year 7)

Such structural issues impacted educators' abilities to develop the strongest language immersion education possible, but they were not mentioned in annual reviews as possible reasons for students' standardized academic achievement scores. On this final point, what was left *out* of the new Director's communications is perhaps most telling. Rather than highlight these system-wide challenges, LICS leaders were shaped by accountability pressures from the Sponsor and state, as well as their goal to serve *all* (Black) children. In turn, they continued to reflect the intertwined ideologies of (Black) *languagelessness* and the need for *standardization* in their proposal for organizational change.

Discussion/Conclusion

Given her prior experiences at LICS, when we began this project, Lisa assumed we would find discourses related to standards, data and accountability. She was also aware of the schools' original focus on social equity and wondered how that had been implemented over time, especially in light of recent conversations she had with Black moms at LICS, who lamented why *their children* were often so explicitly named as the schools' 'problem.' This led to our study using a raciolinguistic perspective and our finding that even with a proclaimed focus on equity in DL education, racialized ideologies retained their power and structural reform was challenging to sustain (Sung, 2018).

At LICS, intersecting racialized ideologies were powerful and prevalent; even social justice advocates and Black leaders sometimes positioned Black youth in deficit ways as they strove for equitable language education. Nearly all documents in this study proclaimed the importance of (1) providing equitable access to multilingual education for all youth *(social equity)*; (2) valuing standard educational outcomes *(standardization)*; and (3) addressing an achievement gap through providing literacy education to Black youth *(languagelessness)*. Leaders used a combination discourses like these to build or (re)develop the schools. As they did so, they deeply believed that they had students' best interests at heart.

That said, the use and juxtaposition of discourses shifted as the leadership changed and institutional accountability mandates strengthened. While the founding African-American Director employed the discourses related to *languagelessness* as she argued for LICS in the charter application, she never drew upon deficit discourses of Black youth in her public discussions. Each of her presentations analyzed here, in fact, positioned Black students as capable youth who *would* become bilingual. This was her 'non-negotiable' and 'audacious' goal from the very beginning. This part of our analysis shows that it *is* possible for DL leaders to take action against inequity and present alternate discourses, but we have to retain such leaders. Discourses related to social equity diminished once Reina left LICS.

As the school's leadership shifted to fewer multilingual leaders of color and when state standardized tests became increasingly high-stakes, the discourse on 'all (Black) students' adapted to how they needed the 'basics' and had to have 'English' before they could be allowed to study in another language. Even when explicitly asked (by Lisa) to remove language in school communications that positioned Black children as the central reason for LICS's 'failure,' the new Director did not (although she did reduce the number of times she named Black students as failing). In this way, the definition of equity itself changed as policymakers more strongly reflected the intersecting ideologies of *standardization* and *languageless*.

In conclusion, we call for further application of the raciolinguistic perspective to understand the power of such ideologies in language education. Schools, policymakers and families should attend to how DL leaders draw upon dueling discourses in their contexts, and how they might fight for equity in light of these discourses (Bernstein *et al.*, 2020). We should consider the importance of having leaders that not only represent the racial communities served, but also embrace purpose-driven (Dantley, 2009) and social justice leadership (DeMatthews *et al.*, 2017; Theoharis, 2007) in ways that resist deficit discourses and work to dismantle systemic racism. We also argue that schools' policies must be examined in comparison to the structural conditions existing in each space (Ball *et al.*, 2012). Too often, we have ignored the material contexts that intersect with racist ideologies and ultimately shape students' educational access and outcomes (Sung, 2018). Finally, we must study our own discourses, look into our own histories and be willing to critique how they shape what *we* say and do in our own fights for equity, for we are all subjected to raciolinguistic forces unbeknownst to us until we interrogate our own words and lives.

References

Aguayo, D. and Dorner, L.M. (2017) Assessing Spanish-speaking immigrant parents' perceptions of climate at a new language immersion school: A critical analysis using 'Thinking with Theory.' *Education Policy Analysis Archives* 25 (112), 1–27.

Alim, H.S., Rickford, J.R. and Ball, A.F. (eds) (2016) *Raciolinguistics: How Language Shapes our Ideas about Race*. New York, NY: Oxford University Press.

Avineri, N., Johnson, E., Brice-Heath, S., McCarty, T., Ochs, E., Kremer-Sadlik, T., Blum, S., Zentella, A.C., Rosa, J., Flores, N., Alim, H.S. and Paris, D. (2015) Invited forum: Bridging the 'language gap'. *Journal of Linguistic Anthropology* 25 (1), 66–86. doi:10.111/jola.12071

Ball, S.J., Maguire, M. and Braun, A. (2012) *How Schools Do Policy: Policy Enactments in Secondary Schools*. New York, NY: Routledge.

Baugh, J. (2003) Linguistic profiling. In S. Makoni, G. Smitherman, A.F. Ball and A.K. Spears (eds) *Black Linguistics: Language, Society, and Politics in Africa and the Americas* (pp. 155–168). London: Routledge.

Bernstein, K.A., Katznelson, N., Amezcua, A., Mohamed, S. and Alvarado, S. L. (2020) Local, global, profit, pride: Dueling discourses of dual language in principals' talk about their programs. *TESOL Quarterly* 54 (3), 652–684. https://doi.org/10.1002/tesq.582

Bonney, E., Dorner, L., Trigos-Carrillo, L., Song, K. and Kim, S. (2019) Developing inclusive and multilingual family literacy events at diverse schools. In E. Crawford and L. Dorner (eds) *Educational Leadership of Immigrants: Case Studies in Times of Change* (pp. 176–182). New York, NY: Routledge.

Burns, M. (2017) 'Compromises that we make': Whiteness in the dual language context. *Bilingual Research Journal* 40 (4), 339–352.

Cervantes-Soon, C., Dorner, L., Palmer, D., Heiman, D., Schwerdtfeger, R. and Choi, J. (2017) Combating inequalities in two-way language immersion programs: Toward critical consciousness in bilingual education spaces. *Review of Research in Education* 41 (1), 403–427.

Consoletti, A. (2011) *The State of Charter Schools: What We Know – and What We Do Not – About Performance and Accountability*. Washington, DC: Center for Education Reform.

Dantley, M.E. (2009) African American educational leadership: Critical, purposeful, and spiritual. In L. Foster and L.C. Tillman (eds) *African American Perspectives on Leadership in Schools: Building a Culture of Empowerment* (pp. 39–55). Lanham, MD: Rowman & Littlefield Education Publishers, Inc.

de Jong, E.J. (2016) Two-way immersion for the next generation: Models, policies, and principles. *International Multilingual Research Journal* 10 (1), 6–16.

Delpit, L.D. (2011) The silenced dialogue: Power and pedagogy in educating other people's children. In K. Afolabi, C. Bocala, R.C. DiAquoi, J.M. Hayden, I.A. Liefshitz and S.S. Oh (eds) *Education for a Multicultural Society* (pp. 123–143). Cambridge, MA: Harvard Educational Review.

DeMatthews, D., Izquierdo, E. and Knight, D.S. (2017) Righting past wrongs: A superintendent's social justice leadership for dual language education along the US-Mexico border. *Education Policy Analysis Archives* 25 (1), 1-28.

Dorner, L.M. (2015) From global jobs to safe spaces: The diverse discourses that sell multilingual schooling in the US. *Current Issues in Language Planning* 16 (1&2), 114–131.

Dorner, L.M. and Layton, A. (2014) '¿Cómo se dice?' Children's multilingual discourses (or interacting, representing, and being) in a first-grade Spanish immersion classroom. *Linguistics and Education* 25, 24–39.

Dorner, L.M. and Layton, A. (2013) What makes a 'good' school? Data and competing discourses in a multilingual charter network. In D. Anagnostopoulos, S. Rutledge and R. Jacobsen (eds) *The Infrastructure of Accountability: Mapping Data Use and its Consequences Across the American Education System* (pp.145–162). Cambridge, MA: Harvard Educational Press.

Fairclough, N.L. (2010) *Critical Discourse Analysis: The Critical Study of Language* (2nd edn). New York, NY: Taylor & Francis.

Fairclough, N.L. (2011) Semiotic aspects of social transformation and learning. In R. Rogers (ed.) *An Introduction to Critical Discourse Analysis in Education* (pp. 119–127). New York, NY: Routledge.

Flores, N. and Chaparro, S. (2018) What counts as language education policy? Developing a materialist anti-racist approach to language activism. *Language Policy* 17 (3), 365–384.

Flores, N. and Rosa, J. (2015) Undoing appropriateness: Raciolinguistic ideologies and language diversity in education. *Harvard Educational Review* 85 (2), 149–171.

Gutiérrez, K. and Orellana, M.F. (2006) The 'problem' of English learners: Constructing genres of difference. *Research in the Teaching of English* 40, 502–507.

Hart, B. and Risley, T.R. (2003) The early catastrophe: The 30 million word gap by age 3. *American Educator* 27 (1), 4–9.

Henderson, K. (2019) The danger of the dual-language enrichment narrative: Educator discourses constructing exclusionary participation structures in bilingual education. *Critical Inquiry in Language Studies* 16 (3), 155–177.

Howard, E., Lindholm-Leary, K., Rogers, D., Olague, N., Medina, J., Kennedy, B., Sugarman, J. and Christian, D. (2018) *Guiding Principles for Dual Language Education* (3rd edn). Washington, DC: Center for Applied Linguistics.

McKenna, L. (2018) *The Long Contentious History of the 'Word Gap' Study*, 15 June, The Atlantic. See https://www.theatlantic.com/education/archive/2018/06/the-long-contentious-history-of-the-word-gap-study/562850/

Martínez, R.A. (2017) Dual language education and the erasure of Chicanx, Latinx, and indigenous Mexican children: A call to re-imagine (and imagine beyond) bilingualism. *Texas Education Review* 5 (1), 81–92.

Menken, K. and Solorza, C. (2014) No Child Left Behind: Accountability and the elimination of bilingual education programs in New York city schools. *Educational Policy* 28 (1), 96–125.

Meshulam, A. and Apple, M.W. (2014) Interrupting the interruption: Neoliberalism and the challenges of an antiracist school. *British Journal of Sociology of Education* 35 (5), 650–669.

Muro, J.A. (2016) 'Oil and water'? Latino-white relations and symbolic integration in a changing California. *Sociology of Race & Ethnicity* 2 (4), 516–530.

Nicoladis, E., Taylor, D.M., Lambert, W.E. and Cazabon, M. (1998) What two-way bilingual programmes reveal about the controversy surrounding race and intelligence. *International Journal of Bilingual Education and Bilingualism* 1 (2), 134–148.

Paciotto, C. and Delany-Barmann, G. (2011) Planning micro-level language education reform in new diaspora sites: Two-way immersion education in the rural Midwest. *Language Policy* 10 (3), 221–243.

Paino, M., Renzulli, L.A., Boylan, R.L. and Bradley, C.L. (2014) For grades or money? Charter school failure in North Carolina. *Educational Administration Quarterly* 50 (3), 500–536.

Palmer, D.K. (2010) Race, power, and equity in a multiethnic urban elementary school with a dual-language 'strand' program. *Anthropology & Education Quarterly* 41 (1), 94–114.

Paris, D. (2016) It was a Black city: African American language in California's changing urban schools and communities. In H.S. Alim, J.R. Rickford and A.F. Ball (eds) *Raciolinguistics: How Language Shapes our Ideas about Race* (pp. 241–253). New York, NY: Oxford University Press.

Pearson, T.M., Wolgemuth, J.R. and Colomer, S.E. (2015) Spiral of decline or 'beacon of hope': Stories of school choice in a 'declining' school. *Education Policy Analysis Archives* 23 (25), 1–27.

Rickford, J.R. and Rickford, R.J. (2000) *Spoken Soul: The Story of Black English*. Hoboken, NJ: John Wiley & Sons.

Rosa, J.D. (2016) Standardization, racialization, languagelessness: Raciolinguistic ideologies across communicative contexts. *Journal of Linguistic Anthropology* 26 (2), 162–183.

Rosa, J. and Flores, N. (2017) Unsettling race and language: Toward a raciolinguistic perspective. *Language in Society* 46 (5), 621–647.

Sung, K.K. (2018) Raciolinguistic ideology of antiblackness: Bilingual education, tracking, and the multiracial imaginary in urban schools. *International Journal of Qualitative Studies in Education* 31 (8), 667–683.

Tedick, D.J. and Wesley, P.M. (2015) A review of research on content-based foreign/second language education in US K-12 contexts. *Language, Culture and Curriculum* 28 (1), 25–40.

Theoharis, G. (2007) Social justice educational leaders and resistance: Toward a theory of social justice leadership. *Educational Administration Quarterly* 43 (2), 221–258.

Thomas, W.P. and Collier, V.P. (2012) *Dual Language Education for a Transformed World*. Albuquerque, NM: Dual Language Education of New Mexico Fuente Press.

Umansky, I.M., Valentino, R.A. and Reardon, S.F. (2016) The promise of two-language education. *Educational Leadership* 73 (5), 10–17.

Valdés, G. (2002) Enlarging the pie: Another look at bilingualism and schooling in the US. *International Journal of the Sociology of Language* 155 (156), 187–195.

Valdés, G. (2018) Analyzing the curricularization of language in two-way immersion education: Restating two cautionary notes. *Bilingual Research Journal* 41 (4), 388–412.

Wall, D.J., Greer, E. and Palmer, D. (2019 online first) Exploring institutional processes in a district-wide dual language program: Who is it for? Who is Left Out? *Journal of Latinos and Education*. doi:10.1080/15348431.2019.1613996

5 Centering Raciolinguistic Ideologies in Two-Way Dual Language Education: The Politicized Role of Parents in Mediating their Children's Bilingualism

Sera J. Hernandez

Latinx[1] populations have a long history of racial, linguistic and economic marginalization in the US, and nowhere is this more evident than in public schools. Participation in ideologically and programmatically subtractive schooling (Valenzuela, 1999) has been the norm for Spanish-speaking Latinx youth in US schools (Gándara & Contreras, 2009; Yosso & Solórzano, 2006) and researchers, policymakers and educators are turning to dual language education programs as pedagogical alternatives that promote bilingualism, biliteracy and biculturalism (Baker & Wright, 2017). With the burgeoning demand for dual language education in the United States, critical researchers argue that we must attend to the ideological polemics at the core of bilingual education debates and realities that on one end illustrate hegemonic imperialist (Flores, 2016) and gentrifying (Valdez *et al.*, 2016) forces that benefit privileged communities and, on the other end, the reclamation of a race radical vision of bilingual education born during the Civil Rights Movement (Flores, 2016).

An examination of the language ideologies behind dual language programming can elucidate the sociopolitical reality for racially and linguistically minoritized populations, where, for example, two-way immersion (TWI) models are lauded because they are designed so that students are integrated across race/ethnicity and class during a time when US society remains highly segregated (Orfield & Lee, 2006). However, despite indication of academic promise and success for students across demographics (Collier & Thomas, 2004), critical investigation of TWI programs has illustrated profound 'competing interests and orientations' that can 'compound issues of inequality' for language minoritized students (Cervantes-Soon *et al.*, 2017: 404). This ideological and social reality has entered public discourse as well, with op-eds framing the current trend as a 'middle class takeover of bilingual education' (Williams, 2017), where 'white,' 'privileged' and 'middle-class' are used synonymously to refer to the population vying for spots in dual language programs. These ideological discourses and practices must be explicitly examined in TWI programming and research to avoid further reproduction of status quo power dynamics in bilingual education in the US (Cervantes-Soon *et al.*, 2017; Delavan *et al.*, 2016; Hernandez, 2017; Valdés, 2018) and to counter the pervasive color-evasiveness[2] (Annamma *et al.*, 2017) racial ideology at the core of a *bilingualism for all* discourse that surrounds these program models.

Previous studies of raciolinguistic ideologies and perspectives reveal how 'privileged white subjects' are normalized in their linguistic practices while 'racialized speaking subjects' are positioned as deviant in their ways with words (Flores & Rosa, 2015: 150). Rather than an analysis of how racialized social actors talk, this chapter interrogates how racialized social actors get spoken about, and specifically the raciolinguistic ideologies behind the naming and participation of parents in TWI programs in two California districts. Previous research has demonstrated that TWI contexts can heighten the trends of stratification of parental engagement across racial/ethnic, class and (im)migrant differences because of the integration of communities in these settings (Hernandez, 2013). In this chapter, I will first bring together the educational literature on parent engagement, social class and school integration to support the idea that a raciolinguistic analysis of the discourse surrounding social actors in TWI is needed and timely. Next, I will present my methodology and data sources drawing from two case studies in schools located in different regions of California. Then, I will share examples of raciolinguistic discourse surrounding the implementation of a TWI program in each case to highlight how race and class ideologies play a role in the conspicuous differences in which diverse parents and families are spoken about in the business of doing school. I illustrate this by highlighting instances where diverse TWI parents' characteristics and practices are overtly or covertly described or named by educational stakeholders, including administrators, teachers and parents themselves. Finally, I argue that a careful examination and analysis of class dynamics are needed when examining raciolinguistic discourses and ideologies as class is co-naturalized with race and language in the business of doing school.

Toward a Raciolinguistic Understanding of Parental Engagement in Two-way Immersion

The study of raciolinguistics in education (Alim *et al.*, 2016; Flores & Rosa, 2015) draws on the perspectives of interdisciplinary fields such as sociolinguistics, linguistic anthropology, ethnic studies and educational linguistics to produce scholarship that foregrounds the role language plays in shaping ethnoracial identities across dynamic social and educational contexts, with the recognition that language and race are connected social processes (Alim, 2016). Specifically, the raciolinguistic agenda is 'dedicated to bringing to bear the diverse methods of linguistic analysis to ask and answer critical questions about the relations between language, race, and power across diverse ethnoracial contexts and societies' and during a time of resegregation (Alim, 2016: 3). The examination of raciolinguistic ideologies, that is, systems of belief that naturalize connections between racialized speakers and linguistic norms (Flores & Rosa, 2015), is an essential component of the agenda. Therefore, this chapter builds on previous studies of raciolinguistics by attending to ideological intersectionality (Crenshaw, 1991) to investigate the intersecting dimensions at the forefront of bilingual education that go beyond language and that shape the structural dynamics of power and inequality in TWI spaces across both group and individual identities. The ideologies behind parental engagement and school integration research indicate that TWI is a promising setting for the investigation of how US schools are addressing ethnoracial and socioeconomic integration as manifested in relationships among schools and the racially and economically diverse families they serve.

Decades of research indicate that dominant paradigms of parent involvement (Epstein, 1992) support government-defined parameters (Mapp, 2012) of what the home–school relationship should entail and provide prescriptive parental roles for ways in which linguistically and culturally minoritized parents with school-aged children should engage in the schooling process. This is unsurprising as minoritized parents have been framed as problems or obstacles in their children's educational paths in the national narrative, stemming from a pervasive ideology that undergirds education policy making (Baquedano-López et al., 2014). For over a century, Latinx, Black, and African-American families have been and continue to be taken up as objects and subjects of federal social and educational policy making (Fine, 1993), and their continued racialization and pathologization continue in interventionist parent involvement programming (Valdés, 1996) as a result of that policy, with explicit attempts to standardize parent involvement programs and practices (de Carvalho, 2001) across the US.

Research on parent engagement also recognizes the mediating role of education in the social mobility process and how schooling can reproduces class inequalities (Bowles & Gintis, 1976). Social and cultural resources and capital are converted into educational advantages (Lareau & Horvat, 1999), and while (im)migrant parents are believed to be positioned as bearers of important knowledge, especially in a TWI setting, this cultural capital (Bourdieu, 1986) can be undervalued due to parents' social location (Lareau, 2003). This is becoming more common as middle-class parents are a growing constituency in urban public schools in general, and particularly in dual language schools in California. Recent research suggests that regardless of intentions, these parents may ultimately exacerbate race and class inequalities in public education (Posey, 2012), yet educators often believe parental involvement initiatives and school practices are neutral and sufficient to promote access and equity to all families (Lareau & Horvat, 1999). With regard to parent engagement initiatives and practices in a TWI setting, Bourdieu's (1986) claim that there are notable differences between 'potential' and 'actualized' resources inherent in social networks rings true, where the mobility of capital and resources requires an exercise of power (Rios-Aguilar *et al.*, 2011).

This is why school integration research matters (Frankenberg *et al.*, 2016) and dovetails well with the programmatic features of TWI as language integration is a cornerstone of the TWI project. Though the de jure *Brown vs. Board of Education* decision of 1954 deemed segregated schools as inherently unequal, segregation is a current de facto reality of schooling in the US. In fact, Latinx students are more likely to attend segregated schools than African-American students and language minoritized students in general often experience *triple segregation* in US schools where they are segregated by race, socioeconomic class and language (Gándara, 2010). School integration is unquestionably a key civil rights issue of our time and has promise as 'a powerful mechanism for developing a more equitable pre-K-16 school system in the United States' (Hopkins, 2016: 3).

A raciolinguistic analysis can offer educational researchers a deeper and nuanced understanding of the current sociolinguistic landscape of TWI integration and inform segregation and integration research that moves beyond the white-non-white binary (Garver, 2016) to take up linguistic and discursive elements of the TWI project. Though language is used as the signifier of difference in a TWI model (e.g. Spanish-dominant, English-dominant), we cannot disentangle the intersectionality of race/ethnicity, class and immigration status in our understandings of how they operate in the business of doing school in general, and in doing bilingual education in particular. That is, in TWI contexts, language often functions as a proxy for race/ethnicity, class and immigration status, and an examination not just of the students that are integrated in these programs, but consideration of how the parents, families and larger communities negotiate these complex processes is needed. Therefore, this chapter's raciolinguistic analysis of parental engagement in TWI will illustrate how language, race and class are strategically taken up or ignored by educational stakeholders as a mechanism of implementation in TWI settings, where communities that differ by language use (i.e. Spanish speakers, English speakers) are strategically placed at the same school to support the goals of two-way dual language programming.

Data and Methodology

This chapter draws from multiple case studies (Yin, 2013) in TWI schools/communities to provide a comparative analysis that critically examines the relationships among race/ethnicity, immigration and class by investigating the language and discourses used to discuss educational practices surrounding parents and students in these bilingual settings. Two levels of analysis inform this chapter: one level centers the voices of parents and educators in TWI programs that illustrate the complex ways race/ethnicity, class and immigration are taken up or ignored in discourse about parents; and the other level seeks to examine how the use of these axes of differentiation inform or reflect the ideologies of educational stakeholders in TWI contexts and facilitate or undermine clear communication and healthy relationships among stakeholders. I chose two cases to highlight in this chapter that vary in numerous ways. The first case provides a view into a middle school in northern California that is part of a district that purposefully integrates its student population by race/ethnicity, class and family education level, and the second case shares data collected within an elementary school located in southern California within a district that is highly diverse but segregated by race/ethnicity and class. The first case draws from a larger study that examined the educational experiences of four Latinx (im)migrant families between 2008–2010. The second case stems from a larger study in 2017–2019 that focused on dual language program implementation during the *Multilingualism for All*[3] era in California. Interview data and participant observation are the data sources for both cases. In acknowledging 'race as always produced in conjunction with class, gender, sexuality, religion, (trans)national, and other axes of social differentiation' (Alim, 2016: 6), the questions that guide the analysis explore how these axes of social differentiation are produced and performed by parents and educators to better understand the dynamics of school climate and home–school relationships in TWI settings. They include: What descriptors are used when educational stakeholders refer to diverse parents in TWI programs? How and when are race, class, immigration/citizenship rendered visible and invisible? How do these intersectional identities get displayed in TWI contexts where families, parents and students are integrated across educational spaces?

Describing Parents in a TWI Middle School

This case highlights how stakeholders in a racially and economically diverse middle school TWI program utilize race/ethnicity, class and immigration to name, frame and explain how they perceive the parents and students being served by the program. Cooper Academy[4] is located in a racially and economically diverse district in northern California and makes explicit efforts to engage parents in culturally relevant ways.

The district is proud of the racial/ethnic and socioeconomic diversity reflected in the schools that are a result of their decades of desegregation efforts. This includes Cooper Academy which at the time of the study offered the only middle school dual language strand in the district. Interview excerpts below demonstrate how race/ethnicity, class and immigration get taken up explicitly and implicitly by educational stakeholders talking about the families and students in the school community.

The Latinx vice-principal of Cooper and the white dual language lead teacher were interviewed to get their general perspectives about the families and students they serve. Both regard the TWI strand at the school as a program that levels the playing field for Latinx students and provides them with a safe space because they and their mostly white, middle-class peers are all learning an additional language, therefore they are all language learners.[5] In an interview with the dual language lead teacher, Maestra Stevenson, it is evident that parents are positioned across different levels of distinctions. When explicitly asked about student demographics in the bilingual program Maestra Stevenson responded:

> *Most of the Spanish-speaking kids are first-generation citizens. So most of their parents I think have immigrated here and were not born here. And most of the kids were born here. And there are exceptions on either end. But it's rare for us so far to have parents who were born here. But it's not super rare to have undocumented kids or newly immigrated Spanish-speaking kids.*

The first demographic descriptor named by Maestra Stevenson when referring to 'most' of the Spanish-speaking students in the program was their immigration status – first-generation citizens – indexing the citizenship status of the students explicitly. This first sentence suggests that their parents have immigrated to the US, confirming with her follow-up statement that they have indeed immigrated and were not born in the US. She reiterates that it is rare for Spanish-speaking parents with children in the program to have been born in the US (another indication that they do not have birthright citizenship), so they may not have documentation. The parents' country of origin is not mentioned, nor their race or ethnicity in general. This leaves the parents' citizenship status open and ambiguous, although the issue of documentation comes up when referring to the students again – 'it is not super rare to have undocumented kids [in the TWI program]' suggesting that their parents are also in the US without authorization. The Latinx (im)migrant parents spoken about represent roughly 50% of the participating families in the program and are initially regarded in terms of their immigration status and the dominant language they speak. She continues by switching her focus to the other roughly 50% of students in the program:

> *The other half tends to be pretty highly educated families of English speakers choosing to immerse their kids in a Spanish bilingual program.*

> So there is just an inherent kind of education gap that we start out with. Because the English speakers who are kind of brave enough and willing to go for it, I think already have a lot of confidence that they can support their kid in a second language. Either they feel that either they already know some Spanish or they feel confident academically themselves. And the demographics show definitely that their parents are mostly all college-educated.

Maestra Stevenson fails to mention that the parents of the English-dominant students are from largely white, middle- to upper-class families, and instead shifts the framing of parents with her use of descriptors. No longer referring to nationality or immigration status, she speaks of these parents in terms of their education level, which could serve as a proxy for class. Additionally, the reference to an education gap in the excerpt above is reflective of the mainstream narrative that gaps in educational achievement exist among students distinguished by their race. Here, though, the teacher is referring to the fact that the families who speak English are highly educated, alluding to the intergenerational reproduction of educational advantage. That is, if parents already know how to navigate the educational system in the US, then they can pass on that cultural capital to their children. The (im)migrant parents, who are purportedly highly uneducated cannot. This ideology fuels the district's need for the many interventionist parent education programs offered, even in a district that strives to be anti-racist and socially just. Maestra Stevenson then shifts back to the Spanish-speaking parents, describing them in terms of economics.

> If a kid is [from] a family of a parent who wasn't born here – a Spanish-speaking parent – they usually qualify for free and reduced lunch. So most of our Spanish-speaking kids are from families that are struggling economically.

Demonstrating her awareness that a family's qualification to receive a subsidized lunch is indicative of low socioeconomic status, she returns to defining the Spanish-speaking parents in terms of social characteristics, while completely avoiding doing the same for the English-speaking parents.

The explicit ways in which parents of privilege are juxtaposed with (im)migrant parents in the program and spoken about in terms of their education levels and attributed agency is striking. Never mentioning their immigration status or generation, the English-speaking families are understood to be highly educated risk-takers (i.e. brave and willing). It is unclear, however, if their 'choice' to enroll their children in a Spanish-English bilingual program is related to their high levels of education, or their 'bravery,' 'willingness' and 'confidence' – all descriptors not used when describing the choice or agency of the Spanish-speaking parents. There is no mention of their bravery or willingness to take risks to (im)migrate to the US, to come out of the shadows (for those without documentation), to enroll their children in a bilingual program despite larger political debates around language use, or to even (im)migrate to the US in the first place despite the personal and social risks involved. Additionally, there was no recognition for the giftedness involved in common interpreting performed by (im) migrant children (Valdés, 2003), the social, cultural and cognitive capabilities of cultural brokering executed by many (im)migrant children (Orellana, 2009), or language minoritized students' linguistic genius (Alfaro & Bartolomé, 2019). Examples like these demonstrate how factors such as racial background, class level, or citizenship status, may be explicitly and implicitly named, depending on the context and the interlocutors involved (Pollock, 2004). In educational policy, parents of school-aged children are often distinguished by their racial, linguistic and economic backgrounds. While marginalized parents are often regarded in terms of these reductionist notions of personhood, the race/ethnicity or class of dominant parents often goes unstated or assumed, with their everyday ways of participating in schools and everyday living as the normalized goal of such policies and practices.

Also critical to our understanding of the raciolinguistics behind parent engagement is examining how parents' participation in schools is described. In an interview, Vice Principal (V.P.), Sanchéz shared his concern that the Latinx families were not involved in the school like other parents:

> *I guess at this particular school it's not strong, the [Latinx] engagement's not strong. But we do have a small cohort of very committed parents and I think if [I'm] not mistaken that's [due to] some of the hard work in the elementary schools. Some of these parents have had some workshops on kind of leadership and kind of just engagement and have been involved in the ELACS[6] from elementary. The participation is coming to observe the school versus coming to question and see how we could improve their students' performance, if that makes sense. It's almost like – and I'm thinking of Back to School Night and I'm thinking of Open House – they come to kind of see versus coming to kind of question how could my kid do better, if that makes sense.*

Patterns of parent engagement behaviors across race/ethnicity and class are well documented in educational studies (Lareau, 2000; Lareau & Horvat, 1999). This idea of questioning and seeing how their children can do better is a middle-class way of being an involved parent. Seen as inadequate ways of engaging families of color (Auerbach, 2009), Traditional Parent Involvement Structures (TPIS) such as Back-to-School Night and the Parent Teacher Association (PTA) ignore the inherent white, middle-class behavior norms in these school-sanctioned practices (Cooper, 2009). Though not stated explicitly, V.P. Sanchéz is comparing the Latinx families to the middle-class (mostly) white families that make up the other half of the program.

Interestingly, the leader of the small cohort of 'committed parents' V.P. Sanchéz refers to was an immigrant mother from Mexico who happened to be the English Language Advisory Council (ELAC) president at the elementary school before her daughter transitioned to Cooper for middle school. Justa (her self-selected pseudonym that means *just* or *fair* in Spanish) attended a district-level training for her leadership position, so therefore had a sophisticated understanding of the federal educational policies that support the committee. For example, she knew how the annual funding was expected to be spent to support English learners and their teachers and the classification process of English learning dictated by the California Department of Education. Though she started engaging at Cooper Academy in middle-class ways, it is important to note that there were several experiences at the school that discouraged her to participate in the 'school-sanctioned' ways like she did when her daughter was in elementary school. For one, she felt that the middle school ELAC functioned differently than the one at the elementary school. She shared:

> *Yo vine a dos juntas y me di cuenta que no vi mucho interés en mi o que no estaba la información. Estábamos enfocados en otras cosas que quizás yo como madre no me interesaban. Porque yo quería saber como, Guadalupe es aprendiz de inglés, yo necesitaba escuchar en algo que le ayudará a mi hija. Y yo no estaba escuchando eso. Yo estaba escuchando que vamos a hacer para Cinco de Mayo, que vamos a hacer cuando los niños se gradúen. Entonces yo como madre de una hija de aprendiz de inglés, para mi, no era algo interesante estar escuchando eso. Yo quería que me dijeran que o miran los niños que no pasaron el examen, les vamos a ayudar con tutoría o vamos a ver en que es lo que salieron mal para poderles reforzar. Eso es lo que quería escuchar.* [I came to two meetings and I realized that I didn't see much interest in me or that there wasn't the information. We were focused on other things that maybe as a mother didn't interest me. Because I wanted to know how, Guadalupe is an English Learner, I needed to hear something that would help my daughter. I was not hearing that. I was hearing about what we were going to do for Cinco de Mayo, what we will do when the children graduate. Then as a mother of a daughter that is an English Learner, for me, it wasn't interesting to be listening to that. I wanted for them to tell me or look at the children that didn't pass the exam, we are going to help them with tutoring or let's see in what they did poorly for them to reinforce. That is what I wanted to hear.]

Justa expressed how the middle school ELAC functioned as a mechanism to get Latinx parents to plan cultural celebrations for the school community rather than focusing on the academic achievement of the students still classified as 'English Learners.' This contrasted from her ELAC experience at the elementary school. Indeed, inherent in the name 'English Learner' Advisory Committee is a marginalized and narrow perspective of what these parents can and should do as they are involved in schools.

EL as a raciolinguistic label that indexes immigrant, non-English and often Latinx, pigeonholes parents into a pathway of involvement that can commodify them as the immigrant other in the business of doing school (Hernandez, 2013).

Another example of raciolinguistics at work is when Justa referred to students and families in the TWI program using raciolinguistic descriptors that index the 'type' of student in the program – a native English or Spanish speaker. Specifically, she explained her frustration with the double-standard around state testing for the students in the program determined by their nationality.

> *¿Por qué a los niños que están en inmersión y hablan inglés – los americanos – no le hacen el test en español? Nada más se los hacen a los latinos?* [Why are the children that are in immersion and speak English – the Americans – don't take the test in Spanish? They only make the Latinos.]

Here Justa used 'American' as a proxy for the white, middle-class students, illustrating how 'whiteness has become the unspoken and profound sense of what it means to be American, thereby Othering all other racialized identities' (Leitner, 2012: 830). Discursively, Justa positioned her daughter as less American, though she is a US citizen – a raciolinguistic example of how she understands that her daughter's first language and EL status render her a racialized Other (Flores & Rosa, 2015), who happens to also be over-tested because of this status (Hernandez, 2017; Zacher Pandya, 2011). That is, in the context of US labeling and subgroup testing festishes, her daughter's home language and ethnic background make her the prototypical (Latinx) English Learner that in this context conveys immigrant non-American status. The discourse around dual language programs reproduces narratives of Spanish speakers as (Latinx) immigrants and the English speakers as Americans, providing a one-to-one correlation between language and national identity, though we know many Spanish-speaking students are born in the US, including Justa's daughter. Justa's daughter was in middle school at the time of the study and was just as much an English speaker as she was a Spanish speaker. Justa provides a sociopolitical critique of the double standards inherent in testing practices that pathologize English learning and celebrate Spanish acquisition for 'los americanos' that is never heard by school officials. As a racialized subject and immigrant Other in this context, Justa is no longer an 'involved parent' in the business of doing US public schooling.[7] For Justa, though she was seen as an advocate and leader in her daughter's elementary school, she was positioned differently at the middle school. Her voice, and the voices of other Latinx parents, were muted in the middle school ELAC, a space that was designated by the federal government through high-stakes educational policies for parents like themselves to have decision-making rights, but ultimately became a space for them to focus on 'food, fun, and fiesta.' The use of axes of differentiation (i.e. race, class, immigration, EL status, etc.) to name and frame educational practices undoubtedly shaped the experiences of the families participating in Cooper's TWI program.

TWI and Privileged Parents' Request for Within-school Segregation

This second case shares data from Hoover Elementary, a school located in an urban district in southern California that also serves racially and economically diverse families but does not strategically desegregate like the northern California district. Unlike Cooper Academy that had an established TWI program well before the study began, Hoover Elementary was just starting its TWI program at the time of this second case study. Everything appeared to be moving forward smoothly to support the reopening of a once English-only public school to a dual language bilingual school that would offer a TWI program at Hoover. The school would start out with a TWI dual language strand (at least one bilingual classroom per grade level – K-2) and would eventually become a fully bilingual school in three years. With a 90/10 model, the goal was for all students to graduate with bilingualism and biliteracy in Spanish and English. While the school was able to successfully follow through with this program plan, the first year was a bumpy road for the administrators and teachers. This case examines ways in which parents were involved in school matters during the first year of implementation of this new TWI program at Hoover Elementary. Interviews with the school's principal and PTA resident reveal the tensions experienced between a group of parents and the district/school leadership during the first year of the program that made it a challenging start to program implementation.

Directora Martínez has decades of experience in education with roles as a teacher, teacher coach and, more recently, as an administrator. Her belief in dual language programs for language minoritized students influenced her decision to become a principal at a school in her district that was to become a fully bilingual, TWI school. District leadership complained that the local charter school was taking many of their students because of the dual language program they offered. With her charge to turn one current school into a TWI school, Directora Martínez had her work cut out for her. For one, there was a one-way dual language strand within a school in the district and parents of these students would need to move their children to this new two-way school from another part of the city. These parents were asked to enroll their children in Hoover Elementary so that their children could continue to receive a bilingual education because their school would no longer offer one.

It was noted early on in the year that a group of parents from the one-way dual language school that was closed were not happy with this change. Señora López, the bilingual PTA president, shared why the parents who transferred to Hoover were upset:

> That first year, from what I understand these parents were upset about, was the fact that, one, they wanted all of their children to stay together, in these classrooms… that they had been promised that they would stay in the classroom together, that the continuity of those children would stay. So that group would always be a group. I don't know if they thought, just in a classroom or what? And [that was] the only thing that I could think of that was different you know, cause I had conversations with them. Like, 'I don't understand, like what's the big problem? What is so difficult? They kept a 90/10 model the way your school was when you came. Right? The only thing that's different with this model is that instead of it being a one-way model it is now a two-way model, meaning that there are children fluent in Spanish or fluent in English, right?' So that was the only difference and the only mix, which I felt was great.

Señora López began her narrative explaining that the main reason this particular group of parents was upset with the new program was because they wanted their children to stay together as one group in the new school. This would be impossible in a TWI program. Many people, including families in dual language programs, are unaware of the various model types under the dual language umbrella. The confusion often lies between the language use percentages and student population. While language of instruction allocations such as 90/10 and 50/50 refer to the language use during the school day, two-way and one-way refers to the student population; that is, a model that serves two different student groups or one student group in terms of language fluency (Baker & Wright, 2017). Whether or not the parents realize the differences in model types, a parallel program was what they appeared to be asking for – a one-way approach for their children and a two-way for other people's children. It is not rare for privileged parents to advocate and sometimes outright demand special treatment for their children, and in this case, this group of middle-class parents was making noise to voice their concerns and the stipulations that they believed their children were entitled.

She continued:

> …the other issue, and maybe I am more understanding in this way. They were upset about details within the way the school was created – you know, 'Why did they pick that site? Why in that area?' You know because it is not the best area of Riverpoint. They didn't like that all of the resources weren't ready and going. They felt that there was a lot of stuff being created as the program went and their children were the guinea pigs in it.

Her commentary reveals other issues that made them upset, most noteworthy is the fact that these parents seemed apprehensive about the school's location and were not happy about bringing their children to this part of town. The demographic landscape of the city, similar to other parts of the region, is highly segregated. In the city of Riverpoint, there are differences between the resources in the center of town and the outskirts of the city. There is a plethora of research in social psychology demonstrating that perceived threat – particularly around the loss of valued resources, whether realistic or symbolic – can be associated with different ethnoracial groups and is thought to trigger negative reactions by one group towards another (Richeson & Sommers, 2016). Hoover Elementary is located along the low-income margin part of town and it appeared that these privileged parents did not want to be integrated with a community of low-income status. The maintenance of this type of group dominance and comfort is achieved through a variety of mechanisms. DiAngelo (2011) explains the comfort of segregation as part of white fragility dynamics where race-based stress can be avoided.

> Whites consistently choose and enjoy racial segregation. Living, working, and playing in racial segregation is unremarkable as long as it is not named or made explicitly intentional….I posit that it is the intentionality that is so disquieting – as long as we don't mean to separate, as long as it 'just happens' that we live segregated lives, we can maintain a (fragile) identity of racial innocence. (DiAngelo, 2011: 62)

White Americans' preference for living in relatively segregated neighborhoods is well documented (Richeson & Sommers, 2016), and this ingroup favoritism is a form of discrimination that helps maintain the status quo and racial disparities in the country. Directora Martínez added some clarity to the integration issue in her interview, sharing candidly:

> *The primary challenge there was that people were uprooted from their community, their school, to go to the school of 'those kids,' the school on the other side of the [town]. Era un clash económico totalmente, era no necesariamente blanco porque había unos Latinos ahí, pero era la mentalidad blanca totalmente menospreciando la riqueza cultural que se había creado en nuestra escuela. Era como 'Por qué mis niños van estar con esos niños? Can we have our own classrooms? Can we have our own teachers? Can they not mix?' And it was always very directed, it was never like, 'Oh let me just put it this way to see if she can infer.' No, 'Can we have separate classrooms? Why are our kids mixed with those kids? Why are we coming to the ghetto to get something we signed up for three years ago?'*[8]

In this interview excerpt, Martínez shares candidly how parents from the one-way dual language school were not shy about expressing their discontent with their children's transition to Hoover Elementary for several reasons. First and foremost, Hoover was on the other side of town, but what first appears to be a larger issue of being uprooted from one school and dealing with change, parents go deeper into the dissatisfaction with the integration across class status for families in the TWI program. Martínez refers to the issue as an 'economic clash' happening at the school in which white and Latinx families of a middle- to upper-class status were interacting with low-income, mostly Latinx families that were served on Hoover's side of town. By speaking up against the district and the school, these parents were requesting to be segregated in the school so that their English-dominant speaking children did not have to mix with the Spanish-dominant speaking children. Ultimately, they were lamenting the social process of integration that is part and parcel of the two-way model, while simultaneously racializing (im)migrant families in this TWI space which ultimately defends white privilege and culture (Leitner, 2012), supporting social, spatial and geographical segregation. Kobayashi and Peake (2000: 393) explain the process of racialization as:

> ...the material processes and the ideological consequences of the construction of 'race' as a means of differentiating, and valuing, 'white' people above those of color... 'Racialization' is therefore the process by which racialized groups are identified, given stereotypical characteristics, and coerced into specific living conditions, often involving social/spatial segregation and always constituting racialized places. It is one of the most enduring and fundamental means of organizing society.

Additionally, the parents bemoaned having to leave their safe space that is socially and geographically distant from the school's location in the 'ghetto,' indexing a hegemonic class ideology that simultaneously racializes communities and languages. As Kobayashi and Peake (2000) remind us, racialization always has a specific geography, and all geographies are racialized (2000: 395). Directora Martínez also points out that this white mentality, which she clarified was held by some of the Latinx parents as well, is why the parents were looking down upon the cultural wealth the school had created, in large part because of the diverse, mostly minoritized student population. In her commentary, Martínez illustrates her awareness of raciolinguistic work and provides an example of raciolinguistics at work. Clear here is that ideologies of whiteness are mediated by other axes of social differentiation, including ethnic background, class and language. When we understand that whiteness is not skin-color, but rather 'a constellation of processes and practices rather than as a discrete entity' (DiAngelo, 2011: 56) then we can accurately locate it in social position (Ignatiev, 1997). Therefore, it is evident that race and class intersect in the production of white ideologies in TWI settings through the ongoing, dynamic nature of discursive relationships in a racialized/classed society. Increasing diversity in the US and within TWI programs can foster an increase in white fragility, opportunity hoarding and integrated schools without the actual integration of communities.

Important to highlight as well in Martínez's interview excerpt is the significance in the use of the demonstratives 'those/esos' which point to a certain kind of 'kids/niños.' She states that the parents were not happy about going to the same school with 'those kids' and then reinforces the idea when she states it again in Spanish ¿*Por qué mis niños van estar con esos niños*? As a linguistic tool with indexical power (Silverstein, 2003) that encodes context (Levinson, 1983), 'those' allows the privileged parents to index race and class in their comments without explicating naming these axes of differentiation. That it, the parents are able to *encode* 'low-income' and 'Latinx' into one word (i.e. those) so that the principal can *decode* meaning successfully. As Martínez was able to successfully understand what was being conveyed in the parents' comments, she interpreted the sentiment as a white mentality/ideology. Though the parents were of different racial backgrounds, they shared a middle-class status that was taken up to advance their agenda of segregation via an ideology that articulated and reproduced hegemonic whiteness, ultimately increasing their social distance from the racialized Spanish-speaking students and their families. Leitner (2012: 830) affirms that 'this politics of belonging is simultaneously a politics about cultural and racial boundaries, boundaries of place and entitlements to economic and political resources. All these elements contribute to defining the boundaries between the "we" and "them" and are at stake in these struggles.'

Putting her focus on other parents in the school community 'that wanted to be there,' as Señora López mentioned in her interview, she explained how she would walk and talk to people outside of the school campus as part of her networking to get more parents involved. In the interview she shared:

> *That was something I did a lot of my first year of PTA because I knew there was a large community that didn't understand what PTA was, didn't understand what it meant to help a school…A lot of parents would tell me in Spanish, 'It's because I can't help them. I don't know the language. Or I can't help at the school because I don't know the language.' I try to really help those parents that felt like, 'Oh, I can't because I don't speak English. I can't be important in the school or a leader in my school because I don't speak English.'*

Señora López shared how she actively tried to get Spanish-speaking parents involved in the PTA and the school, working to convince them that they bring valuable skills to the table. Consider the distinction between Señora López's comment above about the Spanish-speaking parents at Hoover and Maestra Stevenson's statement about the English speakers at Cooper referenced in the first case: *Because the English speakers [parents] who are kind of brave enough and willing to go for it, I think already have a lot of confidence that they can support their kid in a second language. Either they feel that either they already know some Spanish or they feel confident academically themselves.* Yet, parents with linguistic and cultural capital in Spanish in this TWI setting have to be convinced that they have something to offer the school and their children's educational experience, while middle-class English-speaking parents are convinced they should have the principal's ear to suggest institutional changes to a program model that inherently integrates students and families. In the context of TWI, the same behavior – choosing to participate in a TWI program – is seen vastly different by the language and skin one speaks (Delpit & Dowdy, 2002). That is, agency attribution is dependent on multiple axes of social differentiation so that parents are positioned as either active or passive in their children's educational experiences, regardless of the type or quality of the engagement.

Raciolinguistic Ideologies Interest with Class Among TWI Stakeholders

The discourse surrounding parents and students related to educational matters inherently engages class and race whether it is stated explicitly or coded in language covertly in TWI contexts and beyond. The system is structured to highlight and mute certain aspects of linguistic, racial/ethnic and class identities. In the first case shared in this chapter, there was a sharp contrast between the way that parents were spoken about in a social justice-informed TWI program, influenced by the ideologies behind axes of social differentiation. The notable differences when asked an open-ended question about demographics revealed pervasive reductionist notions of personhood (e.g. *the immigrant other, the English Learner*), particularly surrounding minoritized students and families. Though Maestra Stevenson was asked to speak about the demographics of the students in the bilingual program, she utilized very distinct descriptors depending on which group of students she was referring to – the Spanish or the English speakers. She used labels of axes of differentiation to largely describe the demographics of the Latinx families, but used mostly descriptors of virtues when describing the largely white, middle-class families that made up the other side of the two-way program. Perhaps these raciolinguistic and hegemonic class ideologies influenced educational practices at the school, thus impacting the ways in which parents, such as Justa, chose to visibly be involved (or not) in school business.

The second TWI case highlights the ways in which one school, under the leadership of a bilingual Latina principal, negotiated the complaints of privileged parents who believed the school was not doing its job in educating their children. They were concerned with the allocation of resources, the use of classroom space, and blatantly, the mixing of children. At Hoover Elementary, some parents were intentional with their desire to have their children remain segregated from a community with which they felt they were forced to integrate in order to secure bilingualism for their own children, ultimately with the goal of operating two different programs – one for 'our' children and one for 'those' children. This reality demonstrates how educational integration is much more than just inhabiting the same space. This case also complicates our understanding of raciolinguistic ideologies, as the notion of 'our children' and 'those children' was expressed by more than just white parents at the school. Some Latinx parents also expressed this 'white mentality' that Martínez describes. That is, the performance of whiteness as belonging to white bodies muddles the one-to-one mapping of raciolinguistic ideologies, because in this space, privilege was performed by middle-class Latinx parents as well. It is essential to recognize that race and class are not neatly disentangled and the historical reproduction of a classed Whiteness (Spanierman *et al.*, 2013) is a reality in the US.

As illustrated across the two cases, competing discourses on parent engagement and participation in schools exist in TWI programs and are raciolinguistically coded. On the one hand, schools expect all parents to play an active role in their children's education. V.P. Sanchéz expressed his desire for the Latinx parents in the middle school program to become more involved in school sanctioned-ways while, ironically, Justa slowly withdrew as an 'involved parent.' Maestra Stevenson shared her belief that middle-class white parents were committed to their children's education in a way not possible by the (im)migrant parents that didn't know the educational system. Directora Martínez noted how middle-class parents expressed a white mentality that contradicted the efforts of the TWI program to integrate students and foster appreciation for their efforts to integrate children and families and celebrate multiculturalism in authentic ways. PTA President López shared how privileged parents expressed their disappointment with the TWI program and advocated for changes while she actively tried to convince Spanish-speaking Latinx parents that they belonged and were capable of being a valuable contributor to the school. These cases illustrate the hierarchies of cultural privilege (Motha, 2014) and how ideologies of personhood tied to language, race/ethnicity, class and immigration/citizenship status intersect to create binary ways of being and participating in TWI programs – the Americans and the Latinos, the English speakers and the Spanish speakers, the involved parents and the uninvolved parents, those children and our children. Some are overtly stated and others are covert in nature but equally present. It is clear that parental privilege and marginalization is recognized, resisted, or reinforced by school administration as evident in the competing discourses about parent participation present in both TWI cases. These raciolinguistic and class-based discourses and ideologies reflect power dynamics across axes of differentiation that can bring about challenges and explicitly and implicitly send mixed messages to parents across racial/ethnic and class lines. The analysis of these competing discourses on parents necessitate the understanding that race is sociolinguistically constructed and ideologies surrounding TWI programs are naturally racialized and class-based as mirrors of larger societal forces.

As race and language are co-naturalized for marginalized positions in the business of doing school (Rosa & Flores, 2017), the power of class status further reproduces these particular subject positions and these ethnoracial and linguistic identities within TWI contexts. The ethnoracial makeup of the community where 'that school' is located or of the students categorized as 'those children' is not about race/ethnicity alone. We also need to investigate phenomena that do not neatly fit into existing criteria and examine how individuals navigate the raciolinguistic landscape of TWI and other educational settings. We must consider class and immigration/migration in our understanding of raciolinguistic realities to continue to analyze the interconnected and confounding nature of language and race, while attending to other systems of social difference such as class, nationality and immigration status that play important roles. As evident in this chapter, these notions of personhood impact the attributed agency of parents, that is, their participation in educational practices, ones which reside in the home and by presence or performance in school-sanctioned routines and activities. Parents' attributed agency is ultimately stratified by language, class and race. That is, parents as agents in education are facilitated or undermined by these axes of social difference. Recognizing the myriad ways that identities intersect will undoubtedly influence moments of inclusion and exclusion for students in becoming bilingual and parents in becoming involved. To address equity for language minoritized students, any analysis of dual language education, particularly TWI programs, must interrogate the raciolinguistic and sociopolitical characteristics of the educational context in the planning, implementation and evaluation of such models, and especially as they consider family and parent engagement policies and practices.

Notes

(1) I use the term Latinx instead of Latino/Latina as a gender nonbinary pan-ethnic marker of identity.
(2) The racial ideology that one does not see or acknowledge race is traditionally referred to as 'color-blind' though I utilize what Annamma *et al.*'s (2017) term 'color-evasiveness,' because it 'resists positioning people with disabilities as problematic as it does not partake in dis/ability as a metaphor for undesired' (2017: 153).
(3) As opposed to the era of restrictive language policy after Proposition 227 passed in 1998, California's policy changes promoted 'multilingualism' as a goal for all students in a global economy through initiatives such as the Seal of Biliteracy, the passing of Proposition 58, and Global California 2030. See Katznelson and Bernstein (2017) for an unpacking of the discursive shift and rebranding of bilingual education in California.
(4) The names of schools, districts, and educational stakeholders are pseudonyms.
(5) See Hernandez (2017) for an interrogation of the ideology 'all language learners' in dual language education.
(6) The *English Learner Advisory Committee* (ELAC) is a group of parents, staff, and community members specifically designated to advise school officials on English Learner (EL) program services as mandated by the US Department of Education.

Parents of English Learners from each school that receives federal funding to support EL programing are required to participate in the committee to be in federal compliance.
(7) See Hernandez (2013) for documentation of Justa's complex parent involvement journey.
(8) To maintain the sentiment in Martínez's account, I did not translate into English any of her expressions in Spanish. She translanguaged between English and Spanish as many bilinguals do when speaking with other bilinguals (García, 2009).

References

Alfaro, C. and Bartolomé, L. (2019) Preparing ideologically clear bilingual teachers to recognize linguistic geniuses. In B.R. Berriz, A.C. Wagner and V.M. Poey. (eds) *Art as a Way of Talking for Emergent Bilingual Youth: A Foundation for Literacy in PreK-12 Schools* (pp. 44–59). New York, NY: Routledge.

Alim, H.S. (2016) Introducing raciolinguistics: Racing language and languaging race in hyperracial times. In H. Alim, J. Rickford and A. Ball (eds) *Raciolinguistics: How Language Shapes Our Ideas About Race* (pp. 1–30). New York: Oxford University Press.

Alim, H.S., Rickford, J. and Ball, A. (eds) (2016) *Raciolinguistics: How Language Shapes our Ideas about Race*. New York: Oxford University Press.

Annamma, S.A., Jackson, D.D. and Morrison, D. (2017) Conceptualizing color-evasiveness: Using dis/ability critical race theory to expand a color-blind racial ideology in education and society. *Race Ethnicity and Education* 20 (2), 147–162.

Auerbach, S. (2009) Walking the walk: Portraits in leadership for family engagement in urban schools. *School Community Journal* 19 (1), 9–31.

Baker, C. and Wright, W.E. (2017) *Foundations of Bilingual Education and Bilingualism* (6th edn). Bristol: Multilingual Matters.

Baquedano-López, P., Hernandez, S. and Alexander, R.A. (2014) Thinking through the decolonial turn in research and praxis in Latina/o parent involvement: Advancing new understandings of the home-school relation. In P.R. Portes, S. Salas, P. Baquedano López and P. Mellom (eds) *US Latinos and Education Policy: Research-based Directions for Change* (pp. 16–34). New York: Routledge.

Bourdieu, P. (1986) The forms of capital. In J. Richardson (ed.) *Handbook of Theory and Research for the Sociology of Education* (pp. 241–258). New York: Greenwood.

Bowles, S. and Gintis, H. (1976) *Schooling in Capitalist America: Education Reform and the Contradictions of Economic Life*. New York: Basic Books Inc.

Cervantes-Soon, C.G., Dorner, L., Palmer, D., Heiman, D., Schwerdtfeger, R. and Choi, J. (2017) Combating inequalities in two-way language immersion programs: Toward critical consciousness in bilingual education spaces. *Review of Research in Education* 41, 403–427.

Collier, V.P. and Thomas, W.P. (2004) The astounding effectiveness of dual language education for all. *NABE Journal of Research and Practice* 2 (1), 1–20.

Cooper, C.W. (2009) Parent involvement, African American mothers, and the politics of educational care. *Equity & Excellence in Education* 42 (4), 379–394.

Crenshaw, K. (1991) Mapping the margins: Intersectionality, identity politics, and violence against women of color. *Stanford Law Review* 43 (6), 1241–1299.

de Carvalho, M.E. (2001) *Rethinking Family–School Relations: A Critique of Parental Involvement in Schooling*. Mahwah, NJ: Lawrence Erlbaum Associates.

Delpit, L. and Dowdy, J.K. (eds) (2002) *The Skin that we Speak: Thoughts on Language and Culture in the Classroom*. New York: New Press.

DiAngelo, R. (2011) White fragility. *International Journal of Critical Pedagogy* 3 (3), 54–70.

Epstein, J.L. (1992) School and family partnerships. In M. Alkin (ed.) *Encyclopedia of Educational Research* (pp. 1139–1151). New York, NY: Macmillan.

Fine, M. (1993) [Ap]parent involvement: Reflections on parents, power, and urban public schools. *Teachers College Record* 94, 682–710.

Flores, N. (2016) A tale of two visions: Hegemonic whiteness and bilingual education. *Educational Policy* 30, 13–38.

Flores, N. and Rosa, J. (2015) Undoing appropriateness: Raciolinguistic ideologies and language diversity in education. *Harvard Educational Review* 85, 149–171.

Frankenberg, E., Garces, L.M. and Hopkins, M. (eds) (2016) *School Integration Matters: Research-based Strategies to Advance Equity*. New York, NY: Teachers College Press.

Gándara, P. and Contreras, F. (2009) *The Latino Education Crisis: The Consequences of Failed Social Policies*. Cambridge, MA: Harvard University Press.

Gándara, P. (2010) Overcoming triple segregation. *Educational Leadership* 68: 60–64.

García, O. (2009) *Bilingual Education in the 21st Century: A Global Perspective*. Malden, MA: Wiley Blackwell.

Garver, R. (2016) Segregation in segregated schools. In E. Frankenberg, L.M. Garces and M. Hopkins (eds) (pp. 121–134). *School Integration Matters: Research-based Strategies to Advance Equity*. New York, NY: Teachers College Press.

Hernandez, S.J. (2013) When institutionalized discourses become familial: Mexican immigrant families interpreting and enacting high stakes educational reform. Unpublished doctoral dissertation, University of California, Berkeley.

Hernandez, S. (2017) Are they all language learners?: Educational labeling and raciolinguistic identifying in a middle school dual language program. *CATESOL Journal* 29 (1), 133–154.

Hopkins, M. (2016) Advancing equity through integration from pre-K to higher education. In E. Frankenberg, L. M. Garces and M. Hopkins (eds) *School Integration Matters: Research Based Strategies to Advance Equity* (pp. 1–7). New York, NY: Teachers College Press.

Ignatiev, N. (1997) The point is not to interpret whiteness but to abolish it. Paper presented at the Making and Unmaking of Whiteness. UC Berkeley.

Katznelson, N. and Bernstein, K. (2017) Rebranding bilingualism: The shifting discourses of language education policy in California's 2016 election. *Linguistics and Education* 40: 11–26.

Kobayashi, A. and Peake, L. (2000) Racism out of place: Thoughts on whiteness and an antiracist geography in the new millennium. *Annals of the Association of American Geographer* 90 (2), 392–403.

Lareau, A. (2003) *Unequal Childhoods: Class, Race, and Family Life*. Berkeley, CA: University of California Press.

Lareau, A. and Horvat, E.M. (1999) Moments of social inclusion and exclusion: Race, class and cultural capital in family-school relationships. *Sociology of Education* 72 (1), 37–53.

Leitner, H. (2012) Spaces of encounters: Immigration, race, class, and the politics of belonging in small-town America. *Annals of the Association of American Geographers* 102 (4), 828–846.

Levinson, S.C. (1983) *Pragmatics*. Cambridge: Cambridge University Press.

Mapp, K.L. (2012) Title I and parent involvement: Lessons from the past, recommendations for the future. The Center for American Progress and the American Enterprise Institute for Public Policy Research. See http://www.americanprogress.org/issues/issues/ 2012/03/pdf/titleI_parental_invovlement.pdf

Motha, S. (2014) *Race, Empire, and English Language Teaching: Creating Responsible and Ethical Anti-Racist Practice*. New York, NY: Teachers College Press.

Orellana, M.F. (2009) *Translating Childhoods: Immigrant Youth, Language and Culture*. New Brunswick, NJ: Rutgers University Press.

Orfield, G. and Lee, C. (2006) *Racial Transformation and the Changing Nature of Segregation*. Cambridge, MA: The Civil Right Project at Harvard University.

Pollock, M. (2004) *Colormute: Race Talk Dilemmas in An American High School*. Princeton, NJ: Princeton University Press.

Posey, L. (2012). Middle- and upper middle-class parent action for urban public schools: Promise or paradox? *Teachers College Record* 114: 1–43.

Richeson, J.A. and Sommers, S.R. (2016) Toward a social psychology of race and race relations for the twenty-first century. *Annual Review of Psychology* 67: 439–63

Rosa, J. and Flores, N. (2017) Unsettling race and language: Toward a raciolinguistic perspective. *Language in Society* 46 (5), 621–647.

Rios-Aguilar, C., Kiyama J., Gravitt, M. and Moll, L. (2011) Funds of knowledge for the poor and forms of capital for the rich?: A capital approach to examining funds of knowledge. *Theory and Research in Education* 9 (2), 163–184.

Silverstein, M. (2003) Indexical order and the dialectics of sociolinguistic life. *Language & Communication* 23 (3–4), 193–229.

Spanierman, L.B., Garriott, P.O. and Clark, D.A. (2013) Whiteness and social class: Intersections and implications. In W. Ming Liu (ed.) *Oxford Library of Psychology. The Oxford Handbook of Social Class in Counseling* (pp. 394–410). New York, NY: Oxford University Press.

Valdés, G. (1996) *Con Respeto: Bridging the Distances Between Culturally Diverse Families and School*. New York: Teachers College Press.

Valdés, G. (1997) Dual-language immersion programs: A cautionary note concerning the education of language-minority students. *Harvard Educational Review* 67: 391–429.

Valdés, G. (2003). *Expanding Definitions of Giftedness: The Case of Young Interpreters From Immigrant Communities*. Mahwah, NJ: Lawrence Erlbaum Associates.

Valdés, G. (2018) Analyzing the curricularization of language in two-way immersion education: Restating two cautionary notes. *Bilingual Research Journal* 41 (4), 388–412.

Valdez, V.E., Freire, J.A. and Delavan, M. (2016) The gentrification of dual language education. *Urban Review* 48: 601.

Valenzuela, A. (1999). *Subtractive Schooling: US-Mexican Youth and the Politics of Carin*. Albany, New York: State University of New York Press.

Williams, C. (2017, December 28) The Intrusion of White Families into Bilingual Schools. *The Atlantic*. See https://www.theatlantic.com/education/archive/2017/12/the-middle-class-takeover-of-bilingual-schools/549278/

Yin, R.K. (2013) *Case Study Research: Design and Methods* (5th edn) Thousand Oaks, CA: SAGE Publications.

Yosso, T.J. and Solórzano, D.G. (2006) Leaks in the Chicana and Chicano educational pipeline. *UCLA Chicano Studies Research Center*. Latino Policy & Issues Brief, No. 13.

Zacher Pandya, J. (2011) *Overtested: How High-Stakes Accountability Fails English Language Learners*. New York, NY: Teachers College Press.

6 Helping or Being Helped? The Influence of Raciolinguistic Ideologies on Parental Involvement in Dual Immersion

Jazmín A. Muro

Introduction

Melissa, an immigrant mother from Mexico, had two children enrolled at Samuelson Elementary, a Spanish/English dual immersion school in the greater Los Angeles area. Though parental involvement was expected, and most parents were involved with a variety of activities on campus, Melissa was rare in that she was both a member of the Parent Teacher Association (PTA) and the English Language Advisory Council (ELAC) at the school. As a member of both groups, Melissa helped organize events, lead meetings and was well known at the school. Given her regularity on campus and reputation with other parents, Melissa had much to share about the parental involvement at Samuelson. When asked about the PTA and ELAC, she shared how they were 'Igual, es lo mismo' (Same, it is the same). But, after I asked her why they had two organizations, she explained:

> Melissa: Hay dos diferentes porque ELAC se encarga de, no solo es para los Latinos si no es para todos, pues para informar a la gente. Es mas para informar a la gente ELAC. ELAC se encarga de informar a la gente y traer a gente para que les pueda ayudar por ejemplo programas a donde puedan ir los niños gratis o doctores a donde puedan ir. O por ejemplo padres que les ayudan a hablar ingles.
> JM: ¿Clases?
> Melissa: Así. De eso se trata ELAC. Y PTA se encarga de recaudar fondos.
> JM: Mhm.¿Y quienes son miembros?

Melissa:	Ahí es la persona que quiera, no es solamente nosotros Hispanoparlantes- es mas para nosotros hablantes en Español. Pero es cualquier miembro.
Melissa:	There are two different ones because ELAC is in charge of, it's not only for Latinos but for everyone, it's to inform people. It's more to inform the people of ELAC. ELAC is in charge of informing people and bringing people to help them, for example, programs where children can go for free, or doctors where they can go, or for example parents who they help to speak English.
JM:	Classes?
Melissa:	Yes, that is what ELAC is about. And PTA is responsible for raising funds.
JM:	Mhm. And who are the members?
Melissa:	Whoever wants, it is not just us Spanish speakers – it's more for us speakers in Spanish. But it's any member.

Though Melissa insisted that each organization was open to anyone from any racial/ethnic or linguistic background, her comments show her hesitation to commit to one term, despite her acknowledgement that ELAC comprised mostly Spanish speakers. Her explanation illustrates the often complicated way parents and teachers discussed the parent organizations on campus —alluding to racial/ethnic, linguistic and even socioeconomic differences without explicitly stating that the PTA was mostly white parents, locally referred to as 'English doms,' and ELAC was mostly Latinx[1] parents, known at Samuelson as 'Spanish doms.' This careful dance of using language as a proxy for other racial and class markers often led to confusion among other parents on campus, with some asking if the PTA was for 'Americans' and the ELAC was for 'Latinos' (Muro, 2016) and the overall perception that the PTA and its members were 'helpers' to the school, whereas the ELAC and its members needed help from the school.

Existing research on parental involvement at schools highlights how schools tend to value white, middle-class modes of parental involvement (Lareau, 2000; Turney & Kao, 2009) and highlights the lack of non-white parents in formal parents organizations (Li & Fischer, 2017; Turney & Kao, 2009). Additionally, assumptions about languages and their speakers are well documented (Chaparro, 2018; Flores & Rosa, 2015; Rosa & Flores, 2017). But, little attention has been paid to the participation efforts of parents in dual immersion or parent's experiences in immersion more broadly. In this chapter, I examine the participatory patterns of Latinx parents like Melissa and non-Latinx white parents at a Spanish/English dual immersion school. Drawing from both interviews and participant observation at a dual immersion school in the greater Los Angeles area, I find that both Latinx and white parents participate actively, albeit separately, in parent organizations on campus. I show how parent participation on campus is a reflection of the common raciolinguistic ideologies held about 'Spanish doms' and 'English doms' and argue that these ideologies impact how service efforts are perceived at the school. I first show how these local labels function at the school and are perpetuated by both Latinx and white parents. Then, I demonstrate how these ideologies influence parent participation by analyzing how white parents are considered 'helpers' to the school, while Latinx parents are to be 'helped' by the school. Finally, I shed light on the heterogeneity of the Latinx and 'Spanish dom' community in order to complicate the dichotomy most dual immersion programs create and which most research continues. Centering parent experiences contributes to our overall understanding of the consequences of raciolinguistic ideologies and can aid in making dual immersion more equitable for students and their families.

Previous Research

Existing research demonstrates how race and language are often tied together, shaping perceptions of both Spanish and English speakers that can ultimately impact how their linguistic abilities are evaluated (Flores & Rosa, 2015; Rosa & Flores, 2017). Flores and Rosa (2015), for instance, detail how *raciolinguistic ideologies* explain why racialized speakers of particular languages are perceived as deficient in spite of their linguistic abilities and how people are 'positioned as speakers of prestige or nonprestige language varieties based not on what they actually do with language but, rather, how they are heard by the white listening subject' (c: 160). In later work, Rosa and Flores (2017) coin the term *raciolinguistic perspective* to examine how 'the ongoing rearticulation of colonial distinctions between populations and modes of communication that come to be positioned as more or less normatively European' (Rosa, 2018, c: 5). In other words, using a *raciolinguistic perspective* allows us to analyze the coupling of race and language and unpack the assumptions that those in power, in this case non-Latinx whites, hold and enact about both linguistic practices and their speakers. For Rosa (2018), this perspective allows him to illustrate to readers how the linguistic practices of Latinx people are 'construed from the perspective of hegemonically positioned White perceiving subjects' (c: 6). Ultimately, Rosa (2018) describes how these processes lead us to perceive language and race as so intertwined that race can be 'heard' and language can be 'seen.' For Latinx, this practice contributes to the idea that they are a homogenous group and erases the heterogeneity within the population.

Among students, these processes can impact how they are evaluated by educators and can also impact their identity formation and relationships with each other. For instance, Chaparro (2018) has coined the term *raciolinguistic socialization* to elucidate how children learn to 'naturalize [the] connections between ways of speaking and raced and classed backgrounds' that they experience in their own bilingual schooling (c: 2). She finds that the binary of 'Spanish dominant' or 'English dominant' does not adequately fit all speakers – particularly bilingual individuals whose linguistic practices do not fit either of these categories. Because of the connection between an individual's manner of speaking and race/ethnicity, these labels are imbued with evaluations of speaker's practices that may then play out in how students are categorized at the beginning of immersion but that also structure how they are evaluated as they progress through these programs. Often, these raciolinguistic ideologies paint Latinx student's bilingualism as deficient (Rosa & Flores, 2017) and, by extension, paint Latinxs as deficient students (Gándara & Contreras, 2009; Valenzuela, 1999). And while these studies highlight the significant impact these assumptions have on students, it is necessary to remember that students are not the only actors in schools. Teachers, administrators, school staff and students' parents are also a part of the school context and the ties between language, race and class may also influence how they are involved in their school communities.

For instance, we know that parental involvement is not accessible to all parents. Existing research on parental involvement suggests that parental involvement and student academic achievement is positively correlated (Epstein, 2001; Jeynes, 2010; Lareau, 2000). That is, the more that parents partake in the schooling of their children, the better children tend to do in school. But, activities that require significant time or money are not as welcoming to parents who are from marginalized communities including those who are low-income, people of color or immigrants (Posey-Maddox, 2012; Turney & Kao, 2009). According to a 2019 report by the Department of Education, the most commonly cited explanations for low involvement at school for parents included the inability to have time off from work, inconvenient meeting times, lack of child care and a lack of clear communication about what is happening at school. The lack of child care was most pronounced for Latinx families, and the number of Black families who felt that inconvenient meeting times were a barrier to school involvement was higher than for any other group. These results are in line with previous work that shows how parents in advantaged positions in terms of race, nativity and socioeconomic class have higher odds of participating in formal organizations and are more often recognized for their efforts (Jeynes, 2003; Lareau, 2000; Posey-Maddox, 2012). Language and linguistic practices can also play a role; for example, Turney and Kao (2009) demonstrate how a lack of English language ability may hinder immigrant parents from fully participating in their children's schools. For instance, how language abilities are perceived may play a part in how parents participate on campus.

Despite these obstacles, research examining the participation rates of Latinx parents finds that they are just as involved as non-Latinx white parents once you account for differences like educational attainment and class (Terriquez, 2012; Terriquez, 2013). In her nationally representative study of civic engagement, Terriquez finds that 'disparities in mother's educational attainment, rather than factors associated with their racial/ethnic identification, drive unequal patterns of school-based civic participation between Latinas and whites' (c: 676). Despite the barriers Latinx parents face, they do indeed participate in their children's schools. Not only this, studies find that participation for Latinx parents can be enhanced with increased representation in positions of power in parent organizations like the PTA (Shah, 2009) and that parental networks have a significant impact on parent involvement (Li & Fischer, 2017). This work highlights how connecting with other parents on campus can help bolster participation at schools, but, it is also possible that participation can increase parental networks. It also reminds us that how parents feel on campus and whom they know and see there can impact their own patterns of participation.

This chapter builds on previous work by examining the participatory patterns of Latinx and white parents in a Spanish/English dual immersion school in the greater Los Angeles area. Drawing from in-depth interviews and ethnography, I illustrate how both Latinx and white parents partake actively at school, though in segregated Parent Teacher Organizations (PTO). Participation from parents reflects the dominant raciolinguistic ideologies about Latinxs more broadly. These perceptions influence both how they understand their role at the school and how other perceive their efforts on campus. I show how white parents are considered 'helpers' to the school, while Latinx parents are to be 'helped' by the school. Ultimately, these raciolinguistic ideologies exacerbate the disparities in power and influence among dual immersion families.

Methodology and Site Description

Samuelson Elementary, the site of this study, is a K-5 Spanish/English dual immersion school that is located in the greater Los Angeles area and comprised racially/ethnically, socioeconomically and linguistically diverse families. Samuelson became a dual immersion program in the late 1980s in an effort to temper the racial/ethnic isolation at the school and utilize students' Spanish language abilities as an asset. During the time of this study, 2011–2013, Samuelson functioned as a language magnet and drew families all over the Los Angeles area. While some families at the school were part of the neighborhood, many had to obtain district permission to opt out of their 'home' schools and enroll at Samuelson. As a school, Samuelson aims to have equal proportions of native Spanish speakers and native English speakers and operates as a 90/10 model.[2] Approximately 63% of students at Samuelson identify as Hispanic/Latinx, 25% as non-Latinx white, 4% as African American, 2% as Asian and 7% identify as multiracial. About half of the students are categorized as English Language Learners (ELL) and half receive free/reduced lunch.[3] Samuelson is designated a Title 1[4] school because of the high amount of low-income families. Though I was not able to access cross-tabulated data of students by race and class, the principal and teachers relayed that most low-income families were of Latinx origin and that poor or working-class white families were rare. Most low-income families were Latinx immigrants and most US-born Latinxs and white families were middle class or affluent. Most families at Samuelson are of Mexican ancestry, but there were also parents from Latin American countries like Venezuela, Argentina, El Salvador and Peru. Because of this reason, the umbrella term 'Latinx' is used throughout this chapter.

This chapter draws from both ethnography and in-depth interviews. In total, I spent over 20 months conducting participant observation at Samuelson and completed 66 interviews with parents and employees at the school between 2010–2013. As a participant observer, I attended parent organization gatherings, helped with special events and fundraisers on campus and worked as a volunteer teacher's aide in several classrooms. From simple observation to reading to students for story time or helping set up for the annual festival, my role as a participant observer was dependent of the needs of the parents and teachers at Samuelson. As outlined in qualitative research methodology (Berg, 2001; Strauss & Corbin, 1998), I immediately took detailed field notes after each visit to the field, coded broadly for themes and used memos to analyze my data. Using Dedoose, a qualitative coding software, I initially coded for things like 'parent–staff interaction' and 'tensions between groups' and these codes became more specific with increased time in the field.

I also conducted a total of 66 interviews with 68 participants,[5] 42 Latinx origin parents and employees at the school, 19 with white parents or employees, three with parents that identified as Asian and two with African American parents. I recruited participants through contacts I made during the initial period of ethnography and via announcements about the study in meetings and the school newsletter. In order to recruit participants who were not as involved on campus or that had specific characteristics like dominant language, I also utilized snowball sampling where previous participants refer other possible interviewees (Berg, 2001). All interviews were audio recorded and transcribed verbatim. Most interviews took about an hour and most took place in respondent's homes, with a handful at local coffee shops, parks or participant's offices. All participants also completed a demographic information sheet asking about their racial/ethnic identification, children, education, occupation, family income and language(s) spoken.

Findings

As a school, Samuelson Elementary was unique in that parent involvement was high and regularly encouraged. In fact, administrators and teachers told parents that they should plan to spend 20 or so hours per year at the school volunteering or participating in school activities. In her regular update for parents Mrs Martell, the principal, explained how Samuelson needed parents to help out with events and in the classroom in order to supplement the existing resources at the school. Though there was no log or sheet to keep track of the hours each parent contributed, most parents were involved on campus in some way – including but not limited to helping in the classroom, attending and participating in parent teacher organizations and helping plan and execute events and fundraisers.

Though families at Samuelson Elementary are equally encouraged to participate on campus and share an interest in Spanish/English bilingualism, there are clear disparities in how parents participate on campus. Here, I first detail how common raciolinguistic ideologies about Latinx and white parents are deployed and perpetuated on campus by both Latinx and white families in how they use the local labels 'Spanish dom' and 'English dom.' I then describe how these ideologies impact the organizations that parents join and how their work is perceived as either helping the school or receiving help from the school. Finally, I end by problematizing the term 'Spanish dom' by illustrating the diversity within the label and the tensions among Latinx origin parents.

Raciolinguistic ideologies on campus

As a school with an explicit goal of enrolling equal proportions of native Spanish and English speakers, Samuelson has high level of racial/ethnic, socioeconomic status and linguistic diversity. On any given day, you can find wealthy families, low-income families, families from Mexico, Peru, France, parents who are doctors to parents who work as servers in local restaurants. Indeed, participants often mentioned the heterogeneity of the school and its population during interviews and expressed a pride in this diversity. For example, Lisandra, an immigrant mom from Peru, explained how 'Las personas que van aquí son gente de todo tipo... hay de todo, de todo, es una mixtura de todo aquí en esta comunidad' (The people who go here are people of all kinds...there is everything, everything, it's a mix of everything in this community). She elaborated:

> Yo pienso que no hay una clase determinada. Yo pienso que todos los niños vienen en diferentes estatus sociales y eso esta bien. Y todos los niños vienen de diferente tipo de razas, sudamericanos, centroamericanos, Europeos, americanos, de todas partes. No hay solamente uno en especifico. Claro que la mayoría de Latinos aquí son mexicanos y eso es obvio, no? Pero siento que hay una mezcla de varios países.
>
> I think there is no determined social class. I think that all children come from different social status and that's good. And all children come from different types of races–South Americans, Central Americans, Europeans, Americans, from all places. There is not just one specific [place]. Of

course, the majority of Latinos here are Mexicans and that is obvious, no? But I feel that there is a mixture of several countries.

While Lisandra and other parents were cognizant of the heterogeneity among families at the school, common raciolinguistic ideologies about Spanish speakers were evident at school and manifested in everyday interactions between students and families. For instance, the very labels that are used on campus to refer to the two largest communities are indicative of how these ideologies about Spanish speakers undergird perceptions at Samuelson. At Samuelson, it was common to hear about the two most prominent groups on campus as 'Spanish doms' for Spanish-dominant individuals and 'English doms' for English-dominant individuals. Though brief, these local labels were dense with assumptions. At Samuelson, these labels were used as shorthand to talk about the socioeconomic status, nativity, education and ethnoracial background of families on campus. For example, Celina, a US-born Latina mother, detailed how her son was able to enroll at Samuelson as a part of the lottery program. While she and some of her family spoke Spanish, she noted that her writing was 'horrible' and her son did not speak Spanish at home prior to enrolling in the dual immersion program. Because Samuelson aims to have equal proportions of native Spanish and native English speakers, students are evaluated on their language skills once they are accepted into the program and classified as either English dominant or Spanish dominant. Celina shared how her son was classified as 'American because he didn't speak Spanish. He understood Spanish, but speaking – he would say one word. He did not speak Spanish at all.' Scholars have critiqued the notion that individuals must be either/or in terms of bilingualism and the idea that there is an 'appropriate' way to be bilingual (Flores & Rosa, 2015), and yet, even dual immersion schools implement evaluation to categorize speakers. Celina notes that her son was classified as 'American' when the official term at the school is 'English dominant.' Her use of these terms as interchangeable signals the coupling of language and national origin. Though Celina was born in the US and speaks both English and Spanish, her comment implies that 'American' is a proxy or pseudonym for 'English dominant.'

Conflating race/ethnicity, national origin, socioeconomic class and language was not uncommon. In fact, the use of 'Spanish dom' as a stand in for working class/low income, immigrant and Latinx families was the norm at the school. Though I was not able to access cross-tabulated data of students by race and class, the principal and teachers relayed that most low-income families were of Latinx origin and that poor or working-class white families were rare. Most low-income families were Latinx immigrants and most US-born Latinxs and white families were middle class or affluent. Due to these patterns, socioeconomic status, language and race/ethnicity labels were often used interchangeably on campus – for instance, parents might refer to 'Spanish doms' but mean Spanish-dominant Latinx immigrant parents. This local label was also used often when talking about issues of class and whether or not 'Spanish doms' could afford particular activities. In one instance, Candace, the librarian and a former Samuelson parent, noted that yearly silent auctions at the school alienated Spanish-speaking parents because they could not afford to participate. She stated,

> I am not saying it was only the Latino parents that could not afford the items, because there are definitely some Latino families here that could afford it, but some of our families just could not buy what was being sold – so they just wouldn't come.

Though Candace claims that there are Latinx families who can afford the items for sale at the school auction, she first states that they are out of reach for 'Spanish-speaking' or Latinx parents. Candance illustrates how at Samuelson, Spanish speaker, Latinx and working-class status were tied together. Occasionally comments about class and income, or lack thereof, were used to avoid racial terminology and other times the connection between working class status and race were explicit. These language labels nod to racial/ethnic difference without having to use racial terms like Latinx and white explicitly, as parents at this site are aware of what racial/ethnic groups speak each language.

These understandings of 'Spanish dom' families were also affected by the recruitment efforts at the school for both the student population and for parents in organizations on campus. Though Samuelson became a dual immersion school to 'combat' the racial/ethnic isolation of mostly Latinx students in the neighborhood, the school had become very popular with non-Latinx families in the surrounding area. This, combined with the gentrification of the Samuelson neighborhood, contributed to lower numbers of native Spanish-speaking students. While students classified as English dominant had a wait list and lottery, families and employees at the school often described how difficult it was to enroll Spanish-dominant students. For instance, during an ELAC meeting with the principal, one of the co-presidents, Javier, a Latinx immigrant from Mexico, told members how important it was for the school and program to have students that speak Spanish in order to 'stay balanced.' Speaking in Spanish, Javier asks the members to invite Latinxs to bring their kids to Samuelson, stating 'quieren un grupo que hable español' (they want a group that speaks Spanish). The principal then added how 'hay muchos anglo-parlantes que quieren estar aquí pero necesitamos dos grupos para ser balanceados y completamente bilingües' (there are many English speakers who want to be here but we need two groups to be balanced and completely bilingual). Finally, Javier asked members to tell people they knew spoke Spanish – particularly people who worked or lived in the area. He added that there are many Latinx people in that work in nearby restaurants and hotels and that they could bring their kids, since they would be coming daily anyway.

This public exchange illustrates how for many, 'Spanish dom' is a synonym for Latinx and often working class. Note how Javier used the terms 'Latinx' and 'Spanish-speaking' interchangeably and then suggested to invite parents who work or live in the area but was clear in pointing out how many Latinxs in the area work in the service economy. Other parents also fell into using these terms as shorthand. During her interview, Gloria, a US-born Latina, explained:

> [The Westside] is a pretty expensive area to live in so sometimes a lot of the Latino families can't afford to live here. You know, that's why we can't get a lot of these kids…although a lot of people do not know but if you work here you are also able to go to a [Westside] school.

Gloria, like many other parents at Samuelson, spoke about the challenges for 'some families' that were working class and could not afford particular fundraisers or activities for children. These types of comments were always referencing 'Spanish dom' families.

Parents, both US-born and immigrant, Latinx and white subscribed to the notion that Latinx at Samuelson was also working class, Spanish-speaking and immigrant and spoke of this community as homogenous despite the clear variance among Latinxs on campus. Latina immigrant women noted how the disparities in status between the 'English dom' and 'Spanish dom' were clear. Daisy, an immigrant mother from El Salvador, shared how she felt the program facilitated learning between people from different places. She explained how she felt the 'Anglos' were more open minded and speculated it was due to their levels of education. Daisy stated, 'Tenemos menos estudio que ellos…yo veo que la mayoría tienen carrera y nosotros somos babysitters, housekeeping y otros que todavía andan estudiando' (We have less education than them…I see that the majority have careers and we are babysitters, housekeeping and others are still studying). Daisy sees herself as part of the 'Spanish dom' community that has less educational attainment and subsequently less status relative to the 'English doms.'

How Samuelson recruited families for the immersion program undoubtedly impacted the perception of Latinx families on campus and other immigrant Latinx parents also noted the differences. Selena, an immigrant mother from Mexico, shared that some of the women she knew had kids at Samuelson learned about the school because 'eran babysitters de Americanos. Se enteraron de esta escuela porque traían a los niños Americanos' (they were babysitters for the Americans. They found out about this school because they brought the American kids). Selena explained how the women she knew lived near China Town or on the East side of Los Angeles but were able to bring their kids to the school along with the kids they cared for as nannies. That Selena, Daisy and other Latinx immigrant parents used 'American' as a stand in for white was very common at the school and the structure of the relationships between these parents outside of the school undoubtedly influenced perceptions of who was higher status on campus. That is, the interactions and nature of the relationship between some parents who held an employee–employer relationship impacted the relations between parents on campus. And while they may have had children enrolled in the same school, the school itself does not render the power disparities between them invisible – particularly when some Latinx immigrant parents continue to work for white families as domestics, housesitters and care workers.

Common raciolinguistic ideologies about both Latinxs and white families exist on campus and can be seen in everyday language at the school and common explanations for events that happen on campus. In line with previous studies, white families are referred to as 'English doms' and are assumed to be middle class or affluent, with terms like 'American' are used as proxies to describe them (Chaparro, 2018). Latinx origin families are homogenized as 'Spanish doms' who are working class, foreign born and low income. These local labels are imbued with meanings and assumptions about these communities and are used as shorthand or proxies for many other social statuses. These raciolinguistic ideologies are so powerful that they occur despite the explicit valorization of the Spanish language in a Spanish/English dual immersion school and the voluntary nature of the program where all parents desire to raise bilinguals. Moreover, these limited notions of Spanish and English speakers can be found among both Latinx and white families who perpetuate these ideologies by speaking of them as simple realities. More importantly, these assumptions impact how parents are able to participate on campus and how others perceive their efforts.

Helping or being helped? Raciolinguistic ideologies in parent organizations

On any given day, it was not uncommon to see mothers of all racial/ethnic, socioeconomic and linguistic backgrounds on campus. In fact, most volunteer and service efforts were spearheaded and performed by women at Samuelson. While fathers also volunteered, mothers were the majority of the members in both parent organizations and in other service efforts at the school. Most interviewees in heterosexual relationships noted that men would attend things like festivals or back to school night but were not as involved in activities on campus. Alba, an immigrant mother from Spain, noted that 'va por supuesto a las conferencias con los maestros, a los fests, a los eventos y participa ya como voluntario un par de horas pero no tiene tanto tiempo' (he goes to the conferences with the teachers, to the fests, to the events and participates as a volunteer for a couple of hours but he doesn't have much time). Responses like Alba's were common among respondents when it came to discussing time spent on campus. This is not a surprise, as reproductive labor, or the labor needed to sustain a productive labor force, and which includes cooking, cleaning and caring for children is often relegated to women (Nakano Glenn, 1992; Parreñas, 2000).

Service efforts were also structured by other social locations – divisions between parents reflected their personal resources. Latinx immigrant mothers cited helping in the classroom by stuffing parent folders with flyers and other small clerical tasks assigned by teachers and serving as chaperones for school field trips. Latinx immigrant mothers were also responsible for virtually all events that involved food (such as preparation and serving food at events). White mothers described attending meetings, donating money, helping organize events and using their own professional skills as ways they gave back to Samuelson. Field observations also demonstrated white parents handling ticketing at movie nights and events and computer-related tasks such as organizing the online auction. Lastly, US-born Latinx mothers reported attending meetings, helping organize events and translating (both verbally and in writing) as ways they contributed to Samuelson.

Participatory differences between Latinx and white parents were evident to them. For example, Latinx parents mentioned that they were often in charge of staffing for and serving food at events and doing the work that was 'de mano' or by hand (Muro, 2016). More importantly, however, parents attribute value judgments to the work they did on campus. Carla, an immigrant mother from Mexico, for instance, noted how she felt that white parents helped not only the school but also the other, presumably less privileged, parents at the school. She explained how the white parents helped with all of the events and 'todos los eventos que hacen son para ayuda para la escuela' (all of the events they do are to help the school). She continued, 'la verdad si ayudan bastante los gabachos[6]' (truthfully the white people do help a lot). Carla explained how the school had a sort of campaign that encouraged parents to provide funds to help students or what they referred to as 'direct donation.' Though it was not officially recorded or shared, administrators and parents in leadership positions indicated that if each parent donated approximately $300 per student enrolled, the school would have plentiful funds to supplement the funds provided for the school via the district. Carla explained, 'muchos papas no lo damos pero hay muchos gabachos que si dan bastante dinero y ayudan mucho a la escuela' (many of us parents do not give it but there are many white people who do give a lot of money and help the school a lot). While Carla was not denying that Latinx families also participated on campus, her comment both relies on the raciolinguistic ideologies detailed above about Latinx and white parents on campus and implies that the help provided by white parents the school was more impactful than the efforts of parents like her.

The notion that white parents were able to 'help' the school was very common among all parents. For example, almost all discussion of fundraising efforts brought up comments about the vast disparities between families and how these became more obvious during events like the silent auctions. Valerie, a white mother, shared how these silent auctions had become a topic of debate among parents because of how they 'illustrated the economic diversity of families.' Note that many participants did not directly say that it was Latinx families that were working class, but instead relied on proxies to reference this community – labels like 'Spanish dom.' Valerie explained how they would have the 'library set up with all these bidding things, prices to bid on anywhere from $30 to $500 items and you know, you can just bid.' But, despite what she described as the 'really hard work to get donations,' it did not work. Instead, Valerie, continued, 'we found, and the teachers have seen this for years, they're like this doesn't work because what they found was largely, the upwardly mobile people with disposable income and guess what? The majority of them were white.' In this way, white families and particularly white parents involved at the school were perceived as helpers that could plan and execute events to raise money and they were also presented as the individuals most likely to help the school monetarily.

Alternatively, Latinx families at the school were perceived as those to receive help from both the school and other parents. Parent organizations, including the PTA and ELAC reflected these patterns. Both ELAC and PTA had regular meetings every month in the library and both organizations' meetings were open to any Samuelson parents. But, almost all regular members of the PTA were English-speaking white women and almost all regular members of ELAC were Spanish-dominant Latinx immigrant women. When speaking to the principal, Mrs Martell explained that the ELAC was supposed to help the parents of English learner's with any special concerns they might have about their child's educational experience, while PTA was tasked with helping administrators make decisions about the school and increasing parent voice on campus. However, in practice, PTA spent the majority of meeting time talking about and planning for fundraising efforts at the school and deciding where these monies should be allocated. ELAC, on the other hand, functioned as a type of support group for parents and included regular presentations from outside agencies about topics like how to properly discipline children, legal assistance and even nutrition.

Parents were well aware in the differences between these parent organizations and regularly mentioned them during interviews. Daisy, explained that much of content for meetings at ELAC was based on teaching parents about different things. She explained,

> ELAC se encarga de reuniones, como informar a los padres de diferentes cosas – como de abuso domestico, ayudar a los niños en las tareas, como aprender que los niños usen programas en la computadora. Diferentes cosas…ellos no recaudan dinero.

> ELAC handles meetings, like informing parents of different things – like domestic abuse, helping children with homework, how to learn that kids use computer program. Different things…they don't raise money.

Daisy was correct in that most of the ELAC meetings were formatted as workshops for parents on a variety of topics ranging from nutrition, homework and discipline strategies to use with kids to sessions on taxes and citizenship questions. These meetings were almost exclusively in Spanish and when presenters, often visitors from outside of the school, did not speak Spanish, the community liaison translated for parents into Spanish. It was very rare to have English-dominant speakers attend these meetings or request that they be translated into English. Daisy herself noted that she did not know if there were any 'Anglos' but that everyone she knew in ELAC was 'Hispanic.' As noted in the above section, racial/ethnic terms and linguistic descriptors were used interchangeably and help elucidate the common raciolinguistic ideologies at the school.

These raciolinguistic ideologies structured participation in parent organizations so that ELAC was perceived as a place to receive help and PTA was a place to provide it. During my time at Samuelson, I observed presentations on all the topics Daisy mentioned and even workshops like parenting support groups. Consider the following fieldnote from the support group hosted in Spanish:

> The facilitator starts the meeting by telling everyone that everything that is said during these meetings is confidential and that we should not talk about it with anyone outside of the circle, or go around the school telling people's problems. Everyone nods and agrees. He tells us that the group is new and that the idea came from meeting with the 'directora' or principal. They felt it was a good idea to have resources for parents and so came the group, which had only met once before. He tells us the group is to help cope with the problems and stresses that come with parenting, and that sometimes we can feel alone with our problems, but that in sharing them we will find that others have similar challenges. He says that when you try to solve a problem alone there is only one brain at work, but here in the group there are eight powerful brains working to solve problems and that they, the parents, are the experts.

The facilitator is an older immigrant Latino that is a bilingual counselor at the school and speaks Spanish the entire time. Parents share their experience and one mother, a Latinx immigrant mother, shares how she worries about yelling at her kids and her frustration that they only listen when they see she is very upset and raising her voice. The facilitator allows her to share her story, parents nod and the facilitator reassures her that she is a good parent. The following excerpt illustrates his approach as he continued the group:

> The facilitator then jumps in and tells us that parents are the ultimate teachers, and that is why they must answer to their kids or their kids can become misinformed elsewhere. He goes on to say that kids did not grow up the same way they did and those nowadays are more curious and ask much more questions than when they were growing up. He says that parenting now is not only about authority. Ariana chimes in saying that

when she was growing up she would not even be done talking back when her mother was already punishing her/hitting her. Other parents agree and nod their heads. The facilitator responds 'no estamos en otro país hace veinte años' (we are not in another country twenty years ago) and the parents nod their heads in agreement.

The facilitator's comment about being in another country during a time in the past made the audience clear – Latinx immigrant parents. The implication is that their parenting practices, those informed by their own parents in their countries of origin, are outdated and do not fit with their current landscape. Though these support groups were offered in both Spanish and English, the Spanish session was well attended while the English was not – indeed a Latina immigrant mother attended that session and spoke mostly in Spanish. To be clear, the facilitator and the school itself did not assume that English dominant or white parents did not need a support group to help them cope with the everyday pressures and stresses that come with children. But, comments like this illustrate how these types of resources targeted the Latinx origin community and demonstrate how the usage of these services contribute to ideas about who needs help at the school and who can provide help to the school. There is no doubt that white parents also felt stress and pressure when it came to raising their children. But, their absence from groups like this and the fact that they were not subjects to workshops like those in ELAC added to the idea that either they did not need help in the same way or that they could access and afford that help elsewhere. Overall, 'English doms' who were white and often middle class or affluent were constructed as the community at the school who did not need help, either in parent organizations or other venues hosted by the school.

This sentiment was so prevalent, it was echoed among both parents and employees at Samuelson. Gloria, a US-born, bilingual Latina mother, explained in her interview how 'ELAC is meetings, we mostly get these workshops and then the PTA is more like business – this is what's happening, you know? We need to raise money, do this, do that.' Gloria even noted how ELAC offered 'ESL classes for the non-English speaker parents.' Gloria's comments show how other parents understand the differences between the parent organizations and their aim or purpose at the school. Adults understood the PTA organization as a place to get things completed and to help decide where money raised would be allocated. On the other hand, ELAC was a place of support for parents who needed extra help in a range of areas. These ideas were so normative at the campus, that parents were not the only ones on campus who explained the differences between ELAC and PTA this way. In fact, the community liaison, a US-born, bilingual Latina subscribed to these ideas as she explained her role at the school and stated, 'I mean I mostly do stuff for the ELAC parents.' Consider the following field note:

Yaniz tells me that she meets with ELAC parents at the beginning of the year and the parents tell her what topics they would like presented at the meetings. I ask her if there is a presentation at each meeting and she says yes, that parents pick the topics and she is in charge of finding presenters. Each meeting has a theme – she tells me that next week will be about after school opportunities since the school will be under construction and the free childcare they provide will not be available during that time. I tell her the ELAC format is very different from the PTA and she agrees. I ask her if she organizes anything for the PTA and if the PTA has a 'community liaison' as well. She responds, 'Well I am the liaison for everybody but they don't really need me over there…they have more people doing stuff and taking care of things.'

Yaniz makes it clear that the selection process for topics at ELAC is a collaborative effort between her and parents. She arranges time with ELAC leaders and other parents and after they tell her what types of workshops they would like, she invites presenters. But, the structure of ELAC itself does not have to follow this format. More importantly, Yaniz's comment indicates how she feels some parents need help and others do not. While ELAC parents, who are also 'Spanish doms' or parents that are Latinx immigrants need her assistance, she does not feel that parents in the PTA or 'English doms' that are native-born whites require her help.

Ideas about who required assistance and who 'ran' things at the school were also reflected in the knowledge parents had about the parent organizations overall. During interview, it was clear that the PTA was known as an organization to raise money and make decisions at the school. Alba, an immigrant mother from Spain, explained,

> PTA es la asociación de padres y maestros que gestiona todo el dinero, el que se recauda y decide como apoya. Y ELAC es un grupo para gente que el ingles es su segundo idioma y esta mas enfocado como ayudar a los padres para que a los padres después ayuden a sus hijos.
>
> PTA is the association for parents and teachers that manages the money that is fundraised and decides how it is used. And ELAC is a group for people who English is their second language and is more focused on how to help parents so that parents can then help their children later.

Alba was one of the few parents that knew about ELAC's mission or had a firm grasp on its purpose, most parents instead would say they were 'not really sure' about what they did in those meetings or how to become members.

This lack of information about ELAC also contributed to misconceptions about their work to help the school. Recall how Daisy, a Latina immigrant mom, believed that ELAC was a space for information was certain that the group did not fundraise. Daisy was incorrect in her assumption – in fact, ELAC hosted their own events, including a special

Valentine's Day event, and helped PTA fundraise at other events like the Fall Festival and other holiday celebrations. Parents also discussed fundraising during ELAC meetings. For example, during one gathering at ELAC, Rodrigo, a Latino immigrant father, announced to the other parents that they needed donations for the upcoming yard sale they will be putting on as a fundraiser. Another Latino immigrant father, Angel, suggests they sell food at this event or even occasionally at the school to help. He stated, 'Pues nosotros, muchos trabajamos en restaurantes, pues yo trabajo en una pizzería…sabemos hacer muchas cosas diferentes y podemos vender aquí' (Well us, many of us work in restaurants, well I work in a pizza shop…we know how make many different things and we can sell here). To be clear, parents in ELAC did fundraise for Samuelson and helped PTA with their fundraising for the school. The primary difference was that PTA was officially in charge of allocating moneys raised and that PTA received much more recognition for the work they did in order to help the school. These examples are not meant to minimize the contributions of Latinx immigrant parents, efforts by all parents are necessary and meaningful, but rather to highlight how raciolinguistic ideologies about Latinx and white parents are reflected in the work they do on campus and the recognition they garner at Samuelson.

When labels don't fit: Latinx heterogeneity on campus

While common raciolinguistic ideologies impacted how both parents and parent's participation on campus were perceived, these raciolinguistic ideologies did not accurately reflect the complexity of students and their families at Samuelson. Latinxs at Samuelson were not homogenous despite the strong raciolinguistic ideologies about them on campus. Indeed, Latinx families at the school were a heterogeneous group with diverse levels of linguistic abilities, of different generations, socioeconomic backgrounds and countries of origin. These differences allow us to see how raciolinguistic ideologies that pair 'Spanish dom' with working class and immigrant prevail despite the sizeable amount of families that are do not fit this image. Families who did not fit these assumptions commonly mentioned that they were overlooked and served as a kind of floating community depending on their own levels of comfort with each language, socioeconomic class, nativity and even country of origin. For example, Lisandra, an immigrant mother from Peru, explained that her son knew that they were from Peru, 'sabe que nosotros somos de Perú y que el es Peruano, si sabe. Pero también siento que el sabe que el es Americano a la vez, me entiendes? Sabe que el es de los dos' (he knows that we are from Peru and he is Peruvian, he knows. But I also feel that he knows he is American at the same time, you know? He knows he is both). Lisandra was married to a white American man and her son had been born in the US. And while she felt that he knew about their background, he did have questions about the cultural practices he was exposed to at Samuelson. She explained,

> A veces dice 'pero mama nosotros no somos mexicanos,' porque a veces hablan de el día de cinco de mayo o hacen la bandera de México, cosas así, y el 'pero yo no soy de México, verdad mama?' No, no somos de México, yo no soy de México. Y el sabe, se da cuenta que su maestra es de México.
>
> El habla palabras Peruanos como 'casaca' que yo le enseño que es 'jacket' o 'chaqueta' en Mexicano. Su maestra no le entiende, me dice 'Mama pero como se dice esto en Mexicano,' Porque, le digo, 'porque mi maestra no entiende, no entiende cuando yo le digo casaca.' Oh okay... se da cuenta de la diferencia.
>
> Sometimes he says 'but mom we are not Mexican' because sometimes they talk about Cinco de Mayo or they make the Mexican flag, things like that and he goes, 'but I am not from Mexico, right mom?' No, we are not from Mexico. I am not from Mexico. And he knows, he knows his teacher is from Mexico.
>
> He uses Peruvian words like 'casaca' that I teach him, that is 'jacket' or 'chaqueta' in Mexican. His teacher doesn't understand him, he tells me 'mom but how do you say this in Mexican?' Why I ask him, 'Because my teacher doesn't understand, she doesn't understand when I say casaca.' Oh okay...he does notice the difference.

Lisandra's experience with her son reflects another assumption at the school – that all Latinx families are Mexican origin. Well aware that a majority of families at the school are Mexican origin, she acknowledged how her son was learning about particular cultural practices that were not a part of her Peruvian culture. And while Lisandra made it clear in her interview that she did not mind the exposure to other Latinx cultural practices, she did feel her son would experience some confusion, particularly when using slang from Peru. But, more importantly, Lisandra's family does not fit the common assumptions about 'Spanish doms' – she is in fact married to a non-Latinx white man, she is not Mexican origin and she is not working class. This matters because it shows how despite the clear diversity within the Latinx label and the obvious over simplification of the communities at Samuelson, the existing raciolinguistic ideologies gloss over the experiences of families who do not 'fit' and can impact their participation on campus.

Students and families who did not neatly fit into existing raciolinguistic ideologies about 'Spanish doms' or 'English doms' challenged the idea that all Latinx families on campus needed help. Rather, several of these families were middle class or affluent, highly educated and at times expressed concern about the heterogeneity. While parents like Lisandra noted the differences and did not mind the dominance of particular cultures given the concentration of the population, other parents made comments that were not as benign. Intentional or not, some middle-class and affluent Latinx parents made comments about 'Spanish doms' that indicated how they perceived the as less than. For example, Valentina, an immigrant mother from Argentina, shared her concerns that the Spanish available at the school was not up to par. She shared that she was 'not extremely happy with the level of Spanish' and was bothered by the level of Spanish used in written communication. She explained,

> I can't imagine any English-speaking parent getting a flyer with lots of spelling errors, not being appalled. Can you imagine, getting a flyer from your school, with grammatical and spelling errors that are appalling? It bothers me...obviously the teachers don't have time to be translating material, and so they have their staff translating material, who are bilingual, but they're not linguists, and they don't necessarily write in Spanish a lot. Their grammar and their spelling, is not proper grammar and spelling.

Valentina explained that she did not think that the families receiving these materials with mistakes would complain. When I asked her why she felt this way, Valentina responded that most of these families that were Hispanic were probably not at 'the sociocultural level' to comment and complain. She elaborated,

> It's not a priority or maybe they don't necessarily know. I'm not saying they don't know how to read or write, they, they're not necessarily great spellers. I don't know, I think it's an educational, socioeconomic thing. Maybe they might notice. I believe some of them know, but maybe they don't … they're intimidated, they don't want to complain. The parents who say something are people who have a higher level of education, their family is Spanish and they might think, 'Wow, this is …' To me, it's just, I can't believe it.

Though Valentina had grown up in Argentina, her family had the means to pay for private bilingual education and she was fluent in English before ever coming to the US. Given her education, she talked extensively about how disappointed she was in the written materials that were sent home regularly. More importantly, Valentina's comments are loaded with assumptions about fellow Latinx families – about the employees and their abilities, about the types of families that match her in terms of educational attainment, socioeconomic status. For instance, Valentina asserts that Samuelson employees are not all 'fully bilingual.' That is, she worried that many of the support staff did not have the writing skills in Spanish that she expected of the teachers and other professionals like 'linguists.' She polices the Spanish use of her coethnics by indicating that their spelling and grammar is 'not proper.' As Flores and Rosa note, the regulation of 'proper' and 'improper' is a reflection of the raciolinguistic assumptions about people (2015), and this is particular case, one that is enacted by those within the racial/ethnic group. Clearly, Valentina does not 'match' her coethnics in all aspects – she makes this clear by distinguishing herself as a parent who is 'appalled' and thus one who is educated and of a higher socioeconomic status. Her comment also implies that Spanish families, as in those families who are from Spain, are those with higher status and prestige at the school. Alternatively, she assumes that those parents who are not Spanish, who may not have high levels of education and who may be of a lower socioeconomic status, do not have the desire to complain even if they notice errors. These assumptions are problematic overall, but that they are shared by a Latinx parent is particularly telling about the heterogeneity within what Samuelson families perceive as the 'Spanish dom' community and illustrates how incorrect raciolinguistic ideologies can be despite their prevalence.

This type of policing was not unique to Valentina and other parents occasionally mentioned how the written materials were not always perfect or how the Spanish was not at the same level for all teachers or employees. Alba also shared that she believed 'que no debería haber errores en la escuela' (there should not be errors at the school). Alba noted that even the principal did not have the 'perfect Spanish' and thought about asking the teachers 'si ellas son conscientes de su nivel de español' (if they are conscious of their level of Spanish). Valentina named a handful of teachers who she believed had 'good Spanish' –a list that was mostly foreign born and older teachers. She continued to explain that some teachers were not as good and that it was a 'tema delicado' (sensitive subject). Though these critiques were voiced more clearly by middle-class Latinx parents, they were not alone in their observations about the 'quality' of Spanish. For instance, Dulce, a Latina immigrant mother who was working class, explained that she believed educational level could not compare to being a native language speaker. She felt some teachers 'confunden a los niños' (confuse the kids) and despite their years of teaching and despite the fact that they are 'maestros preparados y hablan español bastante bien, pero no lo suficientemente bien para que los niños entiendan mejor' (prepared teachers and speak Spanish quite well, but not well enough for the children to understand better). Dulce felt that many of these teachers, particularly those who were not Latinx origin, did not speak 'el español que hablamos nosotros' (the Spanish we speak).

Comments like the ones made by the participants mentioned above demarcate the boundaries that occur within the Latinx community at Samuelson and that are far more complex than dominant raciolinguistic ideologies at Samuelson would indicate. Boundaries exist within what is imagined as the 'Spanish dom' community around other social locations that include national origin, nativity and socioeconomic status. While parents may identify as Latinx or even as a part of the 'Spanish dom' community at Samuelson, there are important differences and even tensions within these umbrella terms that are often glossed over. This heterogeneity complicates the common idea that 'Spanish dom' families are to be helped on campus and also impact other everyday activities at the school. These differences and tensions impact parental involvement on campus and are important to examine because Latinx heterogeneity if often overlooked in research about dual immersion. Examining parental involvement with a raciolinguistic perspective illuminates the complexity that labels like 'Spanish dom' and 'English dom' erase and demonstrates how these raciolinguistic ideologies impact all individuals in dual immersion, not solely students.

Conclusion

This chapter contributes to previous literature by examining how raciolinguistic ideologies about 'Spanish doms' and 'English doms' impact the way parents are perceived on campus and how their participation efforts are interpreted through these ideologies. Drawing from in-depth interviews and participant observation with Latinx and white parents in a Spanish/English dual immersion program in the greater Los Angeles area, I find that common raciolingusitic ideologies about white and Latinx people are drawn upon and re-articulated on campus. While 'Spanish dom' parents, who are Latinx origin, are assumed to be working class and foreign born, 'English doms' are presented as 'American,' middle class or affluent and white. Here, I demonstrate how both Latinx and white parents at the school espouse these raciolinguistic ideologies and how these contribute to the patterns of parent participation at Samuelson.

The co-construction of race/ethnicity, socioeconomic status and language can be seen in the everyday interactions between parents and even local labels used to refer to these communities. Parents, administrators and teachers used 'Spanish dom' and 'English dom' as shorthand for communities on campus that they spoke of as homogenous. Though it was evident that these labels and the accompanying assumptions were not accurate for everyone at Samuelson, adults continued to use them to insinuate race/ethnicity, nativity, class and linguistic ability. Parents would use 'Spanish dom' to reference families of Latinx origin and in doing so conflate socioeconomic status, nativity and even linguistic abilities. Despite the clear presence of Latinx families from diverse national origins, of varying class statuses and with a wide range of bilingualism, adults at the school contributed to the homogenizing of Latinxs by using 'Spanish dom' almost exclusively to refer to these families. Similarly, the 'English dom' population was not all white, US-born or middle class/affluent. In fact, this label glossed over some of the racial/ethnic diversity at the school and effectively rendered the Asian and Black families on campus invisible.

These raciolinguistic ideologies are perpetuated with daily use and undergird parent's participation in organizations on campus. That parents participate actively in school organizations like the PTA and ELAC is important given then literature that finds formal participation and parental involvement is lower for non-white parents (Posey-Maddox, 2012; Turney & Kao, 2009). In line with studies on Latinx parent participation (Terriquez, 2012, 2013), Latinx parents participated in school as frequently as white parents and were also involved in organizations on campus. The difference between them and white parents, however, was the visibility and power in their service efforts. Officially, ELAC or the English Learning Advisory Council is supposed to serve any parents whose children are learning English. In practice, however, ELAC does not spend the majority of the time discussing English learning and instead Latinx origin parents who were primarily members of ELAC were subject to workshops on how to 'properly' discipline kids, how to access public services for children and other general advice to 'help' them. Alternatively, the almost exclusively white members of the PTA were perceived as 'helpers' for the school that had the power to fundraise and make decisions about these funds. The raciolinguistic ideologies that impact how these activities also help channel parents into separate groups on campus based on the assumptions that come with the 'Spanish dom' and 'English dom' labels.

Finally, I demonstrate how these labels incorrectly homogenize the Latinx population on campus. Latinx families at Samuelson come from many different countries, have varying socioeconomic backgrounds, are US and foreign born and do not all speak Spanish in the same way despite being referred to as 'Spanish doms.' This heterogeneity is not only overlooked, but gives the false notion that there are no tensions among Latinx origin families at the school. In fact, boundaries among 'Spanish doms' hinged on the varying levels and dialects of Spanish and reflected the vast economic disparities between some of the families. These tensions indicated that not all 'Spanish doms' need help and some consider themselves to be in positions to help other Latinx. Highlighting these differences elucidates the complexity that local labels and existing research may not address and helps us understand how these practices affect more than just students in dual immersion.

Overall, this chapter builds on existing literature on dual immersion by centering the experiences of parents of children in dual immersion and demonstrating how using a raciolinguistic perspective can nuance our overall knowledge of inequities within immersion programs. While involvement efforts by all parents are necessary, the disparate power and recognition that these efforts garner highlights the inequalities between parents at the school. The segregation of parent organizations and the disparities in the power they exercise at school ultimately exacerbate the inequalities between them. Inequalities exist even in contexts that value bilingualism and have high levels of racial/ethnic, socioeconomic and linguistic diversity. This work reminds us to be more conscious of how existing labels can contribute to the erasure of Latinx heterogeneity by illustrating some of the consequences of these ideologies and showing how these inequalities are not relegated to students but also extend to parents and families more broadly. By the same token, research on how parents experience immersion can help carve a path of change that may help make dual immersion a more equitable experience for both students and their families.

Notes

(1) I use the term 'Latinx' throughout the chapter except when participants or scholars used Latina/o or Hispanic.
(2) 90/10 models begin with 90% Spanish instruction and ten percent English instruction and increase the amount of English instruction with each grade.
(3) Free or reduced lunch are commonly used measures for poverty among students.
(4) Title 1 is a federal program that provides funding for schools serving large low-income populations.
(5) Two interviews were with heterosexual married couples.
(6) Gabacho is Spanish slang for white Americans.

References

Berg, B.L. (2001) *Qualitative Research Methods for the Social Sciences*. Prentice Hall.
Chaparro, S. (2018) But Mom! I'm not a Spanish Boy: Raciolinguistic socialization in a Two-Way immersion bilingual program. *Linguistics and Education* 50, 1–12.
Epstein, J. (2001) *School, Family, and Community Partnerships: Preparing Educators and Improving Schools*. Boulder, CO: Westview Press.
Flores, N. and Rosa, J. (2015) Undoing appropriateness: Raciolinguistic ideologies and language diversity in education. *Harvard Educational Review* 85, 149–171.
Gándara, P. and Contreras, F. (2009) *The Latino Education Crisis: The Consequences of Failed Social Policies*. Cambridge, MA: Harvard University Press.
Jeynes, W. (2010) *Parental Involvement and Academic Success*. New York: Routledge.
Jeynes, W. (2003) A meta-analysis: The effects of parental involvement on minority children's academic achievement. *Education & Urban Society* 35 (2), 202–218.
Lareau, A. (2000) *Unequal Childhoods: Class, Race, and Family Life*. Berkeley: University of California Press.
Li, A. and Fischer, M. (2017) Advantaged/disadvantaged school neighborhoods, parental networks, and parental involvement at elementary school. *Sociology of Education* 90 (4), 355–377.
Muro, J.A. (2016) 'Oil and Water'? Latino-white relations and symbolic integration in a changing California. *Sociology of Race and Ethnicity* 2 (4), 516–530.
Nakano Glenn, E. (1992) From servitude to service work: The historical continuities of women's paid and unpaid reproductive labor. *Signs: Journal of Women in Culture and Society* 18 (1), 1–44.
Parreñas, R. (2000) Migrant Filipina domestic workers and the international division of reproductive labor. *Gender & Society* 14 4(August), 560–580.
Posey-Maddox, L. (2012) Professionalizing the PTO: Race, class, and shifting norms of parental engagement in a city public school. *American Journal of Education* 119 (2), 235–260.
Rosa, J. (2018) *Looking Like a Language, Sounding Like a Race: Raciolinguistic Ideologies and the Learning of Latinidad*. New York: Oxford University Press.
Rosa, J. and Flores, N. (2017) Unsettling race and language: Toward a raciolinguistic perspective. *Language in Society* 46, 621–647.
Shah, P. (2009) Motivating participation: Estimating the impact of symbolic representation on latino parent involvement. *Social Science Quarterly* 90 (1), 212–230.

Strauss, A. and Corbin, J. (1998) *Basics of Qualitative Research: Techniques and Procedures for Developing Grounded Theory* (2nd edn). Thousand Oaks, CA: Sage Publications.

Terriquez, V. (2012) Civic inequalities? Immigrant incorporation and Latina mothers' participation in their children's schools. *Sociological Perspectives* 55 (December), 663–682.

Terriquez, V. (2013) Latino fathers' involvement in their children's schools. *Family Relations* 64 (October), 662–675.

Turney, K. and Kao, G. (2009) Barriers to school involvement: Are immigrant parents disadvantaged? *Journal of Educational Research* 102 (4), 257–271.

Valenzuela, A. (1999) *Subtractive Schooling: US Mexican Youth and the Politics of Caring.* Albany, NY: State University of New York Press.

7 Hebrew Dual Language Bilingual Education: The Intersection of Race, Language and Religion

Sharon Avni and Kate Menken

One of the main intentions of bilingual education is not only to serve as a site for language learning, but also to foster non-linguistic growth, including the development of cross-cultural understandings and positive attitudes toward the self and others (Baker & Wright, 2017; Collier & Thomas, 2014). These principles are particularly relevant in dual language bilingual education programs (henceforth DLBE), which by definition bring children of two language groups together with the aims of developing bilingualism and biliteracy in both languages (García & Kleifgen, 2018; Hamayan *et al.*, 2013). Advocates point to research showing that DLBE is inherently socially transformative because it provides a space in which minoritized communities' languages, identities, and cultures can be recognized and supported within public schools (Baker & Wright, 2017; García & Woodley, 2015). Along with its documented impact on language maintenance and reversing language shift across generations (Fishman, 2014; Freeman, 1998; Valdés, 2014) as well as on cultural preservation through more 'humanizing pedagogy' (Fránquiz, 2012; see also Baker & Wright, 2017; García, 2009), these programs have garnered the attention of public schools looking for ways to promote diversity and equity. Parents choose to send their children to DLBE programs specifically because they believe that they will be culturally as well as linguistically sustaining (Farrugio, 2010; Gerena, 2011; Paris, 2012).

Yet, at the same time, there is a growing literature that challenges the success of dual language structures as a democratizing force. Despite the 'rich promise' (Lindholm-Leary, 2005) of these programs to attain strong academic achievements for bilingual children through content instruction in the two languages, there is increasing concern that dual language programs are not providing equal educational opportunities, particularly for emergent bilinguals learning English (Boyle *et al.*, 2015; Cervantes-Soon,

2014) – the targeted students for whom bilingual education was originally developed in the United States (Flores, 2016). Studies reveal that dual language programs can perpetuate racial discrimination, linguistic marginalization, and class and ethnic hierarchies in public schooling (Amrein & Peña, 2000; Cervantes-Soon *et al.*, 2017; Fitts, 2006; Hernández, 2015; Palmer *et al.*, 2019; Petrovic, 2005; Valdés, 1997) and reaffirm power asymmetries (Chaparro, 2019; Palmer, 2009; Zúñiga *et al.*, 2018). As Muro (2016: 2) found in her study of a two-way immersion program in a gentrifying community, integration alone did not necessarily lead to equity, but rather resulted in 'symbolic integration,' and what she categorizes as the 'polite, surface-level, interactions that are enjoyable, voluntary, and additive' but that did not ultimately disrupt the durability of prejudice and racial hierarchies. Moreover, although bilingual education would seem to lend itself to the recognition of students' cultural backgrounds and identity through culturally sustaining pedagogy (Paris, 2012), Valdiviezo and Nieto (2015) show how bilingual education does not by definition necessitate multicultural education. To respond to these critiques, researchers are increasingly calling for bilingual education pedagogy, particularly within the context of DLBE programs, that is attentive to imbalances of power, disrupts prevalent raciolinguistic ideologies, and fosters critical consciousness (Cervantes-Soon *et al.*, 2017; Chaparro, 2019; Palmer *et al.*, 2019).

This chapter contributes to these debates about the capacity of DLBE programs to address social asymmetries and offer transformative educational change by examining the unique case of a Hebrew–English program in New York City (NYC). Specifically, it details the creation and implementation of a dual language Hebrew–English program that served Jewish children and Black children at a public middle school, two populations of students that have not traditionally taken part in bilingual education programs in NYC public schools. As Hebrew is closely associated with Judaism and its teaching has widely been restricted to private sectarian schooling, this case study advances raciolinguistic scholarship by bringing religious language ideologies into the dynamics of dual language initiatives in public schooling. Attending to Hebrew language ideologies and what language learning represents to the Jewish and non-Jewish students in this program, this chapter demonstrates how the dual language structure provided a space for communal outreach and identity growth on one hand, while perpetuating raciolinguistic ideologies and racial categories and hierarchies on the other hand (Rosa & Flores, 2017). Although the Hebrew program promoted diversity and effectively carved out a space for a minoritized language group which lacked other options in public schooling, it did so in ways that also contributed to racism and marginalization. With its structural design focused on recruiting Jewish students and instructional approach centered (myopically) on language, this Hebrew–English program did not expand beyond essentialist Hebrew language ideologies, and failed to attend to broader multicultural possibilities.

Context

The site for our research is a traditional NYC public middle school we call 'Multilingual Public Middle School' (MPMS)[1] which in 2012 began to offer DLBE in Mandarin. It extended soon thereafter to Russian and Spanish, and ultimately added Hebrew in 2015. The findings presented in this chapter come from data collected when the Hebrew program was in its second and third years of implementation. Between September 2016 and May 2017, we observed 30 classroom lessons, one all-day professional development workshop (held 8/31/16), and five weekly teachers' meetings. We conducted semi-structured interviews from September 2016 through February 2018 with the principal and the assistant principal of the school, the school's staff developer, the Hebrew and social studies teachers, parents, and students in the Hebrew program. Additionally, we collected sociolinguistic data through a survey to the students and parents, and collected copies of students' written work and pedagogical materials. All of the interviews were recorded with a digital recorder and transcribed. Data for this chapter come primarily from classroom observations and parent, student, and administrative interviews, which were coded and analyzed to identify prevalent themes (LeCompte & Preissle, 1993; Miles *et al.*, 2013). The findings reported here draw from the most prevalent themes having to do with diversity and race.

As we have documented elsewhere (Avni & Menken, 2019; Menken & Avni, 2017, 2019), the impetus for a Hebrew–English bilingual program at MPMS was the result of a confluence of social, economic and linguistic conditions. These conditions included available funding from the NYC Department of Education (NYCDOE) to expand DLBE in the city, strategic moves by the MPMS principal to improve the school's reputation and boost enrollment by attracting new communities of students, and a local Hebrew charter elementary school that had demonstrated proof of concept regarding the feasibility of teaching Hebrew in a public school context without running afoul of the Establishment clause of the Constitution separating church and state. The success of the elementary charter school ignited several Jewish families to push for a Hebrew program at MPMS, a move to which the principal was highly receptive. Collectively, these conditions resulted in the opening of the program, which in its initial years was structured to teach social studies in Hebrew following the NYS Social Studies Curriculum for each grade level, as well as Hebrew language in a class called 'Hebrew Language and Culture' whose curriculum was created by the Hebrew teacher, Ms R.[2] Though it was initially identified and even lauded as a model DLBE program, two years into the program, the school was forced to change the title of their program to a 'heritage language program' because it was not offering sufficient Hebrew instruction to meet the NYCDOE's stringent requirements for DLBE classification. That is, the student population was not '50% English language learners (ELLs)' and '50% English proficient students' as city policy dictated (NYCDOE, 2015). Only one of the students in the program was classified as an 'English language learner' and most students were not traditional 'heritage language learners' in that they did not speak Hebrew at home.[3] In our previous work, we critiqued how this framing of the students, along with the practice of strictly separating languages of instruction in DLBE programs, is rooted in a monoglossic perspective on language that does not recognize the complex languaging practices of bilinguals, and documented how recategorizing the program as 'heritage language' rather than 'dual language' ultimately limited how much Hebrew instruction could be provided (Avni & Menken, 2019; Menken & Avni, 2017, 2019).

The Hebrew program at MPMS mainly comprised low-and middle-income Jews, many of whom were children of immigrants from a wide variety of countries who spoke many different languages at home. Indeed, our survey and interviews revealed that the majority of students came from bi/multilingual homes, where languages such as the following were spoken: Arabic, Bukharian, Carpathian, English, French, Georgian, Haitian Creole, Hebrew, Hungarian, Jamaican 'Patois,' Kavkazi, Persian, Polish, Portuguese, Russian, Spanish, Ukrainian and Yiddish. Data also showed that while most students were born in the US, their families' countries of origin included: Azerbaijian, France, Georgia, Grenada, Israel, Jamaica, Morocco, Puerto Rico, Romania, Russia, Ukraine, UK and Venezuela. The Jewish students were not primarily from Ashkenazi families and did not descend from Germanic, French and/or Eastern European Jewish communities. Many were of Sephardic/Mizrachi ancestry, meaning that their families came from Spain, Portugal, the Middle East and North Africa. While the Jewish students in this program represented diasporic Jewry in all of its multiculturalism and multilingualism, they did not fit the category of affluent white monolingual English speakers – descriptors that have been used for groups that many see as appropriating dual language and removing it from its original social justice mission of serving disadvantaged, minoritized language groups (Cervantes-Soon, 2014; Cervantes-Soon *et al.*, 2017; Palmer, 2009).

Though many of the Jewish students in the Hebrew program at MPMS may be viewed by others (and themselves) as white and benefit from white privilege, their non-Ashkenazi backgrounds point to the complex dynamic of Jewish racialization at work. Racial/ethnic hierarchies within Judaism have led to the symbolic violence of Ashkenazi Jews which deem Sephardic/Mizrachi Jews' identities, histories, customs, and practices inferior and inauthentic forms of Judaism and in need of 'Ashkenazification' – defined as adopting Ashkenazi religious rituals,

Ashkenazi pronunciations of Hebrew liturgy, and Eastern European foods (Sasson-Levy & Shoshana, 2013). The socio-historical normalization of Jews as white, European, and Western has resulted in the marginalization of Jews of other races and ethnicities, a dynamic which means that MPMS students were entangled in racial, ethnic, and class difference even while being subsumed under the Jewish category. Broadly speaking, these Jewish students represented the 'minority within the minority' (Sachedina, 1994) – a term used to describe double marginalization – in this case, the hierarchization of Ashkenazi Jewry over Sephardic/Mizrachi communities.

There is also an assumption in the US to assign a white racial identity to Jews; however, it is important to note that not all Jews are in fact white, nor do they necessarily claim a white identity.[4] This 'racial indeterminacy' (Goldstein, 2006) can be traced back to the 1800s, when American Jews were positioned at a time of fervent pro-nativist sentiments as 'an intermediate race located socially between black and white' (Ignatiev, 2012). Historians (Goldstein, 2006; Rottenberg, 2013; Sicher, 2013) have documented how the emergence of the category of ethnicity in the United States in the early 1920s and postwar period, along with new legislation that enacted fewer restrictions on educational and employment opportunities, enabled American Jews to escape hegemonic racialization as an inferior and degenerate minority. By the mid-1900s, Ashkenazi Jews 'became' white (albeit white Others) as they achieved upward social mobility (Brodkin, 1998); in the process, Jewishness was deracialized and disarticulated from the racial binary between Blacks and whites in American society (Greenberg, 2013). As a result, Jewish ethnicity replaced the perception of Jews as a racial category. Part of this transition of Eastern European Jews to the US at the turn of the 20th century demanded a negotiation of Yiddish and other European languages (the home languages), Hebrew (the sacred language), and English. The sociolinguistic intergenerational shift to English as a means of displaying allegiance to their newly adopted homeland, along with the 'linguistic disinheritance' of Jewish languages (Wirth-Nesher, 2006: 18), were part and parcel of the process of Jews responding to America's postwar social transformation and their becoming an ethnic group in the United States. Like other immigrant groups at the time, shifting to English monolingualism became a marker of Americanness. For the purposes of this chapter, these shifts underscore the historical dimension of Jewish raciolinguistic dynamics and lay the foundation for understanding the complexity of the intersecting categories of Jewishness, language, whiteness, class, and race.

Creating a Jewish Space

All of the Jewish families interviewed expressed favorable views on the establishment of the Hebrew program at MPMS because it carved out a 'Jewish space' for their children in an otherwise non-Jewish large urban public middle school. One reason for the need for this space was the awareness of growing antisemitism, including in the local area.[5] In this excerpt, the Jewish mother of a student in the Hebrew DLBE program at MPMS described her other son's experience attending another New York City public school:

> If I tell you stories about my other son in middle school, which is very unpleasant unfortunately…[R]emarks about the person being Jewish, it's very unfortunate…He just recently told me that the kids are throwing pennies and telling him, 'You pick up this penny. That's what you Jews are for.' (Michelle, parent, interview transcript, 12/22/17)

In this interview excerpt, Michelle described how her son experienced antisemitic bullying based on the negative stereotype of Jews as cheap in a public school that did not offer a Hebrew program. This sense of fear spoke to the diversity of Jewish families that lived in the area in which MPMS was located, which included observant families that adhered to traditional Jewish law (i.e. keeping kosher, observing Shabbat, attending synagogue, and sending their children to yeshivas – private Jewish schools in which secular and religious studies are both taught, often in single sex classrooms). MPMS also attracted secular and religious Israeli–American Jewish families as well as Jewish American families with no connection to Israel who were looking for Hebrew language study. In all cases, the Jewish families actively sought out a safe and identity-affirming Jewish space for their children.

Beyond teaching Hebrew, the families' acceptance and comfort with the program was the direct result of the school administration's welcoming and progressive policies of making kosher food[6] available in the cafeteria and during field trips, letting students hang up religious imagery throughout the year (such as a menorah during Chanukah), and modifying their schedule to fit the Jewish holidays. Acutely attuned to the need to accommodate ex-yeshiva students, the principal boasted that:

> In the first year we had twelve students [from yeshiva]. And the parents were always nervous…I'll tell you a funny story. After three days, she [a yeshiva parent] comes back and she was crying hysterically…She goes, 'The rabbi came to my house last night and he was like – 'Tell me, how can you send your child to a school where there's sex and drugs in the hallways?' Which is totally false…And I spoke to all these twelve students, they all said, 'We like it better here. We like the teachers better. And we feel more comfortable.' That's pretty amazing. After three, four days of being in a new place, they don't want to leave. (Mr D, principal, interview transcript, 9/30/16)

The reported narrative of a rabbi scaring yeshiva families away from public schools (and ostensibly trying to keep them at yeshiva) because of 'sex and drugs in the hallways' is itself reflective of a racialized perspective of non-Jews. The underlying presumption the rabbi was tapping into was that non-Jews are morally flawed and engaging in recreational behaviors that threaten the core of Orthodox religious Jewish life, which focuses on self-control and self-discipline (Fader, 2009). That the principal and staff were able to overcome this fear is significant. Families' level of comfort filtered down into the daily vicissitudes of classroom life. In the words of one mother,

> [MPMS] is very accommodating. The teacher would be like, 'This homework is due next week because we realize there's a few days where some of the kids are unable to write and unable to hand in the homework on time[7]. So, everybody gets to hand in the homework a little bit later'... I think it makes the kids feel like they could be who they are, without feeling like 'I'm the oddball here. I'm the only one handing in my assignment late.' (Leah, parent, interview transcript, 12/2/17)

The availability of Hebrew classes and kosher food, accommodations for Jewish observance, and the school's coordination with an after-school off-site program offering Jewish education, marked MPMS as 'Jewish enough' to offer a viable option for families willing to consider the public-school system. In this way, 'Jewish enough' was a discursive move that assuaged families' perceived fears of public schooling as a threatening assimilatory force and paved the way for families to make the shift. Yet, when heard in light of 'white enough' discourses common in affluent white families' cautious acceptance of dual language programs in gentrifying neighborhoods, it can be read as Jewish families aligning themselves with a form of privilege that enabled them to assert their position without having to acquiesce to a disruption in the social boundaries between Jews and non-Jews.

Overall, despite this sense of reassurance that they would not be forced to change or compromise, the decision to leave the yeshiva elementary context was fraught with trepidation for many observant families. Those who chose to take a chance at MPMS were also buoyed by the school's reputation for rigorous academic standards in secular studies (i.e. math and science), the eschewal of private school tuition, and what some parents perceived as a close-minded and racist perspective in yeshivas toward non-Jews, which they believed was less pervasive in public schooling. Once again, we see an interesting tension at work in the desire for a Jewish educational space with a more open-minded educational context than the yeshiva was presumed to provide. Jewish families also noted that the Hebrew bilingual program offered their children some form of Jewish education, even if religious studies were not a part of the curriculum, and indicated that the Hebrew program at MPMS was their 'chance' to take advantage of language learning programs just like other minoritized communities had throughout the city as the result of the expansion of DLBE programs.

Hebrew Language Ideologies

The conflation of Hebrew learning with Jewish space is premised on a deep-rooted language ideology that positions Hebrew as a primary marker of Jewishness (Avni, 2012). Broadly speaking, Hebrew theologically and culturally occupies a place of privilege and power in defining, creating, and sustaining authenticity in Jewish practices and traditions. Whereas Biblical and older varieties of Hebrew make up the textual tradition of religious Judaism, including the Torah and the prayer book, Modern Hebrew is the product of the Zionist project to (re)create a 'new' language for the Jewish homeland established in Israel in 1948.[8] As an example of Irvine and Gal's (2000) semiotic process of erasure, language ideologies that highlight Hebrew as a fundamental marker of Jewishness across time and space create a Jewish imaginary that erases, or at least downplays, Jewish religious, ethnic, national and linguistic diversity by promoting a common linguistic denominator that all Jews share. One mother at MPMS tapped into this ideology when she stated: 'Hebrew is our language. It represents who we are and where we come from. It represents us Jewish people' (Aviva, parent, interview transcript, 12/5/17). However, as strong as the ideology of Jewish ownership of Hebrew is, it is equally important to note the paradox that the vast majority of American Jews do not speak Modern Hebrew, nor can most read Biblical Hebrew with any comprehension beyond the decoding level.

Nonetheless, the language ideology premised on the co-naturalization of Hebrew and Jewishness had direct implications for the construction of racial hierarchies at MPMS. While each of the dual language programs opened at MPMS were conceived with the goal of recruiting groups of language minoritized students as a means of expanding racial and ethnic diversity in the school (Menken & Avni, 2017),[9] the notion and purpose of diversity did not extend to opening up the Hebrew language and allowing non-Jews to claim it as theirs. In other words, diversity had its limits. On one hand, school administrators, parents, and students espoused views that the language programs at MPMS enabled students 'to hang out with people who have different cultures…and get to know what their religions are like and what they do at home' (Rachel, student, interview transcript, 3/24/17). This capacious definition of diversity and its importance in wider American society was evident for Jewish parents who spoke about their perceived sense that yeshiva education, with its singular focus on accentuating Jewish insularity, promoted racism. As one mother, herself a graduate of public schooling, expressed:

> I feel like in public school I was taught to be very tolerant. And I was taught to be benevolent…I feel like my kids went to yeshiva, yet they didn't walk away from yeshiva with things that I walked away from public school with. And that bothered me. It really bothered me…Kids who go to yeshiva, when they see someone [homeless] in the street or

> whatever, can't even give them a dollar because 'Oh, he's faking it…'. And definitely negative stereotypes about other people. I didn't like that at all in a yeshiva. The use of different words to describe people is just unacceptable by me. (Leah, parent, interview transcript, 12/2/17)

Other parents spoke about the need to take their children out of yeshiva in order to ensure that 'in the world we live in today' their children could 'speak to anybody' without hesitations about 'who they are or what their religion is' (Aviva, parent, interview transcript, 12/5/17). Finally, parents spoke about the disadvantages of racial homogeneity in the yeshiva context.

> There's a lot of African American kids in her class right now, and it's important to me that she doesn't go to a school where everyone is just white and Jewish. At yeshiva everyone would have been the same. The world doesn't function that way. People are different, and I need her to learn how to appreciate everyone's differences and be proud of her own differences and that's fine. (Yael, parent, interview transcript, 5/14/17)

While regarding school integration favorably, Yael speaks about diversity in terms of what it might offer her daughter that a yeshiva would not, thereby commodifying her daughter's African American classmates in ways that echo the commodification of minoritized students and their community's linguistic resources in DLBE programs (Cervantes-Soon *et al.*, 2017; Flores, 2016; Valdés, 1998).

On the other hand, Jewish parents held contradictory views when it came to non-Jews speaking Hebrew, in that Jewish parents were far more reluctant and disinclined to allow non-Jews to claim Hebrew for themselves. From their perspective, Hebrew study was primarily for the benefit of Jewish students. As some Jewish parents indicated, if the program also had non-Jewish students who wanted to learn the language, this was manageable and tolerable, and even came with some degree of curiosity. Put differently, as there were no Black Jewish students, the presence of Black non-Jewish students in the class neither attracted Jewish families to the program nor put them off, as captured in the following mother's comment:

> It wasn't important to me, but I don't care, because I'm used to it from Chile. In Chile, there was a lot of Black kids…It doesn't bother me. I wasn't looking for it, but I accept it. (Tali, parent, interview transcript, 12/8/17)

In fact, the Jewishness of Hebrew study was so taken for granted that Jewish parents erased the presence of students with other religious backgrounds. As one Jewish mother explained, 'The Hebrew program attracts a special group of kids, and I really wanted him to be within that environment' (Ariana, Parent, interview transcript, 12/22/17). When pressed about what type of environment she was referring to, she responded: 'I hate to say it. It might sound wrong. Our kind. I mean the kids like him that have parents that do speak Hebrew, and that might not [speak Hebrew] but that Hebrew is important for them.' (Ariana, parent, interview transcript, 12/22/17). This mother's comment not only assumes that Hebrew is only important to American Jews, but also reflects a more insular, exclusionary, and arguably more overtly racist perspective. Speaking about 'our kind' clearly disabuses any notions that this parent saw the dual language structure as promoting the dissolution of ethnic and religious boundaries. If anything, the DLBE program offered a means to reify those societal divisions.

Interestingly, one Israeli mother from a Sephardic family interpreted our question about diversity in the classroom to refer solely to Jewish diversity, saying the following:

> It's good also for the kids to be exposed to that [diversity]...to other type of kids that come from different houses with different ideas, with different, you know, everything. We are all Jewish at the end of the story, so we all share something. (Aviva, parent, interview transcript, 12/5/17)

Indeed, the default position that the class was for Jewish students, along with the indifference to racial or Christian-Jewish diversity was also reflected in another mother's stark dismissal of diversity: 'I think there's plenty of diversity within the Jewish religion itself. So that's enough diversity for me.' (Edith, parent, interview transcript, 12/5/17). What these quotes make evident is that any goals of DLBE programs regarding the development of cross-cultural understandings or critical consciousness (Palmer *et al.*, 2019) were not a pivotal determining force for some of the Jewish families; instead, the Hebrew DLBE program was attractive because it was perceived as a Jewish space.

Underlying all of these utterances eschewing religious difference is a Hebrew language ideology that speaks directly to raciolinguistic ideologies whose logic affirms the inextricable and impenetrable interrelation between language (Hebrew) and religion (Judaism) in ways that minimalize or ignore other racialized groups and essentialize notions of Hebrew as a solely Jewish language. Significantly, the boundaries around Hebrew and the Hebrew classroom were impervious to any push to disassociate Hebrew from Jewishness. These non-porous boundaries also rejected any challenge to the hegemonic Jewish ownership of the language. Hence, what emerged is the dual language paradox in stark relief: on one hand, the creation of a Hebrew program that emboldened a group of Jewish families who had previously felt unwelcomed in public schooling and who sought it out for the benefits it provided. On the other hand, the creation of conditions that condoned a form of Jewish privilege that obviated the presence of non-Jews and foreclosed on the possibility of opening up language learning as a resource for all.

Non-Jews' Hebrew Ideologies

Attending to language ideologies in the Hebrew class at MPMS reveals hermetic boundaries of racial and religious difference and marginalization. Yet the Jewish families were not the only ones to base their decisions to attend the Hebrew program on beliefs about language, religion, and race. Racialization also played a critical role in how non-Jewish families came to attach particular valences to Hebrew through their own Hebrew ideologies. Because MPMS was a magnet school, attending the Hebrew program was one way for students to gain entry to the highly competitive, integrated school. This meant that for non-Jewish Black parents, Hebrew offered the possibility of admission into a well-resourced school with strong academics, which would open up access to other educational opportunities. In the words of one Black mother:

> I feel like you can get a better chance of education when you go to a diverse school other than, for me, an all African American public school. That's my opinion. Because we don't have the same resources, we don't have the same educators. We don't have the same funding. And I think the diversity provides more funding, more resources for the children. (Yalandra, parent, interview transcript, 12/4/17)

As Yalandra explains, her daughter being admitted into MPMS meant she did not have to go to her locally zoned, predominately Black school and could instead benefit from the additional resources available at MPMS. Hebrew learning in and of itself was tangential; that it is to say, the decision to attend a school with a Hebrew program was not based in the possibility of learning the language per se, but rather in the potential of securing a quality education for their children. Yalandra's perspective is reinforced by research findings that show there are greater resources available at integrated schools than at schools that are predominately Black and/or Latinx (Bohrnstedt *et al.*, 2015; Orfield & Frankenberg, 2013; Roda & Wells, 2013). At the same time, Yalandra's comment suggests that the Hebrew program was a means to gain access to white privilege in terms of funding and opportunity.

Yalandra went on to cite the conflation of Hebrew, Jews, and access when talking about the instrumental benefits of her daughter learning Hebrew:

> The world we live in right now and, you know, career-wise a lot of businesses, a lot of careers, they want you to have two languages. Hebrew is one of them. There's a lot of places are run by them. By Jews, I mean, 'cause it's true. Especially in New York City [*laughs*]… By Jews. And I think Hebrew is one of the main languages…I mean, so I feel like, you know, it would broaden [daughter's name]'s horizon and broaden her chances of getting a job within, you know, the field that she chooses… I mean, when she comes to my job. I work at a nursing home and I'm a nurse at a nursing home, so there it's owned by Jewish, by Jews. And she is able to speak with them when she comes there, in the language… I mean, she can speak good…I think she knows how to speak it well! (Yalandra, parent, interview transcript, 12/4/17)

In this instance, Yalandra tells the story of how her daughter's performance of Hebrew at her workplace endowed her family with social and economic capital.

Another Black parent displayed a more general interest in language learning without a specific interest in Hebrew per se, saying in response to a question about how important learning Hebrew was to her and her family:

> I must say it isn't that important to me. It's just that I'm just happy that she's able to speak another language but not necessarily the fact that it's Hebrew...[Learning Hebrew] was fine with me because it just opened my daughter to more things. I don't know. It didn't bother me. It's using more of her brain. (Laura, parent, interview transcript, 12/10/17)

For this parent, the idea that it 'it didn't bother me' conveys an ambivalence about the inherent worth of knowing Hebrew (as opposed to another language), but recognizes the benefit that this language learning context provided. While Jewish parents sought a space in the public school for religious expression, non-Jewish Black families also saw Hebrew instrumentally and pragmatically. As the comments indicate, Black families saw the Hebrew–English dual language program from an enrichment perspective that could provide their children with access to academic, social, and economic benefits.

This difference in goals exposed a tension between the goals of Black families who enrolled their children in the Hebrew dual language bilingual program and the views of many Jewish families who positioned Hebrew as a Jewish language. Based on the ideologies Jewish families expressed, it seemed that no matter how well Black children were able to master Hebrew it would never afford them Hebrew ownership. What is more, though the non-Jewish families perceived the benefits of learning Hebrew for specific job opportunities, the reality is that Hebrew is not a commonly spoken language in the United States, so the language actually has limited currency in the American marketplace, even among American Jews, who as noted previously, typically do not speak it. All of which points to the differing expectations and motivations of families attending dual language programs, and how these can be deeply entrenched and yet superficially attached to actual language learning and use.

'I Won't Touch It': Avoidance and Silencing Narratives

The previous section showed the importance of the Hebrew program specifically for Jewish families, a minoritized community seeking spaces where their children would be welcomed and their home practices supported in school, and it showed Black non-Jewish families' reasons for Hebrew learning. In this section, we probe how the Hebrew DLBE program existed in tandem with other forms of racism and bias that accompanied students into the school and Hebrew classes and how, in response, topics deemed sensitive such as race, religion and the Arab–Israeli conflict were systematically avoided and silenced by school staff and students' families. We want to underscore that while the linguistic, religious, and cultural diversity of the students in the Hebrew bilingual education program might seem to lend itself to the adoption of culturally sustaining pedagogy (Paris, 2012) and a curriculum that challenges raciolinguistic ideologies (Rosa & Flores, 2017), our findings revealed that this was not the approach taken at MPMS. Topics such as the students' religious or racial diversity and their identities were never explicitly addressed, even though bilingual education and social studies were formal educational spaces where such topics could easily have been woven into the curricula.

In general, all aspects of religious observance were silenced. For instance, during an observation of a 7th-grade social studies class, there was an incident in which a non-religious Jewish boy took a religious boy's skullcap, known as a yarmulke or *kippah*.[10] Our fieldnotes documented the moment:

> 10:14 am: Students are called on to go to smartboard and fill in blanks on the board. There's a moment where another student steals a boy's yarmulke and starts wearing it. The boy grabs it back and says 'Why are you wearing my yarmulke?!' The other boy laughs and says, 'I tried to put it and it doesn't even fit'. The boy says 'give me back my yarmulke!' as he grabs it back himself, and puts it back on. Ms. R doesn't get involved. The religious boy then moves his desk away from the other boy and works in silence until the end of period. (7th-grade classroom observation, fieldnotes, 1/12/17)

When the non-religious boy grabbed the skullcap he threatened his classmate's observance and made a joke of it. By not getting involved, the teacher missed an opportunity to address students' religious diversity.

We also heard from Yalandra, the Black mother quoted previously, about a racist experience her daughter had in the Hebrew dual language program:

> …[A] child that was negative, like was saying racist remarks…That she, you know, I don't, like, he just, he was just saying things. I'm not sure I recall the full story. But I know it was about, you know, Blacks always shooting people and if she sits on the bus should she sit in the front of the bus or the back of the bus, and how Black people can be, they like to shoot each other, to that effect. (Yalandra, parent, interview transcript, 12/4/17)

The student making racist comments to Yalandra's daughter was a Jewish boy in the Hebrew program who had recently moved to MPMS from yeshiva. Yalandra's daughter reported it and the boy was suspended from the school for several days. What these two incidents show is how simply placing diverse students together in a DLBE program did not automatically redress overt articulations of racism or create the conditions in which difference could be discussed and equity promoted.

Faculty in the dual language program at MPMS also did not seek out opportunities to leverage their students' diversity in the service of addressing forms of marginalization occurring at the school, and instead actively sought to avoid and suppress such discussions. Ms R and Ms T, a school administrator, explained that because MPMS was a public school where there was a strict separation of church and state, Judaic religious studies were not permitted in the Hebrew program. At the same time, New York State's Social Studies curriculum complicated this distinction because study of Islam, Judaism, and Christianity is part of the state's middle school social studies curriculum. In the absence of a formal curriculum for the class titled 'Hebrew Language and Culture', Ms R focused her instruction on Jewish holidays and teaching Israeli culture and history, such as Israeli traditional foods and key Zionist leaders in Israel's history, while avoiding explicit discussions about the Palestinian conflict, a fundamental component of Israel's geopolitical reality. In the interview excerpt below, Ms R and Mr A, the social studies teacher with whom she collaborated, discussed their approach.

> SA: Do you have any students who talk about Palestine or, you know, Palestinian rights? Does that ever come up? Like if you're talking about Yom Ha'atzmaut (Israeli Independence Day), does anybody ever say like.../?
>
> Ms R: I'm not touching this issue...Yeah. Even when we teach in Social Studies about slavery, we talk about Black and White. And I ask my husband, can I call White South? And he told me, 'No, don't touch it'...One of the lessons, I found the article about a caricature museum in Holon [a city in Israel]. Cartoon museum. And it was, I showed different pictures caricature. It was pictures like Spiderman, but Superman in black color.
>
> SA: Superman as a Black man?
>
> Ms R: Yeah...And one girl became crazy. As you remember, she became crazy, how I show Black discrimination. It was nuts... She felt like discrimination...
>
> SA: Do you think there'd be a backlash? Like if you were to start talking about how there are people in Israel that consider Yom Ha'atzmaut the Nakba ['disaster' in Arabic, referring to the Palestinian exodus], or something like that?...
>
> Mr A: That's always tricky. These kids are tricky. I almost feel like it would be easier to do it in a non-Hebrew class setting... But maybe I'm making an assumption that a lot probably go home and hear very pro-Israel things. It might be tricky.

Ms R: ...[W]e talk about Ten Commandments, and I told them that actually it was Jewish and Christians took it and ran it through. [Student name] told me, 'It's a lie. My mom knows'...I told him, 'Okay, go to a priest and ask...' (Ms. R and Mr. A, teachers, interview transcript, 2/23/18)

Both teachers described how they actively avoided discussing topics that could be sensitive, such as race, religious differences, and the nationalistic conflict. The teachers responded to students' contestations by dismissing them (e.g. when Ms R responded to the Black student calling her a racist by referring to her as 'nuts' and 'crazy'). While teachers seemed to think it was acceptable to discuss issues such as race or religion in an abstract or conceptual way, they did not invite discussions of these issues in a personal way, and in fact actively shut them down. Moreover, as Mr A suggests, the fact that they were in a Hebrew class ironically made speaking about religious and ethnic conflict more difficult and 'tricky.'

Some parents of children in the program agreed with the teachers' choices, as they too expressed a desire to avoid talking about divisive topics like racism as it pertained to the students in the school. In response to a question of whether teachers should directly address economic, ethnic, religious or racial difference in the classroom, a mother had the following to say:

> If the teacher sees that there is a problem in the classroom, yeah. But if the classroom gets along and everybody's doing well with each other, she shouldn't, again, I don't see a reason for the teacher to like bring it up, you mean, or teach the class about it... (Aviva, parent, interview transcript, 12/5/17)

Like many other parents, Aviva made clear she did not see that student diversity should be a part of the school's curriculum. Although racism and other forms of bias were issues that arose in the school's dual language program, teachers and families maintained that diversity of the students should not be addressed in the MPMS dual language curriculum, and teachers described their explicit avoidance of engaging in conversations about these issues.

Conclusion

The role that Hebrew ideologies, and by extension, a Hebrew–English DLBE program played in both reaffirming racial difference and downplaying its presence were on full display at MPMS. Jewish families were attracted to the program because it carved out a Jewish space in the otherwise non-sectarian public schools of NYC in ways that were extremely important to Jewish families. While they were often racialized as whites, the Jewish families at this school represented Mizrachi/Sephardi backgrounds and were not affluent. At the same time, Black non-Jewish families saw learning Hebrew as access to privilege in the form of educational and economic opportunities, and had less invested in the particular language being taught in contrast to the opportunity that language learning experience offered.

Both perspectives indicate the significance of bilingual education for minoritized communities, and underscore the varying Hebrew ideologies at play. While Jewish and non-Jewish stakeholders at the school held diverging ideologies about Hebrew as a marker of Jewish identity and as an instrument for educational equity and economic opportunity, these Hebrew ideologies allowed the school to promote this program and attract two groups that have traditionally not taken part in bilingual education in NYC public schools. This inclusion of black and Jewish students into DLBE is a positive change. At the same time, while we recognize how meaningful DLBE programs are for the students who have the opportunity to participate in them and their families, analyzing our data through a raciolinguistics lens has clarified specific areas for improvement to support these programs in realizing their potential.

Specifically, the elevation of Hebrew for Jewish students also exposed raciolinguistic ideologies which limited the potential for non-Jewish Black students to claim this language as their own. For the most part, the Jewish students in the Hebrew DLBE program were situated as the normative speaker and non-Jewish Black students as Other, even if language assessments placed them at the same Hebrew proficiency level. In this we see how the Jewish families aligned themselves with privilege (by positioning Black students as linguistic outsiders), even though the Jewish families attending this school had themselves faced and continue to face discrimination and marginalization – particularly in a national landscape where rhetoric of white nationalism once again reminds us of the contested and precarious nature of Jewish whiteness (Green, 2016).

Hence, this chapter underscores the complex relationships among language ideologies, raciolinguistics, and languages like Hebrew that are so closely identified with one particular religious group or nationality. Understanding how DLBE programs impact children from differently racialized, classed, and religious backgrounds offers an important contribution to the growing scholarship on raciolinguistics, which compels us to think about socio-historical dynamics of groups of speech communities and their identifications with particular languages. In this Hebrew classroom, racial, ethnic, and religious difference were both highly visible in determining who the 'authentic' Hebrew learner was, and yet remained virtually absent from any discussions in the class. In fact, the focus on Jewish holidays and Israeli culture and history precluded any discussions about black–white relations or internal Jewish difference. And yet, the issues were present. In this we see the contradictory capacity of DLBE: the ability to uplift one social group and the potential to ignore or downgrade another. The myopic focus on Hebrew learning without acknowledging what the language represented to different stakeholders impeded this classroom's possibilities for being a space for social transformation. Perhaps that is one of the biggest lessons that this Hebrew case study offers. Students from both language groups in DLBE come to these programs with varying backgrounds, differing attachments to their 'own' language, and a range of motivations for learning the other. Sweeping aside these dynamics and presenting them as two neutral languages ignores their specific histories and runs the risk of closing down opportunities for dual language classrooms to be truly inclusive of all students and their languaging practices.

Notes

(1) Pseudonyms are used for the name of the school and all the participants in this study.
(2) Because much of the Hebrew teaching material created in the United States for American children is targeted for Jewish day schools or synagogue after-school programs and explicitly promotes Judaism, there is very little published material available for teaching Hebrew in the public school setting. Ms R not only developed the curriculum for the 'Hebrew Language and Culture' class, but also wrote and/or pulled together materials to use in class from other resources, some of which were taken from pedagogical material used in Israel for new immigrants learning Hebrew. In terms of teaching social studies in Hebrew, she rewrote much of the English material in Hebrew and created her own set of assessment tools in Hebrew.
(3) That only one student was classified an 'English language learner' by the NYCDOE indicated this was not a program established in order to develop proficiency in English among emergent bilinguals. While many students 'test out' of their 'English language learner' designation by the time they begin middle school, it is unusual for a bilingual middle school program in New York to serve so few.
(4) Though the Pew Research Center's 2013 *Portrait of American Jews*, found that 7% of Jews described themselves as Black, Hispanic, or of a different racial background, the recently issued report *Counting Inconsistencies: An Analysis of American Jewish Population Studies, with a Focus on Jews of Color* (2019) – a meta-analysis of national and community level Jewish population studies – found that Jews of color represent at least 12–15% of American Jews. Among its conclusions is that American Jewish population surveys have largely neglected to systematically and consistently ask about the racial and ethnic identities of US Jews, which has led to a lack of knowledge about the composition and size of the population of Jews of color. This report explicitly challenges the racialized assumptions that the vast majority of American Jews identify as 'white.' Though the authors do not frame it from a raciolinguistic perspective, they do note that survey designs have traditionally sampled respondents in ways that likely result in undercounting Jews of color because they relied on sampling 'distinctive Jewish names,' as well as relying heavily on Jewish community lists.
(5) While antisemitism is a frequent concern for Jewish families, our study was conducted prior to the recent surge in antisemitic acts in the United States (Anti-Defamation League, 2017). There have been several recent reports in the media of violence and threats against Jews in the area of New York in which MPMS is located (Rayman & Blau, 2017; Stremple, 2018).
(6) Jewish dietary laws, *Kashrut* (keeping kosher), prohibit the mixture of milk and meat.
(7) According to Jewish *Halacha*, the laws and ordinances that regulate Jewish religious observances and daily life and conduct, observant Jews are forbidden to write on the

Shabbat and Jewish holidays, as it constitutes a form of work. One student reported that the school did not put meat in the oven with dairy foods, and that there was always hummus and pretzels available as an option.

(8) An essential component of the revernacularization of Hebrew as part of the Zionist enterprise was to have a single language that could unite the linguistically diverse Jewish community living in Palestine and then in Israel when the state was established in 1948. For more on the rejection of Yiddish and the erasure of other languages, as well as the extensive language policies that were designed to create a monoglot Hebrew speaking society (see Halperin, 2015; Safran, 2005; Spolsky & Shohamy, 1999).

(9) It is important to note that this objective aligns with city educational goals, as NYC public schools are highly racially segregated (Kucsera & Orfield, 2014), despite the fact that the city school system is the most diverse in the US.

(10) Covering one's head with a yarmulke is a sign of devoutness and a way of honoring god.

References

Amrein, A. and Peña, R.A. (2000) Asymmetry in dual language practice: Assessing imbalance in a program promoting equality. *Education Policy Analysis Archives* 8 (8), 1–17.

Anti-Defamation League (2017) 2017 Audit of anti-Semitic incidents. See https://www.adl.org/resources/reports/2017-audit-of-anti-semitic-incidents (accessed 1 January 2019).

Avni, S. (2012) Hebrew as heritage: The work of language in religious and communal continuity. *Linguistics and Education* 23 (3), 323–333.

Avni, S. and Menken, K. (2019) The expansion of dual language bilingual education into new communities and languages: The case of Hebrew in a New York City public middle school. *Theory Into Practice* 58 (2), 154–163. DOI: 10.1080/00405841.2019.1569378

Baker, C. and Wright, W. (2017) *Foundations of Bilingual Education and Bilingualism* (6th edn). Bristol: Multilingual Matters.

Bohrnstedt, G., Kitmitto, S., Ogut, B., Sherman, D. and Chan, D. (2015) *School Composition and the Black–White Achievement Gap* (NCES 2015-018). US Department of Education, Washington, DC: National Center for Education Statistics See http://nces.ed.gov/pubsearch (accessed 25 January 2019).

Boyle, A., August, D., Tabaku, L., Cole, S. and Simpson-Baird, A. (2015) *Dual Language Education Programs: Current State Policies and Practices*. Washington, DC: American Institutes for Research.

Brodkin, K. (1998) *How Jews became White Folks and What that Says about Race in America*. New Jersey: Rutgers University Press.

Cervantes-Soon, C.G. (2014) A critical look at dual language immersion in the new Latin@ diaspora. *Bilingual Research Journal* 37 (1), 64–82.

Cervantes-Soon, C.G. and Turner, A.M. (2017) Countering silence and reconstructing identities in a Spanish/English two-way immersion program: Latina mothers' pedagogies in El Nuevo Sur. In X. Rong and J. Hilburn (eds) *Immigration and Education in North Carolina: The Challenges and Responses in a New Gateway State*. Boston, MA: Sense.

Cervantes-Soon, C., Dorner, L., Palmer, D., Heiman, D., Schwerdtfeger, R. and Choi, J. (2017) Combating inequalities in two-way language immersion programs: New directions for bilingual education. *Review of Research in Education* 41 (1), 403–427.

Chaparro, S. (2019) But mom! I'm not a Spanish boy: Raciolinguistic socialization in a two-way immersion bilingual program. *Linguistics and Education* 50, 1–12. 10.1016/j.linged.2019.01.003.

Collier, V.P. and Thomas, W.P. (2014) *Educating English Language Learners for a Transformed World*. Albuquerque, NM: Fuente Press.

Elazar, D.J. (1989) *The other Jews: The Sephardim Today.* New York: Basic Books, Inc.

Fader, A. (2009) *Mitzvah Girls: Bringing Up the Next Generation of Hasidic Jews in Brooklyn.* Princeton University Press.

Farruggio, P. (2010) Latino immigrant parents' views of bilingual education as a vehicle for heritage preservation. *Journal of Latinos and Education* 9 (1), 3–21.

Feinauer, E. and Howard, E. (2014) Attending to the third goal: Cross-cultural competence and identity development in two-way immersion programs. *Journal of Immersion and Content-Based Language Education* 2 (2), 257–272.

Fishman, J.A. (2014) Three hundred-plus years of heritage language education in the United States. In T. Wiley, J. Peyton, D. Christian, S. Moore and N. Liu (eds) *Handbook of Heritage, Community, and Native American Languages in the United States* (pp. 50–58). New York: Routledge.

Fitts, S. (2006) Reconstructing the status quo: Linguistic interaction in a dual-language school. *Bilingual Research Journal* 30 (2), 337–365.

Flores, N. (2016) A tale of two visions: Hegemonic whiteness and bilingual education. *Educational Policy* 30 (1), 13–38.

Fránquiz, M.E. (2012) Key concepts in bilingual education: Identity texts, cultural citizenship, and humanizing pedagogy. *New English Reading Association Journal* 48 (1), 32–42.

Freeman, R. (1998) *Bilingual Education and Social Change.* Clevedon: Multilingual Matters.

García, O. (2009) *Bilingual Education in the 21st Century: A Global Perspective.* West Sussex, UK: Wiley-Blackwell.

García, O. and Kleifgen, J. (2018) *Educating Emergent Bilinguals: Policies, Programs and Practices for English Learners* (2nd edn). New York, NY: Teachers College Press.

García, O. and Woodley, H.H. (2015) Bilingual education. In M. Bigelow and J. Ennser-Kananen (eds) *The Routledge Handbook of Educational Linguistics* (pp. 132–144). New York: Routledge.

Gerena, L. (2011) Parental voice and involvement in cultural context: Understanding rationales, values, and motivational constructs in a dual immersion setting. *Urban Education* 46 (3), 342–370.

Goldstein, E.L. (2006) *The Price of Whiteness: Jews, Race, and American Identity.* Princeton: Princeton University Press.

Green, E. (2016) Are Jews white? *The Atlantic*, December 5, 2016.

Greenberg, C. (2013) I'm not White – I'm Jewish': The racial politics of American Jews. In E. Sicher (ed.) *Race, Color, Identity: Rethinking Discourses about 'Jews' in the Twenty First Century* (pp. 35–55). New York: Berghahn.

Halperin, L. (2015) *Babel in Zion: Jews, Nationalism, and Language Diversity in Palestine, 1920–1948.* Yale University Press.

Hamayan, E., Genesee, F. and Cloud, N. (2013) *Dual Language Instruction from A to Z: Practical Guidance for Teachers and Administrators.* Portsmouth, NH: Heinemann.

Hernández, A.M. (2015) Language status in two-way bilingual immersion: The dynamics between English and Spanish in peer interaction. *Journal of Immersion and Content-Based Language Education* 3 (1), 102–126.

Ignatiev, N. (2012) *How the Irish Became White.* New York: Routledge.

Irvine, J.T. and Gal, S. (2000) Language ideology and linguistic differentiation. In P. Kroskrity (ed.) *Regimes of Language* (pp. 35–83). Santa Fe, NM: School of American Research Press.

Kelman, A., Hahn Tapper, A., Fonseca, I. and Saperstein, A. (2019) Counting inconsistencies: An analysis of American Jewish population studies, with a focus on Jews of color. See https://jewsofcolorfieldbuilding.org/wp-content/uploads/2019/05/Counting-Inconsistencies-052119.pdf (accessed 30 May 2019).

Kucsera, J. and Orfield, G. (2014) New York State's extreme school segregation: Inequality, inaction and a damaged future. The Civil Rights Project/Proyecto Derechos Civiles. See https://escholarship.org/uc/item/5cx4b8pf (accessed 17 June 2020).

LeCompte, M. and Preissle, J. (1993) *Ethnography and Qualitative Design in Educational Research* (2nd edn). San Diego, CA: Academic.

Lindholm-Leary, K.J. (2005) The rich promise of two-way immersion. *Educational Leadership* 62 (4), 56–59.

Menken, K. and Avni, S. (2017) Challenging linguistic purism in dual language bilingual education: A case study of Hebrew in a New York City public middle school. *Annual Review of Applied Linguistics* 37, 185–202.

Menken, K. and Avni, S. (2019) Language policy conflicts: New York City's efforts to expand bilingual education amidst English-Only pressures. In T. Ricento (ed.) *Language and Politics in the United States and Canada: Taking Stock on the Occasion of the 150th Anniversary of Canadian Confederation* (pp. 154–172). Cambridge: Cambridge University Press.

Miles, M., Huberman, A. and Saldaña, J. (2013) *Qualitative Data Analysis: A Methods Sourcebook* (3rd edn). Los Angeles, CA: SAGE.

Muro, J.A. (2016) 'Oil and water'? Latino-white relations and symbolic integration in a changing California. *Sociology of Race & Ethnicity* 2 (4), 516–530.

New York City Department of Education (NYCDOE) (2015) *Checklist: Primary Characteristics of Model Dual Language Programs*. New York, NY: Author.

Orfield, G. and Frankenberg, E. (2013) *Educational Delusions? Why Choice Can Deepen Inequality and How to Make Schools Fair*. Oakland, CA: University of California Press.

Palmer, D.K. (2009) Middle-class English speakers in a two-way immersion bilingual classroom: 'Everybody should be listening to Jonathan right now…' *TESOL Quarterly* 43 (2), 177–202.

Palmer, D., Cervantes-Soon, C., Dorner, L. and Heiman, D. (2019) Bilingualism, biliteracy, biculturalism, and critical consciousness for all: Proposing a fourth fundamental goal for two-way dual language education. *Theory Into Practice* 58 (2), 121–133. DOI: 10.1080/00405841.2019.1569376

Paris, D. (2012) Culturally sustaining pedagogy: A needed change in stance, terminology, and practice. *Educational Researcher* 41 (3), 93–97.

Petrovic, J.E. (2005) The conservative restoration and neoliberal defenses of bilingual education. *Language Policy* 4 (4), 395–416.

Rayman, G. and Blau, R. (2017, November 2) Anti-Semitic incidents nearly double in N.Y. since Trump's election: *Daily News*. See http://www.nydailynews.com/new-york/anti-semitic-rates-double-n-y-trump-election-report-article-1.3607636 (accessed 11 June 2018).

Roda, A. and Wells, A.S. (2013) School choice policies and racial segregation: Where white parents' good intentions, anxiety, and privilege collide. *American Journal of Education* 119 (2), 261–293.

Rosa, J. and Flores, N. (2017) Do you hear what I hear? Raciolinguistic ideologies and culturally sustaining pedagogies. In D. Paris and H.S. Alim (eds) *Culturally Sustaining Pedagogies: Teaching and Learning for Justice in a Changing World* (pp. 175–190). New York, NY: Teachers College Press.

Rottenberg, C. (2013) Spaces of ambivalence: Blacks and Jews in New York City. In E. Sicher (ed.) *Race, Color, Identity: Rethinking Discourses about Jews in the Twenty First Century* (pp. 96–112). New York: Berghahn.

Sachedina, A.A. (1994) A minority within a minority: The case of the Shi'a in North America. In Y.Y. Haddad and J. Idleman (eds) *Muslim Communities in North America* (pp. 3–14). New York: State University of New York Press.

Sáenz-Badillos, A. (1996) *A History of the Hebrew Language*. Cambridge: Cambridge University Press.

Safran, W. (2005) Language and nation-building in Israel: Hebrew and its rivals. *Nations and Nationalism* 11 (1), 43–63.

Sasson-Levy, O. and Shoshana, A. (2013) 'Passing' as (non)ethnic: The Israeli version of acting white. *Sociological Inquiry* 83 (3), 448–472.

Sicher, E. (2013) Rethinking discourses about Jews. In E. Sicher (ed.) *Race, Color, Identity: Rethinking Discourses about Jews in the Twenty First Century* (pp. 3–18). New York: Berghahn.

Spolsky, B. and Shohamy, E.G. (1999) *The Languages of Israel: Policy, Ideology, and Practice*. Clevedon: Multilingual Matters.

Stillman, N.A. (1995) *Sephardi Religious Responses to Modernity*. Luxembourg: Harwood Academic Publishers.

Stremple, P. (2018, November 5) Rise in Anti-Semitic crimes across Brooklyn brings condemnation, calls to action from politicians. *Bklyner*. See https://bklyner.com/anti-semitic-crimes/ (accessed 11 June 2018).

Valdés, G. (1997) Dual-language immersion programs: A cautionary note concerning the education of language-minority students. *Harvard Educational Review* 67 (3), 391–429.

Valdés, G. (2014) Heritage language students: Profiles and possibilities. In T.G. Wiley, J. Kreeft Peyton, D. Christian, S.C. Moore and N. Liu (eds) *Handbook of Heritage, Community, and Native American Languages in the United States* (pp. 41–49). New York: Routledge.

Valdiviezo, L. and Nieto, S. (2015) Culture in bilingual and multilingual education: Conflict, struggle and power. In W.E. Wright, S. Boun and O. García (eds) *The Handbook of Bilingual and Multilingual Education* (pp. 92–107). Hoboken, NJ: Wiley-Blackwell.

Wirth-Nesher, H. (2006) *Call it English: The Languages of Jewish American Literature*. Princeton, NJ: Princeton University Press.

Zúñiga, C.E., Henderson, K.I. and Palmer, D.K. (2018) Language policy toward equity: How bilingual teachers use policy mandates to their own ends. *Language and Education* 32 (1), 60–76.

8 Raciolinguistic Positioning of Language Models in a Korean–English Dual Language Immersion Classroom

Jin Sook Lee, Wona Lee and Hala Sun

Dual language immersion programs have been gaining popularity as a promising educational model that can lead to high academic achievement and multilingualism for students from both linguistic majority and linguistic minority backgrounds (de Jong, 2016; Lindholm-Leary, 2001; Steele *et al.*, 2017; Tedick *et al.*, 2011). A core principle of the program rests on the positioning of speakers of English and their partner languages as language models for one another which can also help to balance the power dynamics between language groups (Christian, 1996; Lindholm-Leary, 2001). Yet, studies have shown that despite programmatic intentions of promoting equity and diversity, challenges with differential language status and power dynamics continue to persist in dual language immersion programs (Freeman, 1998; Hadi-Tabassum, 2006; Lee & Jeong, 2013; Potowski, 2007). Moreover, educative practices based on narrow and rigid views of language competence in dual language immersion programs have continued to perpetuate racialization processes that lead to inequitable learning opportunities for students (Cervantes-Soon *et al.*, 2017; Lee *et al.*, 2011; Valdés, 1997).

In this chapter, we join the conversation about race, language and power in dual language immersion settings by taking up raciolinguistic positionings of language models – fluent speakers of the instructional languages who are integral to the viability of dual language immersion programs. Using an ethnographic lens, we present interview and classroom interactional data in a first grade 50/50 Korean–English dual language immersion classroom that make visible how raciolinguistic ideologies shape speaker identities and ability positioning in the teaching and learning processes. To illustrate these points, we first examine parents' raciolinguistic profiling of the classroom teachers, who are self-identified heritage language speakers of Korean and dominant speakers of English. Then, we trace how the teachers construct the notion of appropriate language models among their students, making a distinction in the language modeling practices between native speakers (i.e. students who are not only born into the language and have racial and cultural affiliation with the language, but are also dominant speakers of the first language) and fluent bilingual speakers. Our analysis aims to provide insights into how perceptions of appropriate language modeling are constructed among key stakeholders in dual language immersion programs and how they may perpetuate racialized expectations of students in ways that can affect their learning opportunities.

Theoretical Perspectives

Drawing from the disciplinary fields of sociolinguistics and linguistic anthropology, this study utilizes raciolinguistic perspectives to examine how ideas and expectations of appropriate language behavior influence perceptions of competence among both the speakers and listeners of a language (Flores & Rosa, 2015). Flores and Rosa (2015) argue that the expectations and demands to use only a specific type of discourse in educational settings create unequal learning opportunities for students, especially for racialized students. That is, what is deemed to be 'appropriate' language use in educational settings is often dictated by raciolinguistic ideologies that position certain language speakers and their practices as normative and others as deficient or incorrect. For example, in language learning settings like dual language immersion programs, the native speaker is often upheld as the target language model. However, labels such as native speaker or heritage language speaker must be understood in relation to racialized perceptions that promote a certain kind of language competence as standard or appropriate, which are often unrelated to any empirical linguistic practices (Bonfiglio, 2010; Flores & Rosa, 2015; Rosa & Flores, 2017).

The model of bilingual development in dual language immersion settings that undergirds instructional practices such as the arbitrary separation of the languages of instruction by content, teacher and/ or classroom space or assessment practices that measure bilingual students against monolingual native speaker norms promote the belief that bilinguals consist of two monolinguals in one speaker (Grosjean, 1989; Lee *et al.*, 2008; Valdés, 2005). Such practices reinforce monoglossic language ideologies that limit our imagination of what can constitute rich bilingual language use. Instead, García (2009) proposes a more dynamic understanding of language competence that supports a heteroglossic language ideology to account for the fluid language practices of multilinguals. But in order to do so, changes in linguistic practices and perceptions must happen at both the speaker and listener levels (Flores & Rosa, 2015; Inoue, 2006). In other words, regardless of how closely some speakers are able to follow the ways of native speakers, if listeners are unable to undo their raciolinguistic perceptions, they will continue to be heard as being less than ideal or deficient in some way. Thus, it is imperative that we continue to critically examine the implications of native speaker appropriateness-based standards in dual language immersion programs, if the goal is to truly foster healthy heteroglossic language ideologies and multilingual norms.

Korean–English Context

In comparison to languages like Mandarin or Spanish, Korean dual language immersion programs are much less common and draw a very specific student population, mostly those with heritage ties to Korean. According to Ee (2018), as of 2014, there are 13 K-12 Korean–English dual language immersion schools in the Los Angeles area, and a few more scattered across the United States in areas with high concentrations of Koreans. They present an opportunity to investigate how raciolinguistic perceptions function within a racial group that places divisions between recent Korean immigrants and Korean Americans.

In order to better understand raciolinguistic perspectives commonly observed among Korean people, some historical background is necessary. There has been a long lineage of US influence on the education of Koreans dating from the first entry of an US missionary, Horace Grant Underwood, in 1885 who brought a vision of education that has planted deep roots in ideologies about language and education among the Korean people. Through instruction in science, math and English, which were an indirect means to introduce Koreans to the Bible, literacy rates reached as high as 85–90% (Pang, 2015). Historically, the educational institutions that Underwood established were so highly regarded in the Korean society that even the King of Korea recruited the top two students from these institutions into his service every year (Pang, 2015). In what was known as the 'hermit kingdom,' nicknamed for Korea's strong resistance against foreign influence, the educational practices brought by missionaries became the beginnings of privileging racially white teachers in Korea, an ideology still strong today in education circles where parents choose white teachers over other races, in hopes that their children will learn the 'American ways' (Rondilla, 2009). Moreover, the association of English with societal advancements and access to modernization and power was reinforced during the Korean War when the US became the superpower ally to the South Korean government. These historical events in addition to the recognition of the power of English in the world have fueled what Park (2009: 2) calls 'strange and irrational obsessions which unduly burden every Korean, both emotionally and financially' to learn and speak English well. The status of English has become so prominent as a critical criterion for education and employment that South Korea had even considered adopting English as an official language at one time (Song, 2011).

As such, preferential treatment and attitudes toward whiteness and the belief that white native speakers have superior language and teaching skills, which has also led to discriminatory practices in teacher recruitment in Korea, are prevalent in Korea and among Koreans (Jeong, 2014; Kubota & Lin, 2006; Lee, 2014). Hence, immigrant parents from Korea bring with them the perspective of the 'white gaze' (Paris & Alim, 2014) that views the practices and beliefs of white subjects to be superior in ways that cannot be completely acquired by language-minoritized people even when they are modeled after them (Flores & Rosa, 2015). Such raciolinguistic ideologies are highly relevant for Korean–English dual language immersion programs because they strongly influence the expectations placed on teaching practices and student learning outcomes. Previous studies have found that two primary reasons for sending children to a Korean–English dual immersion program is to develop and maintain ties to their heritage and to facilitate the transition to the US culture and language (Ee, 2016; Lee & Jeong, 2013). Like other dual language immersion programs, although to different degrees, Korean programs also see an imbalance in the status of languages as well as in the expectations of mastery of English and Korean by the teachers and parents for their students. As the data will show, parents and teachers hold different standards and learning expectations for Korean and English proficiency development for children from differing backgrounds.

Research Site

The data come from a nine-month longitudinal study in a first-grade Korean–English dual language immersion classroom at Seaside Elementary School, located in an urban area of Southern California. Seaside Elementary School implements a 50/50 dual language immersion model, where the students are provided with 50% instructional time in Korean and 50% in English on a daily basis in one classroom (i.e. morning instruction in Korean and afternoon instruction in English across content areas, alternating the schedule on a monthly basis). Both teachers identify themselves as Korean Americans and immigrated to the US at a young age. They maintained their Korean as a heritage language via home language use, but never had any formal linguistic training in Korean, although Ms Suh was educated in Korea through her middle school years. They are both credentialed teachers and have some training in bilingual teaching methods, but nothing specific to teaching in Korean. Officially, Ms Kim, who has 10 years of teaching experience, is the lead teacher for Korean and Ms Suh, who has been teaching for 1.5 years, heads the

English instructional time. However, they serve as each other's assistants during their partners' instructional times. Therefore, the students interact with both teachers in English and Korean.

There are 26 students in the first-grade class, which is composed of approximately 25% Korean-dominant, 30% English-dominant and 45% more balanced bilingual students as described by the teachers. Of the 26 students, 20 are of Korean ethnicity, eight were born in Korea and 12 were born in the US. Of the eight born in Korea, two students, Hyun and Yun, had recently arrived to the US in the past year. With the exception of Hyun and Yun, most of the students self-identified as being 'American.' Of the six children that were not of Korean heritage, there was one African American student, one Filipino student, two white students, and two mixed-heritage students (Japanese/white and Chinese/white).

All the parents with the exception of one mother, who was a high school graduate, possessed college degrees. While the parents of the Korean children reported wanting to give their children an opportunity to develop their heritage language, the parents of the non-Korean children commented that they enrolled their children for exposure to a different culture and language because they believed in the benefits of multilingualism. These parents also commented that Korean children tend to achieve high academic outcomes and saw it to be beneficial to expose their children to such an academic culture (Lee & Jeong, 2013). These were general impressions and expectations that the non-Korean parents had at the beginning of their dual language immersion journey. Whether and how such racialized perceptions of Korean students may have evolved throughout their journey remains to be seen.

Data Sources and Analysis

The data consist of two interviews with six Korean parents (once at the beginning and once at the end of the study), who had volunteered to be a part of the study, three interviews with each of the two teachers, and 24 hours of classroom observations, during which we recorded whole group and small group interactions. None of the non-Korean parents were interested in participating in the study formally; however, they did engage in informal conversations with us where they shared their general views about their interest in the Korean–English dual language immersion program.

The interview format was semi-structured and conducted by the researchers in Korean with the parents and in both Korean and English with the teachers, which were the languages of choice by the informants. Each interview lasted approximately an hour. The parents were interviewed about their motivations for their sending their children to a dual language immersion school, their language ideologies, their perceptions of the linguistic and pedagogical competence of the teachers, and the quality of the program. The teachers were interviewed about their motivations for becoming a teacher in a bilingual setting, their assessment of their students' and their own language proficiencies, their language ideologies, their beliefs about language development and teaching, and their experiences teaching content in both languages.

For the purposes of this chapter, a thematic analysis of the interview responses was conducted to identify parents' views of the teachers' linguistic and pedagogical competence as well as their expectations of their children's English and heritage language proficiency (Strauss & Corbin, 1998). Also, the teachers' language ideologies were analyzed through the interview and classroom data to examine their construction of 'appropriate' language models in their discourse and teaching practices. Classroom interaction data were combed through for instances where the teachers or students spoke of language modeling or language proficiency/competence or where teachers engaged in nominations of particular students as language models. The identified episodes were then transcribed and analyzed in terms of how the teachers positioned students' perceived language competence and their abilities.

Findings

Parents' raciolinguistic profiling of teachers as language models

A common theme that reoccurred during the interviews with Korean parents was their raciolinguistic profiling of the teachers' English and Korean as 'not being native enough.' According to Bonfiglio (2010), the native speaker term originated as a time-space-bound construct linking being native to a birthright and a state of monolingualism. From this perspective, a person is not a native speaker if she/he is not born into the language and sustains a pure state of monolingualism in the language. Similar to the 'white gaze,' the parents held what we may term as a 'native gaze' that views the practices and ways of native speaker subjects to be superior over those of a non-native speaker. Their 'native gaze' shaped their perception of the language and teaching abilities of the teachers as not being equal to that of a monolingual native speaker in English or in Korean.

Both teachers are of Korean descent, but were raised in the United States. Ms Suh came to the US at the age of 11 and Ms Kim came at the age of 4, but they both saw themselves as 'native' or 'near-native speakers' of English, and English was clearly identified as their dominant language. Yet, the parents, who interestingly self-assessed their own English proficiency to be low, characterized the teachers' English as being 'different' from white teachers as reflected in the words of one mother who stated '아무래도 영어 사용이 다르잖아요' *(It is inevitable that their English language use is different [from white teachers])*, and wondered how the teachers' 'non-nativeness' would influence their children's acquisition of English.

M-K9: 저는 듀얼 랭귀지면 한국어는 한국 사람이, 영어는 외국 사람이 그렇게 가르켰으면 좋겠어요. 우리는 말을 배우기 이전에, 그 나라 말을 배우면서 그 나라의 이렇게 뭐랄까, 그 나라의 관습도 배우고 그 나라의 manner 도 배우고 그 나라 문화를 배우는 거 아니에요? 그런데 한국 사람한테 영어를 배우면, 그것도 지금 담임 선생님이 중학교까지 한국에서 나왔다 그러더라고요. 그러면은 영어는 물론 여기와서 열심히 해서 하셨겠지만, 이 미국 문화까지 아이들이 그걸 배울수 있을까. 엄마들도 그렇고 우리 아빠도 그렇고 그건 조금 의문이라고 생각해요. 뭐 발음도 물론 열심히 해서 좋아지기는 하겠지만 이 원어민들하고 또 같지 않을 그럴 문제가 있잖아요. 그래서 듀얼 랭귀지니까 한국말은 한국 사람이, 미국말은 미국 사람이 하는 그런 거였으면 더 좋은 교육이겠다 싶어요.

When I think of dual language programs, I would prefer Korean to be taught by a Korean native, and English to be taught by a foreign person [literal translation from Korean word 외국 사람, referring to a non-Korean person that is a native speaker of English in this context]. *Before we learn a language, we need to learn, how should I say, the country's traditions, the country's manners, and the country's culture, right? But when we learn English from a Korean person- as a matter of fact, the homeroom teacher graduated from middle school in Korea I am told- although I'm sure she studied English really hard once she was here, I wonder if our children can learn about the American culture from her. Other mothers and also my husband have doubts about whether that is possible. Of course, if you practice your pronunciation enough, it can get better, but it won't be the same as native speakers, that is the problem. That's why I feel that since it is a dual language program, it would be a much better educational program if Korean was taught by a Korean person and English was taught by an American who speaks the American language.*

This mother clearly lays out her rationale for why languages should be taught by native speakers of the language because she believes that there are fundamental differences in pronunciation and the understanding of the cultures, traditions and mannerisms between 'American' native speakers and Korean speakers of English, no matter how much they study or try. This again demonstrates the prominent 'native gaze' ideology circulating among the parents.

Her views were corroborated by other mothers as well as a father who also commented that '사운드는 약간 미국 애들하고 우리 아시안하고 발음을 똑같이 할 수는 없는 것 같아요 (F-K12)' *(I don't think that the sounds produced by American kids and our Asian kids can ever be exactly the same)*. Interestingly, the Korean parents made a distinction between their ethnically Korean children and 'American' children, a term they used to refer to non-Korean children, although most of their children saw themselves to be 'American.' Their 'native gaze' ideology situates their children's language competence to be somehow different from their white English-speaking peers, yet their desire for 'native pronunciation' and 'perfect grammar' in their children's English was strong. Pronunciation and grammar were constantly brought up by parents as the two English skills that their children must have to succeed in the US. Throughout the interviews, parents alluded to their fear that their children will be disadvantaged in some way because their English will not be exactly the same as their white peers and the fact that they were being taught by non-white teachers exacerbated their concern. Because their children will never have the physical appearance of an English native speaker, it seems that the parents believed that the proof of their children's mastery of the English language was in the way of how their children 'sounded' when they spoke English. Thus, their wish for their children to attain 'native pronunciation' and 'perfect grammar' was based on their belief that by having these two linguistic attributes, their children would not face discrimination from listeners while living in the US. This concern is corroborated by studies that have shown that white listeners have negative attitudes and assign undesirable attributes toward speech varieties associated with low prestige groups or racialized groups that lead to discrimination (Kang & Rubin, 2009; Lindemann, 2002).

In order to compensate for what the parents perceived to be a gap in their children's education, that is, the lack of access to an 'American' English native-speaking teacher, the parents sought out other educational opportunities where their children could be taught by speakers that met their idealized standards of a native speaker of English. For example, through after-school programs via the public library or local church organizations, the mothers were constantly on the lookout for programs that were led by 'white' or 'American' teachers. One mother reported:

> M-K11: 뭐, 영어는 발음이나 이런 것도 중요한 것 같아요. 그러다 보니까 되도록이면 그래도 한국 사람이 쓰는 영어보다는 진짜 미국 사람들이 쓰는 영어로 좀 더 하고 싶은데. Creativity 도 백인 선생님들한테 배울 수 있고, 다른 건 몰라도 summer school, 방학 때만큼은 아예 그거를 보내고 싶어요.
>
> *Well, for English, pronunciation is important. So, whenever I can, I would like to use English that real American people use rather than the English that Korean people use. Also, from white teachers, we can learn creativity, and so during summer school or any vacation opportunities, I want to send my children to programs that offer access to these things [offered by white teachers].*

References to '진짜 미국 사람' (literal translation: *real American person*), '백인 선생님' (*white teacher*), and '외국 사람' (*foreign person*) in the discourses of parents point to a deeply ingrained association of race and language and their perception of the authenticity and superiority of the English spoken by 'real' white Americans. Thus, in contrast to the teachers who never questioned their abilities in English, the Korean parents raciolinguistically profiled the teachers to have less than 'native'

English language competence due to their Korean heritage. Hence, their raciolinguistically charged assessment of the teachers' language competence led them to look for other kinds of learning opportunities outside of school, such as reading clubs at the local public library or bible study at the community church that would give their children direct exposure to white native speakers. In addition, their perception that ethnic Korean teachers, despite the fact that they both went through teacher training programs in the US, differ from white teachers in terms of their 'creativity' or their instructional approaches in working with children appears to have contributed to their decision to later enroll their children in a traditional middle or high school (Lee & Jeong, 2013). They felt that middle and high school years were critical periods in their children's college pathway and wanted their children to be educated in a traditional English-only school that offered the academic curricula and the necessary resources needed for college admissions. The time and effort to learn in Korean in middle and high school were seen to be a distractor from the perceived learning that their children needed for college admissions (Lee & Jeong, 2013).

Moreover, the parents also raciolinguistically profiled the teachers as heritage language speakers of Korean and saw their Korean competence to be flawed as well. The parents unanimously commented on the teachers' Korean language proficiency, noting that conversationally the teachers had no problem communicating with students and parents, but academically their Korean proficiency possessed characteristics of non-nativeness such as misspellings, incorrect grammar, and a lack of more formal academic vocabulary, which are attributes typically ascribed to heritage speakers (Montrul, 2012). For example, one parent brought out a notice written in Korean by the teachers that was sent home. She pointed out several errors in the text – some of which could have been attributed to minor typos, but instead were all seen as products of the teachers' incomplete knowledge of Korean. Similarly, Leeman (2012) found that heritage language users are often stigmatized as being incapable of producing oral or written forms that match standardized language practices. Lee and Shin (2008) note that heritage language speakers of Korean have a linguistic system that is distinct from monolingual Korean speakers and argue for the need to recognize its legitimacy as a unique linguistic repertoire reflective of heritage language speaker practices. Yet, the 'native gaze' of parents led them to worry that their children would acquire the incorrect forms of language. Thus, they were constantly thinking of ways to reinforce the correct forms to their children.

With Korean, the parents felt that they could supplement their children's Korean proficiency at home and 'reteach' the content if necessary as one mother in the following comment states:

M-K10: 얘가 가끔 보면은 좀 틀린 것도 있고, 띄어쓰기 같은 거도 좀 틀려가지고 오면은 제가 가르쳐 주면은. 학교에서 배운 게 맞지 않아

요. 선생님이 가르쳐 주는 게. 한글에 있어서는 엄마가 더 나은데...한국어는 아무래도 선생님들도 한국어 쪽에서는 조금 딸리는, 딸리는 것 같애요. 그래서 좀 집에서...

When my child brings homework [in Korean] and I notice some things that are wrong such as the spacing between words, I can teach it. What they learn in school is not correct. What the teachers teach is not correct. In Korean, I am a better teacher... When it comes to Korean, the teachers are lacking in their competence, there are shortcomings... that is why at home [I reteach a little]...

The parents also mentioned that they are careful not to correct the teachers' language ability or talk about the teachers' Korean proficiency in front of the children because they did not want to detract from the teachers' authority.

M-K11: 아빠가 그러더라고요. 애한테 선생님이 잘못됐다는 건 가르쳐주지 말라고. 선생님이 가르쳐준 것 중에 가끔은 틀릴 수도 있다고, 왜냐면 선생님이 여기 오래 사셨고, 오래 사시는 동안 잊어버릴 수도 있고. 공부를 한다 하더라도 엄마가 집에서 해주는 만큼 안 하실 수 있으니까 표현 잠깐 잘못 쓰셨네 라고 만 알려주지. 틀렸다는 말은 쓰지 말라고.

My child's father said that we shouldn't tell the kids that the teachers taught them something incorrectly. We should say that sometimes it is possible that teachers may teach you something that is not right, because they have lived here [US] for a long time. During this long time, they can forget things. Even if they study so that they do not forget, it probably won't be as good as what we can do for the kids at home. We should just tell them that it was a temporary slip of the tongue, but never say that the teachers were wrong.

In an attempt to save the teachers' face and to not undermine teacher authority, parents commented that they did not explicitly point out the teachers' errors in Korean to their children. Rather they provided recasts with the 'correct' forms. Thus, the parents stated that they assumed the responsibility of re-teaching the content in Korean at home using 'appropriate' or 'correct' Korean. The focus on accuracy and correctness was strong in all of the parents' comments about the teachers' competence as teachers of Korean.

Through a 'native gaze' lens, the parents' felt the teachers' level of Korean proficiency was 'not enough' for teaching, yet many parents commented that the teachers' Korean proficiency as heritage language speakers was more than sufficient to accomplish the communicative demands of a heritage language speaker and hoped that at minimum their own children as heritage language speakers would at least develop as much Korean proficiency as the teachers. In other words, as a teacher of Korean, the parents saw the teachers as inadequate language models, but as heritage language speakers, they felt that the teachers' Korean proficiency was good enough for Korean Americans. Thus, there were differences in expectations for language competence for teachers of Korean and heritage language speakers of Korean as well as between English acquisition and Korean acquisition where the development of native-like Korean proficiency was less critical than English in the minds of the parents for their children in the US context.

> M-K11: 그분이 여기 4살 때 오셨거든요. 근데 한국말 쓰는거는 여기 고등학교 졸업해서 왔다는 사람보다 더 잘하세요. 말씀하시는거나 애들 표현하는거나. 참 그러기 힘든데 나중에 저도 최소한 우리 제니가 그 선생님만큼…
>
> *She [Ms. Kim] came when she was 4 years old, but she speaks better Korean than someone who came after graduating from high school. The way she talks, the ways she uses expressions to the kids. Wow, it is really difficult to achieve that level of proficiency, I hope later Jenny will be as proficient as Ms. Kim…*

In contrast to the parents' views, the teachers, however, saw themselves as good Korean language models for their students. Ms Suh stated that although she was not fully educated in Korea, she takes pride that her Korean is stable and 'strong' due to being an avid reader in Korean. She reported that she is a language model for her students: '제 language 가 model이 되고. 제 writing이 또 model이 되고' *(My [Korean] language becomes their model, my writing is also their model)*. Ms Kim was also proud of her Korean language skills because even though she came to the US at the age of four, she feels that her Korean is better than other Korean Americans enabling her to model the language for her students: '한국어에서는 아이들 한테는 계속 modeling을 좀 해주고' *(In Korean, I continue to model the language)*. Although they both repeatedly mentioned that they are still learners of Korean, they did not see this as a deterrent from their ability to teach in Korean or be language models for their students.

Thus, regardless of the teachers' actual language competencies, due to their English as a second language beginnings and their heritage language speaker status, the parents' 'native gaze' positioned the teachers as inferior language models for their children in both English and Korean. Rosa (2016) describes this as a racialized ideology of languagelessness through which perceptions about particular non-standardized practices work to racialize certain categories of speakers as not being able to produce standard or legitimate language. However, for these parents any shortcomings in the teachers' Korean proficiency were not considered as problematic as the perceived lack of nativeness in English, a domain in which the parents were not able to support their children. Interestingly, the parents' perceptions of the teachers' abilities and their roles as appropriate language models did not align with the teachers' views as will be discussed in the next section.

Teachers' raciolinguistic profiling of students as language models

In contrast to the 'native gaze' that was imposed upon teachers by the Korean parents, the teachers, for the most part, positioned successful Korean American bilingual children like Jenny, who is comfortable in both Korean and English, as the more able language models in class. That is, the teachers did not impose a 'native gaze' on their choice of language models in class. Rather, they selected students who most similarly reflected their own bilingual profiles as the more appropriate language models. For instance, Examples 1 and 2 below illustrate how the teacher positions Jenny as the able speaker and knower of Korean rather than the student who recently arrived from Korea by nominating her over others.

Example 1

Line	Speaker	Verbal interaction	Observation notes
1	Ms Kim	이걸 뭐라고 부르죠?	
		ikel mwerako hatera?	
		How do you call this?	
2		옆에 친구한테 얘기해 주세요.	
		yephey chinkwuhanthey yaygihae cwuseyyo	
		Tell it to your friend next to you.	
3		준비된 친구, 손 머리하고 있으세요	Most of students put their hands on their heads.
		cwunpitoin chingwu, son merihako issuseyyo	
		If you are ready, please put your hands on your head	
4		기쁨아, 이것을 뭐라고 하더라?	Students make moaning sounds that indicated disappointment after Jenny is nominated.
		kippum-a (Jenny's Korean name), ikkeul mwerako hatera?	
		Jenny, do you remember how to say this?	
5	Jenny	온도계	
		ontogye	
		Thermometer	
6	Ms Kim	맞았나요?	
		macassnayo	
		Is she correct?	
7	Students (Ss)	네	
		ney	
		Yes.	

In Example 1, Ms Kim goes over the science homework during Korean instructional time that she has assigned the day before. In this whole class activity, the students are sitting down on the floor in front of the blackboard. In order to review weather-related vocabulary she asks the class what you call 'thermometer' in Korean (line 1) and encourages peer interaction by saying '옆에 친구한테 얘기해 주세요' (*Tell it to your friend next to you.*) (line 2). Then, she asks students to put their hands on their head if they are ready to answer (line 3). Most students put their hands on their head, indicating that they knew the answer. However, Ms Kim calls out '기쁨' (*Kippum*: Jenny's Korean name) and designates her as the knower by asking '이것을 뭐라고 하더라?' (*Do you remember how to say this?*) in line 4. Compared to the previous question in line 1, Ms Kim uses a different sentence ending as she invites Jenny to provide the answer to the whole class. She uses the '더라' (*deora*) ending which expresses the speaker's perception about the listener's epistemic status (Sohn, 1994). In other words, this sentence ending conveys the speaker's knowledge of the fact that the designated student not only knows the answer now but also knew the answer prior to this event and is a stronger reconfirmation of the student's ability to correctly answer the question. Therefore, Ms Kim was validating Jenny's answer as the correct one even before Jenny answered the question. This is just one example of the many instances that the teachers continue to position Jenny as a capable peer who can model the target language. Similarly, Example 2 presents another instance of how Ms Suh positions Jenny as the knower and able language model.

Example 2

Line	Speaker	Verbal interaction	Observation notes
8	Ms Suh	크리스마스 몇 월 몇 일인지 아는 사람 말해줄 수 있어요?	Jenny and Chanyoung raise their hands.
		kurisumasu myech wel myech il inci anun saram malhaycwul swu isseyo	
		Can anyone tell me what date is Christmas?	
9		크리스마스는 몇 월 몇 일이에요?	
		kurisumasunun myech wel myech ilieyo	
		What date is Christmas?	
10		우리 기쁨이가 한 번 말해 보세요.	
		wuri kippumika han pen malhay poseyyo	
		Can our Jenny say it?	
11	Jenny	12월 25일	
		sipiwel isip oil	
		December 25th	

12	Ms Suh	긴 문장으로 한 번 다시 말해 주세요.	Ms Suh elongates the vertical space between her hands to express longer sentence.
		kin mwuncangulo han pen tasi malhay cwuseyyo	
		Can you say it again in a full sentence?	
13	Jenny	크리스마스는 12월 25일이에요.	
		kurisumsunun sipiwel isip oilieyyo	
		Christmas is December 25th.	
14	Ms Suh	잘 알고 있네 기쁨이. 좋아요.	
		cal alko issney, kippumi choayo	
		I knew you would know it well Jenny. Good job.	

While talking about Christmas presents, Ms Suh asks if someone can tell her the actual date of Christmas in line 8. Jenny and Chanyoung, another bilingual child but with a lower level of Korean proficiency than Jenny according to the teachers, raise their hands. Similar to Example 1, Ms Suh grants a turn to Jenny (line 10) referring to her as 'our Jenny' in line 10 and not Chanyoung. Jenny provides the correct day with the proper number classifier for month and day in line 11, Ms Suh makes another request for Jenny to say it in a full sentence in line 12. In line 14, Ms Suh indicates that she knew Jenny would know the correct form demonstrating her positioning of Jenny as a capable model of the target language.

What is interesting is that in other speech recordings of students' language use in class, we observed marked characteristics of heritage language speech in Jenny's Korean such as the lack of use of the null form in referential choices (Clancy, 1993; Sohn, 1994), which is a normative and commonly used form in Korean speech. Yet, despite certain characteristics that marked Jenny's Korean apart from the more fluent speakers of Korean like Hyun, Jenny was still positioned as the able language model by teachers. The teachers constantly praised her for 'knowing' and for 'reading and speaking appropriately and well.' It appears that for these teachers, the standards for language models mirrored those of a successful bilingual model like themselves and were less based on native speaker characteristics.

In fact, the data revealed interesting interactional patterns in the ways in which the teachers categorized and differentiated between Korean students, who were either born in the US or had come to the US at a very early age, and those that had recently arrived from Korea. The recently arrived Korean students were never acknowledged by the teachers as Korean language models during Korean instructional time, and were rather discouraged by the teachers for 'reading or speaking too fast,' because it was deemed that their peers would not be able to follow them. In the following example, the teacher shuts down a display of competence by Hyun, a recently arrived student from Korea.

Example 3

Line	Speaker	Verbal interaction	Observation notes
15	Ms Kim	현, 시작.	Hyun gets a turn to read in his small reading group.
		Hyun, sicak	
		Hyun, start.	
16	Hyun	[엄마는] 아침부터 김밥을 싸시고,	Hyun looks at his book. Jenny looks at her book. Hyun starts to read very fluently.
		[emmanun] achimpwuthe kimpapul ssasiko	
		Mom is making kimbop since early morning and,	
17		나는_삶은_달걀을_가방에_담아요.	Jenny looks at Hyun's book.
		nanun_salmun_talkyalul_kapangey_tamayo	
		I put a hard boiled egg in a bag.	
18		엄마아빠_나는_XX버스를_타고_할머니댁에_갑니다.	Jenny puts her right hand on the page of her book to follow the text as Hyun is reading.
		emma appa nanun XXpesulul thako halmeni taykey kapnita	
		Mom, Dad, and I go to Grandmother's house by XX bus.	
19	Ms Kim	그렇게 읽으면 잘 읽는다고 생각해요?	Ms Kim interrupts Hyun. Hyun looks at Ms Kim
		kulehkey ilkumyen cal ilknuntako sayngkakhayyo?	
		Do you think you read well if you read like that?	
20	Hyun	아니요.	Ms Kim shakes her head.
		aniyo	
		No.	
21	Ms Kim	아니,	Hyun looks at the students to his left.
		ani	
		No,	
22		우리가너무 빨리 읽으면 무슨말 하는지 하나도 못 알아들어요.	Hyun looks disappointed and lowers his head.
		Wulika nemwu ppalli ilkumyen mwusunmal hanunci hanato mos alatuleyo	
		We cannot understand anything if you read so fast.	

After giving turns to other students who have less proficiency in Korean than Hyun, Ms Kim finally grants a turn to Hyun to read in line 15. Compared to the students who read before Hyun, he read his paragraph fluently at a rapid pace without any hesitations. However, in line 19 Ms Kim asks Hyun, '그렇게 읽으면 잘 읽는다고 생각해요?' (*Do you think you are reading well if you read like that?*) and added '우리가 너무 빨리 읽으면 무슨말 하는 지 하나도 못 알아들어요' (*We cannot understand anything if you read so fast*) (line 22). By using the pronoun '우리' (*we*), she included herself with all the other students in the class who were unable to follow Hyun's rapid reading. Ms Kim overtly disqualified Hyun as an appropriate language model. Although in other studies (Martin-Beltran, 2010), highly proficient students are the ones that gain access to participation, in this class, being positioned as too proficient went against the teachers' conception of an appropriate language model. Although both teachers evaluated Hyun's Korean to be very strong, they did not acknowledge his competence in class and found his non-accommodation of the Korean learners in class to be inappropriate as a language model for other students.

Moreover, Ms Kim stated that having Korean children [referring to recently arrived students] in class poses a 'problem' because they know more vocabulary than the other students and they do not give the other '외국 애들' (*foreign kids*) an opportunity to answer. She goes on to state that '걔가 항상 해야 된다는 자기 의무라고 생각해요' (*She/He feels that it is her/his responsibility to always answer or participate*), referring to her assessment that the native Korean-speaking students are dominating the activities. However, what was interesting was that during English instructional time, the English-dominant speakers were actively participating in ways that the recently arrived students from Korea were not given an opportunity to do. In fact, the English-dominant speakers were never characterized as posing a 'problem' for the other students in the process of learning English. For the recently arrived Korean students, Korean instructional time was the space that they could display their competence, yet because of the teachers' beliefs about what constitutes an appropriate language model in this context, students like Hyun had limited opportunities to display their competence publicly.

In contrast, during English instructional time, the teachers' raciolinguistic ideologies that positioned the white native speaker as the capable language model surfaced when they were teaching structures or sounds that they considered to be more complex. In these instances, we noted a pattern for the teachers to call on white native-speaking students to serve as the language models for the rest of the class. For example, as shown in the following transcript, the teachers appeared to regularly nominate various students for content-related or fact-related answers, but when they asked about specific syntactic constructions such as contractions or other language-related questions, they regularly nominated the white native speakers of English.

Example 4

Line	Speaker	Verbal interaction	Observation notes
23	Ms Suh	Ok, who can tell me what day of the month is it today?	Three students raise their hands, but Chris (Korean American student) does not raise his hand.
24		Chris?	Teacher nominates Chris with a rising intonation.
25	Chris	It is the 11th day of the month.	
26	Ms Suh and Ss	It is the 11th day of the month.	The students and teacher repeat the sentence in unison.
27	Ms Suh	Let's use that with a contraction.	Two students are raising their hands including Ana (white student).
28		Ana.	Teacher does not use a rising intonation.
29	Ana	It's the 11th day of the month.	
30	Ms Suh and Ss	It's the 11th day of the month.	The students and teacher repeat the sentence in unison.
31	Ms Suh	Alright boys and girls, what day is it today?	Two students are raising their hands including Jung (Korean student).
32		Jung?	Teacher nominates Jungwoo with a rising intonation.
33	Jung	Today is Thursday.	
34	Ms Suh and Ss	Today is Thursday.	The students and teacher repeat the sentence in unison.
35	Ms Suh	What day of the week is it today?	Seven students raise their hands including Seung (Korean student).
36		Seung?	Teacher nominates Seung with a rising intonation.
37	Seung	It is the fifth day of the week.	
38	Ms Suh and Ss	It is the fifth day of the week.	Both the teacher and students repeat the sentence
39	Ms Suh	Let's use that with a contraction.	Four students raise their hands but Sam (white student) does not raise his hand
40		Sam.	Teacher does not use a rising intonation.
41	Sam	It's the fifth day of the week.	

Example 4 illustrates a particular pattern by which the teacher nominates certain students to provide responses for different types of questions. In line 24, Ms Suh nominates a Korean American child, Chris, who did not have his hand up to answer her question, with a rising intonation suggesting that Chris gives it a try. When he does so correctly in the form she was looking for in line 25, she moves on to ask students to repeat the sentence in line 26. Given that contractions were the syntactic structure the class was working on during the week, in line 27 she asks for the same sentence but using the contraction form of 'it is.' In line 27, we see that two students raise their hands to be nominated, one Korean student and the other Ana, a white student. Using a final declarative intonation in her utterance, indicating a direction, Ms Suh nominates Ana to model the contraction form in line 28. In line 31, the teacher goes back to ask a factual question, 'what day is it today?' and calls on Jung, a Korean student. As she calls Jung's name, her intonation rises indicating an invitation for him to try to answer. She goes on to ask another direct question in line 35 and calls on another Korean student with a rising intonation to answer the question in line 36. However, when she asks for the contraction form of the sentence again, she nominates Sam, the other white student in class, using a final declarative intonation in line 40, despite the fact that there were other students with their hands up. Although in this instance, it is unclear whether Sam's nomination was indeed because the teacher intended to nominate a native speaker of English to model the colloquial uses of contractions or whether it was because she wanted to make sure Sam was paying attention. Yet, we continued to witness subtle ways in which raciolinguistic ideologies appeared to be shaping the teachers' nominations of students during classroom interactions.

The teachers' raciolinguistic ideologies also surfaced in their views about English as the more important language to learn well and accurately as well as in their differential expectations in learning Korean between Korean ethnic children and non-Korean children. For example, both teachers referred to English as the 'prestige language' in the American society that everyone must speak well, which according to them is the reason why '한국 아이들이 한국어를 점점 잃어가는 이유가 그런것 같아요. 더 영어를 많이해야만 인정을 받고' (*Korean children start to forgo their heritage language. Because they have to use more English to be validated in this society*) (Ms Suh). Despite the bilingual ethos of the dual language immersion setting, there was a shared consensus among teachers, parents and students that English was the more important language to focus on due to real social and academic consequences that are associated with non-mastery of the English language.

Moreover, Ms Suh described how she at first held raciolinguistic ideologies that led her to be more fascinated with kids who did not look Korean but were speaking and writing in Korean.

Ms. Suh: 보통 **머리 노란 아이들**이 한국말을 하는것이 더 신기하잖아요. 제가 처음에는 그런 편견이 있었던것 같아요. Ana 나 Sam 같은 경우도 보기에 굉장히 다른 아이가 한국어로 인사를 하고 한국말로 글을 쓰고 그럴때 처음에는 굉장히 신기하고 그랬어요.

In general it is more surprising to see a child with blond hair speaking Korean. I was fascinated by that at first. Just by looking at Ana and Sam who come from a different background, when they greeted me in Korean and when they wrote in Korean I was very fascinated at first.

Throughout the course of the nine months we were in the classroom, it appeared as if the initial 'fascination' persisted and the teachers continued to be impressed with the language growth that non-Korean students made, whereas the language growth in Korean among the Korean ethnic children fell within their scope of expected outcomes. Their fascination was evident in our conversations where they continued to comment on how impressed they were with the Korean language learning progress of the non-Korean children, whereas the Korean language growth among the heritage speakers was hardly ever mentioned.

In sum, the teachers positioned the Korean American students who were fluent heritage language speakers of Korean and also fluent English speakers as the more appropriate language models for peers to emulate, although for certain language forms such as contractions, they relied on the white English-dominant students as the language models. Given that the goals of the program are to develop bilingual speakers in the US, it makes sense that the teachers not only saw themselves as appropriate bilingual language models, but also designated the more fluent bilingual students that were similar to their own linguistic backgrounds as the language models for other students. Yet, although their practices at times seemed to honor the rich and creative language practices of their emerging bilingual students, we also witnessed elements of raciolinguistic ideologies at play in the different expectations and standards of English and Korean development. The 'native gaze' was upheld as the standard to achieve in English for students by both the parents and teachers, but the level of attainment in Korean, unlike English, was not complete mastery. Moreover, in Korean, the expectation for language development differed for Korean and non-Korean ethnic students. Such inconsistencies in expectations shed light on the complex ways in which raciolinguistic ideologies play out in educational contexts.

Conclusion

In this paper, we examined how parents' raciolinguistic ideologies about native speakers and heritage language speakers shaped their assessments of teacher competence in a dual language immersion setting as well as how teachers' raciolinguistically charged ideas about what they considered as appropriate language models led to practices that positioned certain types of children as able language models, which led to instances of inequitable opportunities in the classroom. The data show that even within a racialized group, raciolinguistic ideologies and practices exist among group members to set boundaries between native speakers and heritage language speakers, resulting in different expectations and learning experiences for teachers and students in Korean English dual language immersion settings. The awareness that such raciolinguistic ideologies exist and the understanding of how they influence educational experiences are critical in order to achieve bilingualism for all in ways that promote equity and diversity (de Jong, 2016).

We must continue to work towards creating inclusive discourses that validate and widen our acceptance of different forms of language in educational settings and beyond as well as be prepared to question and challenge prescriptive uses of language. To do so, ideologies associated with the 'native gaze' that are prevalent, but disguised in subtle ways must be surfaced and discussed openly with all stakeholders to minimize the negative ways in which they can influence instructional and evaluation practices and policies, especially in multilingual spaces like the dual language immersion contexts. As Paris and Alim (2014) argue this may require a deep inspection of one's internal belief systems and a willingness to explore, value, and respect the rich and various heritage and community practices. In other words, there needs to be a fundamental shift in the ways we perceive the language practices of multilinguals as legitimate and representative forms of lived experiences of speakers who are embracing and making sense of the complex and dynamic linguistic and cultural worlds that they participate in. Such creative and dynamic forms and uses of language are what makes us uniquely human. Thus, as we continue to advance our understanding of the intricate relationships between race, language, power, and learning, we are encouraged by the potential role of dual language immersion programs to foster the richness and flexibility of our human linguistic capacity.

References

Bonfiglio, T. (2010) *Mother Tongues and Nations: The Invention of the Native Speaker.* New York: Mouton de Gruyter.

Cervantes-Soon, C.G., Dorner, L., Palmer, D., Heiman, D., Schqerdtfeger, R. and Choi, J. (2017) Combating inequalities in two –way language immersion programs: Toward critical consciousness in bilingual education spaces. *Review of Research in Education* 41, 403–427.

Christian, D. (1996) Two-way immersion education: Students learning through two languages. *The Modern Language Journal* 80 (1), 66–76.

Clancy, P.M. (1993) Preferred argument structure in Korean acquisition. In E.V. Clark (ed.) *Proceedings of the 25th Annual Child Language Research Forum* (pp. 307–314). Stanford, CA: Center for the Study of Language and Information (CSLI) Publications.

de Jong, E. (2016) Two-way immersion for the next generation: Models, policies and principles. *International Multilingual Research Journal* 10, 6–16.

Ee, J. (2018) Exploring Korean dual language immersion programs in the United States: Parents' reasons for enrolling their children. *International Journal of Bilingual Education and Bilingualism* 21 (6), 690–709.

Flores, N. and Rosa, J. (2015) Undoing appropriateness: Raciolinguistic ideologies and language diversity in education. *Harvard Educational Review* 85 (2), 149–171.

Freeman, R. (1998) *Bilingual Education and Social Change.* Clevedon: Multilingual Matters.

García, O. (2009) *Bilingual Education in the 21st Century: A Global Perspective*. Malden, MA: Wiley-Blackwell.

Grosjean, F. (1989) Neurolinguists, beware! The bilingual is not two monolinguals in one person. *Brain Language* 36 (1), 3–15.

Hadi-Tabassum, S. (2006) *Language, Space and Power: A Critical Look at Bilingual Education*. Clevedon: Multilingual Matters.

Inoue, M. (2006) *Vicarious Language: Gender and Linguistic Modernity in Japan*. Berkeley: University of California Press.

Jeong, S.H. (2014) 'Only looking for Whites: Stereotypes of private academies', *Segye Ilbo*, news article, 3 December. See http://www.segye.com/newsView/20141203004421 (accessed 15 February 2019).

Kang, O. and Rubin, D.L. (2009) Reverse linguistic stereotyping: Measuring the effect of listener expectations on speech evaluation. *Journal of Language and Social Psychology* 28 (4), 441–456.

Kubota, R. and Lin, A. (2006) Race and TESOL: Introduction to concepts and theories. *TESOL Quarterly* 40 (3), 471–493.

Lee, C. (2014) 'Defining racism in Korea', *The Korean Herald*, news article, 4 September. See http://www.koreaherald.com/view.php?ud=20140904001088 (accessed 15 February 2019).

Lee, J.S., Hill-Bonnet, L. and Gillispie, J. (2008) Learning in two languages: Interactional spaces for becoming bilingual speakers. *International Journal of Bilingual Education and Bilingualism* 11 (1), 75–94.

Lee, J.S., Hill-Bonnet, L. and Raley, J. (2011) Examining the effects of language brokering on student identities and learning opportunities in dual immersion classrooms. *Journal of Language, Identity & Education* 10 (5), 306–326.

Lee, J.S. and Jeong, E. (2013) Perspectives from a Korean-English dual language immersion program: Insights, tensions, and hope. *Language, Culture and Curriculum* 26 (1), 89–107.

Lee, J.S. and Shin, S.J. (2008) Korean heritage language education in the United States: The current state, opportunities, and possibilities. *Heritage Language Journal* 6 (2), 1–20.

Leeman, J. (2012) Investigating language ideologies in spanish as a heritage language. In S. Beaudrie and M. Fairclough (eds) *Spanish as a Heritage Language in the US: State of the Science* (pp. 43–59). Washington, DC: Georgetown University Press.

Lindemann, S. (2002) Listening with an attitude: A model of native-speaker comprehension of non-native speakers in the United States. *Language in Society* 31 (3), 419–441.

Lindholm-Leary, K. (2001) *Dual Language Education*. Clevedon: Multilingual Matters.

Martin-Beltrán, M. (2010) Positioning proficiency: How students and teachers (de)construct language proficiency at school. *Linguistics and Education* 21, 257–281.

Montrul, S.A. (2012) Is the heritage language like a second language?. *Eurosla Yearbook* 12 (1), 1–29.

Pang, S.Y. (2015) The legacy of Horace Grant Underwood. *International Bulletin of Mission Research* 39 (3), 150–153.

Paris, D. and Alim, H.S. (2014) What are we seeking to sustain through culturally sustaining pedagogy? A loving critique forward. *Harvard Educational Review* 84 (1), 85–100.

Park, J.S.Y. (2009) *The Local Construction of a Global Language: Ideologies of English in South Korea* (Vol. 24). New York: Walter de Gruyter.

Potowski, K. (2007) *Language and Identity in a Dual Immersion School*. Clevedon: Multilingual Matters.

Rondilla, J.L. (2009) Filipinos and the color complex: Ideal Asian beauty. In E.N. Glenn (ed.) *Shades of Difference: Why Skin Color Matters* (pp. 106–132). Stanford, CA: Stanford University Press.

Rosa, J. (2016) Standardization, racialization, languagelessness: Raciolinguistic ideologies across communicative contexts. *Journal of Linguistic Anthropology* 26 (2), 162–183.

Rosa, J. and Flores, N. (2017) Unsettling race and language: Toward a raciolinguistic perspective. *Language in Society* 46 (5), 621–647.

Sohn, H.M. (1994) *Korean: A Descriptive Grammar.* London: Routledge.

Song, J.J. (2011) English as an official language in South Korea: Global English or social malady? *Language Problems and Language Planning* 35 (1), 35–55.

Steele, J.L., Slater, R., Zamarro, G., Miller, T., Li, J.J., Burkhauser, S. and Bacon, M. (2017) Dual-Language Immersion Programs Raise Student Achievement in English. *Research Brief* 9903. Santa Monica, CA: RAND Corporation. See https://www.rand.org/pubs/research_briefs/RB9903.html (accessed 15 February 2019).

Strauss, A. and Corbin, J. (1998) *Basics of Qualitative Research.* Thousand Oaks, CA: Sage.

Tedick, D.J., Christian, D. and Fortune, T.W. (eds) (2011) *Immersion Education: Practices, Policies, Possibilities.* Bristol: Multilingual Matters.

Valdés, G. (1997) Dual language immersion programs: A cautionary note concerning the education of language – minority students. *Harvard Educational Review* 67, 391–429.

Valdés, G. (2005) Bilingualism, heritage language learners, and SLA research: Opportunities lost or seized? *Modern Language Journal* 89 (3), 410–426.

9 The Black and Brown Search for Agency: African American and Latinx Children's Plight to Bilingualism in a Two-Way Dual Language Program

Claudia G. Cervantes-Soon,
Enrique David Degollado and Idalia Nuñez

When the classroom became larger it took a toll on the connection... My daughter went from loving school, and 'I'm ready to go to school, I'm a big girl,' to 'I don't want to learn Spanish'... 'I don't want to talk in Spanish mamma', 'such and such is not my friend'.' – Kiana's mother.

In the epigraph, Kiana's mother reveals the sudden change in her disposition towards school. Although Kiana – a Black 4-year-old – loved to attend school with Mr Aguirre, she was now reluctant to learn Spanish and alluded to deteriorating peer relationships. Kianas's mother attributes the devolution of her daughter's schooling experiences to the increase in students in Mr Aguirre's class. Indeed, this was one of many concerns that manifested as the school year progressed in Mr Aguirre's Pre-Kindergarten two-way dual language classroom. Recently, critical scholarship in two-way immersion (TWI) has brought attention to persistent inequities that manifest in these programs (Cervantes-Soon *et al.*, 2017), revealing that many of the inequities are the result of students' differential access to power, resources and status within schooling processes and contexts shaped by white supremacist ideologies and neoliberal pursuits. While these issues still stand and are important to resolve, TWI programs in schools serving students from predominantly low-income African American and Latinx backgrounds have received little attention. Considering that due to persistent residential segregation, Black and

Latinx students are often largely concentrated in schools together (Frankenberg *et al*., 2019), Valdés (2002, 2018) has questioned whether TWI can serve the needs and deliver the promise of bi/multilingualism, high academic achievement and cross-cultural understanding by integrating at least two different linguistic groups who have been subjected to educational malpractice for generations.

To address this question, this chapter draws from a year-long ethnographic study in a school implementing a TWI strand serving African American and Latinx children in a Texas urban community to offer an analysis of factors contributing to TWI kindergarteners' engagement with and investment in their bi/multilingual development. We offer a raciolinguistic analysis of how the interactional dynamics evolved throughout the course of the year in the TWI kindergarten class, to incorporate the hegemonic practices of surveillance and control, despite the teacher's initial attempts to enact a democratic and liberatory pedagogy. Ultimately, we illuminate how racialized, everyday practices and expectations in the larger school context contribute to and often determine the ways in which students experience their languages and bilingual instruction. Such dynamic, we posit, serves to position English as the language of agency and Spanish as the language of silence and invisibility in ways that permeate the TWI classroom.

A Raciolinguistic Perspective: Black and Brown Children in Two-Way Dual Language

We situate our study in raciolinguistics examinations of education processes (Flores & Rosa, 2015; Rosa & Flores, 2017). According to Flores and Rosa (2015) raciolinguistic ideologies 'produce racialized speaking subjects who are constructed as linguistically deviant even when engaging in linguistic practices positioned as normative or innovative when produced by privileged white subjects' (2015: 150). Grounded in settler colonialism, raciolinguistic ideologies are the historical formation of race and language as distinct embodied features that can be categorized and are continually juxtaposed against the western European traditions. Flores and Rosa call for educators to unsettle the appropriateness of the white speaking subject gaze that schools continue to reproduce through their teaching of the normativity of whiteness and monoglossic English ideologies even when perceived as 'codes of power'. This involves moving away from attempts to modify the linguistic practices of racialized populations and toward a broader project of dismantling white supremacy and racial capitalism (Rosa & Flores, 2017).

Such a raciolinguistic perspective enables us to analyze the interactions of Black and Brown children in a dual language classroom in which Mr Aguirre (pseudonyms used for all names) – a Latino teacher – makes attempts, albeit incomplete, to enact counter-hegemonic pedagogies. Rosa and Flores (2017) argue that 'Raciolinguistic approaches to the analysis of intersectional identity formations and assemblages of signs and materialities are deeply anchored in concerns about the ways inequities are reproduced and challenged through institutional and interactional practices' (2017: 17). In this chapter we illustrate how a TWI program's goal to foster bilingualism in children of color, largely failed to promote these goals because it was rooted in the reproduction of a white supremacist framework through which the children's overall behaviors (linguistic or else) were continuously assessed and used to position them as devious or deficient. We posit that the ways in which children's bodies were controlled and their agency restricted – stemming from a long history of racialized expectations of deviant behavior and hegemonic whiteness ideologies ultimately hindered access to bi/multilingualism for all of the children involved. In doing so, even the most well-intentioned teachers may fall short of overcoming the institutional forces that reproduce a focus on order and discipline of racialized children while sacrificing their identities, dignity and potential bi/multilingual goals of participating in a TWI program. Such conditions, we argue, also perpetuate the construction of African American students as unruly and unfit for second-language learning, and position Spanish-speaking Latinxs as subordinate unless they acquire English as soon as possible. At the same time, critical ethnographic approach broadens our raciolinguistic analysis by allowing us to highlight the efforts of resistance and agency of Black and Brown children within the everyday struggles and constraints they face in the school context.

The Black and Brown Battle for Educational Equity

For Black and Latinx children, there exists a longstanding struggle for educational equity (San Miguel & Valencia, 1998). As enslaved people, African Americans were denied education and literacy skills; as colonized peoples, Latinxs have been subjected to the legacies of US imperialism. The minoritized status of Black and Latinx people has rendered them second-class citizens, constructing their cultural and linguistic practices as deviant. The fight for civil rights in the mid-20th century generated new hope for equality in society and education. Yet, despite major reforms (i.e. *Brown v Board of Education*, 1954; Civil Rights Act of 1965; Bilingual Education Act, 1968, etc.) that aimed to ameliorate a legacy of white supremacy in the US, equity through education remains elusive. The material effects of a system of discrimination and prejudice against minoritized populations lingers in American society and manifests in a purported achievement gap that Ladson-Billings (2006) argues has more to do with the accumulation of debt in denied access and resources that has yet to be remedied, and pervasive segregation (Frankenberg *et al.*, 2019).

Education research suggests that the linguistic and cultural resources of Black and Brown children continue to be disparaged through subtractive schooling (Valenzuela, 1999) and deficit thinking (Valencia & Solórzano, 1997). For example, research on the alleged 'word gap' (Hart & Risley, 2003) further perpetuates deficit thinking of communities of color and restricts teachers' pedagogical practices (Adair *et al.*, 2017). While some argue that teaching codes of power (Delpit, 1995) would benefit children of color in schools and society, others (Martínez, 2010) have shown that children's linguistic resources are sources and opportunities to build learning and are even acts of resistance to oppressive and restrictive learning environments.

African Americans in two-way immersion

In recent decades, TWI immersion programs that integrate students from two different linguistic groups to promote bilingualism and biliteracy, high academic achievement, and intercultural competence, have increased in popularity because they can support the home language maintenance among language minoritized students while simultaneously providing opportunities to English speakers for second-language learning, all while arguably reducing achievement gaps. Yet persistent inequities, particularly for Latinx language minoritized students in TWI, have been documented (Cervantes-Soon *et al.*, 2017), and there is little information about Black students' experiences and linguistic trajectories in TWI. On the one hand, language minoritized students' from low-income Latinx families' access to TWI often occurs only insofar as their language skills can be commodified (Cervantes-Soon, 2014; Petrovic, 2005; Valdés, 1997). On the other, systemic barriers tend to keep African American students from low-income families out of TWI (Palmer, 2010; Wall *et al.*, 2019), perpetuating a long history of exclusion of African Americans from foreign language education (Hubbard, 1980).

Much of the TWI literature assumes English speakers to be white, serving to erase the African American perspective from program planning, academic outcome reports, the preparation of bilingual teachers, and curriculum and instruction design, as well as the importance of considering African American Language (AAL) in TWI curriculum (Valdés, 2002, 2018). Paris (2016) defines AAL as a systematic English variety, learned through social interactions overtime by many African Americans across the nation, which is 'intimately connected with oppression and resistance as well as with the rich linguistic, spiritual and literary achievements of African Americans' (2016: 243). However, deficit views about Black youth's everyday language practices contribute to the widespread perception that it is too difficult for African Americans to learn a second language (Huber, 1990; Kubota *et al.*, 2003).

For example, Wiese's (2004) study of a TWI program noted that emphasis on a perceived need of English literacy remediation reduced

Black children's access to Spanish biliteracy instruction because teachers focused on teaching them standardized English (Wiese, 2004). Krause's (1999) study found higher attrition rates in a DL program among African American students, who also presented lower levels of literacy achievement. Krause's analysis attributed this literacy underachievement to the exclusive use of standardized English and Spanish for instruction, suggesting that AAL speakers may have been at a linguistic disadvantage and unfit for the program. Ruling out cultural exclusion by asserting that the program explicitly attempted to include African American heritage in the curriculum, Krause failed to note that lack of attention to AAL was in itself an indicator of the program's absence of cultural responsiveness.

Anberg-Espinosa's (2008) and Rymes and Anderson's (2004) studies have noted the neglect of AAL in TWI programs. Anberg-Espinosa (2008) investigated the motivations of nine African American students in 4th–8th grades – particularly those who spoke AAL – to continue in a TWI program, documenting both students and parents' perspectives about their journey. Despite the program's positive environment and sense of community, Anberg-Espinosa stressed the need for thoughtful attention to the use of AAL and culture beyond the superficial incorporation of multicultural celebrations into the curriculum by involving deeper explorations of one's own identity and courageous conversations around race and equity. Finally, Rymes and Anderson (2004) observed how frictions and hierarchies emerged as teachers rose the status of Spanish speakers while simultaneously invalidating African American students' voices, despite their attempts to participate in both languages, stressing the importance of connecting research on AAL and bilingualism and examining classrooms where both Spanish and AAL are spoken.

Furthermore, there are but a handful of studies that unpack tensions that emerge in TWI programs serving low-income Black and Latinx students (Valdés, 2002). Bender's (2000) study examined teachers' attitudes toward language use and intergroup relations in a TWI program serving low-income students who were entirely African American or Puerto Rican speakers of non-standardized English/Spanish varieties. Her study sheds light on the detrimental role of teachers' deficit views about these students, as well as lack of preparation and understanding of content-based language learning and pedagogy. Parchia's (2000) study of African American families in TWI found that despite an overall satisfaction with the program – due to positive relationships with peers, a less segregated environment and academic qualities – Black parents still lamented a lack of culturally relevant curriculum for their children, noting that the program's goal of multiculturalism tended to prioritize Latinx's culture and academic needs more than to their own.

In sum, whether TWI can serve the needs and deliver the promise of bi/multilingualism, high academic achievement, and cross-cultural understanding to these culturally and linguistically distinct groups who have been subjected to educational malpractice for generations remains largely unexplored. In addition, given that Latinx/Black TWI programs are understudied, we know very little about how such contexts may affect Latinx students. This study aims to contribute to such explorations, making connections between the systemic forms of oppression that often characterize the schooling of children of color in low-income communities and their access to socially just multilingual learning.

The Study

The data that we present here are part of a larger critical ethnographic study that examined the possibilities of TWI programs as generative multilingual spaces for cross-cultural relationships of solidarity between low-income African Americans and Latinx immigrants. Countering popular discourse that emphasizes tensions and divides between Black and Brown communities, Márquez's (2014) posits that 'collective memories of similar forms of subjection' can serve to bond Black and Latinx subjectivities into 'transracial and transethnic subject position' or what we refer to as Black and Brown solidarity, with possibilities for new collective forms of resistance (2012: 12). Márquez emphasizes that context, including sociohistorical legacies of colonialism and environments of increasing competition; the intersections of race, class, gender, language, citizenship and other social categories; and the frame of reference that each group's experience provides for the other constitute the backdrop for Black and Brown relations. Because of schooling's important role in mediating youth's subjectivities and social relations, and the role of language in manifesting cross-cultural/racial solidarity (Paris, 2009), we are interested in how TWI classrooms in low-income Black and Brown communities may foster solidarity through language instruction (Martínez, 2017), and may generate opportunities for young children and families to make sense of their own and their peers' racialized experiences to engage new forms of agency.

The larger study involved two schools and four classrooms in low-income urban communities of a large city in the US Southwest undergoing rapid gentrification in numerous neighborhoods. This chapter draws on data collected over the course of one academic year in Mr Aguirre's TWI kindergarten class at Paseo del Sol Elementary (PSE). While the fieldwork involved various activities, this analysis focuses on approximately 40 hours of participant observational data and fieldnotes, supplemented with video recordings and semi-structured interviews with five focal students, their mothers and Mr Aguirre, the classroom teacher. The observations of the kindergarten class took place at various times during the school day and in a variety of settings, including the classroom, cafeteria, library, gym, music and art classes, the playground and hallways. The children's interviews lasted between 10–25 minutes, with the goal of eliciting their perspectives about becoming bilingual and about their experiences and relationships in school. The teacher interviews focused on Mr Aguirre's personal and professional background, pedagogical orientation, language ideologies, perspectives about teaching his current class and reflections on his experience. The parent interviews delved into their experiences and perspectives about the program and cross-cultural relationships.

Analysis procedures

We analyzed the data through a critical ethnographic approach (Madison, 2005), emphasizing the role of power in the structuring of social relations and discourses that ultimately impact people's understandings, lived realities and identities. Once the year-long fieldwork was completed, we reviewed all fieldnotes and video recordings, marking segments of tacit and discursive data for additional attention that were then re-transcribed on a separate document for close analysis. Initial meaning reconstruction was conducted through low-level coding of such segments, noting a range of meaning possibilities. For example, lesson interruptions were coded by function (to clarify or deepen content, to scaffold language, to redirect attention, to correct behavior, to answer students' questions, to explore a new topic, to engage students' off-topic interests). This was followed by a recursive cycle of pragmatic horizon analysis (Carspecken, 1996), which involved going back to the fieldnotes to recognize meanings in interactions within a context shaped by the interplay of many paradigmatic and temporal factors. Here we also considered the participants' role, body language and demeanor during discourse, the language(s) used and the type and content of speech (spontaneous dialogue, memorized statements such as chants, yelling, etc.). Soon, instances of adult control over the children emerged as the most predominant, repetitive and influential practice in mediating children's interactions and behaviors. Therefore, we paid special attention to interactive and cultural power relations to identify the types of power employed or claimed by participants that were common to the site and the language(s) used in such process, resulting in high-level raw codes, such as 'coercive power (i.e. threat of punishment),' 'normative power (i.e. claim to adult authority),' 'democratic interaction,' 'agency attempt,' 'ignored voices,' 'language of power,' etc.. We then developed the themes that we present in our findings by reorganizing and identifying relationships between codes, focusing on how racialized expectations, discourses and interpretations of behavior served as the frameworks for social relations, norms and language hierarchies that ultimately helped determine their students' degree of access to agency.

The Site: Paseo del Sol Elementary

Established in the late 50s, PSE is located in a historically Black neighborhood of a large urban community in Texas. The neighborhood is predominantly working class and in recent decades has also become home to a growing number of Latinx immigrant families. Therefore, the school serves predominantly low-income African American (30.7%) and Latinx (64.6%) children. The rapid and widespread gentrification that has characterized the city in the past 15 years is now making its way to the PSE's neighborhood, with visible signs in the form of repossessed homes and/or those undergoing remodeling that appear in almost every block.

The district has established TWI programs in many schools since the early 2000s, with the ultimate goal of better serving language minoritized students and lately, as a strategy to combat a sharp decline in student enrollment. While the most popular TWI programs were those in more affluent, English-speaking neighborhoods, PSE was significant considering its high population of students identified as 'English learners' (EL) (44.64%) and that it was the only TWI program that served a large population of African American students in the city. During the year of the study, the school was in its second year implementing their TWI program as a strand, with only one pre-kinder and kindergarten classes designated as TWI. The principal was a Black woman who was enthusiastic about the TWI program and its teachers. Her support for the program stemmed from her collaborations with a long-time desegregation community activist who promoted dual immersion programs and opportunities for African American students to learn Spanish. The assistant principal was a bilingual Latina woman who was able to communicate with Spanish-speaking families, and many of the faculty and staff members who were also Black or Latinx. Thus, PSE seemed to be an ideal setting to explore both challenges and opportunities in TWI for students from low-income communities of color, without the issues of extreme differences in socioeconomic status, access to white power and privilege, and interest convergence common of other contexts more commonly studied. Such exploration, we hoped, would offer considerations for TWI situated within the everyday lives and realities of historically marginalized communities.

Mr Aguirre's kindergarten class

Mr Aguirre's class, initially, had a total enrollment of 19 students. He provided further insights by identifying eight as Spanish-dominant Latinx, ten as English-dominant African Americans and one as a Latina who appeared comfortable in both languages. With a few exceptions, most of the students had been together since pre-K and had already formed relationships and been exposed to a bilingual classroom environment. Given that the TWI program had to be elected by the parents and based on conversations with some of them, it can be safely assumed that the parents of these children were enthusiastic about the goals of the program.

Mr Aguirre was a young, nurturing and gentle-natured teacher whose teaching career began when he obtained his degree in art education approximately five years prior to the study. He had recently completed a master's degree in a program that had deepened his critical perspectives and commitment to an anti-racist/anti hetero-patriarchal education. Yet his ability to view school as a potential emancipatory space for students from historically oppressed groups was first informed by his own experiences as a working-class 'English-learner' and queer Latino transnational learner from Mexico and by the ways in which certain teachers supported his identity and bilingualism. Due to his bilingual skills, Mr Aguirre first taught for three years at a prestigious Spanish-immersion private preschool that served mostly white affluent children, but wishing to serve students of color, he enthusiastically joined PSE the year prior to the study. This was, however, Mr Aguirre's first year in TWI, which he began with passion and excitement. In what follows we present our findings and examine the ways in which hegemonic everyday practices at the school level progressively impacted the TWI kindergarten class.

Findings

'The kids at this school are not like at other schools': Controlling the Savage Child

At the surface, PSE appeared as a culturally responsive school for Black and Latinx children. A quick look at the school events highlighted on social media depicts a dynamic school where caring educators from diverse racial/ethnic backgrounds engaged in meaningful professional development on topics like restorative justice and mindfulness, where staff and families organized around the needs of the community, and where positive experiences were offered to the children. While this was certainly the case, a closer look revealed that the dominant narratives of deficit thinking about students of color prevalent in the larger society still permeated circulating discourses among many of the adults in the school, as well as their everyday attitudes toward the children. We posit that such tacit attitudes provided the framework that defined the value of students' languages and that ultimately hindered their access to bi/multilingualism.

The main manifestation of deficit thinking emerged through overemphasis and routine control of students' bodies and voices. We observed that in almost every school setting outside their classroom school personnel highly restricted student movement and talk, even where one would expect a more relaxed environment or more freedom of movement or interactions. Yelling at students or speaking to them in patronizing ways was a naturalized practice that students were expected to accept without questioning. For example, at lunch time, a woman would stand by the stage, yelling at students over the microphone to eat quietly, calling out individual children and isolating them from their peers at a separate table if they broke the rule. Special classes, like PE, art, music and library time also took place under practices of constant monitoring and control. In fact, more attention was often paid to restricting children's movement and talk than to the quality of instruction. In PE a slight imperfection in the way they sat or lined up immediately constituted infractions. The low expectations of art class were among the most pronounced. From the moment students arrived at the door, the art teacher spoke condescendingly, making constant demands ranging from body posture and silence to limiting students' use of materials and creativity. Students would come out of class with basic drawings they had colored with crayons following strict instructions, and a sticker for those having complied with all the rules – a stark difference from the elaborate art projects and exploration of various techniques and materials offered to other kindergarteners in the district, based on our experience with other schools.

In one occasion while Claudia waited in the library to conduct a parent interview, Ms Rogers, the librarian, approached her to request the use of low voices because 'the kids at this school are not like at other schools; these kids tend to get easily distracted,' Ms Rogers emphasized. This was the second time she had made this request, revealing her apprehension about students' behavior and her generalized assumption that these children were less attentive or self-controlled than others, and offering insight into the tacit emphasis on control. Ms Rogers comment fits the widespread perception noted by Skiba and Williams (2014) that 'students of color being exposed to greater family and community disadvantage are less likely to learn socially appropriate strategies for self-control and interpersonal interactions...[and] are more likely to engage in disruptive behavior or violate discipline codes,' which is often the reasoning used to justify the overrepresentation of Black children subjected to severe discipline measures (2014: 1–2).

The role of race and ethnicity as strong determining factors in the severity and frequency of punishment on school infractions is well documented (Skiba *et al.*, 2011). In fact, African American and Latino boys are suspended or expelled two to four times the rate of their white and Asian male peers; meanwhile, African American girls are six times (12%) as likely to be suspended compared to white girls (2%) and three times as likely as Latinas (4%) (USDE, 2014). While we did not collect quantitative data on the rates of suspension, office referrals, or other exclusionary discipline consequences, the ways in which many of the adults treated the children at PSE suggested an overall assumption that children were out of control and needed strict limits and body restraint.

Nonetheless, research fails to support the common belief that students of color misbehave more or that issues of poverty are the cause of racial/ethnic disparities in school discipline, yet increased punishment may lead to greater disengagement and distress, perpetuating a cycle of low academic outcomes and punishment (Skiba & Williams, 2014). Moreover, Raible and Irizarry (2010) posit that heightened emphasis on testing and accountability create a context that increasingly renders educators as

'agents of surveillance and behavior management,' a role that characterized most of the school personnel with whom Mr Aguirre's kindergarteners interacted. The literature then points out that race, gender, socio-economic status, verbal and non-verbal language differences and ability serve as the lenses through which teachers interpret students' behavior, positioning those from historically marginalized communities highly susceptible to intensified surveillance and harsher sanctions (Delpit 1995; Lewis & Diamond, 2015; Townsend, 2000), even when infractions are minor or highly subjective, such as disrespect, defiance and non-compliance (Raffaele Mendez & Knoff, 2003). Besides wiggling, playfulness or exhibiting the wrong body posture (i.e. laying on the carpet rather than sitting with legs crossed), these were precisely the kinds of infractions that would receive considerable attention and lead to sanctions for Mr Aguirre's kindergarteners in the larger school setting.

Building an agentic classroom community

In the initial weeks, it was evident that Mr Aguirre wanted to build a classroom community of mutual respect and empathy. His interactions with children, at least initially, were particularly salient in the data because they contrasted with the rest of adult–child interactions his students experienced in school, and because he was generally the only school official who spoke Spanish to the children. In general, he strived to maintain democratic interactions, often asking for students' opinions, stressing interdependence, responsiveness and positive behaviors. He used routine phrases to get their attention such as, 'Veo, veo' to which students responded '¿qué ves?' and he would then end with 'veo...' inserting the object of attention, from a new literacy center to note children who were helping each other. He would also often say, 'We do things...' to which students responded 'together' – repeatedly to draw the whole group's attention or to emphasize collaboration.

Mr Aguirre's morning instruction typically consisted of a combination of whole-class teacher-led lessons with students gathered on the rug, and independent activities in centers where students worked in open and interactive ways while he met with small groups. During interviews he expressed that he had no intention of controlling children's every movement, and that he believed in the importance of play in young children's cognitive and linguistic growth. He lamented that the expectations for kindergarteners were progressively denying them those opportunities. Indeed, it was during centers activities that the children engaged in agentic and interactive learning, and they generally did so in very positive ways, crossing language barriers and developing cross-cultural friendships. One could sense the high morale as students built structures with blocks, worked on numbers and math games, or sang 'Despacito' at a listening center.

Mr Aguirre's democratic style was also evident in the way he initially handled conflict. For instance, one morning during centers, Cristina, a Latina, and Dillan a Black boy argued at the blackboard center. Mr Aguirre's response was significant because of Dillan's strong personality – one of us had observed him the previous summer during a two week-long language festival where despite its cultural relevance and engaging activities, Dillan spent much of the time upset and excluded from the activities due to issues of non-compliance or conflicts with other children. Also, three out of the five students interviewed indicated that they did not like to play with Dillan because 'he was mean' or 'es malo'. Other teachers, like the PE coach also policed his behavior, often expecting infractions. When Cristina complained to Mr Aguirre that Dillan was making fun of his picture, Mr Aguirre calmly walked toward Dillan and conversed with him.

> 'How do you think she felt? Or actually, how would you feel?,' Mr. Aguirre asked him.
> 'Angry... sad,' Dillan responded after a brief pause.

Mr Aguirre de-escalated the conflict and in the process helped Dillan develop empathy, taking Cristina's feelings seriously. Dillan apologized to Cristina, and in a few minutes the whole incident was forgotten. This way of handling Dillan corrected his behavior without marginalizing, labeling or punishing him. Instead, both Dillan and Cristina were promptly reincorporated into the classroom community.

Mr Aguirre was also more tolerant regarding students' physical behavior. For example, while he lined up the children, he did not expect them to walk with their hands behind their backs to limit students' physical movement and with 'a bubble in their mouths' – a phrase used in schools that ask students to hold air in their mouths to restrict them from talking – as we observed in other settings. Children were then inevitably wiggly and playful as they walked in line back from lunch or specials. He also showed responsiveness to his students' interests in spontaneous ways. For example, one time as the class returned from PE the students spotted a bee hovering the bush across their classroom door. Commotion ensued as some feared it would bite them. Rather than shushing and rushing them into the classroom, he stopped and allowed the students to gather around the bush and observe the bee, 'Look at what Dillan said. It won't bite unless you mess with it,' he noted.

Mr Aguirre's flexibility also characterized his approach to language. He did not follow a strict language policy and we never observed him correcting students' language. Initially, he spoke in Spanish for most of the day, and drew on students' help to scaffold for each other. While he emphasized Spanish, he often translanguaged and, if needed, spoke to students individually in the language they understood best. Therefore, it was not only his approach and attitudes to student behavior, but also his use of language what distinguished his interactions with students from other adults'. Students certainly seemed more at ease under Mr Aguirre's supervision. They interacted more and moved around the classroom, manipulating materials with greater freedom. They seemed to experience joy. However, they also expected Mr Aguirre to be flexible, so transitions would sometimes take time as Mr Aguirre attempted to get everyone's attention. This was not necessarily a problem until his class composition changed – a pivotal event that redefined the course of his class.

From bilingualism to control

At the end of September, the financial impact of gentrification on the district and under enrollment at PSE led to the reduction of teachers. When one kindergarten teacher had to leave, her class was spread out through the rest of the grade level. Mr Aguirre received five new English-dominant children (four African American, one Latino) who had little to virtually no exposure to Spanish instruction in the past. The addition of these five students without any further support generated a series of difficult challenges that escalated as the months progressed, particularly around issues of behavior and classroom management. Moreover, his reputation as a good teacher of African American students might have been a reason why Hanna, a student who had been identified as having serious behavioral challenges, was one of the new students assigned to his class. With 24 children, his class was now six students above the district's average class size for kindergarten.

From that moment, the decline in student engagement and teacher enthusiasm was quick and steep. By mid-November, Mr Aguirre appeared emotionally overwhelmed and physically exhausted as he unsuccessfully tried to get all of his students' attention for whole-class instruction. He would start with a handful of inattentive students, but by the time he was able to get their attention, the rest (regardless of race/ethnicity, language, or gender), who had been waiting for several minutes to start the lesson, were already bored and distracted. Spanish lessons were worse, as he lost student interest quickly. It would take him about 10 minutes to get all the students to pay attention to the book he was about to read, only to stop half way through the first page to spend a few minutes again redirecting student behavior. The cycle would repeat over and over, exasperating those who made their best effort to engage. Observing such dynamic was excruciating and in more than one occasion the observer left the room to give the class space. During conversations with us, Mr Aguirre often expressed his worries that discipline problems in his classroom could perpetuate the depiction of Black children as unmanageable:

> It has nothing to do with the children. They are not the problem. The problem is simply that we are too many in this classroom, too many for a

dual language class. You just can't have so many students when they are having to learn in a second language. It's just too much.

Nevertheless, in the next few months, Mr Aguirre began to progressively adopt, at least to some extent, the cultural norms and attitudes of control so pervasive in the larger school environment. Rather than improving the quality of instruction and finding culturally relevant forms of engagement to increase student attention, most of his literacy lessons consisted in drilling phonics exercises and decontextualized Spanish language practice that was too repetitive for Spanish speakers and unmotivating for English speakers. Even activities that aimed to support social and emotional learning, such as 'mindful breathing' and 'today I feel...' check-in exercises began to look more like controlling schemes rather than authentic efforts to build empathy and collective positive energy. Mr Aguirre, who once listened carefully to his students, now engaged in interactions of normative power insisting on obedience while delegitimizing or ignoring his students' concerns. The following exchange on one December morning between Mr Aguirre and Montrell, a high-achieving Black boy who typically followed instructions and paid attention no matter how long others took to settle down or how unchallenging or under-stimulating the lessons were, is a good example of the deteriorating interactions between Mr Aguirre and his students.

Teacher: Buenos días chicos y chicas. Buenos días chicos y chicas. [*Good morning boys and girls. Good morning boys and girls*]

Teacher gets students ready for the lesson.

Teacher: Bubble breath, bubble breath.

Montrell looks up quietly but is not doing the breathing exercises.

Teacher: Montrell...

Montrell: I'm feeling a little upset.

Teacher: It helps if you breath out.

Montrell watches teacher do the breathing exercises but does not do the exercises himself.

Teacher proceeds with a lesson on Spanish sounds and syllables. When students get distracted, he claps patterns trying to get students' attention and get everybody to participate.

Chanise: (pointing at Montrell) He's still not doing it.

Teacher: We do things...

Students: together.

Teacher: We do things...

Students: together.

Teacher asks Montrell if he wants to clap a rhythm. Montrell does not respond. Then the teacher does several patterns himself but Montrell does not participate. As the teacher begins to do the syllables again, Montrell does not participate.

While Mr Aguirre never resorted to coercive power to convince Montrell to follow along, he dismisses Montrell's comment that he is upset rather than taking it seriously. Eventually he moves on and Montrell's comment is never addressed. Similar instances occurred with Dillan who grew increasingly frustrated with Mr Aguirre to the point of aggressive exasperation. While he continued to speak respectfully to children, in some occasions he yelled, causing great distress to Félix, one of his quietest Latino students. Mr Aguirre's frustration was nonetheless understandable, given that he was seldom able to complete a lesson due to lack of students' complete attention. But rather than promoting authentic engagement through interesting lessons and hearing from them, exerting control became his main approach to students, giving conflicting messages about what he valued, reflecting a sense of powerlessness, and fostering low classroom morale. Mr Aguirre had also now resorted to texting the administrators at the first sign of Hanna's non-compliance, which resulted in her frequent removal from the classroom and which was the only type of 'assistance' that Mr Aguirre received from the administration in such overwhelming context. While the district assigned DL specialists to support the TWI programs, the whole year passed without one ever visiting this school. Having received no mentorship and little support, toward the end of the year, Mr Aguirre himself expressed disillusionment and disappointment for not being able to teach according to his values.

Children's Constant Search for Agency

In examining the nature of interactive power between children and students, some characteristics consistently emerged. In most interactions authoritarian personnel first claimed normative power in their demands – that is, students were to obey because of cultural norms that positioned children as subordinate. When this did not work, adults relied on coercive power – namely imposed sanctions. And to a lesser extent, adults drew upon interactively established contracts, meaning that children complied in exchange for rewards. With the exception of Mr Aguirre's initial democratic interactive approach, students were rarely asked for their opinions, to express their concerns, or to ask meaningful questions. Their choices were very limited and they were continuously judged on the basis of their compliance.

On the other hand, within every restriction imposed, children enacted a range of agentic actions to reclaim a sense of autonomy over their bodies, voices, and minds. This was particularly true for African American students, and to a lesser extent Latinx children. If forced to draw a pumpkin exactly like the teacher's, they would stick to the format but decorated it drastically different. If they were asked to only draw a face, they would draw one with four eyes. If the PE coach asked them to practice dribbling the ball, some students would bounce it far away so they could expand their range of movement and talk to their friends. And if when observing a bird, Mr Aguirre told them to be quiet to avoid scaring it, someone would try to prove him wrong. Students would often push the limits of their freedom just a bit, until new restrictions were imposed. We view these acts as a struggle for agency, for the right to remain autonomous beings, a resistance to letting others rule their lives and bodies completely or limit their experiences and creativity. This quest for freedom, we argue, was fundamental for their sense of dignity, and motivated much of students' behavior, including their choice of language practices.

Reifying standardized English as the language of agency

While the opportunities for bi/multilingual development do not seem at first sight associated with the emphasis on containment and control, we contend that such landscape created the conditions that helped perpetuate the hegemony of standardized English for all students because that became the only language associated with access to agentic identities.

While our data did not reveal routine policing or stigmatization of students' authentic language practices in the classroom or in other school spaces, and while we do not assume that all African American students were users of AAL, its emergence was quite marginal, appearing only sparingly in our observational data or interviews. Neither did we observe evidence that AAL was being incorporated into the curriculum or pedagogical practices.

Likewise, although at the beginning of the school year emergent-bilingual Latinxs spoke mostly in Spanish, their use of English increased significantly by the end of the fall, as most of their interactions with their English-speaking peers took place in English, and some of them even began to use English with other Spanish speakers. Their quick transition to English preference may have stemmed from a sense of urgency. Considering that virtually all of those who imposed their domination over students did so in standardized English, lack of English proficiency increased the risk of failure to comply and consequently to receiving sanctions. Moreover, the data revealed that when Spanish-dominant Latinxs rose their hand to participate, they were rarely called upon. Usually, these students would be rendered invisible, especially when educators focused their attention on correcting 'misbehavior.'

Mr Aguirre also progressively reduced his use of Spanish. Compelled by the need to communicate effectively with his new English speakers, most of his interactions were in English unless he was teaching Spanish literacy. However, as we have previously noted, these Spanish lessons were far from engaging. Given the importance of involvement and recognition strategies in facilitating second language learning (Rahimi & Karkami, 2015) the fact that Mr Aguirre seldom recognized the efforts made by African American students to participate in Spanish because of a heightened focus on controlling those who were off-task, may have contributed to their disengagement. Also deserving of attention is that just like discipline enforcement was done in English outside the classroom, Mr Aguirre tended to revert to English to redirect student behavior or exert interactive power.

The determining role of motivation in learners' investment in a second language is well documented, with integrative and instrumental aspects – or the desire to communicate with speakers of the language and perceived benefits from learning it – among the most significant (Oxford & Shearin, 1994). Considering the language landscape that was produced at PSE, for African American students, there was little immediate impetus for learning Spanish. The fast pace at which their Spanish-speaking peers were learning English reduced the potential of integrative motivation. Moreover, there was little evidence for the children that Spanish proficiency would further their access to agency and dignity. With only a few exceptions, Spanish speakers were rarely recognized for their achievements (except for being compliant) or contributions, and instead were produced as silent and invisible. Control and domination were exerted by English-speaking adults, and the only Spanish they heard came from, Mr Aguirre, who seemed increasingly powerless. Moreover, Spanish was challenging to them; it restricted their ability to express themselves in an already restrictive space.

Under these conditions, it was not surprising that Estela, a quiet Spanish-dominant student now tried to speak English during the final interviews even when we asked questions in Spanish. And that Kiana, the spunky petite Black girl who at the beginning of the year was eager to speak to us in Spanish and rejoiced in being read Spanish books, by December repeatedly expressed her refusal to learn Spanish and would cry during drop off not wanting to enter the classroom. These are examples of a trend that helped perpetuate the cycle of English hegemony and the perception that African American students are unmotivated and unfit for second language learning.

From Spaces of Control to Radical Healing and Solidarity

The findings we have presented are attempts to understand the complex dynamics underlying the intersectionality of race and language in power exchanges in TWI programs serving predominantly low-income children of color. Although in this setting teachers did not speak in deficit terms about the students' languages, the way in which several new students were added to the class in the middle of the year without any support from the school administration or the district's DL specialists revealed the lack of seriousness given to the program and the students it served. Such actions were untypical at other TWI programs in the district serving more white and affluent neighborhoods. Thus, the emphasis on controlling the behavior of students' racialized bodies and the lack of validation of Spanish-speaking children in the larger school context was what framed the program. The attention given to behavior unfortunately resulted in the silencing of Latinx students who were now embodying 'good behaviors'; in Black students, it resulted in disengagement with the learning of Spanish, the minoritized language. In other words, in changing the practices, surveillance centered on controlling the bodies of students, superseding the larger TWI goals of bilingualism, biculturalism and biliteracy. We posit that such context, within the larger neoliberal view of language as profit, created a linguistic economy that reinforced the continuous marginalization and silencing of Latinx Spanish speakers and thus positioned Spanish as irrelevant and often in opposition to students' of color access to agency. In this way, students' motivation declined and opportunities to develop bilingualism, biliteracy and solidarity dwindled.

The findings in this chapter are but one slice of what we learned and a much smaller fraction of the work that still needs to be done in order to offer robust recommendations, or to determine the value of TWI for schools serving predominantly low-income Black and Brown communities. Yet we share them with urgency as we consider them significant for those, like PSE, who strive to create socially just, dual language programs for historically marginalized communities. Through this work, we hope to illuminate ways in which raciolinguistic analyses can consider the convergence of language and the tacit white gaze that perpetuates Black and Brown criminalization that materialize through policies and practices. Such analyses must foster reflection on how such ideological context can suffocate even the most critical, and deeply caring educators, but should also move us to actions of possibility.

As we move forward in dual language education, it will be imperative to imagine new futurities outside of the colonial matrix of power that constructs education programs as well as children of color with the idealized white English-speaking subject as the point of reference. This requires moving beyond recognizing inequities to engaging in a radical imagination (Kelley, 2002) of what dual language should look like beyond conventional prototypes. We argue that taking this call seriously entails envisioning and intentionally building dual language education for communities of color as *radical healing spaces*. Ginwright (2010) defines Radical healing as 'building the capacity of young people to create [the] type of communities in which they want to live' (2010: 78). Drawing on Thompson (1995), Ginwright also posits that such kind of healing is fueled on the one hand by the hopes, aspirations, imagination and dreams that youth of color hold for themselves, their families and their communities. And like Valenzuela (1999), he emphasizes that such healing revolves around a collective kind of care that emphasizes not only trusting relations but also political solidarity and critical consciousness.

Dual language programs in Black and Brown schools have the unique opportunity to not just engage in culturally sustaining practices that legitimize the agentic language practices that emerge in marginalized communities (Paris, 2009), but also to truly build relations of political solidarity. Such solidarity may emerge first among educators and families, by thoughtfully exploring issues of power and identity and raciolinguistic ideologies, but also by taking a deep look at the histories of Black and Brown communities and the ways in which they connect and diverge. Such process of critical consciousness-raising also involves acknowledging the various ways in which poverty, joblessness, immigrant hostility, racism and sexism, police brutality and other forms of violence, as well as the many subtle and blatant forms of school-sponsored violence and silencing affect young children of color. With this collective understanding, educators and families may consider the kind of changes, practical actions, and curriculum that are necessary to dream of and to build different futures. As DelaRosa (2018) argues, 'Once our individual [communities of color] can recognize that our hope is intertwined, we can start moving from "mythical" to "critical," from [surviving] to simply "thriving," from mere "wellbeing" to a deeper "radical healing"' (2018: 87). In sum, dual language education can and should aim for more than bilingualism, to the creation of healing spaces built on love, critical consciousness and political solidarity.

References

Adair, J.K., Colegrove, K.S.S. and McManus, M.E. (2017) How the word gap argument negatively impacts young children of latinx immigrants' conceptualizations of learning. *Harvard Educational Review* 87 (3), 309–334.

Anberg-Espinosa, M. (2008) Experiences and perspectives of African American students and their parents in a two-way Spanish immersion program. Unpublished PhD dissertation. Retrieved from ProQuest Dissertations and Theses.

Bender, L.A. (2000) Language planning and language policy in an urban, public school: The interpretation and implementation of a dual language program. Unpublished PhD dissertation. Retrieved from ProQuest Dissertations and Theses.

Carspecken, P. (1996) *Critical Ethnography in Educational Research: A Theoretical and Practical Guide*. New York: Routledge.

Cervantes-Soon, C.G., Dorner, L., Palmer, D., Heiman, D., Schwerdtfeger, R. and Choi, J. (2017) Combating inequalities in two-way language immersion programs: Toward critical consciousness in bilingual education spaces. *Review of Research in Education* 41 (1), 403–427.

DelaRosa, T. (2018) Lessons of 'radical imagination': What the Filipinx community can learn from the Black community. *Asian American Policy Review* 28, 83–83.

Delpit, L. (1995) *Other People's Children: Cultural Conflict in the Curriculum*. New York: The New Press.

Flores, N. and Rosa, J. (2015) Undoing appropriateness: Raciolinguistic ideologies and language diversity in education. *Harvard Educational Review* 85 (2), 149–171.

Frankenberg, E., Ee, J., Ayscue, J.B. and Orfield, G. (2019) *Harming our Common Future: America's Segregated Schools 65 Years after Brown.* The Civil Rights Project: Projecto Derechos Civiles. www.Civilrightsproject.ucla.edu

Ginwright, S.A. (2010) Peace out to revolution! Activism among African American youth: An argument for radical healing. *Young* 18 (1), 77–96.

Hart, B. and Risley, T.R. (2003) The early catastrophe: The 30 million word gap by age 3. *American Educator* 27 (1), 4–9.

Huber, B. (1990) Incorporating minorities into foreign language programs: The challenge of the nineties. *ADFL Bulletin* 21 (2), 12–19.

Hubbard, L.J. (1980) The minority student in foreign languages. *Modern Language Journal* 64, 75–80.

Kelley, R.D. (2002) *Freedom Dreams: The Black Radical Imagination.* Boston, MA: Beacon Press.

Krause, E.M. (1999) Two-way bilingual education: Analysis of an inner-city program. Unpublished PhD Dissertation. Retrieved from ProQuest Dissertations and Theses.

Kubota, R., Austin, T. and Saito-Abbott, Y. (2003) Diversity and inclusion of sociopolitical issues in foreign language classrooms: An exploratory survey. *Foreign Language Annals* 36 (1), 12–24.

Ladson-Billings, G. (2006) From the achievement gap to the education debt: Understanding achievement in US schools. *Educational Researcher* 35 (7), 3–12.

Lewis, A.E. and Diamond, J.B. (2015) *Despite the Best Intentions: How Racial Inequality Thrives in Good Schools.* Oxford University Press.

Madison, D.S. (2005) *Critical Ethnography: Ethics, Methods, and Performance.* London: Sage.

Márquez, J.D. (2014) *Black-brown Solidarity: Racial Politics in the New Gulf South.* University of Texas Press.

Martinez, D.C. (2017) Imagining a language of solidarity for Black and Latinx youth in English language arts classrooms. *English Education* 49 (2), 179.

Martínez, R.A. (2010) 'Spanglish' as literacy tool: Toward an understanding of the potential role of Spanish-English code-switching in the development of academic literacy. *Research in the Teaching of English* 45 (2), 124–149.

Oxford, R. and Shearin, J. (1994) Language learning motivation: Expanding the theoretical framework. *The Modern Language Journal* 78 (1), 12–28.

Palmer, D. (2010) Race, power, and equity in a multiethnic urban elementary school with a dual-language 'strand' program. *Anthropology & Education Quarterly* 41, 94–114.

Parchia, C.T. (2000) Preparing for the future: Experiences and perceptions of African Americans in two-way bilingual immersion programs. Unpublished PhD dissertation. Retrieved from ProQuest Dissertations and Theses.

Paris, D. (2009) 'They're in my culture, they speak the same way': African American Language in multiethnic high schools. *Harvard Educational Review* 79 (3), 428–448.

Paris, D. (2016) 'It Was a Black City': African American Language in California's changing urban schools and communities. In S. Alim, J. Rickford and A. Ball (eds) *Raciolinguistics: How Language Shapes Our Ideas About Race* (pp. 241–254). New York: Oxford University Press.

Petrovic, J.E. (2005) The conservative restoration and neoliberal defenses of bilingual education. *Language Policy* 4 (4), 395–416.

Rafaelle Mendez, L.M. and Knoff, H.M. (2003) Who gets suspended from school and why: A demographic analysis of schools and disciplinary infractions in a large school district. *Education and Treatment of Children,* 30–51.

Rahimi, M. and Karkami, F.H. (2015) The role of teachers' classroom discipline in their teaching effectiveness and students' language learning motivation and achievement: A path method. *Iranian Journal of Language Teaching Research* 3 (1), 57–82.

Raible, J. and Irizarry, J.G. (2010) Redirecting the teacher's gaze: Teacher education, youth surveillance and the school-to-prison pipeline. *Teaching and Teacher Education* 26 (5), 1196–1203.

Rosa, J. and Flores, N. (2017) Unsettling race and language: Toward a raciolinguistic perspective. *Language in Society* 46 (5), 621–647.

Rymes, B. and Anderson, K. (2004) Second language acquisition for all: Understanding the interactional dynamics of classrooms in which Spanish and AAE are spoken. *Research in the Teaching of English*, 107–135.

San Miguel, Jr., G. and Valencia, R. (1998) From the Treaty of Guadalupe Hidalgo to Hopwood: The educational plight and struggle of Mexican Americans in the Southwest. *Harvard Educational Review* 68 (3), 353–413.

Skiba, R.J. and Williams, N.T. (2014). Are Black kids worse? Myths and facts about racial differences in behavior. *The Equity Project at Indiana University*.

Skiba, R.J., Horner, R.H., Chung, C.G., Rausch, M.K., May, S.L. and Tobin, T. (2011) Race is not neutral: A national investigation of African American and Latino disproportionality in school discipline. *School Psychology Review* 40 (1), 85–107.

Thompson, A. (1995) 'Caring and Color Talk: Childhood Innocence in White and Black', in S. Walker and J.R. Snarey (eds) *Racing Moral Formation; African American Perspectives on Care and Justice* (pp. 23–37). New York: Teachers College Press.

Townsend, B.L. (2000). The disproportionate discipline of African American learners: Reducing school suspensions and expulsions. *Exceptional Children* 66 (3), 381–391.

US Department of Education Office for Civil Rights. 2014 'Civil Rights Data Collection Data Snapshot: School Discipline.' U.S Department of Education Office for Civil Rights.

Valdés, G. (1997) *Con Respeto: Bridging the Distances Between Culturally Diverse Families and Schools: An Ethnographic Portrait*. New York, NY: Teachers College Press.

Valdés, G. (2002) Enlarging the pie: Another look at bilingualism and schooling in the US. *International Journal of the Sociology of Language* 155 (156), 187–195.

Valdés, G. (2018) Analyzing the curricularization of language in two-way immersion education: Restating two cautionary notes. *Bilingual Research Journal* 41 (4), 388–412.

Valencia, R.R. and Solórzano, D.G. (1997) Contemporary deficit thinking. In R. Valencia (ed.) *The Evolution of Deficit Thinking: Educational Thought and Practice* (pp. 160–210). Abingdon, OX: Routledge Farmer.

Valenzuela, A. (1999) *Subtractive Schooling: Issues of Caring in Education of US-Mexican Youth*. State University of New York Press.

Valenzuela, A. (2010) *Subtractive Schooling: US-Mexican youth and the politics of caring*. New York: Suny Press.

Wall, D.J., Greer, E. and Palmer, D.K. (2019) Exploring institutional processes in a district-wide dual language program: Who is it for? Who is Left Out? *Journal of Latinos and Education* 18 (3), 1–16.

Wiese, A.M. (2004) Bilingualism and biliteracy for all? Unpacking two-way immersion at second grade. *Language and Education* 18 (1), 69–92.

10 Who Gets to Count as Emerging Bilinguals? Adapting a Holistic Writing Rubric for All

Margarita Gómez and Kristina Collins

'The crisis is not about education at all. It is about power.' – James Baldwin during the National Invitational Symposium on the *King* decision, 1981.

The intentions of a dual language are for '1) students to develop high levels of language proficiency and literacy in both program languages, 2) to demonstrate high levels of academic achievement, and 3) to develop an appreciation for and an understanding of diverse cultures,' according to the Center for Applied Linguistics (2016). Yet, schools – public and private, parochial and secular – within the United States are inherently hegemonic and unequal because of their social underpinnings that directly mirror the social structures of the society in which all schools find themselves situated. In other words, schools are microcosms of the larger society's beliefs related to race and ethnicity, class, gender, ability, sexual orientation, age, etc. It is unavoidable even when the school's mission, vision and curriculum promote and proclaim otherwise. The reason for this is because each of us, in Western culture, colonized locations and American society specifically, are conditioned to the hegemony of white supremacy so much that we unconsciously uphold it even when we think we are not. As Robin DiAngelo (2018) suggests, 'We are all swimming in the same racialized waters'. Bilingual schools therefore face the same challenges and are not immune to issues of racism, classism, sexism, censorship, etc. – of which their purpose suggests will mitigate.

While the research on language diversity and writing has proliferated and much has been learned about the ways in which honoring language diversity is integral to the identity development of emerging bilinguals (EB) students' literacy practices (Ball & Lardner, 2005; Escamilla, 2006; Lee, 2007; Nieto, 2000), little has changed in terms of reconciling this research with classroom writing pedagogy, especially at the elementary level (Flores, 2010; Swearingen & Pruett, 2003; Willis, 2003). The adoption of the Common Core State Standards in many states, privileges 'standard' English (SE) commonly associated with white, middle-class perspectives often at the expense of non-standardized varieties of English and minoritized languages (Paris, 2016). This phenomenon occurs in dual language programs as well, in which a certain variation of the target language is seen as the 'standard' and where service delivery often follows a model that focuses on a strict separation of languages being learned. Thus, while the literature calls for building on EB students' 'funds of knowledge' (Moll & Gonzalez, 1994), frequently dual language programs similarly ask students to bifurcate their 'funds of knowledge' by language. This division of target language instruction also extends into assessment practices. The typical rubrics used to assess students, particularly in writing, miss fundamental opportunities to truly access students' literacies. Traditional writing rubrics, such as the Six Traits Writing Rubric assess traits from a SE discourse perspective (Spandel, 2008) and do not offer spaces to document students' holistic cultural and linguistic features, features of unique dynamic bilingualism/bidialectalism in action (Escamilla *et al.*, 2014; García, 2009; Paris, 2016). As the introduction notes, dual language schools are often seen as places where racism, classism, sexism, etc. can be mitigated by virtue of developing an appreciation of diversity, however as long as traditional monolingual rubrics measure uses of standard languages then the assets of bilingual/bidialectal EBs will continue to go unacknowledged. Further, nothing will change, and the so-called benefits of learning languages will continue to be used to exploit minoritized students. In the specific dual language school site for this study, where there were a large number of African American and black and brown Latinx student populations, African American language (AAL) was included as one of the multiple languages students' used in school among the students, and why we include AAL within the identification of EBs. While the dual language program encouraged dual language development, it did not always recognize AAL as a language to be used in the classroom and/or in writing. As Sledd (1969) aptly notes about bidialectalism, 'Nothing the schools can do about black English or white English either will do much for racial peace and social justice as long as the black and white worlds are separate and hostile' (1969: 1315). This points to the dilemma that arose as teachers at a dual language school began grappling with how to assess the writing, and in essence language, and race, of bilingual/bidialectal EBs and confront their own raciolinguistic perspectives.

This chapter focuses on a two-year ethnographic exploration, during the 2015–2017 school years, of developing assets-based writing rubrics to assess the writing of the student population in a two-way immersion school, St. Lucy,[1] in which there was a significant proportion of African American students, many of whom use AAL. We use the term AAL, in keeping with the work of Paris (2016), Rickford (1998) and Smitherman (2001) to honor the relationship to West African languages and emphasize it is a complete language system. The chapter reports on the efforts to become more critically conscious (Cervantes-Soon et al., 2017) of teachers' raciolinguistic perspectives (Flores & Rosa, 2015). Findings include initial absence of knowledge and misunderstandings by the teachers of the features of AAL and the challenges that emerged as the school worked to develop and implement a more holistic writing rubric for all (Soltero-González et al., 2012).

St. Lucy is an urban dual language (Spanish, English) K-8 school located in the mid-Atlantic region. At the time of the study, student enrollment was approximately 200 students, with the demographics reflecting 56% Latinx, 33% Black, 4% multiracial/Other, 3% Asian/Pacific Islander and 3% White. Of the approximately 200 students, we selected five of the African American students that demonstrated emblematic instances of the features of AAL. The full-time18-member faculty (including instructional aides) demographics during the consecutive school years from 2015–2017 were 94% female. Ethnically and racially the faculty were 33% Latinx, 11% Black, 5% multiracial/Other and 50% White, with no Asian/Pacific Islander representation for both school years. Each year there were 16 faculty members, with a 12.5% attrition rate between 2015–2016 and 2016–2017 school years. Teachers and staff met bimonthly after school for the entire school year to discuss student writing and create a writing rubric that would acknowledge the unique features and repertoires of the students in the school. Data sources include observational notes on the professional development sessions, teacher surveys and reflections, and student writing samples from the 2015–2017 school years. Data were initially analyzed using open coding (Charmaz, 2000). Each of the two authors reviewed the data separately and then discussed the codes. After reviewing the codes, themes were identified by both authors and multiple data sources were used to triangulate and confirm interpretations (Saldaña, 2012).

This project draws from various sociocultural theories and frameworks that position language differences as assets and seek to recognize students' rights to their own language (Kinloch, 2005; Smitherman et al., 2003) and identities. Thus, we draw on literature that discusses the holistic features of AAL and cultural modeling (Lee, 2007). Additionally, we frame our work within holistic bilingual perspectives such as translanguaging (Canagajarah, 2010; Escamilla et al., 2014; García, 2009; Hornberger & Link, 2012). Finally, as we merge these areas of cultural modeling and bilingualism we also draw upon raciolinguistic perspectives toward a vision of equitable assessment practices for bilingual/bidialectal speakers (Flores & Rosa, 2015; Paris, 2016).

Sociocultural Theories of Language and Literacy Development

A sociocultural perspective views language and literacy development as socially constructed experiences that are shaped by the broader cultural context (Bakhtin, 1986; Gee, 1996). Bakhtin (1986), best known for describing the interrelated links within and between speech and written communication, posits that it is not only speech that enters into written genres, but that the relationship is more complex and interrelated. Recent sociocultural research on the language and literacy development of EB learners suggests that schools and classrooms must find ways to capitalize on EB students' hybrid interrelated repertoires of practice, voice(s) and literate identities when teaching academic literacies (García, 2009; Kinloch, 2005; Moll & Gonzalez, 1994; Paris, 2010). Additionally, this research calls for viewing language and literacy development as dynamic rather than static (García, 2009; Young, 2010). Such dynamic views of multilingualism acknowledge that language users are not the sum of two or more monolinguals, instead they make use of all the linguistic and cultural resources to strategically find the features necessary to communicate effectively (García, 2009; Grosjean, 1982).

One way that research in sociocultural theories of language and learning has responded to the call of challenging deficit notions of diverse language use has been to provide evidence of the multilingual nature of language, even SE(s) (Canagarajah, 2007; Young, 2010). Canagarajah (2007) analyzed the work of native English speakers and documented the variety with which students adopted other dialectal and non-standard varieties of English when writing. For example, Canagarajah identifies how students used sarcasm and humor as a way to resist 'lessons that treat them [students] as passive' (2007: 929). Similarly, Young (2010) also documents the use of a variety of English among white, middle-class and how these variations went unnoticed when compared to the variations utilized by African Americans, thus pointing to the inequities afforded to White, middle-class discourses and their variants. To illustrate, Young (2010) points to real estate agent, Chris Ann Cleland's remarks on Obama's economic plan when she states, 'Nothing's changed for the common guy, I feel like I've been punked.' Young uses this example to show the contradiction touted in schools when children are told that vernacular language is for the playground and here we see it being used in the *Washington Post*. These studies demonstrate that even within what is considered 'standard' English there are variations and that speakers vary their use depending on context. Thus, proving that there really is not one 'standard' English.

Features of AAL

In addition to the works of Geneva Smitherman (1977), William Labov (1966) and others in relation to research surrounding AAL, John

R. Rickford (1999) offers a clear guide in his book *African American Vernacular English* to help non-linguists understand the nature of AAL and that it is, in fact, a language. First, he makes it clear that we should not ascribe AAL to only being a list of features. He states, '[AAL] is more than a list of features and notes the expressive use to which [AAL] is put to serve a wide variety of functions by a wide cross section of people within the African American community' (Rickford, 1999: xv). Rickford (1999) also suggests that researcher and layman alike must understand that just as African Americans are not monolithic, neither is AAL. Not every African American speaks or uses AAL, and not every aspect of AAL is used all the time by AAL speakers (Rickford, 1999). Highlighted in Table 10.1 are several phonological and grammatical features associated with AAL as listed in Rickford's text that students at St. Lucy School frequently used verbally and in their writing.

Although AAL has been the language utilized by generations of many African Americans, it historically has not received such recognition in education. Counterintuitive to both empirical and qualitative research to support why AAL is a language and should be recognized as such, politically deeming it as a language has been strenuous at best and vilified at worst. One need only to look at the mid-late 1990s Oakland School District Ebonics controversy and the public's reaction to substantiate how confrontational a declaration of AAL as language can be. Placing AAL on the same level as Standard American English (SAE also SE) is a direct threat and

Table 10.1 Features of African American language (Rickford, 1999: 4–9) found at St. Lucy

Phonological features	Grammatical features
'Reduction of word final consonant clusters, i.e. *pas* + /t/ for standard English (SE) *passed*'	'Absence of copula or auxiliary'
'Realization of final *ng* as n in gerunds, i.e. *talkin* for *talking*'	'Use of invariant *be* or *bees* for habitual aspect'
'Realization of voiced *th* as /d/ or /v/, i.e. *dat* for *that*'	'Invariant *be* for future'
'Realization of *thr* sequence as *th*, i.e. *thodown* for *throw down*'	'Unstressed *been*' and 'stressed *BIN*'
'Transposition of adjacent consonants, i.e. *aks* for *ask*'	'Use of *done* to indicate completion of an even or action'
'Merger of short /i/ and short /e/, i.e. *pin* for *pen*'	'Use of *had* to indicate simple past'
'Realization of syllable-initial str as skr, i.e. *skreet* for *street*'	'Generalization of *is* and *was*'
	'Absent third person singular present tense -s'
	'Use of *y'all [y'alls], mines,* and *they* to indicate possession'

assault to white supremacy (Sledd, 1969). Because of the historical and sociocultural policies and structures that support white supremacist ideologies that influence everyday institutions – including schools – AAL has a long-standing history of being relegated to being marginalized slang, substandard vernacular or dialect, or simply deemed as 'bad' English within Western culture (Van Keulen *et al.*, 1998). The continued preference by individuals within positions of power throughout education and government to position AAL as an inferior form of English only highlights the racial myth inherently ingrained within American society that anything 'Black' or associated with 'Blackness' is inferior. Education in general and some educators specifically continue to perpetuate this myth today. For example, if a student writes, 'We ready for y'all,' for an assignment at school in many traditional cases, even in a bilingual school from the authors' experience, this statement is marked as deficient or as an error. On the contrary, this is not an error when one considers that the student is following AAL grammatical structure by omitting the copula *are* and using *y'all* to indicate second-person plural object pronoun.

Outside of school, at least for entertainment purposes, the same statement can be heard in a recent commercial to promote the 2018–2019 National Football League (NFL) playoffs. The chant 'We Ready' originated with a group of predominantly African-American high school football players getting ready for a game. The original video was posted online, went viral and was then co-opted by the NFL. The chant is a perfect example of how black culture, which includes language, is often used as a tool for entertainment and subsequent financial profit for corporations, many of which are white owned. AAL in this example is celebrated and highlighted not for its own sake, but because it is a tool to promote one of the major sporting events in the United States. In other words, as long as AAL is used to gain profits for predominantly white owned businesses such as the NFL, it is worth using. But when the AAL language is used as a form of self-expression, political empowerment, and to solidify the bonds of community, then it is a problem and deemed unacceptable, especially within schools. Like many second language learners within American schools, some ultra-correct version of SE continues to be the lingua franca of education. As such, many traditional schools force second language learning students to learn SE or fail. Dual language schools also run the risk of maintaining these traditional practices when they fail to recognize, celebrate and utilize AAL in their schools. There is a general disconnect in what is deemed acceptable in schools (i.e. academic language, SE, etc.) and what authentic discourse is actually taking place in the world beyond school (Flores & Rosa, 2015). This disconnect demonstrates how traditional schooling supports white supremacy and the ideology of meritocracy. When Dual Language schools dismiss AAL and thus its speakers, they also perpetuate these hegemonic ideals that they purport to diminish or eliminate.

In truth, by AAL standards the sentence, 'We ready y'all,' is syntactically correct and can be semantically understood like many of the examples of student writing samples mentioned earlier in this chapter. But these are not the standards used in schools. In a vast majority of schools (bilingual schools included), SE is the norm and is normed, like many other aspects of traditional education, to white, middle and upper-class students. Anything outside of those language and cultural norms is therefore seen by society and perceived by teachers as a deficit and error. Students that commit such 'errors' often suffer academically until they conform to the norms. Similarly, for many marginalized – typically black, brown and/or low income – members of society who use SE regardless of race/ethnicity or socioeconomic status – their peers hear whiteness. Hence, the age-old question many people of color who utilized SE have often heard from their sociocultural peers, 'Why you talk white?'

EB students, including those that speak AAL, who use their native marginalized language and SE are then subject to criticism in school for using their native language and by their cultural peers for using SE. EBs walk a fine line because neither language is accepted in the social and academic spheres in which they find themselves. Therefore, schools – bilingual schools specifically – must re-examine holistically their purpose not only in relation to a student's language but also to a student's culture.

Holistic Perspectives on Bilingualism

Holistic perspectives on bilingualism view language as part of a unified system rather than as separate systems, or a parallel monolingual view in which languages operate separately and independent of one another. This conceptualization of language as a unified system, or as a continua of biliteracy (Hornberger, 2003) is different from previous notions of languages as separate registers. Hornberger and Link (2012) argue that, 'it is in the dynamic and sometimes contested spaces along and across continua that most biliteracy use and learning occur' (2012: 243). García and Kleifgen (2010) describe this as dynamic bilingualism in which EBs use all their linguistic tools to develop language, including SE, adding that when viewing language from this perspective, 'students are given agency to negotiate their linguistic repertoires' (2010: 25). The significance of this research is that it seeks to document the complex uses of the language of the students, what García (2009) refers to as 'languaging' and 'translanguaging.' Languaging acknowledges that language is always changing and growing to meet the needs of its interlocutors, rather than seeing it as a static non-changing entity (García, 2009). Building on Williams (1994) work describing translanguaging as a pedagogical tool, García (2009) defines translanguaging then as multilingual learners' ability to use all available repertoires within a unified system. In sum, holistic views of language and literacy development are fluid and flexible use of registers and languages, or languaging/translanguaging, that should be seen as the norm.

More recently, García *et al.* (2017) have offered suggestions and ways in which translanguaging can be used not only as a theoretical stance, but also a pedagogical tool that guides instruction. They describe starting with the students' languaging practices as the translanguaging 'corriente' or positive energetic current that EBs bring to learning. Then, García *et al.* describe the teacher's ability to recognize the complex language use and shift to further language (play with the multiple languages) in order to help the student not only learn language but also acknowledge this as part of identity development. Likewise, Celic (2009) documents her experiences teaching third and fourth graders that speak a variety of languages (Spanish, Chinese and Nepalese). She purposefully pairs students by home language and heterogeneous English language abilities. She provides dynamic scaffolding in which she allows the students to discuss and pose questions in their heritage language so that it can be understood fully before requiring the students to produce English texts. In this way, the students are using their full bilingual repertoires to access the content and help each other work to develop their English literacy. Soltero-González *et al.* (2012) have also explored bilingual literacy development from a holistic, translanguaging frame and this has begun to influence the work of teaching writing to bilingual leaners. Recent research on privileging bilingualism (Hopewell & Butvilofsky, 2016) to understand biliteracy and that of using translanguaging to develop the academic language of students shows how bilingualism can be useful versus the deficit concept that it interferes with literacy. Paris (2016) also contributes to this holistic perspective adding that AAL is also included, 'Recent linguistic, educational, and cultural scholarship has pushed against the tendency to assume unidirectional correspondence between race, ethnicity, language and cultural practice; and in the tradition of this chapter, has shown that such relationships must be understood as dynamic and varied rather than as fixed and monolithic' (2016: 249). Thus, drawing attention to the need for more flexible frameworks for the teaching and learning of languages and cultures in a globalized society. It is [1] important to note that in mixed communities, Latinx students also use features of AAL in speech, which appears in writing as noted by the research of Paris (2016). Below are writing samples from various AAL and Latinx students (Figures 10.1–10.5) that demonstrate some of the uses of AAL discussed in Table 10.1.

The Process of Developing a Holistic Rubric for ALL at St. Lucy

St. Lucy School is a small, K-8 private, parochial school situated in an urban area in the eastern United States. The community surrounding the

Grammatical features

'Stressed BIN (been) (Rickford, 1999: 6).' *We been doing this for years*, indicates the practice started in the remote past and continues until the present.

Figure 10.1 Written sample of AAL grammatical feature, Ashton, grade 8

school is experiencing burgeoning growth in population and diversity, gentrification and socioeconomic stratification. St. Lucy's school has been designated a dual language Spanish immersion school since 2010. Consistent with other dual language schools, St. Lucy follows a traditional two-way immersion service delivery model, whereby students receive instruction in two languages and have a balance of students who are native speakers of each (or both) of the two core languages.

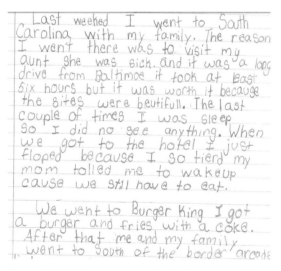

Phonological features

'Deletion or vocalization of *r* after a vowel (Rickford, 1999: 5),' i.e. *Baltimoe* for Baltimore

'Deletion of unstressed initial syllables (p.5)', i.e. *I was sleep* for I was asleep

Pronunciation and, thus, spelling of told as *tolled* (Hudley & Mallinson, 2011: 86)

Figure 10.2 Written sample of AAL phonological features, Jordan, grade 5

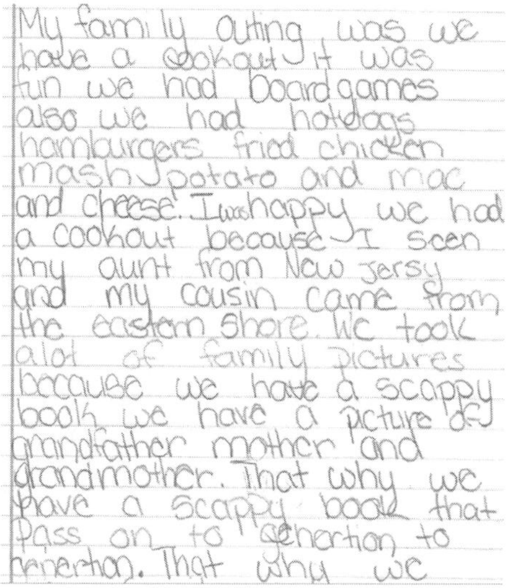

[handwritten sample:]

> My family outing, was we have a cookout it was fun we had board games also we had hotdogs hamburgers, fried chicken mash, potato and mac and cheese. I was happy we had a cookout because I seen my aunt from New Jersy and my cousin came from the eastern shore. We took a lot of family pictures because we have a scappy book, we have a picture of grandfather mother and grandmother. That why we have a scappy book that pass on to generation to generation. That why we

Phonological features

'Reduction of word-final consonant clusters (p. 4),' i.e. Mash for mashed

Grammatical features

'Absence of plural -s (p. 7),' i.e. potato for potatoes

'Use of past participle form (V-en) as past tense or preterite (p. 7),' i.e. I seen my aunt for I saw my aunt

'Absence of possessive -s (p. 7),' i.e. grandfather mother for grandfather's mother and grandmother

Figure 10.3 Written sample of AAL phonological feature, Blair, grade 5

In St. Lucy School, professional development was conducted for two school years on the pedagogical and instructional practices necessary to teach writing to a vast variety of students in the Spanish-immersion Pre-K 8th-grade dual language school. Demographically and linguistically diverse, the school consistently maintains a population of Latinx, African American, white, African and children of two or more races. Similarly, socioeconomic status and family structures of the children represented in St. Lucy is also diverse. Linguistically, the students range from first- and second-generation Spanish-speaking to third- and fourth-generation

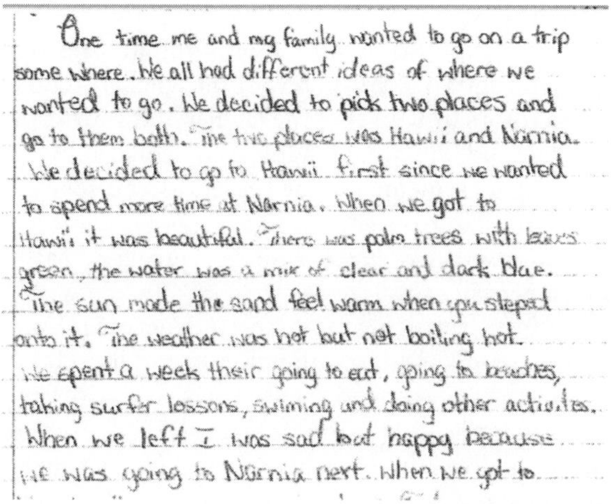

[handwritten sample:]

> One time me and my family wanted to go on a trip some where. We all had different ideas of where we wanted to go. We decided to pick two places and go to them both. The two places was Hawaii and Narnia. We decided to go to Hawaii first since we wanted to spend more time at Narnia. When we got to Hawaii it was beautiful. There was palm trees with leaves green, the water was a mix of clear and dark blue. The sun made the sand feel warm when you stepped onto it. The weather was hot but not boiling hot. We spent a week their going to eat, going to beaches, taking surfer lessons, swimming and doing other activities. When we left I was sad but happy because we was going to Narnia next. When we got to

Grammatical features

'Generalization of is and was instead of are and were (Rickford, 1999: 7),' i.e. *The two places was..., There was palm trees.., or We was going to...*

Figure 10.4 Written sample of AAL grammatical feature, Kelly, grade 6

> I went out with my friends and we went to Six Flags. We went in the pool, got on roller coaster, walked around, eat, talk, laugh, play around, and cuss. We also had woached the fire works. I had fun because I seen People that I use to see almost every day. I like that my mom trusted me to be by my self and hang with my friends without her being with me or being annoying and kept calling me.

Grammatical features

'The use of had to mark simple past (Rickford, 1999: 6),' i.e. *We also had watched the fire works* for We also watched the fireworks.

'Use of past participle form (V-en) as past tense or preterite (p. 7),' i.e. *...I seen people that I use to see almost every day.*

Figure 10.5 Written sample of AAL grammatical feature, Marley, grade 3

bilingual, or monolingual English speaker. The population also includes AAL-speaking students regardless of their race because of sociocultural and residential proximity, and socioeconomic status as referenced in Paris (2016) (Le Moine & Hollie, 2007; Paris, 2016). Some of the features of AAL were found in the verbal conversations of students regardless of race or ethnicity during social interactions as well as in their writing samples (see Figures 10.1–10.5). It must be noted that use of AAL by non-African American students does not equal inclusion into African American identity. This utilization of AAL across ethnic and racial boundaries is based on social context, peer communication and other social functioning either positive or negative (Paris, 2010).

The sixteen faculty and staff at St. Lucy were equally diverse, having teachers that identify as Latinx, African and White. The teachers also identify as speaking different varieties of Spanish, English, and Yoruba. Similarly, the teachers are also socioeconomically diverse and include immigrant, first and second generation and monolingual English-dominant speaking faculty and staff. However, few of the teachers identified as speaking AAL. The authors were part of the faculty and staff at the school, one served as a teacher and later dual language coordinator, while the other was a university faculty member that served as the school's mentor. The authors were participant-observers at the school, interacting with faculty and staff while also writing reflective memos during and after sessions to learn from the experience.

Historically, writing had been a struggle for many students at St. Lucy, and it was more apparent as students matriculated into middle school. Prior professional development was devoted to reading instruction and assessment. However, reading and writing are interrelated. The school mentor along with the administration and teachers agreed it was time to tackle writing instruction and assessment across the curriculum to address the problem of student writing at St. Lucy. The school mentor identified research-based assessment and instructional practices to effectively analyze and teach writing with AAL speakers (LeMoine & Hollie, 2007; Smitherman, 1994) and sought to reconcile these with holistic bilingual features (Soltero-González et al., 2012). These practices include building linguistic awareness of prominent features of AAL and second language writing that might be found in both oral and written form. Additionally, the focus of the professional development was to identify features of interlanguage (Gort, 2006), interlanguage being the application of rules of one written language when learning and writing the other (i.e. phonology, syntax and semantics), as strengths and thus used a balanced approach to literacy that incorporated linguistic and cultural awareness (LeMoine & Hollie, 2007). Taking the elements suggested by Smitherman (2003) and LeMoine and Hollie (2007) a step further, the St. Lucy faculty, with guidance and support from its school mentor, worked to create a writing rubric to effectively evaluate student writing in a bilingual context for both elementary and middle school students from a holistic perspective that included both linguistic and cultural features (see Figure 10.6: English writing rubric and Figure 10.7: Spanish writing rubric). These rubrics developed out of a process of using resources and websites such as the World Class Instructional Design and Assessment (WIDA) Consortium and the Education Northwest six plus one trait rubric (Culham, 2003), as well as the holistic rubrics in Escamilla et al. (2014). These resources were mined to include aspects that would help identify areas of writing that went beyond spelling, capitalization and punctuation.

As suggested by Smitherman (2003), writing instruction and the act of writing by students was supposed to happen each school day. St. Lucy teachers across all grade levels and content areas began to examine how much writing instruction was actually happening during the school day. They, along with the school mentor and administration, discovered that explicit writing instruction in both languages at the elementary level was often relegated to grammar instruction. At the middle school level, writing was only explicitly taught in English and Spanish language arts. Although students within both levels were consistently receiving writing assignments to complete in class or outside of class for homework; the expectations for what that writing should look like was vague. Hence, the need for writing professional development.

With these observations in mind, St. Lucy faculty were tasked with attending monthly professional development sessions regarding writing instruction, drafting a writing rubric for elementary and middle school levels, and collecting at least two writing samples every other week for the purpose of analyzing student writing that would inform the development of the writing rubrics. The rubrics were designed by teachers and the school mentor to help teachers evaluate where students were on the writing continuum for the multiple elements such as ideas, organization, word choice, sentence fluency, conventions, but also to look at the inter-and

232   Bilingualism for All?

	Achieving	Bridging	Expanding	Developing	Beginning	Entering
Content Genre-Specific Elements						
Ideas	Fully describe the main idea or purpose. My supporting information is fully developed and includes relevant facts, reasons, details, etc. appropriate to the genre. My supporting details are accurate, relevant and helpful.		Describes the main idea or purpose. My supporting information is based on research, reading and/or personal experiences and is appropriate to genre. Some supporting details are accurate and helpful.		There is a hint at a main idea or purpose. My supporting information is based on things I already know. I include some details that might be repeated or off topic.	
Organization	Everything connects. All my ideas flow from beginning to end. My writing has structure that strengthens and supports purpose/format. The writing is connected (uses variety of appropriate connectors (i.e logical, sequential, etc.)) throughout and appropriate to genre.		My introduction ties to grab the reader's attention. My writing has structure and fits purpose/genre. I have transitions/connectors that are appropriate to genre. Conclusion is present and somewhat linked to main idea/purpose (as appropriate to genre).		My introduction is not clearly stated. My writing seems to go in many directions (note that this might be an instance of circumlocution in AAE writers; or building argument in Latinx students writing). Connectors do not connect ideas or are not appropriate for genre. May or may not include conclusion (as appropriate to genre)	
Voice	I take the audience into account and use topics, details, and language to connect with the audience.		Show enthusiasm about my topic. My writing is interesting and informative (as related to genre)		I have little confidence or enthusiasm about my topic. Parts of my writing are boring. Not sure about my audience and appropriateness related to audience.	

Figure 10.6 Holistic Writing Rubric (English)

Who Gets to Count as Emerging Bilinguals? 233

	Achieving	Bridging	Expanding	Developing	Beginning	Entering
Word Choice	I use specific and interesting words clearly to create imagery and meaning.		Some of the words I use are exact and make meaning clearer. I use well0chosen words that fit purpose and audience. I use vocabulary linked to genre/content.		My words confuse my reader. I use simple language when I need specific words. I incorrectly use vocabulary of content area, etc.	
Sentence Fluency	My sentences have purposeful and varied beginnings. I use a variety of sentence types and lengths. My sentences are all well constructed (for purpose, format, audience).		I use a variety of sentence types, sentence beginnings, and lengths. My piece can be read with little difficulty.		I use some "choppy" sentences have some tense agreement issues, or are dangling modifiers (no clear subject/verb agreement). My sentences start the same way and are of similar lengths and types.	
Conventions	I avoid misspelling words. I include correct punctuation. I pay attention to grammar.		I have a few errors, but they don't make my writing difficult to understand. I need some editing. I use a variety of conventions correctly.		I have many errors that make it hard to understand my writing. I need to edit each line.	
Presentation	The presentation of my writing is clear. I include appropriate visuals, multimedia to support the writing.		My writing is clear (either handwriting, or typewritten (no typos). My spacing is correct and the font/style is appropriate to purpose/audience. My visuals help the reader with ideas.		It is difficult to read my handwriting or understand the typewritten words. The font, size and spacing make it difficult to read. My visuals do not support the reader in making sense of my ideas.	

Figure 10.6 (*Continued*)

Monitoring Bilingual Strategies in Written Language Development

☐ Intersentential Codeswitching: Example I love my new ropa. I been seeing my friends. How many times is this present in the students' writing? _____
Is it intentional or developmental _____

☐ Intrasentential Codeswitching. Example Student begins in one language and ends in another. How many times is this present in the students' writing? _____ Is it intentional or developmental? _____

☐ Bidirectional phonetic transfer. Example japi for happy, tolled for told How many times is this present? _____

☐ Bidirectional syntax transfer. Example The bike of my sister. How many times is this present? _____

☐ Cultural Discourse Patterns: Circular pattern How many times present? _____

Circumlocution, Example: How paper was made includes personal experiences with making paper airplanes, etc. How many times present? _____ ; Narrative Interspersion: Use of personal anecdotes/experiences in an expository text. How many times is this present? _____ Recursion: Use of different images and words for same thing- Example, Dr. Martin Luther King's I have a dream speech. How many times is this present? _____

☐ Other: What other strategies or uses of language are present in the student's writing?
_____ Other: What other strategies or uses of language are present in the student's

Figure 10.6 (*Continued*)

	Comprensivo	Desarrollando	Iniciando
Contenido Elementos del genero de escritura (narativo, poesia, etc.)			
Enfoque/Ideas	Describe completamente la idea principal de acuerdo a experiencias personales o otras investigación o lecturas. Los detalles apoyan la idea principal y son relacionados uno al otro.	Describo o trato describir la idea principal (dibujo) basado en algunas experiencias personales, investigación o lectura. Incluyo algunos detalles que apoyan la idea principal que son correctos.	No tengo idea principal o detalles. No escribe sobre el tema o pedido.
Organización	Incluye introdución que llama la atencion del lector. Desarollo desenlace la idea principal satisfactorio Esta organizados en parafos de acuerdo a las ideas principales Mi conclusion es efectivo para el tipo de escritura.	Hay titulo, transiciones y conclusion pero algunos no son entrelizadas. Tengo conclusion basica o comun.	No hay titulo, no hay introduccion. La composicion esta confuse. No tengo conclusion (si es un requisite al tipo de escritura).
Voz	Mi escritura no tiene proposito, solo escribe oraciones simples y alguna veces aburidas.	Mi escritura es interesante, informativo y mantiene la atencion de lector.	Mi escritura tiene una mezcla de ideas interesantes e informativas y algunas veces son aburido.
Enlaboración/Vocabulario	Uso vocabulario relacionado con el tema. Uso palabras mas apropriada al tema.	Falta uso de vocabulario/ palabras espacifico al tema. Casi simple uso palabras bien escojidas pero a veces uso palabras basicas para escribir ideas.	Mis palabras no ayudan al lector entender mi escritura. Uso palabras basicas.
Fluidez de oraciones	Uso una variedad de oraciones para comenzar que pueden ser leidas sin dificultad.	Uso comienzos communes que se leen con alguna dificultad.	Mis oraciones iniciales no tienen sentido y es dificil de leer.
Convenciones	Casi no tiene errors de mayuscula, uso punctuacion, y ortografia. (Editar)Tengo muy pocos errores de corregir	Tengo algunas errors en mayuscula, punctuacion, y ortografia. (Editar) Tengo que hacer muchas correcciones. Los errores son aceptables para tu nivel.	Tengo tanto errores en mayuscula, punctuacion y ortografia que es dificil leer lo que has escrito. (Editar) Hay que volver de escribir.
Presentacion	Mi caligrafia y presentacion facilita la lectura. Los dibujos refuerzan el escrito y las ideas principales.	Mi caligrafia y presentacion necesita mas espacio, tamaño y nitidez entre letras para facilitar la lectura. Algunos de los dibujos apoyan las ideas principales.	No se puede leer la caligrafia. Si uso dibujos no va con las ideas principales.

Figure 10.7 Holistic Writing Rubric (Spanish)

Monitoring Bilingual Strategies in Written Language Development (See Soltero-González, Escamilla, Hopewell, 2012)

☐ Intersentential Codeswitching: Example I love my new ropa. How many times is this present in the students' writing? _____ Is it intentional or developmental _____

☐ Intrasentential Codeswitching. Example Student begins in one language and ends in another. How many times is this present in the students' writing? _____ Is it intentional or developmental? _____

☐ Bidirectional phonetic transfer. Example japi for happy. How many times is this present? _____

☐ Bidirectional syntax transfer. Example The bike of my sister. How many times is this present? _____

☐ Other: What other strategies or uses of language are present in the student's writing? _____

Figure 10.7 (*Continued*)

intra-sentential codeswitching, and the bidirectional phonetic and syntax transfer (Culham, 2003; Soltero-González *et al.*, 2012). These features were discussed with specific examples of features listed above, such as the interdental fricative sound in -th versus the labiodental fricative found in –f, which could impact the phonetic spelling of a word. Another element added to these that was not part of prior research was the addition of the cultural aspect and cultural discourse patterns as these could impact the ideas and organization of the text, such as circumlocution (Ball, 1992), narrative interspersion, recursion and circular discourse patterns found in Spanish narratives (Montaño-Harmon, 1991). Ball (1992) explains the first three patterns as those found in the discourse patterns of African Americans. Circumlocution refers to ideas and topics that are connected and signaled through the use of 'and' (Ball, 1992). Ball (1992) defines narrative interspersion as an oral or written pattern within an expository text is interspersed with narrative elements (i.e. personal experience related to the topic). Finally, she identifies recursion as a pattern where a speaker or writer repeats topic but uses different images and words to describe the topic/idea. Montaño-Harmon (1991) did a contrastive analysis between different language patterns and found that Spanish discourse patterns follow a more circular narrative, in which a topic is stated and then other examples and images build on the topic. This pattern was distinct from 'standard' English patterns, which were found to be more linear in nature. Because these patterns are found in the oral and written language of diverse speakers of languages, the mentor decided to include these as a feature that could potentially influence ideas and organization of writing. The rubrics were created for both the English and Spanish language arts classrooms but were not limited to just the language arts discipline. The rubrics were designed to be customizable for use across multiple disciplines in the school setting (see Figures 10.6 and 10.7 writing rubrics).

In the professional development sessions, teachers worked diligently crafting the rubrics and fine tuning them to meet the demands of a bilingual program and the diverse student body. After the professional development, however, it was the implementation phase where the rubrics and the collection of writing samples proverbially died. After taking so much time to craft and refine the rubrics, some teachers were either not collecting writing samples or not collecting samples consistently. This indicated both to the school administration and the school mentor that writing instruction was not a daily or consistent practice as they believed it should be. Additionally, the rubrics were not used in the classrooms by all teachers, but were only utilized during professional development sessions with the school mentor. There was no consistency in implementation or accountability. A survey on using the writing rubric and the analysis of EBs' writing for the features identified in the professional development was given. Teachers were given the choice to add their name or respond anonymously.

Teachers' Responses to Implementation of the Rubric and Analysis of EBs' Writing

There were mixed responses as to both the implementation of the rubric and the analysis of the features of EBs' writing. While there was an overall feeling that the rubrics did give students, 'an opportunity to get a grade based on where they are – Achieving through Entering,' several teachers complained that using the rubrics was, 'too much work or extra work.' Some believed that the work of examining student writing was only beneficial to the school mentor. One female middle school teacher said, 'The mentor is only collecting the samples for her research. Why should we be doing her research for her?' In the professional development sessions, teachers pushed back on the need to look at AAL and acknowledge it as a multilingual strategy, the same middle school female teacher that complained stated, 'I've never heard that that was a language.' Not surprisingly, after presenting the research on AAL, some teachers still thought that this was a matter of opinion, 'That is just slang. They have to learn how to write proper English anyway.' This sentiment again reinforces the underlying bias some teachers have towards AAL. Subconsciously and consciously many educators have been socially conditioned to view anything associated with Blackness as inferior. Another male middle school teacher at the school also indicated that he was unfamiliar with AAL and the features of the language. These comments reinforce that there was a mismatch in understanding and that there was resistance not just to the rubric, but to the idea of holistic bilingualism and seeing the assets students were bringing to the writing of either English or Spanish. The notion that there is only one 'proper' English in the statement made by the female middle school teacher shows that this teacher's thinking did not waver in relation to the idea of multiple Englishes. This same teacher stated that she would 'throw it [the rubric] out' because 'honestly, none of these [the holistic features] are strengths.' Another teacher stated that in relation to holistic features, 'No, I did not see much of this in the writing samples. Spelling and conventions were quite weak though.' Despite the resistance from teachers, teachers at the meeting were still asked to discuss the samples and to mine them to find how students were using holistic bilingual strategies, including those of AAL, and to discuss these as assets. More practice and familiarity with the features of holistic bilingualism helped some of the teachers more easily identify holistic bilingualism and feel comfortable with them as assets. For example, one teacher recognized when AAL speakers were drawing on what they knew to write in Spanish and stated, 'I noticed a few of my students use words that [they think] are cognates. I treated them like the real word needed for the writing and encouraged students to use the glossary I provided in the beginning of the school year when writing.' This statement shows that discussing strategies EBs would draw upon, even the use of false cognates, was helpful in recognizing how interlanguage worked and its influence on the language development process.

Writing samples included a variety of uses of language for a variety of purposes. Above we included some of the samples and discussed the use of language. It is interesting to note, however, that while we did find some examples of AAL in written form it was difficult to find use of AAL in more writing samples despite more students that were known to use it orally throughout the school day. This is something that both LeMoine and Hollie (2007) and Smitherman (2000) also found in their work, and it is more likely that given that students understood that some of their teachers did not understand the usefulness or purpose for including more AAL in their written assignments. Additionally, students were also taught to use 'proper' English, what the teacher identified as 'standard' English, and thus, felt that they could not use it in their written discourse and that it was not an asset. Again, pointing to the need to develop and introduce translingual approaches that recognize the multilingual resources students bring to schools.

Prior to the year-long professional development centered on writing, the faculty had multiple professional developments centered on developing school culture, recognizing and changing biases towards students and families, appreciating language varieties, and how to implement culturally responsive pedagogical strategies in the classroom among other topics related to teaching culturally and linguistically diverse students (Herrera *et al.*, 2014). Why, after all this professional development that was rooted and grounded in research related to intersectionality, bilingual education, culturally responsive pedagogy, etc. was there such resistance to changing how teachers teach and evaluate student writing, for all students, in a bilingual school setting that proclaims to honor all languages and cultures? The results from the survey, the comments in the professional development and the absence of more consistency with the use and analysis of student writing in more holistic terms begged the question about whether the reluctancy in the case of St. Lucy School teachers had less to do with tiredness and more to do with raciolinguistic biases that enforce and maintain the status quo of appropriateness (and thus whiteness) of SE that bilingual education programs proclaim to resolve or lessen. The results of our findings led to more questions.

Vision for Inclusive Writing Assessments and Practices

As school demographics continue to become more diverse and as we better understand how race, ethnicity and language are intersectional (Collins, 2016), we realize the major implications that this work can have on schools and communities. Positioning EBs as competent in all the linguistic repertoires they bring to school can create opportunities for developing more humanizing approaches toward the education of all learners. Paris (2016) notes, 'we must understand that beyond linguistic and historical knowledge, ethnic pride, and interethnic respect, AAL can be a powerful educational resource in learning the DAE [Dominant American English] language and literacy skills demanded in schools' (2016: 249). The use of students' repertoires as sources for ethnic pride and interethnic respect are critical to achieving more liberatory pedagogy (Freire, 1996; Lee, 2007).

Our hope and vision for dual language education, and education in general, is that it resists racialization of language and, subsequently, the discrimination of students that speak or write using marginalized and stigmatized languages or language varieties. Dual language education can be more inclusive beyond the surface acknowledgement of language differences or using native language to learn SE (Flores, 2016). Educational leaders can make an effort to be more inclusive by examining and evaluating writing assessments and teaching practices by looking for bias, equity, inclusivity, accuracy and reliability. Going a step further, educators must also commit to implementing culturally relevant strategies that challenge and dismantle those biases, thus performing an act of liberation for themselves and their students. Dr Gloria Ladson-Billings (2009) states:

> The notion of 'cultural relevance' moves beyond language to include other aspects of student and school culture. Thus, culturally relevant teaching uses student culture in order to maintain it and to transcend the negative effects of dominant culture. (2009: 19)

Therefore, writing assessments must provide students the opportunity to utilize all of their linguistic skills in any language they chose. This further empowers students to understand the choices they have as writers, and for them to be critical of the stylistic decisions they make in their discourse. Furthermore, the tools used to evaluate such assessments must examine student work holistically, taking into account and appreciating their language choices by gauging when, where, and why the student used either language and for what purpose and for whom, not if the language used is 'proper' or 'academic' enough.

This chapter is not suggesting we should not have bilingual or dual language schools. On the contrary, the existence of such schools is encouraging that we are trying to move in the right direction of equality and liberation in education. We are suggesting that just because a school is designated bilingual does not mean they are free and clear from the structures that support white supremacy and language subordination (Flores & Rosa, 2015; Flores, 2016). Validating languages and cultures is not enough, and bilingual programs cannot stop there. We need to move from teaching AAL speakers coping strategies such as code-switching for survival to teaching them to use all of their linguistic repertoires to change the status quo and to gain liberation (Alim & Baugh, 2007). Additionally, we critique how English-speaking teachers use implicit bias towards AAL, but not towards Spanish, calling attention to the fact that when students used Spanish in the hallway, their language was never corrected, however that was not the case when students used AAL. Moreover, heritage Spanish-speaking teachers showed implicit bias in the variety of Spanish, and those biases also indicate preferences by teachers towards 'correct English and correct Spanish.' The results of teachers' responses to the professional development and their analysis of student writing, indicated that more work exploring the links between race, language, culture, socioeconomic status and identity are a necessity.

Note

(1) All names (both of the school and the people involved) are pseudonyms.

References

Alim, H.S. and Baugh, J. (2007) Black language, education, and social change continuing the struggle for equal language rights 50 years after Brown. In H. Samy Alim and John Baugh (ed.) *Talkin Black Talk: Language, Education and Social Change* (pp. 1–12). New York: Teachers College Press.
Bakhtin, M.M. (1986) The Bildungsroman and its significance in the history of realism. *Speech Genres and Other Late Essays* 10, 21.
Ball, A.F. (1992) Cultural preference and the expository writing of African-American adolescents. *Written Communication* 9 (4), 501–532.
Ball, A.F. and Lardner, T. (2005) *African American Literacies Unleashed: Vernacular English and the Composition Classroom*. Carbondale, IL: SIU Press.
Canagarajah, S. (2007) Lingua franca English, multilingual communities, and language acquisition. *The Modern Language Journal* 91, 923–939
Canagarajah, A.S. (2010) A rhetoric of shuttling between languages. In B. Horner, M-Z. Lu and P.K. Matsuda (eds) *Cross-language Relations in Composition* (pp. 158–179). Carbondale, IL: Southern Illinois University Press.
Celic, C. (2009) *English Language Learners Day by Day K-6: A Complete Guide to Literacy, Content-Area, and Language Instruction*. Portsmouth, NH: Heinemann.
Center for Applied Linguistics (2016) Two-way immersion. See http://www.cal.org/twi/ (accessed 22 January 2019).
Cervantes-Soon, C.G., Dorner, L., Palmer, D., Heiman, D., Schwerdtfeger, R. and Choi, J. (2017) Combating inequalities in two-way language immersion programs: Toward critical consciousness in bilingual education spaces. *Review of Research in Education* 41 (1), 403–427.
Charmaz, K. (2000) Grounded Theory: Objectivist and constructivist methods. In N. Denzin and Y. Lincoln (eds) *Handbook of Qualitative Research* (2nd edn). (pp. 509–535). London: Sage Publications.
Collins, P.H. and Bilge, S. (2016) *Intersectionality*. Chichester: John Wiley & Sons.
Conference on College Composition and Communication (1974) Students' Right to Their Own Language. CCC 25, 1–32.
Culham, R. (2003) *6 + 1 Traits of Writing: The Complete Guide Grades 3 and Up*. New York, NY: Scholastic Inc.
DiAngelo, R. (2018) *White Fragility Why It's So Hard for White People to Talk About Racism*. [Audiobook]. Beacon Press.
Escamilla, K. (2006) Semilingualism applied to the literacy behaviors of Spanish-speaking emerging bilinguals: Bi-illiteracy or emerging biliteracy? *Teachers College Record* 108 (11), 2329.

Escamilla, K., Hopewell, S., Butvilofsky, S., Sparrow, W., Soltero-González, L., Ruiz-Figueroa, O. and Escamilla, M. (2014) *Biliteracy from the Start: Literacy Squared in Action* (pp. 25–26). Philadelphia, PA: Caslon Publishing.

Flores, N. (2010) Chicana/Latina education in everyday life: Feminista perspectives on pedagogy and epistemology. *Gender and Education* 22, 469–470. DOI: 10.1080/09540253.2010.496155

Flores, N. (2016) A tale of two visions: Hegemonic whiteness and bilingual education. *Educational Policy* 30, 13–38.

Flores, N. and Rosa, J. (2015) Undoing appropriateness: Raciolinguistic ideologies and language diversity in education. *Harvard Educational Review* 85, 149–171.

Freire, P. (1996) *Pedagogy of the Oppressed* (revised). New York: Continuum.

García, O. (2009) Emergent bilinguals and TESOL: What's in a name? *TESOL Quarterly* 43 (2), 322–326.

García, O., Johnson, S.I., Seltzer, K. and Valdés, G. (2017) *The Translanguaging Classroom: Leveraging Student Bilingualism for Learning*. Philadelphia, PA: Caslon.

García, O. and Kleifgen, J.A. (2010) *Educating Emergent Bilinguals: Policies, Programs, and Practices for English Language Learners*. New York: Teachers College Press.

Gee, J.P. (1996) Discourses and literacies. *Social Linguistics and Literacies: Ideology in Discourses* 2, 122–148.

Gort, M. (2006) Strategic codeswitching, interliteracy, and other phenomena of emergent bilingual writing: Lessons from first grade dual language classrooms. *Journal of Early Childhood Literacy* 6 (3), 323–354.

Grosjean, F. (1982) *Life with Two Languages: An Introduction to Bilingualism*. Cambridge, MA: Harvard University Press.

Herrera, S.G., Perez, D.R. and Escamilla, K. (2014) *Teaching Reading to English Language Learners Differentiated Literacies* (2nd edn). London: Pearson.

Hopewell, S. and Butvilofsky, S. (2016) Privileging bilingualism: Using biliterate writing outcomes to understand emerging bilingual learners' literacy achievement. *Bilingual Research Journal* 39, 324–338.

Hornberger, N.H. (ed.) (2003) *Continua of Biliteracy: An Ecological Framework for Educational Policy, Research, and Practice in Multilingual Settings*. Clevedon: Multilingual Matters.

Hornberger, N. and Link, H. (2012) Translanguaging and transnational literacies in multilingual classrooms: A bilingual lens. *International Journal of Bilingual Education and Bilingualism* 15, 261–278.

Hudley, A.H.C. and Mallinson, C. (2011) *Understanding English Language Variation in US Schools*. New York: Teachers College Press.

Kinloch, V.F. (2005) Revisiting the promise of 'students' right to their own language': Pedagogical strategies. *College Composition and Communication* 57, 83–113.

Labov, W. (1966) Hypercorrection by the lower middle class as a factor in linguistic change. *Sociolinguistics* (Vol. 84, p. 102). The Hague: Mouton.

Ladson-Billings, G. (2009) *The Dream-Keepers Successful Teachers of African American Children*. San Francisco, CA: Jossey-Bass.

Lee, C.D. (2006) 'Every good-bye ain't gone': Analyzing the cultural underpinnings of classroom talk. *International Journal of Qualitative Studies in Education* 19 (3), 305 Vol. 84, p. 102327.

Lee, C.D. (2007) *Culture, Literacy, & Learning: Taking Bloom in the Midst of the Whirlwind*. New York: Teachers College Press.

LeMoine, N. and Hollie, S. (2007) Developing academic English for standard English learners. In H.S. Alim and J. Baugh (eds) *Talkin Black Talk: Language, Education and Social Change* (pp. 43–55). New York: Teachers College Press.

Moll, L.C. and Gonzalez, N. (1994) Lessons from research with language-minority children. *Journal of Reading Behavior* 26 (4), 439–456.

Montaño-Harmon, M.R. (1991) Discourse features of written Mexican Spanish: Current research in contrastive rhetoric and its implications. *Hispania* 74 (2), 417–425.

Nelson, N.W. (2010) Changes in story probes written across third grade by African American and European American students in a writing lab approach. *Topics in Language Disorders* 30 (3), 223–252.

Nieto, S. (2000) Culture, identity, and learning. In S. Nieto and P. Bode *Affirming Diversity* (pp. 138–188). New York, NY: Longman.

Paris, D. (2010) 'The second language of the United States': Youth perspectives on Spanish in a changing multiethnic community. *Journal of Language, Identity, and Education* 9, 139–155. doi:https://doi.org/10.1080/15348451003704883

Paris, D. (2016) 'It was a black city': African American language in California's changing urban schools and communities. In H.S. Alim, J.R. Rickford and A.F. Ball (eds) *Raciolinguistic: How Language Shapes our Ideas about Race* (pp. 241–253). New York: Oxford University Press.

Rickford, J. (1998) Holding on to a language of our own: An interview with linguist J. Rickford. In T. Perry and L. Delpit (eds) *The Real Ebonics Debate: Power, Language and the Education of African American Children* (pp. 59–66). Boston: Beacon Press.

Rickford, J. (1999) *African American Vernacular English*. Malden, MA: Blackwell Publishers

Saldaña, J. (2012) *The Coding Manual for Qualitative Researchers*. London: Sage.

Sledd, J. (1969) Bi-dialectalism: The linguistics of white supremacy. *The English Journal* 58 (9), 1307–1329.

Smitherman, G. (1977) *Talkin' and Testifyin': The Language of Black America*. Boston, MA: Houghton Mifflin.

Smitherman, G. (1994) 'The blacker the berry, the sweeter the juice': African American student writers. In A.H. Dyson and C. Genishi (eds) *The Need for Story: Cultural Diversity in Classroom and Community* (pp. 80–101). Champaign-Urbana, IL: National Council of Teachers of English.

Smitherman, G. (2001) *Talkin that Talk: Language, Culture, and Education in African America*. New York, NY: Routledge.

Smitherman, G., Villanueva, V. and Canagarajah, S. (2003) *Language Diversity in the Classroom: From Intention to Practice*. Carbondale, IL: Southern Illinois University Press.

Soltero-González, L., Escamilla, K. and Hopewell, S. (2012) Changing teachers' perceptions about the writing abilities of emerging bilingual students: Toward a holistic bilingual perspective on writing assessment. *International Journal of Bilingual Education and Bilingualism* 15, 71–94.

Spandel, V. (2008) *Creating Writers: Through 6-trait Writing Assessment and Instruction* (2nd edn). Boston: Pearson Allyn and Bacon.

Swearingen, C.J. and Pruett, D. (2003) Language diversity and the classroom: Problems and prospects, a bibliography. In G. Smitherman and V. Villanueva (eds) *Language Diversity in the Classroom: From Intention to Practice* (pp. 134–148). Carbondale, IL: SIU Press.

Valdés, G. (1999) Incipient bilingualism and the development of English language writing abilities in the secondary school. In C.J. Faltis and P. Wolfe (eds) *So Much to Say: Adolescents, Bilingualism, and ESL in the Secondary School* (pp. 138–175). New York: Teachers College Press.

Van Keulen, J.E., Toliver Weddington, G. and DeBose, C.E. (1998) *Speech, Language, Learning, and the African American Child*. Needham Heights, MA: Allyn & Bacon.

Williams, C. (1994) Arfarniad o Ddulliau Dysgu ac Addysgu yng Nghyd-destun Addysg UwchraddDdwyieithog, [An evaluation of teaching and learning methods in the context of bilingualsecondary education]. Unpublished doctoral thesis, University of Wales, Bangor.

Willis, A.I. (2003) Parallax: Addressing race in preservice literacy education. In S. Greene and D. Abt-Perkins (eds) *Making Race Visible: Literacy Research for Cultural Understanding* (pp. 51–70). New York: Teachers College Press.

Young, V.A. (2010) Should writers use they own English? *Iowa Journal of Cultural Studies* 12 (1), 110–17.

11 One White Student's Journey Through Six Years of Elementary Schooling: Uncovering Whiteness and Privilege in Two-Way Bilingual Education

Suzanne García-Mateus, Kimberly A. Strong, Deborah K. Palmer and Dan Heiman

Introduction

The rise and gentrification of two-way immersion bilingual education (TWBE) is due to the interest of upper middle-class, white [1] parents and an increased general understanding of the value in raising bilingual children (Cervantes-Soon, 2014). It is urgent that we examine the stakes involved when integrating children from the dominant group with children from Latinx [2] and other marginalized communities. This paper describes an examination of the way one white student from an English-speaking home navigated a TWBE program over the course of her elementary school years from 2010 through 2016. What does this kind of integration mean for students of color and those that belong to the dominant group? What does it mean for the future of bilingual programs?

Reyes and Vallone (2007) describe the TWBE program design as being constructed based on four theoretical pillars, the first three of which are: (a) teaching language through content, (b) cognitive and academic development, and (c) the development of a positive cross-cultural attitude. However, it is the fourth pillar – identity construction – that informs the basis of our analysis:

> Through an examination of research on identity construction in childhood and adolescence, particularly as seen through the critical pedagogical lens, it will be proposed that there exists a fourth and relatively unexamined component: identity construction. (p. 4)

In response to inequalities that have emerged in TWBE contexts a related but uniquely different fourth 'pillar' or goal was recently proposed that highlighted the urgency of the development of critical consciousness for all TWBE stakeholders (Cervantes-Soon *et al.*, 2017; Palmer *et al.*, 2019). Critical consciousness, or *conscientizacao,* as Freire (1997) terms it, is an awareness of the structural inequalities that shape the material conditions of our lives and our social relationships due to differences in power and privilege, and includes an acknowledgement of one's own role and complicity in structuring inequalities.

TWBE boasts that it offers speakers of minoritized languages an opportunity to develop or maintain their family's heritage language while simultaneously offering monolingual English speakers the chance to acquire and/or develop a new language (Lindholm-Leary & Block, 2010). This is a beautiful ideal, and in many cases offers a rich and engaging program for students and teachers. Yet the situation is never this simple nor this dichotomized, particularly in diverse and multilingual contexts. Issues of inequity have been demonstrated to emerge in many TWBE programs (Cervantes-Soon *et al.*, 2017). As a team, we are fascinated by the complexity and the possibility of TWBE as a laboratory for understanding the development of skills for negotiating diverse global communities with equity and justice; we therefore have been exploring the kinds of pedagogies that appear to leverage the diversity of the TWBE context for the development of critical consciousness among all students.

This chapter draws on ethnographic observation, interview, and discourse data to track the experiences of one young white student through her six years of elementary schooling. We examine how she was, and in many cases was not, challenged to develop a sense of critical consciousness over the course of her elementary school years through her interactions with heritage speakers of Spanish and her teachers – and how she embodied and enacted whiteness in the TWBE space. We consider the ways that white students impact TWBE programs and the role of pedagogy in developing spaces for the development of critical consciousness. We begin with a brief historical account of the concept of whiteness in the US.

Literature Review

The historical position(ing) of whiteness in the US and in bilingual education

The material benefit to the 'possession' of whiteness emerged in the US during the period of chattel slavery, when whiteness as a racial marker represented 'non-Black' and thus designated the legal right to freedom from being defined as property and all of the economic and social benefits therein (Harris, 1992). The creation of racialized identities to legitimate economic and social inequalities are uniquely Western ideals which were exported via Western imperialism throughout the world, producing a globalized system of white supremacy in which whites enjoy unquestioned, unearned advantages and non-European decendents are Othered, exploited and dehumanized (Allen, 2001). This white supremacist social order is maintained and reproduced both discursively and institutionally, such as through the promotion of physical and ideological sameness centering unmarked white normativity that is prevalent in white-dominated institutions (Ahemd, 2007).

In these institutions, as well as in education, one of the ways that white supremacy is enacted is through the creation and maintenance of hierarchically ranked racial categories, invisible or otherwise. Since in the post-Civil Rights era such explicit racialization is typically frowned upon, the same end is commonly accomplished through ostensibly 'non-racial' categorization and ranking such as the valuing of some linguistic practices as more 'correct' or 'complex' than others, despite linguists' position that such differences are social and political (and, we contend, racial) (Lippi-Green, 2004). This results in the linguistic practices of racialized, bilingual and/or classed communities being seen as 'wrong' and thus warranting the censure and segregation of these speakers in educational settings (Poza, 2015), regardless of these speakers' actual linguistic practices (Rosa, 2016).

Such linguistic ideologies and the hierarchization they purport to justify do not reflect objective linguistic reality any more than the racial ideologies used to legitimate white supremacy; rather, they reflect dominant discourses. Although various and competing ideological discourses exist in any social space, not all can be 'heard' or otherwise considered true and valid (Bourdieu, 1991): only those produced by speakers who already enjoy disproportionate power will be publicly legitimized as 'true' or 'correct' (Blommaert, 2014; Fairclough, 1995; Foucault, 1971; van Dijk, 1993). This conception extends the panopticon of the 'white gaze' to the 'white seeing and listening subject,' an ideological rather than literal figure imbued with the authority to evaluate the linguistic practices of racialized speakers as either legitimate or deviant (Rosa & Flores, 2017) as measured against the nonexistent, idealized linguistic practices of 'standard' white and monolingual speakers (Flores & Rosa, 2015).

As with white supremacy, these linguistic ideologies and the disparate power relationships they represent are most commonly maintained discursively and institutionally rather than through overt force. For example, since identities are co-constructed through interaction (Ochs, 1993), the discursive positioning (Davies & Harré, 1991) of some speakers as embodying the 'correct' linguistic practices and others as 'deviant' implies that the former speaker thus enjoys more authority to authenticate her own and others' identities, linguistic practices, and the worldviews therein (Bucholtz & Hall, 2005). Such positioning and authentication are especially prevalent in linguistically heterogeneous institutional settings such as bilingual schools, where hegemonic racial and linguistic hierarchies are both reflected and reproduced if not intentionally interrupted (Leonardo, 2009).

In TWBE classrooms, unless white students are challenged to take a critical or empathic stance, they play out their roles as white listening subjects (Rosa & Flores, 2017). On the other hand, when they are challenged, they hold potential to serve as allies in the struggle. In this chapter, we examine the ways in which a public school with a TWBE program ratified – and occasionally challenged – a normative whiteness that privileged white students' linguistic resources while minimizing those of bilingual students of color. This chapter pursues the following research question: *In what ways does Tessa (pseudonym), a white, English-dominant student, evidence (a) the white listening subject and (b) the development of critical consciousness in her interactions with classmates, teachers, and researchers over the course of her elementary school years in a TWBE classroom?*

Methods

Context

Our six-year ethnographic and discourse analytic study was inspired by the implementation of a new TWBE program at Hillside Elementary School (all names are pseudonyms), in a historically segregated but rapidly gentrifying city in Texas. In particular, we followed the progression of the first cohort of students in the TWBE program from kindergarten through fifth grade. The demographics of Hillside appeared to mirror those of the city, undergoing dramatic population changes due partly to local gentrification and partly to the growing popularity of the new TWBE program. For example, in the year before the TWBE program was implemented approximately 87% of the students at Hillside were Latinx, with nearly 60% coming from Spanish-dominant homes, yet only seven years later the Latinx population had dropped to 58%, with only 23% of students coming from Spanish-dominant homes. However, this change in population was not due to a dropping enrollment: during this time period, the net population at the school grew by over 97%, largely due to the influx of white, middle-class families eager to participate in the TWBE program.

These dynamics inspired our closer look into one focal student named Tessa, who, as a white, middle-class, English-dominant speaker whose family had elected to come to Hillside during its first year of TWBE implementation, represented the demographic shifts characteristic of both the school and the city during our study. Although English was the only language spoken in Tessa's home, her family had intentionally sought out bilingualism for her, placing her in Spanish-immersion childcare beginning in infancy and continuing until she entered Hillside (Parent Interview, 5/15/16). This exposure likely helped her acquire the label of an

Table 11.1 Changes in school demographics and focal student during span of study

Tessa		Hillside Elementary				
Grade and Year	Teacher	School Net Pop.	Latinx Pop.	White Pop.	Low SES Pop.	Spanish Speaking Pop.
Kindergarten 2010–2011*	Ms Ortega	188	87%	7%	92%	60%
First 2011–2012*	Ms Jackson	220	81%	12%	79%	51%
Second 2012–2013*	Ms Epett	293	74%	20%	70%	40%
Third 2013–2014*	Ms Morales	300	70%	26%	63%	38%
Fourth 2014–2015	Michelle	285	66%	30%	52%	33%
Fifth 2015–2016*	Michelle	302	64%	30%	45%	30%

Note: Use of asterisk indicates years during which researchers actively collected data at site. All data represent percentages of total school population except 'Total Student Population' category, which is reported as a raw number.

academically strong emergent bilingual, testing in the fall of her kindergarten year at 'above grade level' in English and 'reading at level expected by the end of the first grade' in Spanish according to her scores on the Developmental Reading Assessment (DRA) and its equivalent in Spanish.

Table 11.1 documents the changes that occurred at Hillside as we followed the focal student throughout her elementary education.

Data collection

Although the focus of the larger study from which these data emerge was schoolwide, Suzanne, Dan and Deb all collected data at Hillside that included Tessa. Suzanne collected data related to the development of bilingual/biliterate identities of six focal children, of which Tessa was one, from kindergarten through third grade. She spent at least 6 weeks each school year in their classroom, collecting field notes and audio/video recordings of interactions and occasional interviews with children, their parents, their teachers and administrators. Suzanne also formally interviewed Tessa in second grade, using cued video to ask her about her development of bilingualism in kindergarten and first grade.

With an aim to understand how a team of two teachers and their young students were making sense of a brand-new program and policy, Deb also spent significant time in Tessa's kindergarten classroom, collecting video recordings of student interaction and writing thick descriptive field notes. She interviewed both TWBE teachers and the school principal.

Dan carried out a nine-month critical ethnography with Tessa's fifth-grade teacher and her class which spanned the entire 2015–2016 academic year. Dan spent time in Tessa's class three days per week to document the ways that the teacher integrated critical pedagogy with her diverse group of emerging bilingual students. Tessa appeared in 10 instances in his field notes where she was an engaged participant in the teacher's dialogical pedagogy, and we selected these instances for inclusion in this analysis.

Data analysis

We analyzed Tessa's appearances across all our data, exploring how she engaged in this bilingual/bicultural community with an aim to understand (a) how her bilingualism and her race/class identities were interpreted (by herself and others), and (b) how she challenged others or was challenged in dialogue toward critical consciousness (Freire, 1997; Palmer *et al.*, 2019). To do so, we drew on a range of qualitative methods: Suzanne and Deb used a microethnographic approach – in particular Erickson's whole to part inductive analysis (Erickson, 2004; Johnstone, 2008) for video analysis to make connections between micro-level discourse and macro-level processes, while Dan engaged in a thematic analysis (Miles & Huberman, 1984), working closely with the fifth-grade classroom teacher, Michelle, as an 'anthropological confidant' (Foley & Valenzuela, 2005).

All these types of data were then analyzed to identify interactions of Tessa engaging in discourses that privileged or challenged her bilingualism and whiteness. We examined Tessa's whiteness and language use with Latinx and emergent bilingual students, considering her positionality as the white listening subject (Rosa & Flores, 2017) and how it reinforced or deconstructed power dynamics in the TWBE classroom.

Findings

Kindergarten: The foundation for 'Looking like a Language and Sounding like a Race'

In Jonathan Rosa's (2019) book, *Looking like a Language, Sounding like a Race,* he argues that the normalization of white, middle-class language practices has historically scrutinized the language practices of People of Color (POC). Rather than continue to focus on the language practices of POC, Rosa proposes that we shift our focus on to the white listening subject in order to problematize how white, middle class subjects' perceptions impact the ways that we, as a society, internalize and understand the language practices of POC.

Tessa's Spanish-language kindergarten teacher, Ms Ortega, was a bilingual Latina raised in an immigrant family in a large city a few hours from the school. During the Spanish Language Arts block, which took place in the morning, Ms Ortega used Spanish for the vast majority of the time. The kindergarten teachers maintained fairly strict fidelity to the TWBE program's stated policy of language separation by content area. Likewise, students were assigned a label as either 'Spanish expert' or 'English expert' based on the Language Assessment Scales-Oral (LASO) scores and parent/teacher input. They were assigned to their literacy instructional block according to this label; 'English' speakers received literacy instruction in English, while 'Spanish' speakers received literacy instruction in Spanish. The children's names were color coded throughout the classroom, with blue labels for Spanish speakers and red labels for English speakers (see Palmer, 2019 for a close examination of this labeling process and its implications). It is noteworthy that Tessa carried the 'Spanish expert' label, most likely because she had participated in a Spanish immersion childcare since infancy and the fact that her parents advocated for her to be included in the Spanish literacy block.

Every day in kindergarten in this TWBE program, children engaged in bilingual learning centers, which was an open exploration time in which students together in 'bilingual pairs' chose from among a variety of activities such as games/puzzles, art projects, role play centers, or library corner. In the excerpt below, Tessa's 'bilingual pair' was Clarita, who interestingly carried an 'English expert' label despite our observations (and the teacher's confirmation) that she was a simultaneous bilingual Latina who spoke both Spanish and English in her home.

In the interaction below, Tessa and Clarita were counting and measuring beans at a bilingual center. Ms Ortega came over to help them count (in Spanish) how many spoonfuls of beans were needed to fill the different containers. Clarita stumbled as she attempted to count in Spanish, prompting Ms Ortega to ask Tessa, the officially designated 'Spanish expert,' to help. When Tessa did not know, another 'Spanish expert' at a nearby station named Cesar offered the correct number. Tessa repeated it for Clarita and Ms Ortega.

Excerpt 1: (Tessa and Clarita scooping beans into plastic cups while Ms Ortega watches.)

1) Clarita (counts scoops):	Nueve, diez, once, doce, catorce./*Nine, ten, eleven, twelve, fourteen*
2) Ms Ortega:	¿Catorce? Trece. ¿Catorce? luego ¿qué sigue Tessa? ¿Catorce....?/*Fourteen? THIRteen. Fourteen? Now what comes next Tessa? Fourteen...?*
3) Tessa:	¿Dieciseis?/*Sixteen?*
4) Ms Ortega:	No, no.
5) Cesar:	Quince./*Fifteen.*
6) Tessa:	Quince./*Fifteen.*

Ms Ortega positioned Tessa as the 'Spanish expert,' calling upon her to help with counting and inadvertently positioning Clarita as less bilingual and/or in need of help. Although it is a relatively common and innocuous interaction, with the teacher most likely merely trying to encourage the young girls to interact as they worked side by side, we argue that in these positionings Ms Ortega inadvertently reinforced a higher valuing of Tessa's bilingualism and academic skills than Clarita's, thus making visible the 'white listening subject' (Malsbary, 2014; Rosa & Flores, 2017). Because Tessa carried the 'Spanish expert' label and was an English-dominant, white child with a middle-class background, she was frequently called upon to share expertise and support her classmates in both languages. The institutional labeling of children in this case aligned with white supremacist notions of sanctioned speakers: Tessa's bilingualism was celebrated and honored, while Clarita's was made invisible and problematized.

Classrooms are complicated spaces, of course, and Ms Ortega also at times flouted the institutionally imposed labels and white supremacist notions; Deb documented (and wrote about in a different place) an instance in which Ms Ortega seemed to intentionally honor and celebrate Clarita's bilingualism, drawing on Clarita's expertise to support the Spanish language development and science understanding of her peers (see Palmer, 2019).

First grade: Becoming part of a bilingual speech community

Tessa's first-grade Spanish teacher, Ms Jackson, was bilingual and identified as Latina. This was her second year as a dual language teacher, although at the time of the study she had been a transitional bilingual teacher at Hillside throughout her eleven-year career and had been involved in advocating for the implementation of TWBE there. Growing up near the Mexico/US border, Ms Jackson moved fluidly between Spanish and English.

Ms Jackson, more than either Tessa's kindergarten or second-grade teacher, drew on critical consciousness to engage students to dialogue about social inequities by including multicultural and multilingual children's books that explored the oppression of undocumented immigrants in the US (García-Mateus, 2020) In doing so, she entered the experiences and backgrounds of her Latinx emerging bilingual students in her curriculum and instruction. The excerpt below took place during a lesson related to the children's picture book, *¡Sí se puede!* (Cohn & Delgado, 2002), a story about a boy whose mother took part in the Los Angeles 'Justice for Janitors' movement. After reading part of the book, Ms Jackson asked her students to break into groups and re-enact a scene in which Carlitos begs his mom to accompany her as she strikes with her fellow janitors to demand better wages and working conditions.

Tessa's group comprised three girls (all of whom were focal students in Suzanne's study): herself, Elizabeth (a bilingual Latina) and Valentina (a middle-class biracial and bilingual white/Latina). Tessa, though not evident in this brief passage, played the role of Carlitos' abuelita (grandma), taking on the persona of an older Latina. Elizabeth acted as Carlitos, and Valentina was Carlitos' mom. Their teacher hoped that the activity, part of a larger set of lessons involving process drama (Dunn & Stinson, 2011) might push the children to develop empathy and critical awareness about some of the challenges that Latinx workers face in the United States.

Excerpt 2: ¡Sí se puede!

(1) **Valentina (to Elizabeth):**	¿Puedes ayudar? / *Can you help?*
(2) **Tessa:**	You can gather people.
(3) **Elizabeth:**	You can gather people?
(4) **Valentina:**	Pero, es muy peligroso. / *But, it's very dangerous.*
(5) **Tessa:**	You can… [something inaudible].
(6) **Elizabeth:**	What?
(7) **Tessa:** [whispering to Elizabeth]	Pero, yo puedo hacerlo. / *But I can do it.*
(8) **Elizabeth:**	Pero, yo puedo hacerlo. / *But I can do it.*
(9) **Valentina:**	Pero, es muy peligroso porque si alguien te agarra no podemos encontrarte…y la persona que te agarre no va a devolverte / *But, it's very dangerous because if someone kidnaps you we won't be able to find you… and the person who grabs you isn't going to return you.*
(10) **Tessa** [whispers in Elizabeth's ear]:	…Abuela no…Abuela no…
(11) [Elizabeth quickly whispers in Tessa's ear and Tessa nods in agreement]	
(12) **Elizabeth:**	Pero, mi Abuela me puede llevar. / *But my grandma can take me.*

Two things are clear in the above exchange. First, Tessa and peers interacted bilingually, focused upon negotiating meaning related to the text. Tessa was therefore embraced by these two Latina peers as a member of this bilingual community, and clearly saw herself as belonging to it, engaging as needed across the two languages that she and her peers were learning in school. Second, the theme of *helping/ayudar* seemed to play throughout this passage, with Valentina (in her role) initiating a request for help from Elizabeth, and then with Tessa positioning herself in the role of Elizabeth's helper as they work out what each character should say or do. This became relevant when Suzanne, the following year, shared the video of this interaction with Tessa and asked her to explain what was happening.

The process of developing critical consciousness, referred to by Freire (1997) as *praxis*, is messy and complex – and cyclical. We inquire, we explore, we try something, we reflect and come to deeper understandings, and then we begin again. Tessa's process, though certainly advanced by lessons like the above that occurred throughout her first-grade year, was of course by no means straightforward.

Second grade: Hegemonic discourses in retrospective interviews

During Tessa's second-grade year, students rotated between three classroom teachers for their different content areas, two of whom taught in English, either entirely or partially. For example, Ms Cardenas taught entirely in Spanish, Ms Epett, a bilingual Latina who grew up in a large metropolitan city in Texas, was the designated Spanish teacher for language arts, science and social studies. The third teacher taught language arts and math entirely in English. Unlike the prior two years when Spanish was used extensively, during the second-grade year Tessa's Spanish teacher, Ms Epett, rarely spoke Spanish during her designated content areas. This was due to her concern that the (largely white) English-dominant students who for the previous two years had been receiving their language arts instruction in their 'home' language would not have the adequate Spanish language comprehension to follow her instructions in Spanish, prompting her to teach entirely in English. This choice reflects the power of the 'white gaze' in this space, given that as a dual language program by definition teachers were expected to teach children bilingually with an enrichment, linguistically sustaining orientation, and yet the teacher's concern for her white students compelled her to abandon this goal in favor of ensuring their full comprehension of instruction even during a time designated for Spanish language arts. Valdés (1997) worried about this very possibility – that teachers would defer (or accommodate their use of Spanish) for white, English speakers, essentially watering down instruction in Spanish.

Because there were few Spanish language arts lessons to observe, student interviews compose the bulk of the data that Suzanne collected during the second-grade year. Suzanne brought the video recording of the above first-grade scene (Excerpt 2) into an interview with Tessa. After watching the video with her, Suzanne asked Tessa why she and Elizabeth were whispering to one another in the scene from first grade. Tessa replied:

Excerpt 3:

(1) **Tessa:** …when Valentina (as the mom) said it was too dangerous for Elizabeth (as the son) [to strike], Elizabeth didn't know what to say. I kind of helped her a little and when I didn't know what to say, Valentina told me something.

(2) **Suzanne:** Was she telling you in English or in Spanish?

(3) **Tessa:** I think in Spanish.

(4) **Suzanne:** Do you ever use Spanish and English at the same time in class?

(5) **Tessa:** Yeah, probably because a lot of people don't know Spanish and our teachers want them to learn it so it gives them more practice and they want people to know different languages so you can speak to more people.

It is possible that Tessa, who was aware of her label as a 'strong' emergent bilingual, sensed the teacher's fear that the English-dominant students were unable to follow Spanish-language instruction and thus attempted to position herself as a 'helper' to both her teacher and her peers alike. We argue that such advantageous positioning is evidence of how Tessa's bilingualism was privileged in ways that her Latinx peers' bilingualism may not have been.

For example, in the above excerpt Tessa described herself as a 'helper' of Elizabeth, a bilingual Latina, because Elizabeth 'didn't know what to say.' She explained that she and Valentina, a bilingual white/Latina, helped each other. But Elizabeth was not mentioned as 'helping.' In this interview, Tessa appeared to be unaware of the disproportionate privileges she enjoyed as compared to her Latinx peers. On the contrary, she positioned Elizabeth as less capable than herself (i.e. as someone who 'didn't know what to say') and in need of help, while she herself was a strong bilingual who could help her less bilingual classmates to learn Spanish (or, presumably, English), in line with the teachers' goals. We argue that Tessa's description of her own and Elizabeth's language use is intersectional: both race and class influence the white listening subject's perception of Spanish speakers. Although invisible to her, these privileges characterize her school experience, from how she gains and maintains membership to bilingual communities to how her developing bilingualism is recognized and rewarded by those around her (Bartlett & García, 2011; Orellana, 2009; Valdés, 1997).

Third grade: Whiteness leveraging positionality

In the third grade students were divided in two cohorts: (a) English-dominant or (b) Spanish-dominant and strong bilinguals. Tessa, as she had since kindergarten, was placed in the second group and thereby labeled as a 'strong bilingual.' Only three of the fifteen original kindergarten students who came from a working class, Latinx and Spanish-speaking background remained in this group; others were either placed in the 'English-dominant' cohort, had moved away, or had been retained in second grade, as often happened with children who did not appear prepared for the high stakes tests that began in third grade in Texas schools. The criterion to be placed in the Spanish rather than English third-grade classroom was not about Spanish command so much as academic skills. This academic designation was dictated by the accountability policy used by the school district and the state of Texas, which not surprisingly was a monoglossic, single-measure accountability system aligned with dominant (monolingual) notions of achievement rather than with the TWBE program or with the language and cultural practices of marginalized Latinx youth (Palmer *et al.*, 2015). Ms Morales' classroom seating arrangement was a reflection of this criterion. When asked how students were assigned seating she said, 'Students did not get to choose where they sat, we choose according to ability and language....for me I did it more based on ability given that for me it was more important that academic learning occurred rather than some learning Spanish' (E-mail, 2/25/15).

The third-grade teacher, Ms Morales, strongly identified as a heritage speaker of Spanish and Chicana and spoke primarily in Spanish during classroom interactions and instruction. She was raising her own children bilingually in Spanish and English and had entered her daughter into Hillside's TWBE program during the program's first year of implementation in 2010 (her daughter was a year ahead of Tessa's class). Ms Morales had come to Hillside after a career change, leaving social work in order to complete a respected, local alternative certification program to become a bilingual teacher. In fact, she completed the student teaching practicum for her certification program at Hillside with Tessa's kindergarten class. Consequently, as a parent, student-teacher, and professional, Ms Morales had observed the demographic changes at Hillside with a unique conflux of lenses and had a strong relationship with Tessa and her classmates.

In the excerpt below, Tessa's positionality as the white listening subject (Rosa & Flores, 2017) is evidenced in her ability to position herself as a Spanish language expert at the expense of her teacher Ms Morales, who was consequently (re)positioned as not a legitimate bilingual. During this language arts lesson, although Ms Morales tried in certain moments to challenge Tessa to take on a more critical stance, Tessa nonetheless played out the role of the white listening subject, contesting her teacher's command of Spanish and hence her linguistic authority. This exchange unfolded as the class was debating whether certain words rhyme during a discussion of poetry. Here, Ms Morales began to explain rhymes in an assertive teacher voice before being challenged by Tessa.

Excerpt 4:

(1) Ms Morales:		Alright. cinco, cuatro, tres, dos, uno. La rima no puede estar en el mismo verso. Cuando es una rima, va a estar en un verso al otro. Hasta puede ser así (pointing to screen), o así, y éstos o éstos. O estas dos. O estas dos. Pero rimas no van a existir en el mismo verso. ¿Okay? Okay. Vamos primero a comenzar con la pregunta que tienen todos. ¿Rima? ¿Hablar y llorar? / *The rhyme cannot be in the same verse. When there is a rhyme, it will be in one verse or another. It can even be like this (pointing to screen), or like this, like these and these. Or these two. Or these two. Rhymes will not exist in the same verse. Okay? Okay. Let's begin with the question everyone has. Do they rhyme? Talk and cry?*
(2) Class: [together]		Síií. / *Yes.*
(3) Ms Morales:		No rima [pointing to *hablar* and *llorar*]. / *They don't rhyme.*
(4) Tessa:		Yeah, it does! Because it ends with the same letters (pointing to screen) and it sounds the same.

What began as a debate between students at different tables about whether or not *hablar* and *llorar* are words that rhyme evolved into a discussion solely between Ms Morales and Tessa. Tessa (of her own volition) moved to the front of the class while pointing at the poem that was displayed on a projector. Ms Morales and Tessa went back and forth, repeating *hablar* and *llorar*.

Excerpt 5:

(1) Ms Morales:	Pero en esta…. calle, nadie. Abuelo, buñuelo. Abuela, ciruela. Tía, sandia. Primo, pepino. Hermana, manzana. / *But in this one…street, no one. Grandpa, pastry. Grandma, plum. Aunt, watermelon. Cousin, cucumber. Sister, apple.* [all words that rhyme in Spanish]
(2) Tessa: [still in front of the class]	Well, that's clearly a rhyme.

(3) **Ms Morales:** [referring to hablar/llorar] Sí. Pero, ésta, como que no se oye mucho, quizás yo estoy equivocada. Voy a consultar... / *Yes. But, this one, I can't really hear it, maybe I'm wrong. I am going to consult...*

(4) **Tessa:** [still in front of the class] ... with a Spanish expert.

When Tessa walked to the front of the class she was 'holding the floor' and carrying out a privileged activity, challenging the teacher's command of Spanish and drawing on a sense of authority as a speaker of 'standard' English. This was exemplified by her strong and confident use of English throughout this Spanish language lesson. This classroom was a translanguaging space in which such bilingual interactions were normalized; however, Tessa was not only afforded the possibility to translanguage without any resistance from the teacher; she was also permitted to question the teacher's use and knowledge of Spanish *in English*.

Tessa's linguistic move can also be described as a power move that distances her from Latinx and bilingual speakers, like Ms Morales. Tessa was making more than a claim that the two words did in fact rhyme: she was also making a claim to her privileged background as a bilingual and middle-class white student, entitled to certain ways of speaking, including standing in front of the class to argue with the teacher and even claiming expertise in Spanish. Tessa, as the white listening subject, perceived Ms Morales as not understanding which words rhyme and challenged her, a self-identified Latina from the border, and Tessa's teacher (Interview, 12/17/13). Tessa's persistent questioning provoked Ms Morales to question her own understanding of Spanish as she ultimately decided to check with a 'Spanish expert.' Tessa co-constructed this conclusion with her teacher, seeming to affirm that the teacher was not such an expert (while perhaps Tessa might be).

Thus, in kindergarten Tessa was constructed by her teacher as the helper for her Latinx and bilingual partner. In her second-grade interview, Tessa demonstrated her perception that her first-grade Latinx bilingual partner needed her help. In third grade, she seemed to perceive her Latinx and bilingual teacher as needing her help and, therefore, seemed to feel free to challenge her authority. Institutions that embody whiteness normalize this perception (Malsbary, 2014; Matias *et al.*, 2014) that whites command authority and expertise related to language practices – even those that are not, in some ways, their own.

Fifth grade: Gentrification as a generative theme: Tessa moves into more critical terrain

During the sixth year of TWBE implementation, the number of students grew to 331 and less than a third were considered Spanish speakers.

Hillside Elementary was now 61% Latinx and 30% white, although it should be noted that many, at least half of the Latinx and bilingual students present came from upper middle-class backgrounds. As gentrification processes continued to alter the landscape of Hillside Elementary and the surrounding community, by fifth grade many of Tessa's Latinx classmates had been pushed out of the neighborhood into surrounding districts due to soaring rents, and essentially replaced in the classroom by upper middle-class students from Latinx backgrounds (Heiman & Yanes, 2018).

Tessa's fifth-grade teacher, Michelle, was a Canadian citizen of Salvadoran descent who grew up as a refugee in Toronto. She was in her eleventh year of teaching and it was her second year at Hillside Elementary working with Tessa's class, as she had looped with them from fourth grade. Much like Ms Jackson in first grade, Michelle was a bilingual (actually a trilingual) who naturally engaged in translanguaging practices, and did not curb this practice in the classroom despite the TWBE's program mandate to separate languages during instruction. And more than any of Tessa's prior teachers, Michelle took an openly critical stance in her pedagogy, which intentionally and actively privileged students from working-class and Latinx backgrounds, and in her interactions with children, parents, and colleagues at Hillside (Heiman & Yanes, 2018). This provided Tessa with access to a critical narrative about her reality over a two-year span.

The rapid gentrification and its obvious impact on the class prompted Michelle and Dan, who was carrying out a critical engaged ethnography in her class during Tessa's fifth-grade year, to decide in April of the study year to design and carry out a unit together about how these gentrification processes were impacting students and their families. By positioning gentrification as a 'generative theme' (Freire, 1997), i.e. an interdisciplinary topic of study that emerged directly from the realities of students' contexts, they exposed students to historical processes that became platforms for inquiry, dialogue and struggle. This in turn contributed to their development of critical consciousness (Cervantes-Soon *et al.*, 2017). A key element in the gentrification unit was the inclusion of 'testimonios' (Delgado Bernal *et al.*, 2012) from a parent directly impacted by gentrification and two Latinx activists in the community, one of whom was a member of the School Board for the district.

A few days after the School Board member provided a 'testimonio' around the city's history of displacing Latinx and Black populations, Michelle mentioned that this systemic displacement was impacting affordable housing in the Hillside community. This encouraged Ernesto (a bilingual Latinx student) to mention how his friend and classmate Néstor used to live in a nearby apartment complex that was 'getting worked on' and in the process had displaced tenants like Néstor and his family. Michelle then pulled up a map of the neighborhood, and students named more apartment complexes that were impacted by gentrification. These interactions were dominated by the Latinx students who no longer lived in the Hillside neighborhood, as there were only a few comments from middle-class white students. Nonetheless, the aesthetics of one particular refurbished complex impressed the middle-class white students, including Tessa:

Excerpt 6:

(1) **Zuleima:** They're pretty now!
(2) **Ofelia:** They're new! They're really pretty!
(3) **Tessa:** Oh yeah I was about to, yeah, they have like this firefly jar!
(4) **Anita** Yeah
(5) **Ofelia:** Yeah

Michelle took note of the comments from Zuleima (middle-class Colombian Korean), Ofelia (middle-class Uruguayan American) and Anita (white upper middle-class) about 'pretty' aesthetics, but emphasized how they were 'really expensive' and how it was all 'kind of scary.' This spurred students to focus more intently on the economic impact of gentrification in the Hillside community. This re-direction of the conversation back to more critical terrain offered Tessa an opportunity to move beyond 'pretty' aesthetics to the economic impact of the generative theme:

Excerpt 7:

(1) **Tessa:** What's going to happen when all the people move out of [City] because it's just...
(2) **Alina:** But not, people are coming into [City]
(3) **Michelle** So who's moving to [City]?
(4) **Alina:** Californians!
(5) **Ernesto** Rich people!
(6) **Michelle:** Not just Californians! People that have money, so what's going to happen when people who can't afford to live in [City] don't live here?
(7) **Tessa:** It's just gonna become a rich city
(8) **Michelle:** It's gonna become a very rich city!
(9) **Anita:** Might be a big giant mess

Michelle nudged Tessa into a more perplexed space around the generative theme, as her observations of the 'pretty' aesthetics diverged into more empathetic listening (Palmer *et al.*, 2019). Michelle and Ernesto challenged Tessa to think in deeper, more nuanced ways about asymmetrical power relations impacting her classmates, as it impacted her differently than students like Ernesto and other Latinx students pushed out of the Hillside community. Michelle then went on to historicize the notion of bilingual education in a gentrifying Hillside, as she recalled a comment made by a City Council member, Mr Salazar, during his recent visit to the classroom, about finding one's voice and using it with conviction:

> Mr Salazar, so that to me was powerful, no todos estamos en Hillside dual language sólo para aprender español, ese es mi idioma, ese el idioma de Karina, right, pero lo estamos compartiendo con todos, right, ese es nuestro idioma. Que yeah like Larry puede usarlo that's cool, pero ese es mi voz and I'm gonna use it to fight for what's right. Y hoy que gente como Larry o Katie sabe mi idioma, [*We aren't all at in Hillside's DL program just to learn Spanish, this is my language, it's Karina's language, right, but we're sharing it with everybody, right, this is our language. Yeah like Larry can use it that's cool, but this is my voice and I'm gonna use it for what's right. And today like Larry or Katie know my language*]. Well then, now it's your job to fight for what's right, and that's what Natalia (local activist who talked with students about gentrification) says; that the more languages you have in a classroom the more bridges you can make. This is our language. I grew up with this language. Karina grew up with this language. Javier grew up with this language. Like we grew, this is my language, and now I'm sharing it with you; so now you also have to stand up with me, and like fight for what's right. He said find your voice and use it with conviction. What is conviction?

Michelle seemed to direct her 'language-as-empowerment' stance around bilingualism (Heiman & Yanes, 2018) toward her white, middle-class students, as she encouraged them to go beyond a 'language-as-resource' (Ruíz, 1984) orientation to a more activist and social justice one that worked against the white norm at Hillside. We are hopeful that Michelle's race radical stance around Bilingual Education (Flores, 2016) impacted students like Tessa over the two-year period in which she taught them.

Yet, Tessa's reaction to Michelle's rousing speech was one brief utterance expressing confusion, several turns later, when she interjected into the group dialogue: 'Is it, like, well?' We find Tessa's confusion to be a fitting conclusion to her six-year trajectory in Hillside's dual language program, as in spite of some critically minded teachers and encouraging signs of deeper reflection around power and privilege, ultimately there was little evidence that she moved beyond the 'aesthetics' of a dual language construct steeped in whiteness. Most importantly her inability to move beyond the 'aesthetics' reveals that TWBE's fourth goal of critical consciousness needs to go beyond the classroom level and become an integral facet of processes at *all levels for all stakeholders* in TWBE contexts (Palmer *et al.*, 2019).

Discussion

This investigation explored the question: *In what ways were Tessa's experiences during her elementary school years evidence of both (a) her role as the white listening subject and (b) the need to develop of critical consciousness in TWBE classrooms?*

By focusing on how one white, English-dominant student learned alongside her bilingual, Latinx peers and teachers, this study provides additional insight as to how whiteness can impact TWBE programs, highlighting both the imperatives of and challenges for developing critical consciousness in such racially and linguistically heterogeneous spaces. We hope that Tessa's interactions with Latinx bilingual students explored here demonstrate the crucial role teachers can play in beginning conversations aimed at developing critical consciousness as well as the need for educators to prioritize this kind of learning in TWBE programs.

Teachers at all age levels can support white students to develop critical consciousness. They can, for instance, use labels flexibly; as noted, elsewhere we have shown how Tessa's kindergarten teachers did just that by positioning Clarita, a simultaneous bilingual, as an 'expert' in both her languages (Palmer, 2019). Teachers could have explicit conversations with children about the ways their families use Spanish (and English) at home and their communities. These conversations could be facilitated by multilingual and multicultural books, as they were during the first-grade year; books that reflect positively the ways that simultaneous bilinguals use language. Teachers could more intentionally center the use of Spanish, reinforcing the completion of activities and assignments in Spanish even for children who are still early learners of the language, rather than accommodating beginning Spanish learners by teaching in English (as Tessa's second-grade teacher resorted to doing) (Garcia *et al.*, 2017). Teachers can (re)position students, especially heritage speakers of Spanish, such that they become linguistic ethnographers of their community and classroom for ways Spanish is and can be used.

Institutional and ideological aspects of whiteness (Malsbary, 2014) in this TWBE program setting positioned Tessa as a 'balanced' bilingual by labeling her in kindergarten as a 'Spanish-speaker' and by placing her into the 'Spanish cohort' in the third grade. Tessa maintained this label even as our evidence suggests she rarely displayed her bilingualism, interacting primarily or exclusively in English. Even so, this did not position Tessa as an inadequate bilingual. In fact, Tessa even seemed to discursively position herself as a 'Spanish expert' in her third-grade classroom at the expense of her bilingual Latina teacher.

As a fifth grader, Tessa testified before the local school board in favor of bilingual education when the school district was contemplating implementing a DLBE program at the middle school; she did so using neoliberal discourses that conflate language with economic and symbolic capital. Explaining why the TWBE program was beneficial for them, Tessa explained the following in Spanish:

> Yo sé español porque mis padres querían que yo aprendiera español. Aprender español me ha ayudado a poder comunicarme con mis campaneros en Hillside que solo hablan español. Cuando tuvimos un estudiante nuevo en tercer grado y el vino de México yo pude comunicarme con el porque los dos hablamos en español. También hablo español para poder ayudarles a mis padres cuandos salimos de viajes. Una vez el verano pasado fuimos á españa y yo tuve que traducirles todo a mis padres y a mi hermana mayor.
>
> [*I know Spanish because my parents wanted me to learn it. Learning Spanish has helped me to be able to communicate with my classmates that only speak Spanish at Hillside elementary. When we had a new student in third grade and he came from México I was able to communicate with him because we both spoke Spanish. I also speak Spanish when I need to help my parents when we travel. One time, last summer, we went to Spain and I had to translate everything for my parents and my older sister.*]

Tessa's class and race privilege are clearly evident in her framing of the ways that being bilingual has benefited her. Despite Michelle's efforts to reframe bilingualism and the Spanish language as a cultural heritage and to convince Tessa and her white classmates to 'stand up with' their Latinx peers, Tessa continues to frame it as a simple economic commodity that allows her to enjoy foreign travel and to help less-fortunate (immigrant, Latinx) classmates. In her framing of her own bilingualism and her positioning within her school, she remains a white listening subject. If her school had been more successful at deconstructing the institutional practices of whiteness, would her – and her fellow white classmates' – understandings of the purposes of bilingualism and the meaning of biculturalism have better reflected Michelle's vision? If *all* her teachers had shared a unified vision and set of critical pedagogical practices aimed at developing critical consciousness, would they have been more successful at leveraging the TWBE program to benefit the Latinx working class community?

Conclusions

It is evident from Tessa's experiences that it takes tremendous effort and consistent struggle to support young white students on their path to developing the critical consciousness necessary to, as Tessa's fifth-grade teacher encouraged, 'fight for what's right… find [their] voice and use it with conviction.' White supremacy is built into the structures of schooling in US contexts; in a sense, we are struggling against a tidal wave. Therefore, supporting white students – actually, *all* students – to develop critical consciousness is crucially important if we wish to make the distribution of power and status in our increasingly gentrified TWBE programs more equal.

Alim and Paris (2017) suggest that schools can intentionally disrupt normative whiteness through Culturally Sustaining Pedagogies (CSP). Instead of merely teaching traditional liberal multiculturalism with its narrow view on tolerance or celebration of difference (Sleeter & Grant, 1987), CSP strives toward critically exploring racial, linguistic, cultural and class oppression as a means of promoting 'explicitly pluralist outcomes that are not centered on white middle-class, monolingual/monocultural norms and notions of educational achievement' (Alim & Paris, 2017: 12). If practitioners incorporate CSP into everyday lessons, students will begin to develop critical consciousness. Likewise, teachers themselves will develop deeper empathy and critical awareness as they work to embrace CSP and concomitantly confront their own ideologies of white supremacy.

If we are committed to the integration that comes with two-way bilingual programs we must be committed to the work of ensuring that these programs serve the needs of historically marginalized populations just as much as they serve the needs of dominant-group students. Advocates of TWBE programs often point out that white, middle-class students and their families bring resources and social capital into bilingual schools; while this is true, at the same time it is evident in this analysis that these same students *tax* the resources of their Latinx teachers and peers in significant ways. It is important that as educators increasingly embrace two-way models, they go into the project with open eyes.

Notes

(1) This article symbolically lowercases the word white to disrupt social norms that are embedded within structural inequities that affect communities of color.
(2) We use the gender-neutral label, Latinx, to promote the concept that identity construction is not static. This article capitalizes Latinx to give credence to the struggles of a racialized group that shares cultural, political and historical experiences.

References

Ahmed, S. (2007) A phenomenology of whiteness. *Feminist Studies* 8 (2), 150.
Alim, H.S. and Paris, D. (2017) What is culturally sustaining pedagogy and why does it matter? In D. Paris and H.S. Alim (eds) *Culturally Sustaining Pedagogies: Teaching and Learning for Justice in a Changing World*. New York: Teachers College Press.
Allen, R.L. (2001) The globalization of white supremacy: Toward a critical discourse on the racialization of the world. *Educational Theory* 51 (4), 467–485.

Bartlett, L. and García, O. (2011) *Additive Schooling in Subtractive Times: Bilingual Education and Dominican Youth in the Heights*. Nashville, TN: Vanderbilt University Press.

Blommaert, J. (2014) Orders of indexicality and polycentricity. In A. Jaworski and N. Coupland (eds) *The Discourse Reader* (pp. 497–510). Abingdon: Routledge.

Bourdieu, P. (1991) *Language and Symbolic Power*. Cambridge, MA: Harvard University Press.

Bucholtz, M. and Hall, K. (2005) Identity and interaction: A sociocultural linguistic approach. *Discourse Studies* 7 (4–5), 585–614.

Cervantes-Soon, C.G. (2014) A critical look at dual language immersion in the new Latin@ diaspora. *Bilingual Research Journal* 37 (1), 64–82.

Cervantes-Soon, C.G., Dorner, L., Palmer, D., Heiman, D., Schwerdtfeger, R. and Choi, J. (2017) Combating inequalities in two-way language immersion programs: Toward critical consciousness in bilingual education spaces. *Review of Research in Education* 41 (1), 403–427.

Cohn, D. and Delgado, F. (2002) *¡Sí se puede! = Yes, we can!: Janitor strike in L.A.* El Paso, TX: Cinco Puntos Press.

Davies, B. and Harré, R. (1991) Positioning: The discursive production of selves. *Journal for the Theory of Social Behavior* 20 (1), 43–63.

Delgado Bernal, D., Burciaga, R. and Flores Carmona, J. (2012) Chicana/Latina testimonios: Mapping the methodological, pedagogical, and political. *Equity & Excellence in Education* 45 (3), 363–372.

Dunn, J. and Stinson, M. (2011) Not without the art! The importance of teacher artistry when applying drama as pedagogy for additional language learning. *Research in Drama Education: The Journal of Applied Theatre and Performance* 16 (4), 617–633.

Erickson, F. (2004) Definition and analysis of data from videotape: some research procedures and their rationales. In J. Green, G. Camilli and P. Elmore (eds) *Complementary Methods for Research in Education*. Mahwah, NJ: Lawrence Erlbaum & Associates.

Fairclough, N. (1995) *Critical Discourse Analysis: The Critical Study of Language*. London; New York: Longman.

Flores, N. (2016) A tale of two visions: Hegemonic whiteness and bilingual education. *Educational Policy* 30 (1), 13–38.

Flores, N. and Rosa, J. (2015) Undoing appropriateness: Raciolinguistic ideologies and language diversity in education. *Harvard Educational Review* 85 (2), 149–171.

Foley, D. and Valenzuela, A. (2005) Critical ethnography: The politics of collaboration. In N.K. Denzin and Y.S. Lincoln (eds) *Handbook of Qualitative Research* (pp. 217–234). Thousand Oaks, CA: Sage Publications.

Foucault, M. (1971) Orders of discourse. *Social Science Information* 10 (2), 7–30.

Freire, P. (1997) *Pedagogy of the Oppressed*. Translated from Portuguese by MB Ramos. New York: Continuum.

García, O., Johnson, S.I. and Seltzer, K. (2017) *The Translanguaging Classroom: Levering Student Bilingualism for Learning*. Philadelphia: Caslon.

García-Mateus, S. (2020) 'Yeah, things are rough in Mexico. Remember we talked about hard times?' Process drama and a teachers role in critically engaging students to dialogue about social inequities in a dual language classroom. *The Urban Review*.

Harris, C. (1992) Whiteness as property. *Harvard Law Review* 106 (8), 1707–1791.

Heiman, D. and Yanes, M. (2018) Centering the fourth pillar in times of TWBE gentrification: 'Spanish, Love, Content, Not in That Order'. *International Multilingual Research Journal* 12 (3), 173–187.

Johnstone, B. (2008) *Discourse Analysis*. Malden, MA. Blackwell Publishing.

Leonardo, Z. (2009) *Race, Whiteness, and Education*. New York: Routledge.

Lindholm-Leary, K. and Block, N. (2010) Achievement in Predominantly Low SES/Hispanic Dual Language Schools. *International Journal of Bilingual Education and Bilingualism* 13 (1), 43–60.

Lippi-Green, R. (2004) Language ideology and language prejudice. In E. Finegan and J. Rickford (eds) *Language in the USA: Themes for the Twenty-First Century* (pp. 289–304). New York: Cambridge University Press.

Malsbary, C. (2014) Will this hell ever end? Substantiating and resisting race-language policies in a multilingual high school. *Anthropology & Education Quarterly* 45 (4), 373–390, ISSN 0161-7761, online ISSN 1548-1492.

Matias, C.E., Mitchell, K., Wade-Garrison, D., Tandon, M. and Galindo, R (2014). 'What is critical whiteness doing in OUR nice field like critical race theory?' *Equity & Excellence* 47 (3), 289–304.

Miles, M.B. and Huberman, A.M. (1984) *Qualitative Data Analysis: A Sourcebook of New Methods*. Beverly Hills, CA: Sage.

Ochs, E. (1993) Constructing social identity: A language socialization perspective. *Research on Language and Interaction* 26 (3), 287–306.

Orellana, M.F. (2009) *Translating Childhoods: Immigrant Youth, Language, and Culture*. New Brunswick, NJ: Rutgers University Press.

Palmer, D. (2019) 'You're not a Spanish speaker!/We are all bilingual' The purple kids on being and becoming bilingual in a dual-language kindergarten classroom. In J. MacSwan and C.J. Faltis (eds) *Code-Switching in the Classroom: Critical Perspectives on Teaching, Learning, Policy, and Ideology*. New York: CAL and Routledge.

Palmer, D., Cervantes-Soon, C., Heiman, D. and Dorner, L. (2019) Bilingualism, biliteracy, biculturalism… and critical consciousness for all: proposing a fourth fundamental principle for two-way dual language education. *Theory Into Practice* 58 (2), 121–133.

Palmer, D.K., Henderson, K., Wall, D., Zúñiga, C.E. and Berthelsen, S. (2015) Team teaching among mixed messages: Implementing two-way dual language bilingual education at third grade in Texas. *Language Policy*, 1–21. https://doi.org/10.1007/s10993-015-9361-3

Poza, L. (2015) Barreras: Language ideologies, academic language, and the marginalization of Latin@ English language learners. *Whittier Law Review* 37, 401.

Reyes, S.A. and Vallone, T.L. (2007) Toward an expanded understanding of two-way bilingual immersion education: Constructing identity through a critical additive/bicultural pedagogy. *Multicultural Perspectives* 9 (3), 3–11.

Rosa, J.D. (2016) Standardization, racialization, languagelessness: Raciolinguistic ideologies across communicative contexts. *Journal of Linguistic Anthropology* 26 (2), 162–183.

Rosa, J. and Flores, N. (2017) Unsettling race and language: Toward a raciolinguistic perspective. *Language in Society* 46 (5), 621–647.

Rosa, J. (2019) *Looking Like a Language, Sounding Like a Race: Raciolinguistic Ideologies and the Learning of Latinidad*. New York: Oxford University Press.

Ruíz, R. (1984) Orientations in language planning. *NABE Journal* 7, 15–34.

Sleeter, C. and Grant, C. (1987) An analysis of multicultural education in the United States. *Harvard Educational Review* 57 (4), 421–445.

Valdés, G. (1997) Dual-language immersion programs: A cautionary note concerning the education of language-minority students. *Harvard Educational Review* 67 (3), 391–429.

van Dijk, T. A. (1993) Principles of critical discourse analysis. *Discourse & Society* 4 (2), 249–283.

Conclusion: Bilingualism for All? Revisiting the Question

Nelson Flores, Nicholas Subtirelu and Amelia Tseng

The title of this volume takes a slogan that is sometimes used by proponents of the expansion of dual language education in the United States and turns it into a question. This question mark serves two functions. On one level, it is questioning the feasibility of making bilingualism available for all students in a society plagued by racial and economic inequities. Yet, on a deeper level it is calling into question the very premise of any political project that promotes bilingualism that refuses to explicitly engage with these racial and economic inequities. In short, the question mark seeks to challenge the idea that efforts to promote bilingualism are inherently anti-racist and socially transformative. Through their adoption of a raciolinguistic perspective, the contributions to this volume offer a counter-narrative to this dominant framing. What they suggest is that if dual language programs aim to build microcosms of cross-cultural understanding among children who live and grow within larger institutional and societal settings marked by inequity, then the task is much bigger than addressing what takes place within the walls of the classroom or even within the walls of the school. In short, dual language education programs can thrive only in contexts where children, families and the broader community can thrive.

In this spirit, the contributions to this volume make it clear that a movement to build equitable dual language education programs can only be one part of a movement to build equitable communities and institutions and, thus, should be deeply connected to movements that address other relevant concerns such as policies at various levels related to housing, migration, standardized testing and educational funding among other things. For example, over the past few decades, gentrification in US metropolitan areas has resulted in the displacement of economically, racially and linguistically marginalized communities with serious consequences for dual language programs. The lesson that we believe should be drawn from this is that the struggle for equity in dual language programs is a struggle that intersects with other political struggles, such as the fight for plentiful, affordable housing in diverse communities. This recognition should shape both how educators and activists go about planning for dual language programs in their communities as well as how scholars conceptualize and document dual language education. Fortunately, we are not without historic precedent. For example, Trujilio (1996: 120) outlines how, during the 1970s, Chicano activists sought to 'to empower the Chicano community' living in areas occupied by the United States during the Mexican–American war (1846–1848). Their political aspirations were broad including ensuring greater access to 'housing, mental health, health care, economic, and educational programs' (1996: 120). As Trujilio argues, Chicano activists conceptualized bilingual education as an important site for the socialization of a politically aware and culturally informed population of Chicano youth who would grow into the future leaders of the region and continue the struggle against colonization and racial domination. By learning about historical and contemporary examples like this from the US and elsewhere, we as scholars and educators can begin to forge a new politics of language education that imagines educational change inside of larger transformational and emancipatory ends, rejecting the narrow parameters of advocacy that are dominant within the field (Morgan, 2016).

In line with efforts to imagine a new politics of language education, scholars have begun to call for a reconsideration of the pillars of dual language education. In addition to (1) bilingualism/biliteracy, (2) grade-level academic achievement and (3) sociocultural competence (Howard *et al.*, 2018), these scholars have called for (4) critical consciousness which 'draws strong attention to the power dimensions, hegemony of English and standardized languages, and subalternization of minoritized communities in bilingual education' and thereby 'offers a decolonizing and humanizing framework for the future' (Cervantes-Soon *et al.*, 2017: 421). This volume offers insights into the implications of a raciolinguistic perspective in informing this critical consciousness for how we conceptualize dual language education. In particular, the raciolinguistic perspective utilized in this volume raises critical questions about the first three pillars. These include questions as to what counts as bilingualism/biliteracy, who decides what counts, and how race and social class are implicated in these judgments. This interrogation of what counts as bilingualism/biliteracy must also necessitate a critical examination of the normative assumptions that go into determinations of academic achievement and the ways that standardized assessments have historically and continue to be used to pathologize the language practices of racialized students. In particular, these standardized assessments have often failed to capture the sociocultural competence that children from racialized communities develop as part of their lived experiences navigating a white supremacist world. In short, the raciolinguistic perspective adopted in this book calls into question the ideological assumptions that undergird seemingly objective designations such as bilingualism/biliteracy and academic achievement in the hopes of pointing to the ways that schools and classrooms have historically and continue to be sites of raciolinguistic policing that serve to maintain the white supremacist status quo.

While this may seem like a radical assertion, there is a long history within our field of adopting definitions of bilingualism and biliteracy that reject normative assumptions. For example, Hornberger (1990) defined biliteracy as 'any and all instances in which communication occurs in two (or more) languages in or around writing' (1990: 213). Building on this perspective Edelsky (1996) argued that conceptualizations of biliteracy privileged in schools typically were measuring 'test-wiseness' leading to children who engage in biliteracy practices on a daily basis being labeled as not literate in any language. More recent discussions of translanguaging have built on this tradition in order to both document the complex language and literacy practices of racialized bilingual students and their communities and to develop pedagogical approaches that build on these rich linguistic and literary practices (García & Wei, 2014; Hornberger & Link, 2012). By beginning from the perspective of actual bilingual people living in bilingual communities, this perspective exposes the ideological underpinning of any discourse that calls into question these practices. From this perspective, researchers, advocates and educators do not need to disprove deficit discourses being used to describe racialized bilingual students but can begin from the premise that these discourses are inherently racist.

What a raciolinguistic perspective adds to this existing body of literature is a more explicit focus on the white perceiving subject position that informs these deficit discourses and its role in shaping school and classroom dynamics. By bringing attention to the white perceiving subject, a raciolinguistic perspective is able to elucidate the common racialization processes that shape the experiences of racialized bilingual students and racialized students who are positioned as monolingual. This is not to say there are not important differences between these groups or within them. Yet, the white perceiving subject calls into question the legitimacy of all their language practices.

Bringing attention to this ideological subject position points to the many challenges that confront any efforts to raise critical consciousness in dual language classrooms. For one, the habitus (Bourdieu, 1977) associated with dual language programs and classroom practices are shaped by the broader society and can be difficult to challenge both conceptually but perhaps more significantly in practice. That is, dual language educators have, alongside the broader society, been socialized to perceive and respond to the language practices of racialized students from a deficit perspective and, as chapters in this volume illustrated, it can be difficult to change these behaviors. This leads to an inherent contradiction that dual language educators must confront on a daily basis. On the one hand, these programs have an explicit goal of affirming and building on the language practices of racialized students. On the other hand, they are situated within institutions that have historically and continue to rely on metrics that produce deficit discourses and encourage remedial services for these very students. In this way, it is impossible to affirm the language practices of racialized students within schools produced within a white supremacist society leaving dual language teachers with an unresolvable dilemma. What this volume shows is that the only way to resolve this dilemma at the classroom level is to transform the broader institutional practices of the school, which, in turn, requires the transformation of the institutional practices of the broader society.

This is not meant to suggest that dual language teachers and school leaders cannot do anything to challenge raciolinguistic ideologies. On the contrary, the chapters in this volume all point to concrete policy changes that schools and classrooms can adopt that can help challenge existing raciolinguistic ideologies even while recognizing the fact that schools and classrooms cannot do this on their own. For one, school leaders can work to ensure a positive school climate that resists the criminalization of racialized youth and, instead, acknowledges and builds on their existing cultural and linguistic practices. Part of these efforts would be ensuring that all teachers receive professional development that offers a counter-narrative to the white perceiving subject position of the standardized assessments teachers use to evaluate their students by bringing attention to the complexity of these cultural and linguistic practices. It would also be to ensure that all families have equal access to the school and to develop mechanisms for ensuring that more privileged families do not co-opt the school agenda in ways that marginalize others. This broader inclusive context could then be used as a point of entry for promoting equity within the dual language program itself. For one, this broader inclusive context would help to create a school culture that ensures that all students have equal access to the dual language program regardless of their race, social class or ability/disability status. It would also create a context where dual language teachers are primed to listen for cultural and linguistic strengths rather than cultural and linguistic deficiencies when interacting with racialized students. These individual-level interactions may not lead to the social transformation that is necessary to ensure that all children can thrive. For that, we will need to focus on broader structural changes, centering the struggle against inequity and injustice in our field's collective politics. At the same time, these individual-level interactions can have a significant impact on the educators and students who engage in them and help to promote the type of critical consciousness that will push these educators and students to fight for social change.

In short, adopting a raciolinguistic perspective to dual language education entails adopting new ways of thinking and working that challenge powerful assumptions about the nature of education scholarship, policy and practice. The work of realizing the slogan 'bilingualism for all' is work that will cross academic disciplines and requires us to reject the notion that scholarship can be neutral or objective. It will also cross policy contexts with language education policy connected to broader policy efforts to combat poverty and structural racism. Finally, it will challenge the white perceiving subject positions educators are often expected to inhabit and provide tools for them to develop alternative subject positions that perceive the language practices of their racialized students as inherently valuable. In this way, a raciolinguistic perspective is not a pessimistic perspective in the ways that some skeptics might suggest. On the contrary, it seeks to imagine and struggle for a racially just world where all communities thrive. What could be more optimistic than that?

References

Bourdieu, P. (1977) *Outline of a Theory of Practice*. New York, NY: Cambridge University Press.

Cervantes-Soon, C., Dorner, L., Palmer, D., Heiman, D., Schwerdtfeger, R. and Choi, J. (2017) Combating inequalities in two-way immersion programs: Toward critical consciousness in bilingual education spaces. *Review of Research in Education* 41, 403–427.

Edelsky, C. (1996) *With Literacy and Justice for All: Rethinking the Social in Language and Education*. New York, NY: Taylor & Francis.

García, O. and Wei, L. (2014) *Translanguaging: Language, Bilingualism and Education*. New York, NY: Palgrave Macmillan.

Hornberger, N. (1990) Creating successful learning contexts for bilingual literacy. *Teachers College Record* 92, 212–229.

Hornberger, N. and Link, H. (2012) Translanguaging and transnational literacies in multilingual classrooms: A biliteracy lens. *International Journal of Bilingual Education and Bilingualism* 15, 261–278.

Howard, E., Lindholm-Leary, K., Rogers, D., Olague, N., Medina, J., Kennedy, B., Sugarman, J. and Christian, D. (2018) *Guiding Principles for Dual Language Education* (3rd edn). Washington, DC: Center for Applied Linguistics.

Morgan, B. (2016) Language teacher identity and the domestication of dissent: An exploratory account. *TESOL Quarterly* 50, 708–734.

Trujilio, A. (1996) In search of Aztlán: Movimiento ideology and the creation of a Chicano worldview through schooling. In B. Levinson, D. Foley and D. Holland (eds) *The Cultural Production of the Educated Person: Critical Ethnographies of Schooling and Local Practice* (pp. 119–152). Albany: State University of New York Press.

Afterword: What is the Magic Sauce?

Guadalupe Valdés

It is a very special privilege to write the afterword to this important work. I applaud not only the goal of the volume: 'developing a vision for dual language education that most effectively promotes racial equity' (p. 4), but also its attention to macro, meso and micro issues including discourses and structural phenomena, program development, program implementation and classroom practices. I am especially delighted to engage with the thinking of young scholars whose work pushes me to consider new ways of engaging with perennial problems.

The articles in this volume have as their purpose documenting, analyzing and making sense of the far-reaching impact of until-recently unexamined raciolinguistic perspectives (Flores & Rosa, 2015; Rosa, 2018; Rosa & Flores, 2017) that directly and indirectly impact the design, implementation and everyday practices of dual language education or two-way immersion programs (DLE/TWI). Such analyses are essential for those committed to the education of immigrant-origin, linguistically diverse children because it is not clear (as Flores and Tseng suggest in the introduction) that DLE can help dismantle racial and class privilege.

In reading the articles, I am struck by the differences between the programs that have been implemented and are described as DLE/TWI programs. Many of these programs were designed and implemented for mainstream, English-speaking monolingual children (most of whom are white); others were designed for the children of educated bilingual professionals of various ethnic and racial backgrounds; while still others purport to be designed to benefit working-class, immigrant origin children, a group that is itself diverse and multidimensional.

What is clear is that there is much interest in DLE/TWI across the world. Privileged parents want to give their children the 'gift of language' providing them with access to what Flores and Tseng (this volume) refer to as 'white bilingualism'; that is, the bilingualism that is applauded as a special accomplishment for privileged children analogous to excelling at playing the violin or competing on a winning swim team. It signals to the world that the children's parents are preparing them well to compete and win in the national/international contest currently focused on identifying 'talent.' As Reardon (2013) maintains, high-income families must increasingly invest in their children's education because such investments secure their future.

As pointed out by Delvan, Freire and Valdez (this volume), DLE/TWI (as it has expanded to entire states over the last several years and increasingly become an investment for majority, mainstream parents) now 'follows the policy logic of the foreign language lineage of second language education that draws on the Canadian foreign language immersion model, whose traditional focus has been on building multilingualism within majority language speakers of the national context' (p. 20). Not surprisingly, when compared to the largely unsuccessful outcomes of typical traditional foreign language study, there is much to applaud in the outcomes that have been documented for DLE/TWI. This is especially the case in states, like Utah, where there is a tradition of actual language use in missionary activities by young people.

But it is important to stress that DLE/TWI is also attractive to educated bilingual professionals, the other group of advantaged parents I described above. These individuals have a specific interest in their children's maintaining their heritage language and culture. As several authors in this volume have pointed out (e.g. Lee *et al.,* Avni & Menken, this volume), in DLE/TWI programs that are designed for youngsters whose backgrounds include a still-used family heritage language, expectations about the language competencies to be developed by students go much beyond those of the world-language profession. Educated bilingual professionals aspire to have their second- (or even third -) generation children develop language capabilities that will allow them to participate successfully in the monolingual, class-based worlds they left behind. Parents worry, therefore, as the article by Lee *et al.* illustrates, about the quality of the home language spoken by American (second-generation) heritage-origin teachers. They do not want their children to acquire stigmatized ways of speaking that will be looked down upon by relatives and friends.

Importantly, while these educated bilingual parents are discussed in this volume drawing from the five components of the raciolinguistic perspective, in this case, both the historical and contemporary co-naturalization of race and language and perceptions of racial and linguistic difference may operate in ways that are not parallel to what has been assumed by traditional analyses of the American context. More importantly still, the design of DLE/TWI programs to maintain or preserve heritage languages may not actually have as one of its purpose challenging relations of power either in the United States or in the original countries of origin.

By comparison, the third group of parents whom I referred to above includes largely first-generation, working-class immigrant-origin parents. They are the parents of children whose bilingualism is expected (and consistently found wanting). I would argue that they too seek to invest in their children's education. Their investment, however, may sometimes include decisions and actions that elite educators and researchers disagree with, including, for example, opposing the enrollment of their children in both traditional (still essentially compensatory) bilingual education programs *and* DLE/TWI. Among many others, Ochoa and Rhodes (2005), for example, describe this position as follows:

> ...parents of ELL students may often be hesitant to have their children placed in instructional settings that are anything other than English only. Many parents have endured the educational and emotional hardship that often accompanies limited English proficiency and earnestly desire their children to learn English as rapidly as possible. A viewpoint frequently expressed to the authors by parents is that they will assume responsibility for home-language maintenance if the school will assist in the development of English-language proficiency. (2005: 86)

For this third group of parents (who are impacted by what Delvan, Freire and Valdez refer to as 'the bilingual education lineage') matters of interest go beyond language development per se. The issue is the degree to which DLE/TWI can deliver on its transformative promise of purposeful integration of children from diverse cultures, backgrounds and needs, the efficient and timely development of both English *and* the partner language while at the same time ensuring educational effectiveness.

Implications for Scholars, Researchers, and Latinx Activist Educators

For scholars, researchers and Latinx activist educators, the implications of this volume are many. Racism is real. It lives in schools, and it directly affects the present and the future of non-white children who are poor and disadvantaged. In Trump's America, the fairy tales about equal opportunity have lost their sparkle. There are haves and have-nots, high income families who can home-school their children *and* send them to school, and families who live in terror of being deported. Many youngsters in today's schools are the children of Mexican men and women who were surplus workers in their county and were forced by circumstances to become money migrants and supporters of their families back home (Minian, 2018). They want their children to be educated. They have understood the roots of their own exploitation and aspire to much more for their children. In spite of what is often said by those who do not know this population well, Mexican parents *do* care about education.

But the education landscape, for just the Latinx population as an example, is much more complex. It includes Puerto Rican-origin children who are not immigrants and who bring to school rich bi-linguistic repertoires. It also includes other children, recently arrived from Central America, whose linguistic resources may include indigenous languages unknown to educators in this country and possibly only rudimentary capabilities in Spanish. We are told that many of these youngsters after being locked in cages for many months, are now being spread out around the country, some sent to relatives, others to strangers, but all of them, at some point, are entering American schools. To no one's surprise, we have learned from a recent *Washington Post* article (Miller, 2019) that the American heartland has not exactly welcomed these new immigrant children enthusiastically. Many residents of small towns are not pleased. Schools are overcrowded. Dark-haired children look very different from their own, and paying for expanding school services will require raising taxes. For farmers already suffering from the impact of policies that have imposed tariffs on Chinese goods, the cost of educating new immigrants is much too high.

As has been the case since the middle of the last century, for these newly arrived children the point at issue continues to be: can American schools actually educate children who do not speak or understand English? Is it possible? Is it commonplace? What combination of circumstances and resources need to be in place? Moreover, given accountability policies, testing requirements, teacher availability and funding priorities, what can scholars, researchers and Latinx activist educators say to the American heartland, to the parents of newly arrived children, and to the children themselves?

If development of competences in a named language, English, is essential in the process, (and many would argue that it is), concerns surrounding the education of vulnerable, non-English-speaking, immigrant children fundamentally center around two main issues:

- What types of instructional arrangements can make the development of English language resources the most efficient and least painful for children?
- What types of instructional arrangements can offer students, who are in the process of acquiring English, the opportunity to learn, to take up ideas of substance, and to develop both intellectually and emotionally?

I maintain that in spite of our many efforts, we still do not know the answers to these questions. We continue to engage in research that persuades us (but not others) how best to design instructional programs to accelerate English language development. We argue about language, about what it *is* or is *not*, and we generalize from our own experience as educators or researchers about the characteristics of minoritized non-English-speaking <u>and</u> multicompetent children in other school settings very different from our own. And in volumes such as this one, we may at moments make assumptions about the power of instructional arrangements to dismantle racial hierarchies.

In the course of writing this afterword, I found myself deeply concerned about the many unrealized promises that have been made to the parents of vulnerable children about bilingual education in all of its many instantiations (i.e. program models) including DLE/TWI. As I reread my early cautions about DLE/TWI (Valdés, 1997), I once again found Snow's (1990) argument fundamental to the positions we must take today on bilingual education:

> Poor quality bilingual programs do not work any better than poor quality ESL or submersion programs. Language minority children are typically at considerable educational risk for reason that have nothing to do with their bilingualism, so they need the best quality instruction available to ensure their continued progress. (1990: 73)

The editors of this volume conclude their introduction by stating that these chapters ' clearly demonstrate that there is nothing inherently transformative about efforts to promote dual language education and that, on the contrary, these programs can serve to reproduce and even exacerbate existing racial hierarchies.' They emphasize, however, that, their reaching this conclusion does not mean that ' that we should abandon efforts to promote dual language education.' Instead, they situate the work as a loving critique forward that urges the field to engage in efforts that are multiscale and aimed at 'transforming education in individual interactions, classroom practices, community connections, school culture and curriculum, and broader policies affecting students and education.'

I agree with this position, but as I have recently suggested (Valdés, in press), specificity is essential in instructional arrangements directed at supporting language development, particularly the development of majority-language competences by vulnerable children. As scholars, researchers and educators we need to identify the magic sauce. When bilingual education (variously defined and implemented) is found to be the key factor accounting for superior educational achievement in minoritized children (e.g. Umansky *et al.*, 2016), what is it *exactly* that made a difference? I am arguing that, if we are to learn about elements that make a difference in children's lives, program descriptions must include detailed information about what counts as language exposure and/ or language instruction, what the specific language, cultural and social characteristics of the students are, and what are the ways in which both content and language learning is supported for different groups of learners.

Specificity is essential to our work as researchers, educators and activists because we cannot understand the impact of racial and linguistic injustice without clear details about the children who are being instructed, the pedagogies used in instruction, the language background and proficiency of teachers, and the ways in which both language development and academic achievement outcomes were assessed and documented. As Rolstad *et al.* (2005) so clearly point out:

> The lack of consistency in program labels and definitions nationwide creates a thorny obstacle to research synthesis. A program labeled 'English immersion' may provide several hours of native language instruction per

day, while a program labeled 'bilingual education' may provide no native-language instruction at all but rather a bilingual classroom aide for occasional translation support. A researcher interested in determining the effectiveness of a given program must often rely on guesswork when insufficient detail is provided in program evaluations, and different information may be provided depending on the needs and interests of various evaluators. (2005: 48)

Lack of specificity is also an issue in the case of research on DLE/ TWI programs. The summary of the 2018 UCLA Forum on Equity and DL Education held December 7–8, 2018 (https://www.civilrightsproject.ucla.edu/events/2018/confronting-the-equity-issues-in-dual-language-immersion-programs) estimates that there are 2000 programs nationwide in dozens of languages. The report notes that, because DLE/TWI is a strategy that has emerged quickly, rules of enrollment and effective decisions about placement, program implementation and language use vary widely. Of concern is that:

There remain some serious gaps and flaws in research on academic outcomes. Many studies, particularly those from the 1990s and early 2000s, were suspect because of a failure to adjust for selection bias. DLI programs have not been particularly attentive to collecting systematic data on DLI students making it difficult for researchers to investigate longitudinal data. We have very limited research that is able to control for the differential effects by race, ethnicity, or other factors such as poverty. (p.6)

The papers in this volume have provided us with clear evidence that, in spite of good intentions, the original aim of DLE/TWI may not be leveling the playing field or transforming schools and school districts through 'the purposeful integration' of immigrant-origin partner language students and privileged, white-identified, English-speaking children (Arias & Markos, 2018). This is important evidence on which can build to contest or reform current implementations of DLE/TWI.

For activist scholars, interrogating and contesting is an important first step. For activist educators, the challenge is greater. They must involve themselves in finding what I am rereferring to as *the magic sauce*, the program design and implementation elements that can support language development, intercultural understanding, racial and linguistic justice, and academic achievement. In moving forward, and in responding to this volume's 'loving critique,' I would suggest that activist educators must carefully take into account the various interacting mechanisms (Valdés, 2017, 2018a, 2018b) that are involved in the design and implementation of all programs that focus on language development in instructed settings (i.e. language curricularization). These elements include (a) contemporary conceptualizations of language, (b) theoretical perspectives on the development of language practices and resources, (c) understandings of bi/

multilingualism as a human condition and (d) ideological positions (e.g. raciolinguistic perspectives) as they impact on both pedagogies and assessments. If we are to serve the needs of vulnerable, immigrant-origin children in today's America, the task before us demands that we reimagine our work (Pelo & Carter, 2018) and that we advance the conversation among researchers, educators, administrators, policy makers and funders in ways that will help us to nurture the strengths and unique potential of immigrant-origin children who have no choice but to develop additional language resources in order to grow, thrive and contribute to the societies in which they now live.

DBE/TWI may or may not be part of the answer. Racism and classism are unlikely to disappear in the near future. Can and will programs intended for both haves and have nots make it better? Will opposing them and contesting them lead to less support for vulnerable children who have only their language proficiencies in partner languages to offer to the future success of 'cream puff children'?[1] Compromise may be essential and necessary. Theoretical and ideological purity may need to give way to the realities of Monday morning, monolingual teachers, prejudiced bus drivers and very frightened young children.

Note

(1) I am indebted to Margaret Spellings (Secretary of Education under George, W. Bush) for this description of well-to-do, privileged children.

References

Arias, M.B. and Markos, A. (2018) Recent research on the three goals of dual language education. In M.B. Arias and M. Fee (eds) *Profiles of Dual Language Education in the 21st Century* (pp. 3–19). Bristol: Multilingual Matters.
Flores, N. and Rosa, J. (2015) Undoing appropriateness: Raciolinguistic ideologies and language diversity in education. *Harvard Educational Review* 85 (2), 149–171.
Gandara, P. *Confronting the Equity Issues in Dual Language Immersion Programs:* A summary of the 2018 UCLA Forum on Equity and DL Education December 7–8, 2018.
Miller, M.E. (2019, September 22) Immigrant kids fill this town's schools. Their bus driver is leading the backlash. *The Washington Post*.
Minian, A.R. (2018) *Undocumented Lives: The Untold Story of Mexican Migration*. Cambridge MA: Harvard University Press.
Ochoa, S.H. and Rhodes, R.L. (2005) Assisting parents of bilingual students to achieve equity in public schools. *Journal of Educational and Psychological Consultation* 16 (1–2), 75–94.
Pelo, A. and Carter, M. (2018) *From Teaching to Thinking*. Lincoln, NE: Exchange Press.
Reardon, S.F. (2013) The widening income achievement gap. *Educational Leadership* 70 (8), 10–16.
Rolstad, K., Mahoney, K.S. and Glass, G.V. (2005) Weighing the evidence: A meta-analysis of bilingual education in Arizona. *Bilingual Research Journal* 29 (1), 43–67.

Rosa, J. (2018) *Looking Like a Language, Sounding like a Race: Exclusion and Ingenuity in the Making of Latino Identities*. New York; London: Oxford University Press.

Rosa, J. and Flores, N. (2017) Unsettling race and language: Toward a raciolinguistic perspective. *Language in Society* 46 (5), 621–647.

Snow, C.E. (1990) Rationales for native language instruction. In A.M. Padilla, H.H. Fairchild and C.M. Valadez (eds) *Bilingual Education: Issues and Strategies* (pp. 60–74). London: Sage Publications.

Umansky, I.M., Valentino, R.A. and Reardon, S.F. (2016) The promise of two-language education. *Educational Leadership* 73 (5), 10–17.

Valdés, G. (1997) Dual-language immersion programs: A cautionary note concerning the education of language-minority students. *Harvard Educational Review* 67 (3), 391–430.

Valdés, G. (2017) From language maintenance and intergenerational transmission to language survivance: Will 'heritage language' education help or hinder? *International Journal of the Sociology of Language* 2017 (243), 67–95.

Valdés, G. and Parra, M.L. (2018a) Possible goals and pedagogical approaches in teaching language to heritage speakers: towards the development of an analytical framework. In K. Potowski (ed.) *The Routledge Handbook of Spanish as a Heritage Language* (pp. 301–330). New York: Routledge.

Valdés, G. (2018b) Analyzing the curricularization of language in two-way immersion education: Restating two cautionary notes. *Bilingual Research Journal* 41 (4), 388–412.

Valdés, G. (2019) Sandwiching, polylanguaging, translanguaging, and code-switching: Challenging monolingual dogma in institutionalized language teaching. In J. MacSwan and C.J. Faltis (eds) *Code-Switching in the Classroom: Critical Perspectives on Teaching, Learning, Policy, and Ideology* (pp. 114–147). New York: Routledge.

Index

Ability
  Ableist 10, 64, 66, 81
African American Language (AAL) 4, 7, 9, 15, 105, 202–203, 214, 221–231, 238–241
Aurality
  Propertied aurality 22
  Propertied white aurality 6, 19, 22–23, 25, 28, 30–32, 34–35
  White aurality 21–23, 25, 28, 30–35

Bilingualism
  Dynamic bilingualism 221, 226
  Emerging bilingual(s) 195, 220, 248, 251
  Holistic bilingualism 222, 231, 238
  White bilingualism 2, 271

Class (e.g. social class)
  Class privilege 9, 10, 217
  Class-based discourse & ideology 32, 127
  Classed whiteness 14, 127
  Classing 19–22, 25, 35
  Classism 22, 220–221, 277
  Middle-class 9–10, 13–15, 22, 30, 35, 64, 74–75, 81, 89, 112, 114, 116–120, 122, 124–127, 133, 137, 139, 142, 146, 149–152, 157, 221, 223, 226, 244, 247, 249, 251–252, 257–260, 263
  Raceclass 19, 22
  Raciolinguistic classing 20
  Second-class 201
  Upper-class 3, 117, 124, 226, 244, 258–259
  Working-class 9–11, 24, 30, 137, 139–142, 144, 148–149, 151–152, 206–207, 255, 258, 262, 271–272
Colonial

Colonial 4–5, 12, 23, 25, 31, 35, 45, 49, 134, 216
Colonialism 6, 11, 16, 22, 35, 43–44, 56, 200, 204
Colonization 23, 32, 267
Colonize 201, 220
(De)colonizing 19, 23, 267
Critical consciousness 8, 16, 58, 157, 165, 217, 245, 247, 249, 251, 253, 258, 260–263, 267–269

Disability
  Critical disabilities framework 66
  Disabled 14, 63–66, 69–70, 80
  Learning disability 71, 78
  People of color with disabilities (POCwD) 66–67, 79
Discipline 144–145, 153, 162, 201, 208, 211, 215

Emergent bilinguals labeled as disabled (EBLADs) 64, 67–70, 72–74, 76–81
English as a second language (ESL) 28, 50, 68–69, 73, 78, 146, 275
English language learners (ELL) 72–74, 77, 79, 136, 273

Gap
  Achievement gap 71, 96–97, 104, 106, 201–202
  Education gap 117
  Knowledge gap 63
  Language gap 96
  Word gap 202
Gentrification 3–4, 13, 24, 32, 75, 140, 204, 206, 211, 228, 244, 247, 257–260, 266
Globalized human capital 35, 48, 85

Hegemony
  Normative hegemony 67
  Raciolinguistic hegemony 10
Heritage
  Heritage discourse(s) 21, 24, 30, 32, 34, 56, 58
  Heritage language (learners, speakers, & users) 90–91, 93, 159, 178, 180–182, 185–187, 190, 194–195, 227, 245, 272
  Heritage-origin teachers 425
Heteroglossic 178

Immersion
  One-way immersion 27, 32, 34, 88, 121–123
  Two-way immersion (TWI) 25, 27, 30, 32, 34, 63, 111–112, 114, 121–122, 124, 126, 157, 199–200, 202, 221, 228, 244, 263, 271
Immigration 42, 44, 48, 52–53, 114–117, 121, 127–128
Indigenous languages 4, 44, 56, 274
Interdiscursive 40, 44, 46, 48–49, 51–52, 54
Intersectionality 10, 19, 24, 26, 70, 76, 113–114, 215, 239
Intertextual analysis 40, 42–44, 55–56

Language
  Dominant language 27, 29, 45, 116, 137, 182
  Home language 7, 72–74, 79, 88, 94, 100, 105, 120, 180, 202, 227, 253, 272–273
  Interlanguage 231, 239
  Language minoritized 20, 40–41, 53, 56, 65, 112, 114, 118, 121, 128, 163, 180, 202, 206
  Languagelessness 7, 89–91, 96–98, 100–101, 104–106, 187
  Languaging 23, 34, 37, 159, 172, 226–227
  Partner language 10, 26–28, 32–33, 273, 276
  Translanguaging 222, 226–227, 257–258, 268
Liberal multicultural discourse 51, 57
Literacy

Biliteracy 2, 50–51, 54, 56, 70, 73, 76, 81, 88, 111, 121, 156, 202–203, 216, 226–227, 267–268
Literacy (under)achievement 203
Literacy development 223, 227
Literacy practices 220, 268
Seal of Biliteracy 49

Monoglossic
  Monoglossic 159, 178, 200, 255
  Monoglot 45, 48, 51, 56–57
  Monoglot ideology 40, 42, 44–49, 55, 57
  Monoglot standard 45
Multilingualism
  Elite multilingualism 30–31, 33
  Folk multilingualism 29

Native
  Native gaze 15, 182–183, 185–188, 195–196
  Native pronunciation 183–184
  Nativism 40, 44–45, 47–48, 55, 57
  Nativist ideology 46
Neoliberal(ism) 12, 14, 24–25, 29–31, 35, 63, 199, 216, 262

Parent(s)
  Dominant parent(s) 118
  Immigrant parent(s) 9, 94, 135, 140–142, 146, 148, 180
  Marginalized parent(s) 37, 118
  Minoritized parent(s) 113
  Privileged parent(s) 121–123, 125–127, 143, 271
Proper spelling 150

Raciolinguistic(s)
  Critical disabilities raciolinguistic perspective 11
  Intersectional raciolinguistics 19–20
  Raciolinguistic discourses 21, 112
  Raciolinguistic enregisterment 8–9
  Raciolinguistic ideology 4, 6–7, 15, 37, 45, 57, 111–113, 126–127, 132–136, 138–139, 142–143, 145, 148–149, 151–153, 157, 165, 168, 171, 177–178, 180, 192, 194–196, 200, 217, 269

Raciolinguistic perspective 1–2, 4–8, 10–11, 13, 16, 19, 21–22, 40, 43, 47, 65–66, 76, 89, 92, 96, 106–107, 134, 152–153, 200, 266–270, 272
Raciolinguistic socialization 134
Raciolinguistic spectrum 35
Raciolinguistics 19, 21, 65–67, 112–113, 118, 120, 124, 171, 200
Reading
    Formal reading 28
    Grade-level reading 102, 248
Religious language ideology 15, 157

Sociocultural competence 12, 88, 267
Standardization 22–23, 35, 89, 91–93, 96–98, 101, 103–104, 106–107

Test(s)
    High stakes test(s) 14, 107, 255
    Standardized test(s) 7, 14, 54, 69, 94, 101–103, 107, 266–267, 269
    Test-wiseness 268
Top-down model 13, 20, 26, 37

Whiteness
    Hegemonic whiteness 6, 43, 56–58, 125, 201
    White bilingualism 2, 271
    White fragility 123–124
    White gaze 21, 65–67, 180, 182, 216, 246, 253
    White listening subject 21, 134, 247, 249, 251, 254–255, 257, 261–262
    Whiteness 6–7, 9, 11, 14, 19, 21–22, 25, 30, 40, 43–45, 47–49, 55–58, 65, 67, 120, 124–125, 127, 160, 171, 180, 200–201, 226, 239, 244–245, 247, 249, 255, 257, 260–263
    White privileging discourses 14
Writing
    Assets-based writing rubric(s) 221
    Holistic writing rubric 222
    Writing assessment(s) 239–240
    Writing continuum 231
    Writing rubric(s) 221–222, 231, 237
    Writing samples 222, 226–227, 230–231, 237–239